Prompting FastAPI for Backend Development

Build Production-Ready FastAPI Applications with Async Python, REST APIs, Authentication, Testing, Deployment, and AI Prompt Engineering

Fabio Nelli

www.orangeava.com

First Published: August 2026

Published By: Orange Education Pvt Ltd, AVA®

Address: 9, Daryaganj, Delhi, 110002, India

275 New North Road Islington Suite 1314 London,
N1 7AA, United Kingdom

ISBN (PBK): 978-81-69646-45-1
ISBN (E-BOOK): 978-81-69646-46-8

Scan the QR code to explore our entire catalogue

www.orangeava.com

Get a Free eBook

We hope you're enjoying your recent book purchase! Your feedback is incredibly valuable to us and helps other readers discover books that truly make a difference.

If you found this book useful or enjoyable, we'd greatly appreciate it if you could leave a short review with a 5-star rating on Amazon. Your review supports our work and allows us to reach more learners worldwide.

As a thank-you, we're happy to offer you a **free digital copy of this book** plus a **30% discount code** for your next purchase on our official websites:

www.orangeava.com

www.orangeava.in (For the Indian Subcontinent).

☑ **How it works:**

Leave your review on Amazon, take a screenshot of the confirmation or use the following link to submit the claim and email it to **info@orangeava.com.** Once received the required detail, we will send your rewards within 24 hours, **along with one month free subcription to the book on AVA SkillShelf!**

Claim Form
https://rebrand.ly/4d2477

Thank you for your support—it truly means a lot to us.

Downloading the code bundles and colored images

Please follow the links or scan the QR codes to download the
Code Bundles and Images of the book:

https://github.com/ava-orange-education/Prompting-FastAPI-for-Backend-Development

The code bundles and images of the book are also hosted on
https://rebrand.ly/4ajgd41

In case there's an update to the code, it will be updated on the existing GitHub repository.

Errata

We take immense pride in our work at **Orange Education Pvt Ltd,** and follow the best practices to ensure the accuracy of our content to provide an indulging reading experience to our subscribers. Our readers are our mirrors, and we use their inputs to reflect and improve upon human errors, if any, that may have occurred during the publishing processes involved. To let us maintain the quality and help us reach out to any readers who might be having difficulties due to any unforeseen errors, please write to us at:

errata@orangeava.com

Your support, suggestions, and feedback are highly appreciated.

Dedicated to

My Wife, Pamela
And
My Son, Valerio

About the Author

Fabio Nelli is a multidisciplinary technologist, educator, and author with a Master's degree in Chemistry and a Bachelor's degree in IT and Automation Engineering. His career bridges scientific research, software development, and technical education, enabling him to work at the intersection of data science, Artificial Intelligence (AI), programming, and engineering.

Over the years, Fabio has collaborated with universities, research institutes, and private organizations, providing training and consulting in data analysis, data visualization, scientific computing, and modern software development. He specializes in helping professionals and organizations transform complex technical challenges into practical, actionable solutions.

A passionate educator, Fabio has spent much of his career teaching programming, data science, Machine Learning (ML), and software engineering to students, researchers, and industry professionals. His teaching philosophy emphasizes hands-on learning and real-world applications, making advanced technical concepts accessible and engaging.

Fabio is the founder of Meccanismo Complesso, an educational initiative focused on programming, AI, mathematics, data science, and scientific computing. The project continues today through a collection of open-source resources and learning materials shared on GitHub. He is also an active contributor to the developer community, creating software tools, simulation models, technical articles, and open-source projects that support learning and innovation.

As an accomplished author, Fabio has written numerous books covering Python Programming, AI, ML, computer vision, data science, software development, and modern programming frameworks.

When not teaching or writing, Fabio enjoys exploring emerging technologies, and developing educational content that helps others learn more effectively.

About the Technical Reviewer

Anjani Nandigam is a Principal Engineer and Systems Architect specializing in large-scale distributed systems, enterprise platforms, telecommunications infrastructure, and AI-integrated architectures. Her work focuses on designing scalable backend systems, identity lifecycle management platforms, activation security frameworks, and resilient architectures supporting large-scale customer and device ecosystems.

She is an inventor on multiple U.S. patents spanning activation security, eSIM lifecycle orchestration, predictive customer care systems, and subscriber-centric connectivity architectures. Her innovations have been cited by leading technology, telecommunications, and enterprise organizations, reflecting their relevance across multiple industries.

Anjani works at the intersection of core infrastructure and applied AI, with interests in generative AI, agentic systems, LLM-powered applications, API platforms, observability, and cloud-native architectures. As a technical reviewer and engineering evaluator, she reviews publications and technology initiatives with a focus on architectural rigor, scalability, security, and operational resilience.

Acknowledgments

Writing a book is never the work of a single person. Although the words on these pages are mine, many people contributed to making this project possible.

First, I would like to thank the publisher and the entire editorial team of Orange Education Pvt Ltd for their trust, guidance, and support throughout the development of this book. Their professionalism and commitment helped transform an idea into a finished work.

My sincere thanks also go to the technical reviewer, whose careful feedback, critical observations, and attention to detail significantly improved the quality of the manuscript. Many of the refinements presented in these pages are the result of that collaborative review process.

I am deeply grateful to all the colleagues, students, readers, and members of the technical community who, over the years, have encouraged me to continue learning, teaching, writing, and sharing knowledge. Their curiosity, questions, and enthusiasm have been a constant source of inspiration.

Finally, I would like to thank everyone who believed in my abilities, and gave me the opportunity to pursue projects like this one. Your trust and support have played an important role in the successful completion of this book.

Preface

Software development is changing rapidly. Today, developers have access to AI systems that can generate code, explain concepts, review implementations, and assist in solving technical problems. Yet many people encounter the same difficulty when using these tools, such as obtaining code is easy, but understanding it, validating it, and improving it is much harder. This book was written to address that challenge.

Rather than treating AI as a tool for producing instant solutions, this book presents AI as a learning and development partner. The objective is not simply to build a FastAPI application, but to learn a repeatable process that can be applied to any technology. FastAPI provides the practical environment in which that process is explored, refined, and validated.

The book follows an execution-first approach. Instead of beginning with extensive theory, readers start by asking questions, generating working code, running it, observing its behavior, and gradually improving it. Through this process, AI becomes more than a code generator: it becomes a guide for exploration, experimentation, review, and continuous learning.

As the chapters progress, a simple API evolves into a structured, testable, secure, and production-aware system. Along the way, readers learn how to use prompts effectively, how to evaluate AI-generated code critically, how to identify weaknesses, and how to improve systems through iterative refinement.

The book is divided into twelve chapters:

Chapter 1 introduces FastAPI through prompts, and establishes the AI-assisted workflow used throughout the book.

Chapter 2 focuses on setting up a working development environment by using AI as a guided setup assistant.

Chapter 3 guides readers in generating their first functional API, and obtaining observable results as quickly as possible.

Chapter 4 demonstrates how to understand the generated code through targeted questions and structured exploration.

Chapter 5 shows how to organize and refactor an API project using AI-assisted guidance.

Chapter 6 introduces concurrency, asynchronous endpoints, background tasks, and real-time workflows through practical examples.

Chapter 7 adds persistence by integrating databases, and building data-driven APIs.

Chapter 8 introduces authentication, authorization, and security considerations for API systems.

Chapter 9 focuses on testing, deployment, and creating systems that can be verified and executed reliably.

Chapter 10 demonstrates how to use AI as a senior reviewer to debug, optimize, and improve the existing implementations.

Chapter 11 explores production-oriented thinking by evaluating scalability, reliability, and real-world constraints.

Chapter 12 extracts the broader method developed throughout the book, and shows how it can be reused to learn new technologies independently.

Thus, by the end of the book, readers will have built much more than a FastAPI application. They will have developed a practical framework for learning, building, reviewing, and improving software with the assistance of AI. The specific technology may change, but the process remains the same: start small, execute, observe, improve, and repeat.

I hope this book helps you become not only a more productive developer, but also a more confident and independent learner.

DID YOU KNOW

Did you know that Orange Education Pvt Ltd offers eBook versions of every book published, with PDF and ePub files available? You can upgrade to the eBook version at **www.orangeava.com** and as a print book customer, you are entitled to a discount on the eBook copy. Get in touch with us at: **info@orangeava.com** for more details.

At **www.orangeava.com**, you can also read a collection of free technical articles, sign up for a range of free newsletters, and receive exclusive discounts and offers on Print Books and eBooks.

PIRACY

If you come across any illegal copies of our works in any form on the internet, we would be grateful if you would provide us with the location address or website name. Please contact us at **info@orangeava.com** with a link to the material.

ARE YOU INTERESTED IN AUTHORING WITH US?

If there is a topic that you have expertise in, and you are interested in either writing or contributing to a book, please write to us at **business@orangeava.com**. We are on a journey to help developers and tech professionals to gain insights on the present technological advancements and innovations happening across the globe and build a community that believes Knowledge is best acquired by sharing and learning with others. Please reach out to us to learn what our audience demands and how you can be part of this educational reform. We also welcome ideas from tech experts and help them build learning and development content for their domains.

REVIEWS

Please leave a review. Once you have read and used this book, why not leave a review on the site that you purchased it from? Potential readers can then see and use your unbiased opinion to make purchase decisions. We at Orange Education would love to know what you think about our products, and our authors can learn from your feedback. Thank you!

For more information about Orange Education, please visit **www.orangeava.com**.

Table of Contents

CHAPTER 1
From Zero to an API Using Prompts

Introduction

This chapter intentionally does not start with code. Before writing an Application Programming Interface (API), setting up an editor, or installing dependencies, there is a more basic problem to solve: understanding where to begin effectively. When FastAPI and Artificial Intelligence (AI) tools appear together, beginners are often overwhelmed not by complexity but rather by a lack of orientation.

In this chapter, you will not learn syntax or configuration. You will learn how to ask the right questions to move from uncertainty to clarity. Each section will start with a realistic need and show how a simple prompt can produce useful answers—answers that guide decisions rather than merely generate finished solutions.

By the end of the chapter, you will know what FastAPI is for, where it fits in real systems, what kind of API you will build in this book, and how AI will be used throughout the journey. This groundwork is what makes the next chapters faster, safer, and easier to follow. With that in mind, we can start where every real project starts: with a question.

Structure

In this chapter, we will cover the following topics:

- From Zero to an API Using Prompts
- Setting Expectations: AI Utilization
- Building a Mental Model of FastAPI
- The Purpose of FastAPI
- Problems Solved by FastAPI in Real Projects
- FastAPI's Position in Real Systems

- A Concrete Use Case: The API We Will Build
- Connecting This Chapter to Real Development Tools
- From Questions to Action: Using Prompts to Move Forward
- The Workflow We Will Use throughout the Book
- Key Takeaways and Next Steps

From Zero to an API Using Prompts

Most readers open this book with a vague yet concrete intention: they want to build something that works. Maybe they need an API for a web or mobile application. Maybe they have heard that FastAPI is the "right tool" and that AI can speed things up. What they often lack is not motivation or intelligence, but rather a starting point that feels safe and actionable.

The first obstacle is psychological rather than technical. When everything is new, the question is not how to do things, but rather where to begin. Faced with FastAPI, AI tools, and modern workflows, beginners do not yet know what matters and what can be ignored. In this situation, opening documentation or watching tutorials often increases confusion instead of reducing it.

Today, the most natural reaction is to ask an AI assistant. Instead of searching for guides, the reader asks a question...

Weak Prompt

Tell me everything about FastAPI.

This request is too broad and unfocused. The answer will likely be generic, overwhelming, or poorly aligned with the reader's actual need.

Better Prompt

I'm a beginner. I want to build APIs but I don't know where to start. Can you explain what FastAPI is and how I should approach it?

This prompt is intentionally simple. It is not optimized, constrained, or carefully engineered. It reflects a real mental state: uncertainty mixed with intent. The AI assistant responds by offering an overview—describing FastAPI as a Python framework for APIs and highlighting performance, ease of use, and automatic documentation.

At this stage, that answer is enough. Its purpose is not precision, but rather orientation.

This version provides context, intention, and a clear learning goal. The AI can now respond in a way that matches the reader's experience level and immediate needs.

However, something important happens here. The reader does not yet write code, but they already act. By asking this question, they externalize confusion and turn it into a conversation. The AI becomes a tool for reducing ambiguity and guiding early decisions, not simply for producing artifacts.

This moment defines the core idea of the book. We do not begin by installing software or memorizing syntax. We begin by shaping understanding through prompts. The API does not yet exist, but the mental model that will guide its construction is already forming. *Figure* 1.1 shows a simple progression: Unclear goal → Natural question → AI explanation → Initial mental model. The emphasis is on movement, not on completeness.

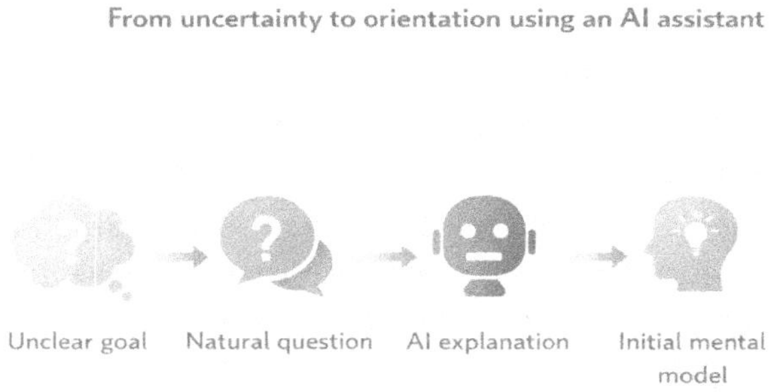

Figure 1.1: *From Uncertainty to Orientation Using an AI Assistant*

At this point, the reader is no longer stuck at "I do not know anything." They now know what FastAPI roughly is and why it might be useful. This is enough to move forward. The next step is not just to write code, but also to refine understanding: to clarify what FastAPI is actually for, and what kind of problems it is meant to solve.

That refinement is where we go next...

Setting Expectations: AI Utilization

After orientation, a new kind of uncertainty often appears. The reader now knows what FastAPI is, but another question emerges almost immediately: What role will AI actually play in this book? Is it a shortcut, a replacement, or just an occasional helper?

This doubt is healthy. Many developers have already experimented with AI tools and experienced both excitement and frustration. They have seen impressive results, but also vague answers, incorrect code, or outputs that looked right but failed in practice. Before moving forward, expectations must be set clearly.

Once again, the natural move is to ask.

Prompt (Clarifying Expectations)

If I use AI to help me learn and build a FastAPI project, what should I realistically expect it to do and what not?

The AI's response is usually reassuring but generic. It explains that AI can generate code, explain concepts, and speed up development, but also that human judgment is still required. This answer is correct yet incomplete. It describes capabilities, not boundaries.

This is where the book's position must become explicit. In this workflow, AI is neither treated as an autonomous developer, nor as a magical solution. This prevents over-reliance and improves long-term understanding. It is treated as an amplifier.

It accelerates what is already clear and struggles where intent is vague. The clearer the question, the more useful the answer. The moment ambiguity appears, the responsibility shifts back to the human.

What matters is not that AI is used, but rather how. Throughout the book, AI will be asked to explain, generate, and suggest. It will never be asked to decide what is correct without verification. For example, blindly accepting generated code or architectural decisions without understanding them is considered a misuse of AI assistance. Code produced by AI is always considered provisional until it is understood and accepted.

Figure 1.2: *Responsibility Split in an AI-Assisted Workflow*

Figure 1.2 shows two parallel lanes. On the left: AI assistant → "Generate", "Suggest", "Explain". On the right: Human → "Decide", "Verify", "Integrate". A clear boundary separates suggestions from responsibility.

By making this division explicit early, we avoid two common traps. The first is blind trust, where speed replaces understanding and problems accumulate silently. The second is total rejection, where AI is ignored, and its benefits are lost. The workflow used in this book deliberately sits between these extremes.

At this point, the reader should feel oriented not only to FastAPI but also to the rules of engagement with the AI assistant. There is no pressure to be perfect, and no expectation of passive acceptance. Interaction is iterative, intentional, and always reversible.

With expectations set, we are ready to focus on the framework itself. The next section addresses a fundamental question that almost every beginner asks, often implicitly: What is FastAPI actually for—beyond the buzzwords?

Building a Mental Model of FastAPI

After clarifying expectations about AI, the reader encounters a different kind of difficulty. They may know that FastAPI is "a framework for APIs," but this definition is still fragile. Without a mental model, every new concept feels isolated, and every detail seems equally important. This is where many beginners get stuck—not because the material is difficult, but rather because there is no map.

Once again, the first step is not to study, but to ask.

Prompt (Seeking a Mental Model)

Explain FastAPI like I'm a beginner. I don't need details yet—just help me understand what it is in simple terms

The AI's response tends to rely on analogies. FastAPI is often described as a translator between HTTP requests and Python code, or as a gatekeeper that controls what enters and leaves the system. These metaphors are not technically precise in every detail, but they serve a fundamental purpose: they reduce initial complexity to something manageable.

At this point, it is important to pause for a moment. The value of this response does not lie in its formal accuracy, but rather in its function. A good mental model does not explain everything; it explains just enough to allow orientation without the fear of making mistakes.

From a human perspective, we can refine this intuition. FastAPI can be thought of as a boundary layer. It is not where deep business logic lives, nor where long-term data resides. It is the point where the outside world meets your system. Its primary role is to transform messy and unstructured requests into reliable and structured data and to transform internal results into clear and consistent responses.

This idea of a "boundary" is crucial. It explains why FastAPI places so much emphasis on validation, types, and explicit contracts. It also explains why it integrates so well with automated tools, including AI assistants. When rules are visible and declared, both humans and machines work better. *Figure* 1.3 shows a simple diagram: on the left, the "External World" (such as clients, browsers, and mobile apps); in the center, FastAPI as a boundary layer that validates and structures requests before they enter the system; on the right, the "Internal System" (such as business logic, databases, and services). This boundary ensures that all external input is validated before reaching the core application logic. The goal is to visualize FastAPI not as a whole system, but rather as a controlled interface.

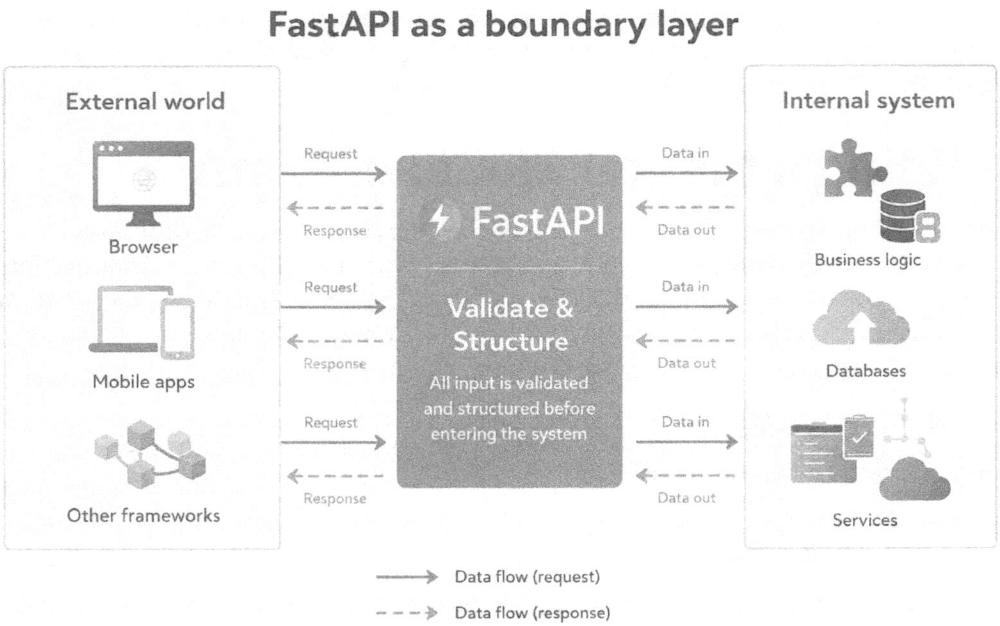

Figure 1.3: *FastAPI as a Boundary Layer*

With this mental model in place, many future details fall naturally into position. Automatic documentation, data validation, and consistent error responses are not isolated features; they are direct consequences of the role FastAPI plays.

At this point, the reader has not written a single line of code yet, but has gained something far more important: a conceptual map. With it, every new element encountered in the following chapters will have a clear place.

The next step is to make this model concrete—to understand not only what FastAPI is, but what it is actually for in real projects. This is where we move to the next section.

The Purpose of FastAPI

At this point, the reader has a basic mental model of FastAPI, yet a practical doubt remains. Knowing what something is does not automatically explain why it should be used. Many beginners reach this book because they have heard FastAPI mentioned repeatedly, or because they need to build APIs for the web, and FastAPI keeps appearing as a recommendation as shown in *Table* 1.1.

Why Developers Choose FastAPI?

Framework	Main Strength	Typical Use Case
Flask	Simplicity and flexibility	Small web applications and custom APIs
Django	Full-featured ecosystem	Large web platforms with many built-in features
Express.js	JavaScript ecosystem integration	APIs and backend services in Node.js
FastAPI	Modern API development with validation and automatic documentation	High-performance APIs and AI-driven applications

Table 1.1: *Comparing FastAPI with Other Widely Used Web Frameworks*

In this situation, the reader's need is not technical depth but rather justification. They want to understand whether FastAPI is a good fit for their goals before investing time and effort.

Once again, the instinctive move is to ask a direct question.

Prompt (Seeking Relevance)

I want to build web APIs in Python. What is FastAPI actually for, and when does it make sense to use it?

The AI's response usually highlights speed, simplicity, and automatic documentation. These points are useful, but still sound like features listed on a product page. They explain what FastAPI offers, not why those offerings matter in practice.

This is where human interpretation becomes essential. FastAPI is neither about writing endpoints quickly, nor about being the fastest framework in isolation. It is designed for situations where the API itself is the product, or at least a critical contract between systems. When an API is consumed by different clients, maintained over time, and evolved by multiple developers, clarity and correctness at the boundary become more important than flexibility.

FastAPI shines when you need to be explicit—about what data you accept, what you return, and what happens when something goes wrong. Instead of hiding assumptions inside code paths, it forces them to be declared. This differs from frameworks such as Flask, where developers often have more flexibility but also more responsibility for structuring validation and documentation themselves. This is why beginners often feel that FastAPI is strict at first, and why experienced teams grow to appreciate it.

This perspective also explains why FastAPI pairs naturally with AI-assisted development. When contracts are visible and enforced, AI tools have less room to guess and more structure to work with. The framework does not just help humans avoid mistakes; it also helps machines generate more reliable code.

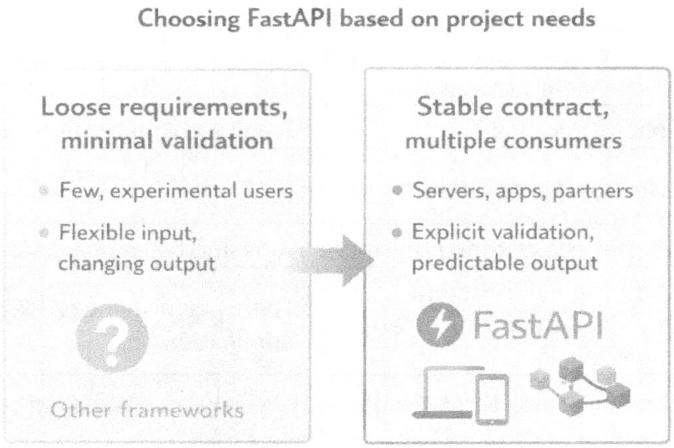

Figure 1.4: *Choosing FastAPI Based on Project Needs*

Figure 1.4 shows a simple decision-oriented diagram: on one side, projects with loose requirements and minimal validation; on the other, projects where the API is a stable contract with multiple consumers. FastAPI is highlighted in the second category, emphasizing explicit boundaries and contracts.

By reframing the question from "What features does FastAPI have?" to "What kind of problems does it address?", the reader gains a more durable understanding. FastAPI is not chosen because it is trendy, but rather because it aligns with a specific way of building and maintaining systems.

With this clarity, the reader is ready to go one level deeper. The next section will focus not on abstract suitability, but rather on the concrete problems FastAPI solves in real projects, and why those problems tend to appear sooner than expected.

Problems Solved by FastAPI in Real Projects

Once the reader understands what FastAPI is for in principle, a more grounded concern naturally emerges. Abstract motivations are helpful, but real projects fail for very concrete reasons. Beginners and experienced developers alike have often seen APIs become fragile, inconsistent, or difficult to evolve. The question now is not whether FastAPI is good, but rather what kinds of recurring problems it is meant to address.

This need often surfaces when something has already gone wrong in the past. The reader may have built an API before and struggled with validation logic scattered across the codebase, unclear error responses, or documentation that quickly fell out of sync with reality. These experiences create a very pragmatic question.

Prompt (Connecting Past Pain to a Solution)

In real-world API projects, what problems does FastAPI help avoid or reduce?

The AI assistant typically responds by mentioning validation, documentation, and performance. These answers are correct, but taken alone, they risk sounding generic. The key is to reinterpret them through the lens of lived experience.

Consider input validation. In many projects, validation starts as a quick check and slowly spreads everywhere. Each endpoint adds its own rules, error formats differ, and edge cases multiply. Imagine a small application with separate endpoints for user registration, profile updates, and account recovery. At first, each endpoint validates input independently. One checks whether an email is present, another verifies password length, and another formats error messages differently. Over time, the same validation rules are repeated in multiple places, and inconsistencies begin to appear.

FastAPI addresses this problem by centralizing validation around declared data models. Instead of scattering validation logic across the application, developers define the expected structure once and reuse it consistently. Validation is no longer an afterthought; rather, it becomes part of the contract itself.

Another common problem is documentation drift. APIs evolve continuously, but documentation often freezes at an early stage. Clients are forced to guess, test manually, or read code. FastAPI eliminates much of this friction by deriving documentation directly from the same definitions that drive runtime behavior. When the API changes, the contract changes with it.

A third problem is ambiguity at the boundary. Many APIs accept almost anything and fail deep inside the system, far from the source of the error. FastAPI pushes failure to the edge. Incorrect input is rejected early, explicitly, and consistently. This reduces debugging time and makes systems more predictable.

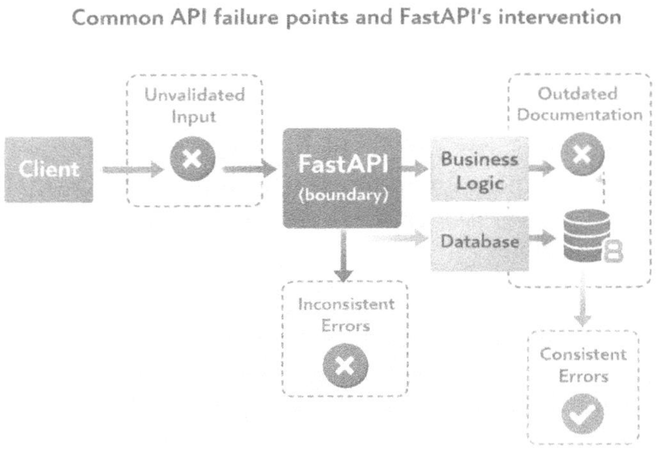

Figure 1.5: *Common API Failure Points and FastAPI's Intervention*

Figure 1.5 shows a simplified request flow with typical failure points highlighted: unvalidated input, inconsistent errors, and outdated documentation. FastAPI is shown acting early in the flow, preventing these issues at the boundary.

It is important to notice that these problems are not advanced or rare. They appear quite early—even in small projects. FastAPI's value lies in making good practices the default, rather than optional add-ons that are introduced later under pressure.

This problem-oriented view also reinforces AI's role in the workflow. When constraints are explicit, and validation is declarative, AI-generated code becomes easier to reason about and safer to adapt. The framework reduces ambiguity not only for humans but also for machines.

At this stage, the reader should recognize a pattern. FastAPI consistently positions itself at the boundary, solving problems before they propagate inward. The next logical step is to see where this boundary typically lives in real systems and how FastAPI fits alongside other components in production environments.

FastAPI's Position in Real Systems

After understanding which problems FastAPI solves, the reader is ready for a broader question. Even a well-designed framework can feel abstract until it is placed inside a real system. Beginners often imagine an API as the application itself, while in practice, it is only one piece of a larger architecture. Clarifying this position early prevents misunderstandings later.

At this stage, the reader's need is contextual. They want to understand how FastAPI relates to other components they may already know or will soon encounter: databases, frontends, background workers, and external services.

The instinctive question reflects this need for orientation.

Prompt (Seeking Architectural Context)

Where is FastAPI typically used in real-world systems?

The AI's response usually places FastAPI at the entry point of a system. It describes FastAPI as the layer that exposes functionality to web frontends, mobile applications, or other services. This answer is accurate, but its importance is easy to underestimate if left unexplored.

From a human perspective, this placement explains many of FastAPI's design choices. FastAPI is not responsible for storing data long-term, running background jobs, or implementing complex business workflows. This Separation of Concerns (SoC) is intentional. In modern architectures, different parts of the system are designed to handle different responsibilities. FastAPI focuses on the API boundary: receiving requests from the outside world, validating and structuring them, and then handing clean, predictable data to the internal parts of the system.

This boundary role is critical in real systems because most failures originate at the edges. Inputs are incomplete, malformed, or simply unexpected. If these problems are allowed to leak inward, they complicate every layer that follows. FastAPI's job is to stop that leakage as early as possible.

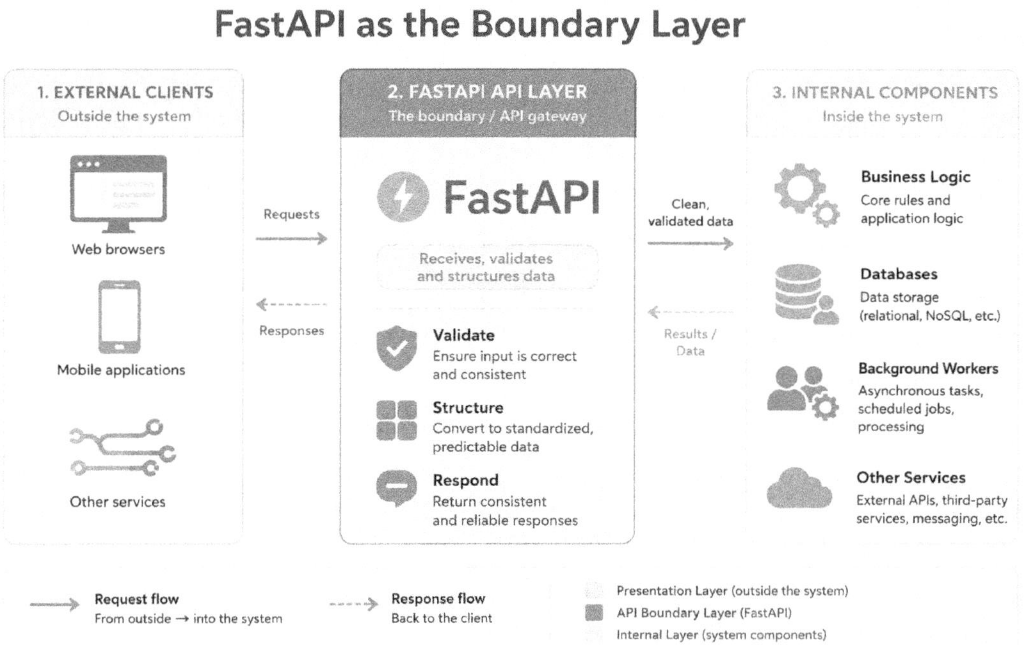

Figure 1.6: *FastAPI inside a Typical Web System*

Figure 1.6 shows a layered system: clients (including browser, mobile app, and other services) on the left, FastAPI as the API layer in the middle, and internal components (including business logic, databases, and background workers) on the right. Arrows emphasize that FastAPI is a controlled gateway, and not the entire system.

This perspective helps the reader to avoid a common beginner's mistake, that is, overloading the API layer with responsibilities it should not have. When FastAPI is understood as a boundary rather than a core engine, design decisions become clearer. Validation belongs here. Authentication starts here. While heavy computation and long-running tasks usually do not.

It also clarifies how AI fits into the workflow. When the role of FastAPI is well-defined, prompts become more precise. Instead of asking the AI to "build the whole system," the reader can ask it to focus on well-scoped tasks at the boundary: defining endpoints, validating input, and shaping responses. This naturally leads to better results.

With this architectural context in place, the reader now has a complete conceptual picture: what FastAPI is, what it is for, which problems it solves, and where it lives. The next step is to anchor this understanding to a concrete project that will evolve throughout the book. That is the focus of the next section.

A Concrete Use Case: The API We Will Build

At this point, the reader has a coherent conceptual picture, yet there is still a risk. Without a concrete destination, understanding can remain suspended and detached from action. Many technical books fail here: they explain well, but never clearly answer the question: "What am I actually going to build?"

To avoid this, we can now make the goal explicit.

A beginner—having reached this stage—often asks a very practical question, which is not about FastAPI in general, but rather about this book.

Prompt (Seeking Concreteness)

What kind of API will I actually build if I follow this book from start to finish?

The AI's response might suggest a generic CRUD API or mention common examples such as users or products. That answer is fine, but the important part is not the specific domain—rather, it is the commitment to continuity.

In this book, we will build an API for managing a product catalog. This choice is intentional. Product-based APIs appear in many real systems: e-commerce platforms, inventory services, internal tooling, and data pipelines. They involve structured data, validation rules, evolving requirements, and multiple consumers. In other words, they are simple enough to start with, but rich enough to grow.

For example, a mobile application might ask the API for information about a specific product, such as its name, price, and availability. The API receives the request, validates it, retrieves the relevant information, and returns a structured response that the application can display to the user.

Even this simple interaction already reflects the core responsibilities of an API: receiving external requests, validating input, coordinating with internal systems, and returning predictable results.

The API will allow clients to create, read, update, and list products. At first, the data will be stored in memory, keeping the complexity low. As the chapters progress, the same API will be extended with persistence, concurrency, security, testing, and deployment concerns. Nothing is thrown away. Each chapter adds constraints to the same system, mirroring how real software evolves.

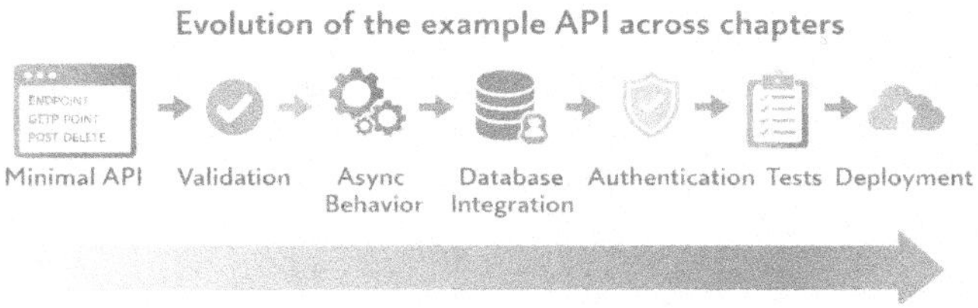

Figure 1.7: *Evolution of the Example API across Chapters*

Figure 1.7 shows a horizontal timeline. On the left: a minimal API with a few endpoints. Moving right: added validation, async behavior, database integration, authentication, tests, and deployment. The visual emphasizes growth through refinement, not replacement.

This continuity matters for two reasons. First, it allows the reader to see the cause and effect. Decisions made early will influence later chapters—sometimes in unexpected ways. Second, it provides a stable context for interacting with the AI assistant. Prompts are no longer abstract requests; rather, they are grounded in a shared project with known assumptions.

By defining the use case early, we remove ambiguity. The reader knows what they are building, why it matters, and how it will evolve. From here on, every prompt, explanation, and code fragment serves a clear purpose.

With a destination in place, the final step of this chapter is to define the method that will guide us there. The next section will introduce the workflow that connects intent, prompts, and implementation into a repeatable process.

Connecting This Chapter to Real Development Tools

Up to this point, everything in this chapter has happened at a conceptual level. You have asked questions, refined your understanding, and built a mental model of FastAPI and the AI-assisted workflow. This is deliberate, but it naturally leads to another question—one that many readers are already forming, even if silently.

Where does all of this actually happen?

So far, prompts may feel like something you type into a chat window, which is detached from real development. However, software is not built in isolation. It is built while looking at files, reading errors, navigating folders, and running commands. If prompts are meant to guide action, they must live inside that environment, not outside it.

At this stage, the reader often asks a practical question.

Prompt (Anchoring Prompts to Reality)

When I'm actually building a FastAPI project, where do prompts fit into my day-to-day development work?

The answer is not a single tool, but rather a shift in perspective. Prompts are not a separate phase that happens before or after coding. They are woven into the development loop itself. They appear when you open an unfamiliar file, when an error message does not make sense, when you hesitate about structure, or when you want to confirm a design decision before committing to it.

In this book, the primary environment where this interaction happens is the development editor—typically tools, such as Visual Studio Code or PyCharm. The editor is where code lives, where errors surface, and where decisions accumulate. It becomes the natural place for dialogue with AI assistants. Instead of switching contexts constantly—reading documentation in one place, asking questions in another, and writing code somewhere else—the conversation converges around the project itself.

This is why modern Integrated Development Environments (IDEs) integrate AI tools directly. Whether the assistant is embedded in the editor, connected to the repository, or aware of the current file, the important aspect is the context. When the AI sees the same code that you see, its answers become more relevant. When prompts refer to the actual files, functions, or errors, they stop being abstract questions and become concrete problem-solving tools.

It is important to be explicit about one thing: using AI inside an IDE does not change responsibility. The assistant can suggest changes, explain what a piece of code is doing, or help you explore alternatives, but it does not own the project. Decisions still belong to the developer. The editor simply becomes the shared space where intent, code, and feedback meet.

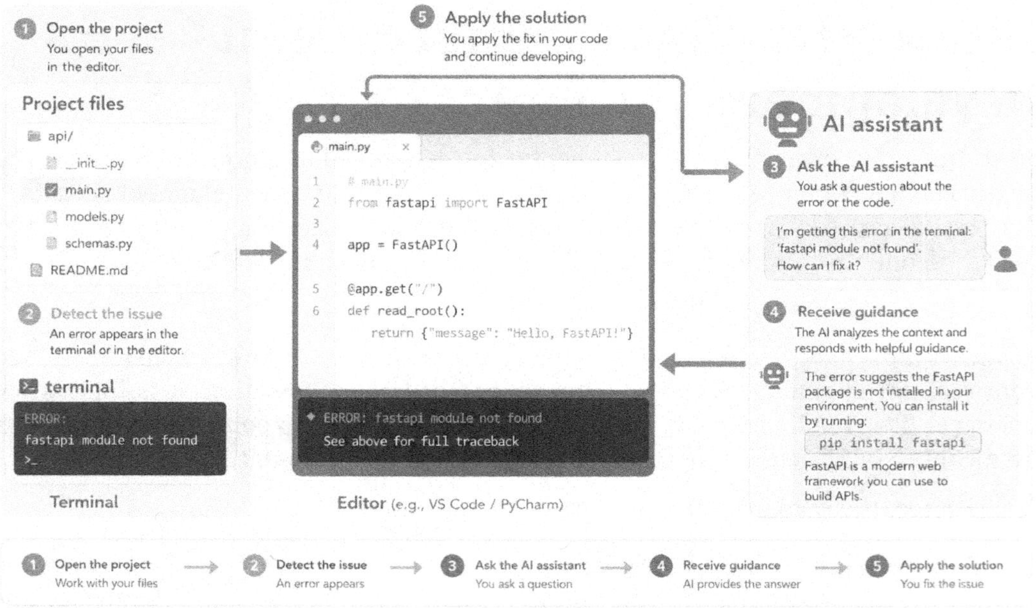

Figure 1.8: *AI inside the Development Environment*

Figure 1.8 shows the development editor at the center. On one side are project files, error messages, and the terminal. On the other side is the AI assistant. Bidirectional arrows connect them, emphasizing that prompts arise from real project context and responses flow back into concrete decisions. The message is that AI is not outside the workflow, but rather embedded within it.

Understanding this connection removes a subtle source of friction. Prompts are no longer something that you do before you start or when you are stuck. They are part of the same loop as reading code, running commands, and refining structure. This is what makes the workflow sustainable beyond learning exercises.

With this bridge in place, the next step becomes obvious. Once prompts are grounded in real tools and real context, they can be used to move from understanding to action. That transition—from knowing what to do to actually doing it—is where we will go next.

From Questions to Action: Using Prompts to Move Forward

Now that the destination is clear, a subtle yet important shift occurs. The reader is no longer asking abstract questions about FastAPI or APIs in general. They are asking "how to move." The system to be built is defined, the role of FastAPI is understood, and the AI assistant is already part of the picture. What remains unclear is how these elements connect in practice.

At this point, beginners often experience a moment of hesitation. They know what they want to build, but they do not yet know the sequence of steps. Traditional tutorials respond by listing commands or instructions. In this book, the approach is different. The first action is not typing code, but rather asking the right kind of question.

Prompt (Turning Intent into Action)

I want to build a small product API with FastAPI, but I'm a beginner. What should be the first concrete step I take?

The AI assistant typically answers by suggesting setup-related actions: installing Python, choosing an editor, creating a virtual environment, and starting with a small API example.

Expected AI output

A good way to begin is with a very small API.

Create a file called main.py and define a simple endpoint that returns information about a product.

Then:

- install FastAPI and the local development server,

- run the application,

- open the API in your browser.

For example, visiting:

http://127.0.0.1:8000/products/1

could return a JSON response containing:

- a product ID,

- a product name,

- and a sample price.

At this stage, your goal is not authentication, databases, or deployment. The goal is simply to understand the basic request/response cycle of an API.

This answer is useful, but what matters more is why it is useful. The prompt did not ask for code. It asked for direction. The AI responded by proposing a path rather than a solution.

This illustrates a pattern that will repeat throughout the book. Prompts are not only used to generate artifacts, but also to decide what to do next. They act as a navigation tool. When the reader is unsure, they ask. When the answer is too broad, they refine the question. Action emerges from iteration, not from a single perfect instruction.

From a human perspective, this is where responsibility remains firmly in the reader's hands. The AI can suggest steps, but it cannot know the reader's environment, constraints, or prior knowledge. The developer's role is to evaluate suggestions, select what applies, and ignore what does not. This is not a limitation of the AI; rather, it is a design feature of the workflow.

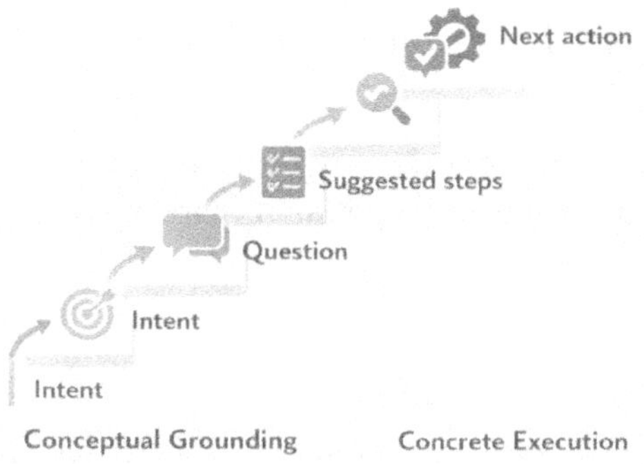

Figure 1.9: *Prompt-Driven Progression from Intent to Execution*

Figure 1.9 depicts a simple staircase: Intent → Question → Suggested Steps → Human Selection → Next Action. Each step represents a prompt-response cycle, emphasizing gradual movement rather than a single leap.

By using prompts in this way, the reader avoids a common trap: waiting until everything is understood before starting. Instead, understanding and action advance together. Each question reduces uncertainty just enough to allow the next step to happen safely.

At this stage, the reader has everything needed to move into concrete work. They know what they are building, how the AI assistant will be used, and how prompts translate uncertainty into progress. The remaining task in this chapter is to make this workflow explicit and repeatable so that it can be applied consistently from setup to deployment. That will be the focus of the next section.

The Workflow We Will Use throughout the Book

After seeing how questions turn into action, the reader is ready to recognize a pattern. What has happened so far is not accidental. Each step followed a rhythm: uncertainty, question, response, interpretation, and then movement. This rhythm is the workflow that will guide the entire book.

At this point, a beginner often asks a meta-question—not about FastAPI, not about the project, but rather about the process itself.

Prompt (Seeking a Method)

What is the general workflow for using AI effectively while building a FastAPI project?

The AI assistant usually responds with a list: ask questions, generate code, test, and iterate. While correct, this answer hides an important detail. A workflow is not defined by steps alone, but also by where responsibility changes hands. Without this clarity, AI-assisted development quickly becomes chaotic.

From a human perspective, the workflow used in this book can be understood as a loop with clear roles. It always begins with intent. Before writing code or asking for a generation, the developer decides what problem needs to be solved. That intent is then expressed as a prompt. The AI responds with suggestions, explanations, or code. At that point, generation stops and evaluation begins.

Evaluation is the most critical step. The developer reads the output, checks whether it aligns with the project's goals, and verifies its behavior. Only after this verification does the output become part of the system. If something is unclear or incorrect, the prompt—not the code—is refined first. This keeps the system coherent and prevents any silent drifts.

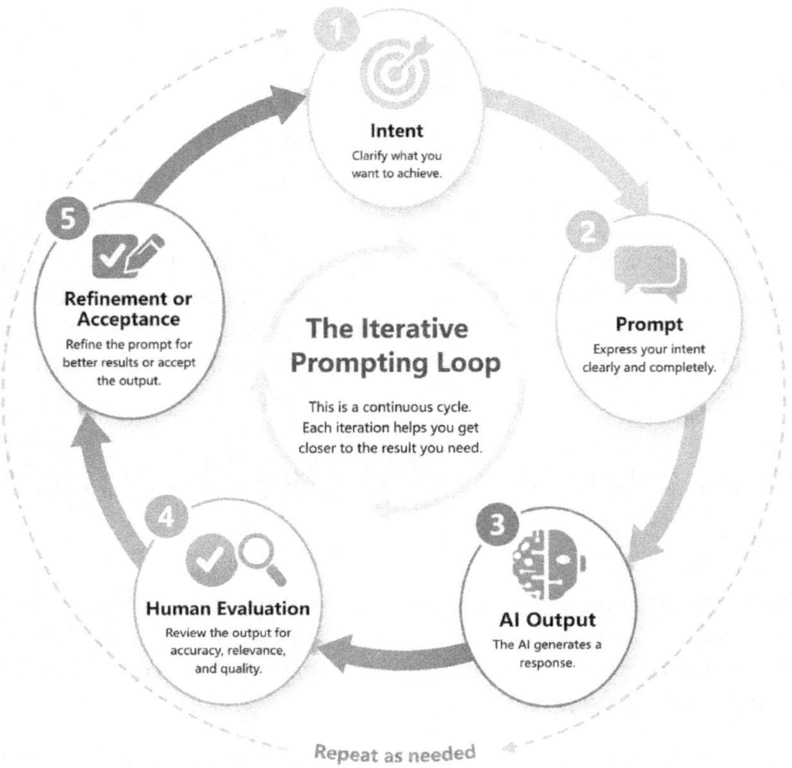

Figure 1.10: *The Prompt-Evaluation Loop*

Figure 1.10 shows a circular flow. This loop emphasizes that progress happens through repetition, and not through one-shot generation.

This workflow intentionally avoids extremes. The AI is neither ignored nor blindly trusted. It accelerates exploration and reduces friction, but it never replaces judgment. By repeating this loop consistently, the reader develops two skills at once: the ability to ask better questions and the ability to recognize good answers.

Another important consequence of this method is stability. As each step is small and verified, errors surface early. Misunderstandings do not propagate silently across chapters. The system grows through accumulation, not through leaps of faith.

By the end of this section, the reader should recognize that the workflow itself is one of the main takeaways of the book. FastAPI is the concrete medium, but the method—intentional prompting followed by deliberate evaluation—is reusable far beyond this specific framework.

With the workflow now explicit, the chapter can close by taking stock of what the reader has gained so far and preparing for the transition from conceptual groundwork to concrete setup. That transition will happen in the final section.

Key Takeaways and the Next Steps

At the end of this chapter, it is reasonable to ask a simple question: What has actually changed? You have not installed anything yet. You have not written code. Yet, you are no longer in the same position as when you started.

The most important shift is not technical, but cognitive. You now understand FastAPI not as a collection of features but rather as a boundary layer with a precise role inside real systems. You know what kind of problems it is meant to solve, where it fits architecturally, and why it pairs naturally with an AI-assisted workflow. This removes much of the anxiety that typically accompanies the first steps with a new framework.

Equally important, you have also experienced a method. You have seen how a beginner's uncertainty can be turned into progress through simple and honest prompts. Not perfect prompts, not optimized prompts—just the right questions at the right moment. You have also seen where the AI helps and where it must stop. Understanding emerges not from a single answer, but rather from iteration and interpretation.

This chapter has deliberately avoided any premature actions. That is not a delay; rather, it is a preparation. By resisting the urge to install tools immediately, you have built a mental structure that will make every concrete step easier to understand and correct when something goes wrong.

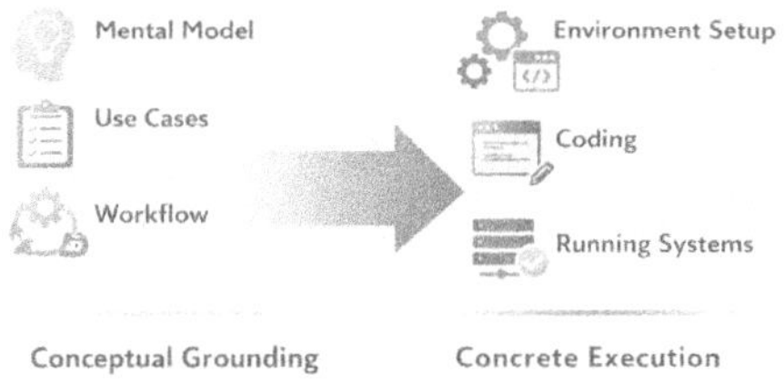

Figure 1.11: *From Orientation to Execution*

Figure 1.11 shows a clear transition: on the left, conceptual grounding (with mental model, use cases, and workflow); on the right, concrete execution (with environment setup, code, and running systems). The arrow between them emphasizes readiness rather than completion.

At this point, you should feel oriented rather than overwhelmed. You know what you are building, how you will interact with the AI assistant, and what kind of discipline will guide each step. Nothing depends on memorization. Everything depends on understanding roles, boundaries, and intent.

The next chapter is where ideas become tangible. You will set up your development environment and verify that it works, using the same prompt-driven approach you have already practiced—this time with observable results. If something fails, it will fail in a controlled and understandable way.

You are done preparing the ground. In the next chapter, you will start building for real.

Conclusion

In this chapter, you did not learn how to write a FastAPI application; rather, you learned how to approach one.

You built a first mental model of what FastAPI is used for, where it fits in real systems, and why it works particularly well with AI-assisted workflows. More importantly, you learned how to turn uncertainty into progress by asking clear and purposeful questions instead of searching blindly for solutions.

This way of working—starting from intent, using prompts to clarify decisions, and validating results step by step—will guide everything that follows. From now on, the focus will gradually shift from understanding what to doing how, without losing control of the reasoning behind each choice.

In the next chapter, we will move from orientation to action. You will set up your development environment and use AI as a guided assistant to reach a working FastAPI setup, quickly and confidently.

Points to Remember

- FastAPI is best understood as an API boundary, not as syntax.
- Prompts reduce uncertainty before coding begins.
- AI assistants guide and suggest; developers decide and verify.
- Good prompts turn vague ideas into actionable direction.
- FastAPI is valuable when validation and predictable behavior matter.
- AI workflows depend on iteration: prompt → evaluate → refine.
- The product catalog API will evolve throughout the book.
- Clear mental models make setup, coding, and testing easier.

Multiple Choice Questions

1. What is the primary goal of the first chapter of this book?
    a. To teach FastAPI syntax in detail
    b. To configure a production-ready environment
    c. To build a mental model and define how AI will be used throughout the book
    d. To compare Python frameworks line by line

2. Why does the book introduce FastAPI before showing detailed code examples?
    a. Because FastAPI is simpler than other frameworks
    b. Because understanding purpose and context prevents mechanical coding
    c. Because AI cannot generate code without a theory
    d. Because FastAPI does not require configuration
3. In this book, what is the main role of prompts?
    a. To replace documentation
    b. To automatically write perfect code
    c. To externalize questions and guide learning and decision-making
    d. To avoid understanding the framework
4. Why is an execution-first approach preferred over a theory-first one?
    a. It produces shorter chapters.
    b. It avoids mistakes completely.
    c. It helps readers see concrete results early and refine understanding progressively.
    d. It removes the need to learn fundamentals.
5. How should AI-generated answers be treated according to this chapter?
    a. As authoritative and final
    b. As suggestions that must be reviewed and validated
    c. As experimental code that should never be run
    d. As documentation replacements
6. What makes FastAPI particularly suitable for AI-assisted development?
    a. Its popularity on GitHub
    b. Its automatic use of databases
    c. Its explicit structure, type hints, and OpenAPI-based contracts
    d. Its built-in frontend system
7. A beginner asks an AI assistant: "I want to build APIs, but I don't know where to start." What makes this prompt effective?
    a. It contains advanced technical terminology.
    b. It clearly communicates uncertainty, intent, and learning goals.

   c. It asks the AI to generate a complete production system.
   d. It avoids giving any context.

8. A developer copies AI-generated code directly into a project without reviewing it. According to this chapter, what is the main problem with this approach?
   a. AI-generated code cannot run correctly.
   b. FastAPI requires manual validation.
   c. The developer loses understanding and responsibility for decisions.
   d. AI tools cannot generate APIs reliably.

Answers

1. c
2. b
3. c
4. c
5. b
6. c
7. b
8. c

Questions

1. Why is it useful to understand what a framework is *for* before learning how to use its syntax?
2. How does using prompts change the way a beginner approaches a new technology compared to traditional documentation-first learning?
3. What are the risks of treating AI-generated answers as authoritative instead of as starting points for reasoning?
4. In what situations is asking a "theoretical" prompt more effective than immediately asking for code?
5. How does FastAPI's explicit structure (such as type hints, clear routing, and OpenAPI) support learning through exploration and questioning?
6. Why does this book emphasize observable results early, even before full understanding?
7. How can asking better questions reduce frustration and cognitive overload when learning backend development?

8. What responsibility remains entirely human when using AI tools during software development?

Key Terms

- **Application Programming Interface (API):** An interface that allows different software systems to communicate through well-defined requests and responses, typically over HTTP.
- **FastAPI:** A modern Python framework for building APIs, designed around type hints, automatic validation, and OpenAPI standards.
- **Endpoint:** A specific URL and HTTP method combination that defines how an API responds to a request.
- **Prompt:** A natural-language instruction given to an AI tool to obtain explanations, guidance, or generated code.
- **Prompt Engineering:** The practice of crafting clear and structured prompts to obtain useful, reliable, and reproducible AI outputs.
- **AI Assistant:** A Generative AI (GenAI) tool (such as ChatGPT, GitHub Copilot, or Amazon Q Developer) used to support reasoning, learning, and development tasks.
- **Mental Model:** A simplified internal representation that helps understand how a system works and how its parts relate to each other.
- **Execution-First Approach:** A learning strategy that prioritizes producing observable results early, refining understanding progressively rather than starting from theory.
- **Type Hints:** Python annotations that describe expected data types and are used by FastAPI for validation, documentation, and tooling support.
- **OpenAPI:** A standardized specification used to describe REST APIs, enabling automatic documentation and client generation.
- **Swagger User Interface (UI):** An interactive web interface automatically generated by FastAPI to explore and test API endpoints.
- **AI-Assisted Development:** A workflow where AI tools support coding, learning, and decision-making, while final responsibility remains with the developer.

CHAPTER 2
Setting up by Asking the Right Questions

Introduction

After understanding what FastAPI is and why it fits in modern backend development, the next step is not necessarily to write code immediately; rather, it is to ask the right questions. Setting up a development environment is often treated as a mechanical prerequisite: install this, configure that, copy a list of commands, and move on. In this book, the setup is approached differently. It is treated as the first concrete application of the same method that will guide the entire project. This chapter will continue the workflow introduced in *Chapter 1, From Zero to an API Using Prompts*, using prompts not only to generate answers but also to shape understanding and guide decisions step by step. Instead of starting with instructions, we will start with intentions. We ask what we need to build, run, and observe a FastAPI application. We translate those intentions into prompts, turn the answers into concrete actions, and validate them by observing what works.

This chapter applies the prompt-driven development cycle for the first time. The object of development is not yet the application itself, but rather the workshop in which it will be built: the editor, the environment, the tools, and the assistants that will support us throughout the journey.

By the end of this chapter, you will have a working setup, a running FastAPI application, and most importantly, a clear and repeatable way to move from questions to working software. From here on, every chapter will follow the same pattern, gradually growing the application while refining your understanding at each step.

Structure

In this chapter, we will cover the following topics:

- The Prompt-Driven Development Cycle
- The Method of This Book: Developing through a Continuous Cycle

- Setting up the Workshop: Virtual Studio (VS) Code, Git, and AI Assistants
- The Roles of Chat, GitHub Copilot, and Amazon Q
- Letting the AI Read Your Code without Copy-Paste
- The First Concrete Objective
- The First Prompt: Starting a FastAPI Project
- Translating the Prompt into Reality: VS Code
- Writing the First Endpoint
- Running the Application
- Stopping to Understand What Happened
- Completing Multiple Prompt Cycles

The Prompt-Driven Development Cycle

Before writing any code, this book introduces a precise way of working. Not a framework, not a tool, but rather a cycle that will be repeated throughout the entire development of the application.

The idea is simple: FastAPI is not learned in isolation, and it is not applied by following a fixed sequence of instructions. Instead, it is used through a continuous loop that connects intention, questions, code, and understanding.

This loop has the following five moments, always in the same order:

1. Intention
2. Prompt
3. Code
4. Observation
5. Understanding

It starts with an **intention**. An intention is not a technical specification, but a concrete need: wanting to start a project, wanting to see if an application runs, wanting to understand why a response looks a certain way. At the beginning, intentions are deliberately small. They only need to be clear enough to justify the next step.

From the intention comes a **prompt**. The prompt is how the intention is expressed as a question to the Artificial Intelligence (AI). At this stage, precision matters more than completeness. The goal is not to ask for the perfect solution, but rather to ask a question that allows progress.

The prompt produces **code**. This code is not theoretical or hypothetical. It is written into real files, inside a real project, by using a real editor. The code may be incomplete, naïve, or temporary. That is expected.

Once the code exists, it is executed, which then leads to **observation**. Something observable always happens: a server starts, a request fails, a response is returned, and an error message appears. Observation is the moment when the system answers back.

Finally, observation leads to **understanding**. This does not mean mastering every detail, but rather recognizing what happened and why it happened at a basic level. Understanding closes the loop and, almost immediately, generates the next intention. *Figure* 2.1 shows a development loop in which intentions are transformed into prompts, prompts into code, code into observable behavior, and observation into understanding.

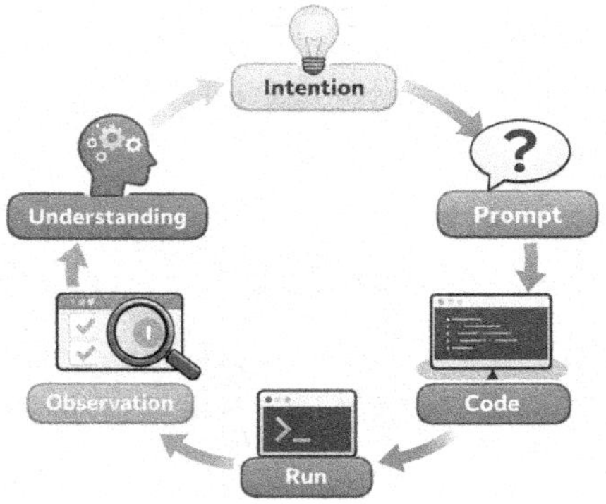

Figure 2.1: *The Prompt-Driven Development Cycle*

This cycle is not linear, and it is not meant to be completed once. It is iterative by nature. Each pass through the cycle slightly improves both the application and the mental model.

What matters is that progress does not come from knowing everything in advance, but rather from completing cycles. A small intention followed through to observation and understanding is more valuable than a large plan that never reaches execution.

Throughout the rest of this chapter — and throughout the rest of the book — FastAPI will be approached in this exact way. Each new feature, architectural decision, and refactoring will be introduced as the result of a new intention, expressed through a prompt, materialized in code, observed in execution, and only then explained.

With this cycle in place, we can now move to the first concrete intention: starting a FastAPI application from scratch that responds to something real.

The Method of This Book: Developing through a Continuous Cycle

The previous section defined the prompt-driven development cycle. This section will explain why the book is built around it, and what changes when you adopt it as your default way of working.

Most beginners approach a new framework as a checklist. They collect features, memorize syntax, and try to follow tutorials step by step. The result is often brittle knowledge: it works as long as the example matches the reality and collapses the moment something changes. This book takes the opposite approach. It treats development as a sequence of small, complete iterations—with each starting from a concrete intention and ending with observable behavior and a clearer mental model.

This is how real projects are built. Developers rarely move in straight lines. They try something, they see what happens, and they adjust. The presence of an AI assistant does not replace this pattern. It accelerates it only if the developer stays engaged in the loop: asking the next question, applying the next change, and validating it through execution. In this method, prompts are not magic commands. They are a way to turn uncertainty into the next actionable step.

FastAPI is particularly well-suited to this approach because it makes the system's boundary explicit and testable, capable of providing immediate feedback through HTTP responses. Requests come in, code runs, and responses go out. Small changes produce immediate and visible effects. This tight feedback loop makes it easier to connect what you wrote with what the system did, and what the system did with what you now understand. *Figure* 2.2 shows how each iteration crosses the FastAPI boundary: a request enters the system, code is executed, and a structured response is returned and observed. For example, changing a product price in the code and immediately seeing the updated JSON response in the browser helps the developer to verify both the behavior and their understanding of the system.

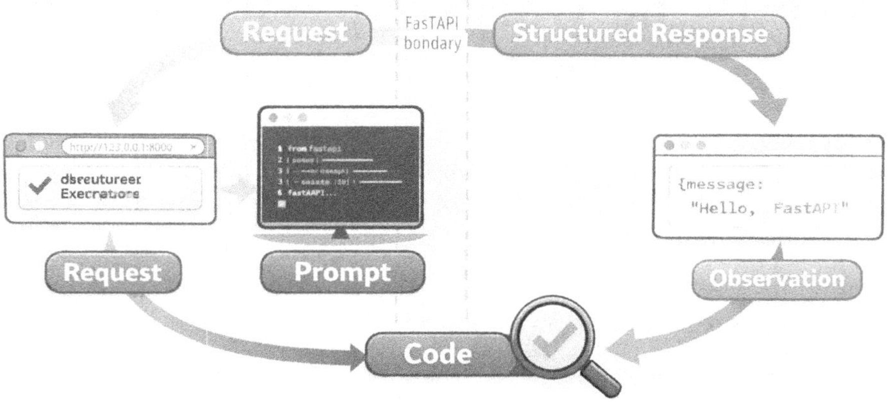

Figure 2.2: *The Cycle Applied to a FastAPI Application*

Over time, repeating this cycle does more than grow the application. It trains a habit: before asking for code, you clarify the intention; before trusting an answer, you execute; and before moving forward, you explain what happened. This is the core skill the book aims to build. *Figure* 2.3 shows how the application evolves step-by-step—with each cycle adding a small piece of functionality and refining the developer's mental model.

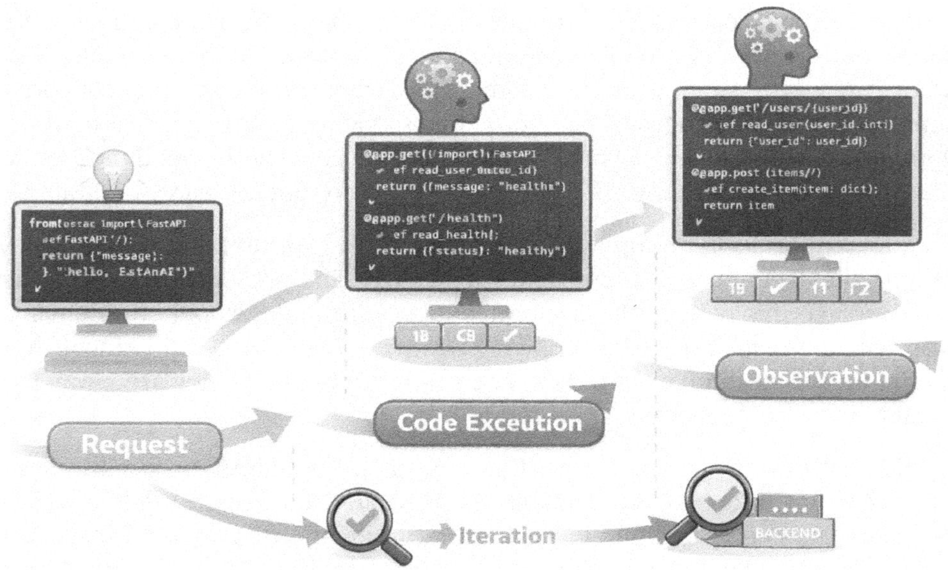

Figure 2.3: *Incremental Growth of the Application through Repeated Cycles*

With this method in place, we can move to the first concrete objective. That is not to design an entire application, but rather to complete a first iteration by starting FastAPI, executing it, and observing a real response.

Setting up the Workshop: Virtual Studio (VS) Code, Git, and AI Assistants

Before we write any FastAPI code, we need a place where the cycle can actually happen. "Intention → Prompt → Code → Observation → Understanding" is not an abstract idea: it requires a concrete workshop where we can write files, run commands, inspect outputs, and collaborate with our AI tools without friction.

The intention of this section is simple: prepare a working environment that makes every next step in the book executable and observable.

A bad way to start could be as follows:

Bad Prompt

How do I install FastAPI?

This question is too narrow and lacks context. It does not explain the intended workflow, the development environment, or the actual goal of the setup. Instead, a good way to start is to ask the AI for a practical checklist. Not a long guide, just the minimal set of actions needed to get from "nothing" to "I can run a FastAPI app from VS Code."

Good Prompt

I'm starting from a clean machine, and I want to build a FastAPI project step by step.

I will use VS Code.

Give me the minimum steps to: create an isolated Python environment, install FastAPI + an ASGI server,

run the app from the integrated terminal and connect an AI assistant in the editor.

Keep it practical and ordered: do I install FastAPI?

This version provides the AI with just enough context to produce a focused and actionable setup plan.

Expected Output Summary

A practical setup usually includes:

1. *Install Python*
2. *Install VS Code*
3. *Add the Python extension*
4. *Create a virtual environment*
5. *Install FastAPI and Uvicorn*
6. *Run the application from the integrated terminal*
7. *Optionally connect Git and an AI assistant extension*

The goal is not to build a complete production environment yet, but to create a clean workspace where development, execution, and feedback can happen quickly.

A useful answer will converge on the same essentials: Python, a virtual environment, FastAPI + Uvicorn, VS Code with the Python extension, and (optionally) Git plus AI extensions. The point is not to follow the response blindly, but rather to implement the minimum that makes progress possible.

We begin by creating a project folder and opening it in VS Code. In this book, we will use the following name:

```
fastapi_app/
```

Inside VS Code, open the integrated terminal (that is, Terminal → New Terminal). From now on, every command we run will be executed from this terminal, and every file we edit will live inside this folder. The first technical decision is to create an isolated Python environment. This prevents dependency conflicts and makes the project reproducible.

FastAPI works best with modern Python versions (Python 3.11 or newer is recommended).

From the project root (**fastapi_app/**), run the following command:

```
python -m venv .venv
```

This creates a folder called "**.venv**," containing a private Python installation for this project, as shown in *Figure 2.4*.

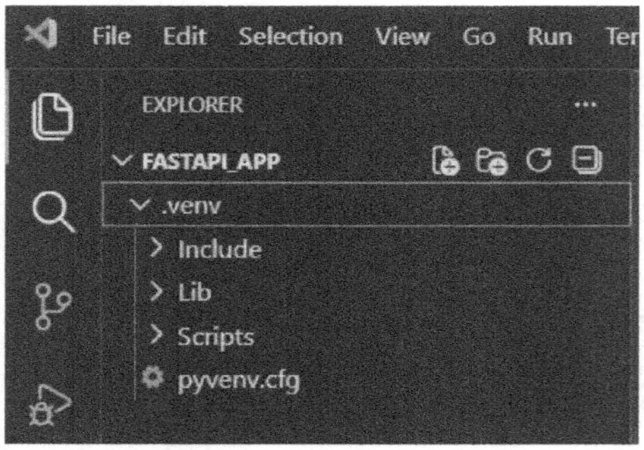

***Figure 2.4:** In VS Code Explorer, You Can Follow the Project Structure*

Your project now looks as follows:

```
fastapi_app/
└── .venv/
```

Now, activate the environment. If activation fails, check the execution policy (Windows).

On Windows (PowerShell):

```
.\.venv\Scripts\Activate.ps1
```

On macOS/Linux:

```
source .venv/bin/activate
```

You should see the environment name appear at the beginning of your terminal prompt. This is a small yet important observation: it confirms that the commands you run next will affect this project and nothing else (refer to *Figure 2.5*).

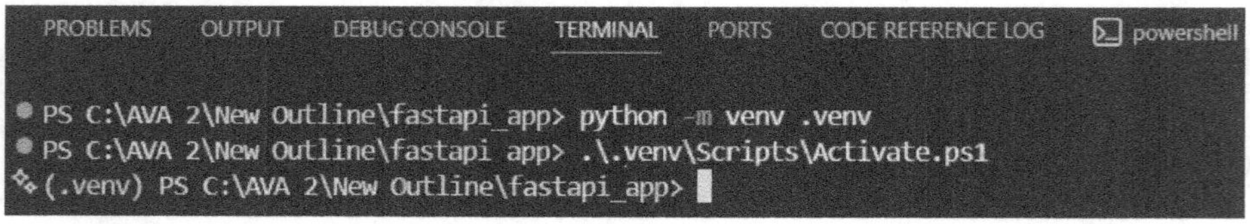

***Figure 2.5:** In the VS Code Terminal, You Can Run Commands in the New Virtual Environment Created Specifically for This Project*

Now, install the minimum dependencies needed to run FastAPI:

```
pip install "fastapi>=0.115" "uvicorn[standard]>=0.30"
```

Pinning minimum versions reduces compatibility issues and makes the setup more reproducible across different environments. At this point, we want a quick sanity check—something observable that confirms the installation worked and that VS Code is using the correct Python environment, which is as follows.

```
python -c "import fastapi; print(fastapi.__version__)"
```

This command verifies the following two things at once:

- FastAPI is actually installed, and
- The active Python interpreter can access it correctly.

If this prints a version number, similar to the following:

```
0.128.7
```

The environment is alive, and FastAPI is available. However, if you see an error such as "**`ModuleNotFoundError: No module named 'fastapi'`**," the most common cause is that the virtual environment is not activated, or VS Code is using a different Python interpreter.

Next, we will make VS Code aware of this environment. VS Code must run and analyze Python using the interpreter inside the "**`.venv`**" file; otherwise, the editor and the terminal will disagree about what is installed.

In VS Code, open the Command Palette (*Ctrl+Shift+P* on Windows/Linux, *Cmd+Shift+P* on macOS) and choose "Python: Select Interpreter" (as shown in *Figure* 2.6). Select the interpreter that includes **`.venv`** in its path. This is one of those small steps that prevents hours of confusion later. If you ever see a mismatch—FastAPI imports work in the terminal but not in the editor, or the opposite—this interpreter selection is usually the cause.

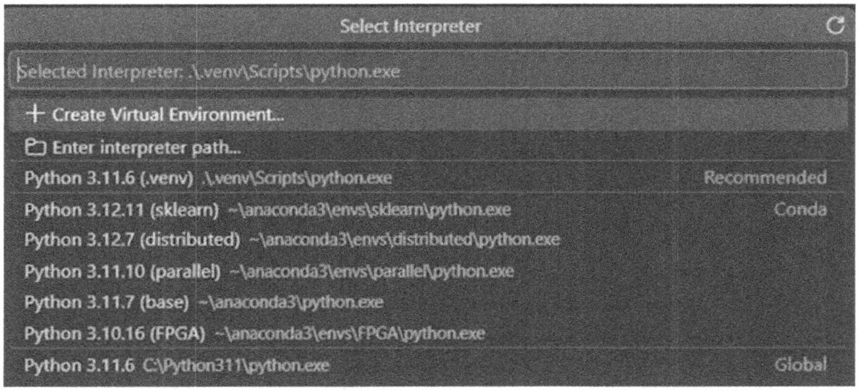

Figure 2.6: *The VS Code Command Palette, the Central Hub for Editor Commands.*

With the environment ready, we will add one more foundational tool: Git. Not because we need a complex workflow, but because Git provides an extremely useful form of "observation" about the project's state. It will also give us checkpoints as the app grows chapter by chapter.

From the project root, initialize a repository in the following way:

```
git init
```

At any moment, we can inspect the current project state with the following command:

```
git status
```

This command helps us observe which files are new, modified, or not yet tracked by Git.

Now, add a "**.gitignore**" file, so that we do not commit the virtual environment or other generated artifacts. The "**.venv**" folder contains a local Python installation that can be recreated automatically, which may differ across operating systems and machines. Ignoring it keeps the repository smaller, cleaner, and more portable. Create a file named:

```
fastapi_app/.gitignore
```

and then, place this minimal content inside:

```
.venv/
__pycache__/
*.pyc
.DS_Store
```

Your project now looks as follows:

```
fastapi_app/
├── .gitignore
└── .venv/
```

Commit this baseline as the first checkpoint in the following manner:

```
git add .gitignore
git commit -m "Initialize project structure"
```

If this is your first time committing on this machine, Git may ask you to configure your name and email. That is normal. Do it once, and it will not interrupt you again.

Now, we will connect the "**assistants**" that will accompany the rest of the book. The point here is not to teach each tool in depth, but rather to ensure that the workflow is real: you can ask questions and receive help inside your environment.

Install the VS Code Python extension (published by Microsoft) if it is not installed yet. This extension is not optional in practice: it enables interpreter selection, linting, debugging, and a smooth experience with virtual environments (as shown in *Figure* 2.7).

Figure 2.7: *From VS Code's Extensions Marketplace, You Can Install Many Useful Tools That Integrate into Your Development Environment*

Next, enable at least one AI assistant inside VS Code. Which one you choose is less important than having a working assistant to interact with. Beginners do not need to use multiple tools immediately—starting with a single assistant is enough. In this book, we will refer to the following three tools:

- **ChatGPT** (external, best for explanations and structured reasoning)
- **GitHub Copilot** (in-editor code suggestions)
- **Amazon Q Developer** (in-editor assistant with strong AWS awareness)

You can use one, two, or all of the preceding three tools. The workflow remains the same. *Figure* 2.8 shows the Copilot sign-in flow in VS Code, marking the moment when the assistant is enabled and connected to the editor.

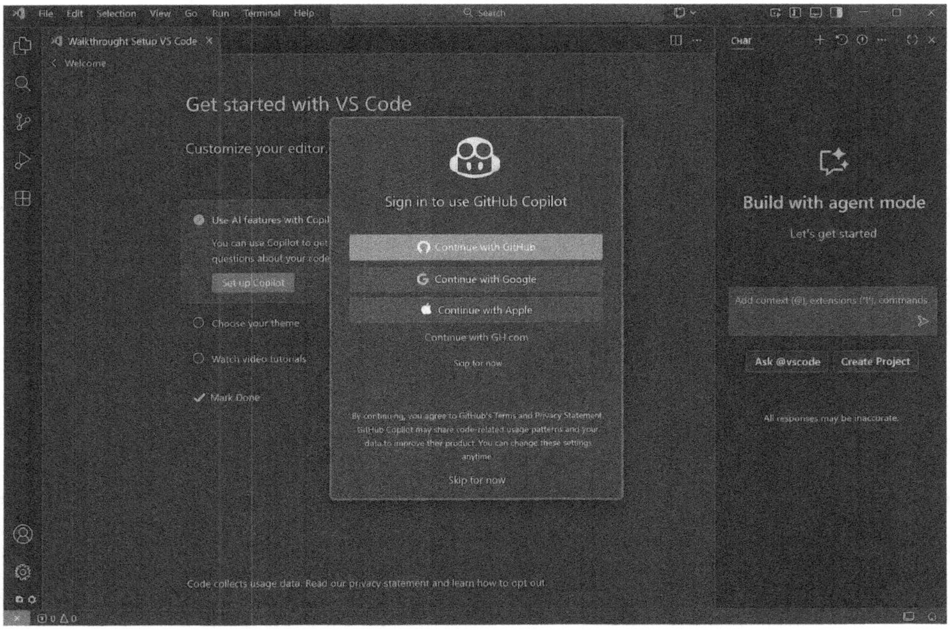

Figure 2.8: *VS Code and GitHub Copilot Activation*

Once Copilot is active, verify that it responds to context. Create a temporary file named:

```
fastapi_app/scratch.py
```

and then, type a single comment such as:

```
# create a function that returns the factorial of a number
```

You should see an inline suggestion appear. Accepting it is optional—the goal is simply to observe that the tool is connected and responsive. *Figure* 2.9 shows an inline completion generated from a Python comment, demonstrating that suggestions appear in real-time.

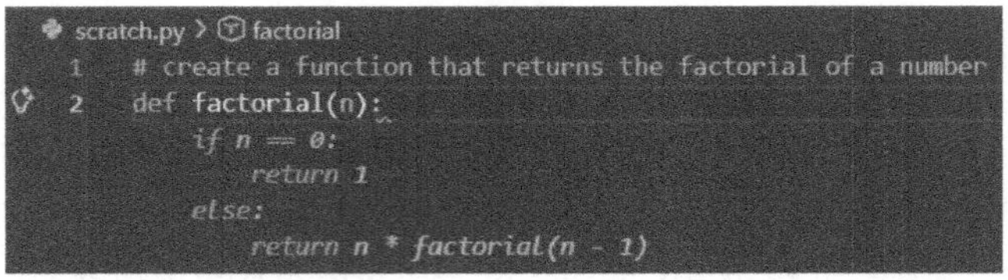

Figure 2.9: *Copilot Suggests Code from a Natural Language Context*

If you want Amazon Q Developer, install the "Amazon Q Developer" extension from the VS Code marketplace and authenticate. Again, the goal is not to write AWS code yet—only to verify that the assistant is available. *Figure* 2.10 shows the extension enabled and connected, confirming that Amazon Q can assist inside the Integrated Development Environment (IDE).

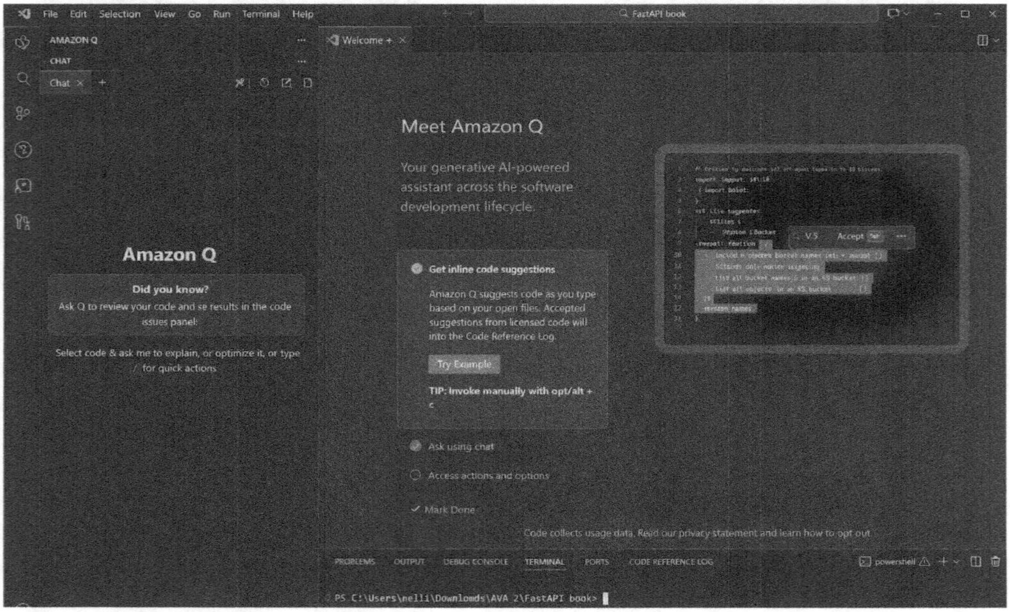

Figure 2.10: *Amazon Q Developer Installed and Authenticated in VS Code*

At this point, the workshop is ready. We have a project folder, an isolated Python environment, FastAPI and Uvicorn installed, VS Code configured to use the correct interpreter, Git initialized for checkpoints, and at least one AI assistant available for prompts and suggestions.

This completes the following first full cycle introduced earlier in the chapter, even though we have not written the application yet:

- The **intention** was to create a space where development can happen.
- The **prompt** provided a minimal setup checklist.
- The **code and commands** created the project structure and environment.
- The **execution step** happened in the integrated terminal.
- The **observations** appeared through terminal outputs, interpreter selection, Git status, and AI responses inside the editor.
- The resulting **understanding** is now practical: we know where work happens, how it runs, and how we will collaborate with assistants.

With the workshop prepared, we can move to the next objective: starting FastAPI and obtaining our first real response.

The Roles of Chat, GitHub Copilot, and Amazon Q

At this point, the workshop is ready. The editor is open, the environment works, and AI tools are available. This is exactly where a new and practical set of questions naturally arises for the reader, which are as follows:

- Why am I using more than one AI assistant?
- Which one should I talk to?
- Which one writes code?
- Which one explains what I already have?

Typical Roles of Each AI Tool

Tool	Best Used For	Typical Interaction
ChatGPT	Explanations, planning, reasoning, debugging concepts	"Explain why this API design is failing."
GitHub Copilot	Inline code suggestions and autocomplete	Writing functions, routes, and repetitive code
Amazon Q Developer	IDE assistance and cloud-aware workflows	AWS integration, infrastructure, and project guidance

Table 2.1: *Typical Roles of AI Assistants in the Development Workflow*

The important idea is not to memorize strict boundaries, but rather to understand that different assistants are optimized for different kinds of interaction. Without clear answers, the risk is not underusing AI, but rather using it inefficiently—asking the right question to the wrong tool, or expecting a tool to do something it was never designed to do.

This book uses three different kinds of AI assistance, which are not interchangeable. They overlap in appearance, but not in role. Understanding this distinction early makes every prompt more effective and reduces frustration.

A good way to clarify this is to turn the confusion itself into a prompt.

Prompt

I'm building a FastAPI app in VS Code.

I have ChatGPT, GitHub Copilot, and Amazon Q available.

What is the role of each one during development, and when should I use which?

A clear answer does not describe features. It describes actions.

Chat-based AI is best used when you need to think. It is the tool you turn to when the problem is still fuzzy: when you are trying to understand what to build, why something behaves a certain way, or which direction to explore next. It does not see your project unless you show it explicitly, but it excels at reasoning, explanations, and high-level guidance. Chat is where intentions become clearer questions.

GitHub Copilot, on the other hand, does not wait for questions. It works silently, inside the editor, while you type. Its role is not to explain or decide, but to assist during writing. Copilot reads the current file, nearby code, comments, and patterns, and suggests what usually comes next. It intervenes directly in the code, proposing concrete implementations. It is not conversational, and it does not reason aloud. Its strength is speed and continuity.

Amazon Q sits in between these two roles. It is conversational as a chat-based AI, but context-aware as Copilot. It can see the file you are currently editing and reason about it without requiring you to copy and paste code. Its role is to explain, navigate, and clarify existing code inside the project. When something already exists, and you want to understand it better, Amazon Q is usually the right tool.

The distinction becomes clearer if we frame it around common development needs, as shown in *Figure 2.11*.

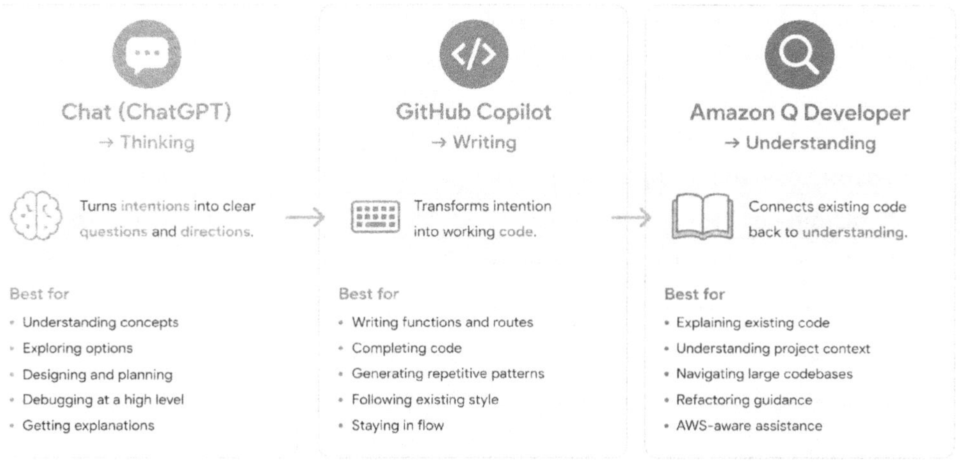

Figure 2.11: *Complementary Roles of AI Assistants in the Development Workflow*

When you are unsure what to do next or why a concept exists, chat-based AI is the right starting point.

When you are actively typing code and need help to complete it, Copilot is the right companion. When code already exists, and you want it explained or inspected in context, Amazon Q is the most efficient choice.

Each tool intervenes at a different moment in the cycle, demonstrated as follows:

- Chat shapes the intention and refines understanding.
- Copilot transforms intention into code.
- Amazon Q connects existing code back to understanding.

Figure 2.11 shows how Chat-based AI supports reasoning and planning, Copilot assists while writing code, and Amazon Q explains and navigates existing code inside the editor.

It is important to notice what these tools are not meant to do. Copilot should not be expected to explain architectural decisions. Chat should not be expected to know the current state of your project without being shown. Amazon Q should not be treated as a replacement for thinking about design. Each tool is powerful precisely because it is specialized.

Using multiple assistants is not redundant. It is a division of labor.

Once this mental map is clear, prompts become sharper. Instead of asking a generic question to whichever tool is closest, the developer chooses deliberately: Who should answer this question, why, and at which point in the cycle.

Choosing the Right Assistant for the Task

Situation	Best Tool
Understanding a concept or planning an API	ChatGPT
Writing or completing code quickly	GitHub Copilot
Explaining existing project code	Amazon Q Developer
Exploring architectural alternatives	ChatGPT
Generating repetitive implementation patterns	GitHub Copilot
Understanding a file already open in the editor	Amazon Q Developer

Table 2.2: *Selecting the Appropriate AI Assistant for Different Development Tasks*

With this distinction in place, we can now address a related and practical concern: how these tools see your code, and how much context you actually need to provide for them to be useful.

Letting the AI Read Your Code without Copy–Paste

Once the different roles of the AI assistants are clear, a practical question inevitably follows. It is a question that every developer asks the moment they start working with AI inside an editor: How does the AI actually see my code?

More specifically, do I need to copy and paste files into a chat every time I want an explanation? Does the assistant know which file I am looking at? And why does one tool seem to understand the code without me providing it, while another does not?

These questions matter because they directly affect how prompts are written and how often the developer is forced to break focus. The answer is simple, but the implications are important: not all AI tools operate with the same level of context, as shown in *Figure 2.12*.

Figure 2.12: *Different Levels of Context Awareness in AI Development Assistants*

At this point in the chapter, a real file exists in the project: `app/main.py`. It contains a minimal FastAPI application, and the reader is looking at it inside VS Code. This is the perfect moment to understand how different tools interact with that same piece of code.

Chat-based AI tools operate outside the editor. They do not see your project, your files, or your terminal. They only know what you explicitly give them. If you want such a tool to explain a piece of code, that code must be included in the prompt.

Prompt

Here is a FastAPI endpoint.

Explain what it does and why it returns JSON.

from fastapi import FastAPI

app = FastAPI()

@app.get("/")

def read_root():

return {"message": "Hello, FastAPI"}

This works well when the goal is conceptual understanding, comparison, or reasoning which is detached from the current project state. The trade-off is friction: you must decide what to include, keep the pasted code up-to-date, and constantly move information in and out of the editor.

GitHub Copilot works in a completely different way. It does not wait for questions or explain. It continuously reads the file you are editing, along with nearby context, and reacts to what you type. Its prompts are not questions, but rather comments and partial code written directly in the file.

When you write something in the following manner:

```
# add a new GET endpoint that returns a status message
```

Copilot interprets this as intent and proposes code inline. It intervenes directly in the writing phase of the cycle. What it will not do is explain why the code works or describe the behavior of an existing file. Copilot is optimized for continuation, not reflection.

Amazon Q operates somewhere in between. Similar to chat-based AI, it can answer questions, and similar to Copilot, it is embedded in the editor. The crucial difference is that it can see the file you are currently working on without requiring you to paste anything.

This enables a different kind of prompt—shorter, more natural, and explicitly contextual.

Prompt

Explain what this FastAPI file does and how the response is generated.

In this case, "this FastAPI file" refers to the open editor tab. The assistant already has access to the code and can reason about it directly. This makes Amazon Q particularly useful during the observation and understanding phases of the cycle, when something has already happened, and the developer wants to know why. *Figure* 2.13 shows how an editor-embedded assistant can reason about code in context without manual copy-paste.

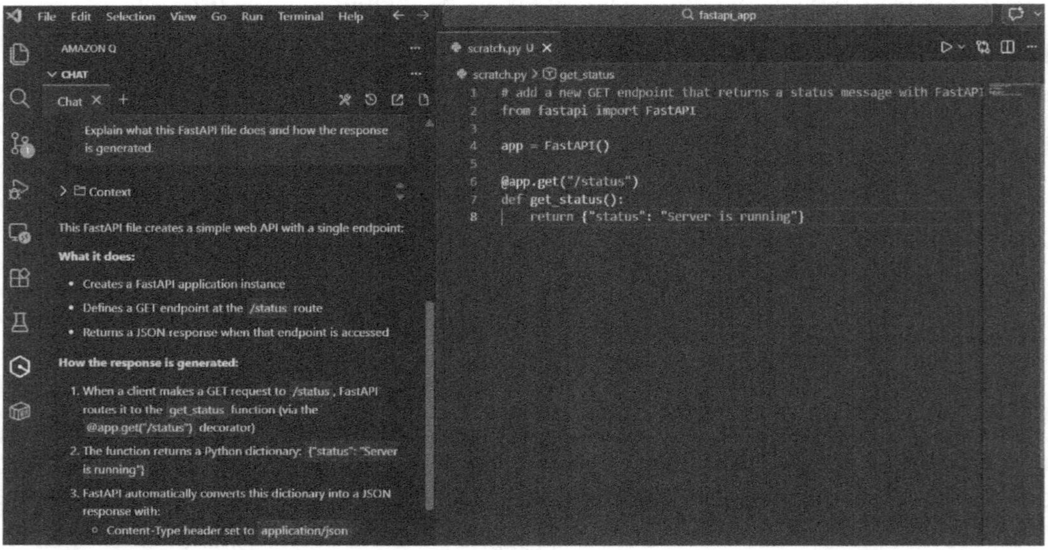

Figure 2.13: *Asking an AI Assistant to Explain the Currently Open File*

The difference between these tools is not about intelligence, but rather about context. Chat-based AI requires explicit input. Copilot requires no explicit input, as it only helps while writing. Amazon Q requires an open file and supports explanation and navigation inside the project. *Figure 2.13* shows how some AI tools operate only on information explicitly provided in the prompt, while others derive context directly from the editor.

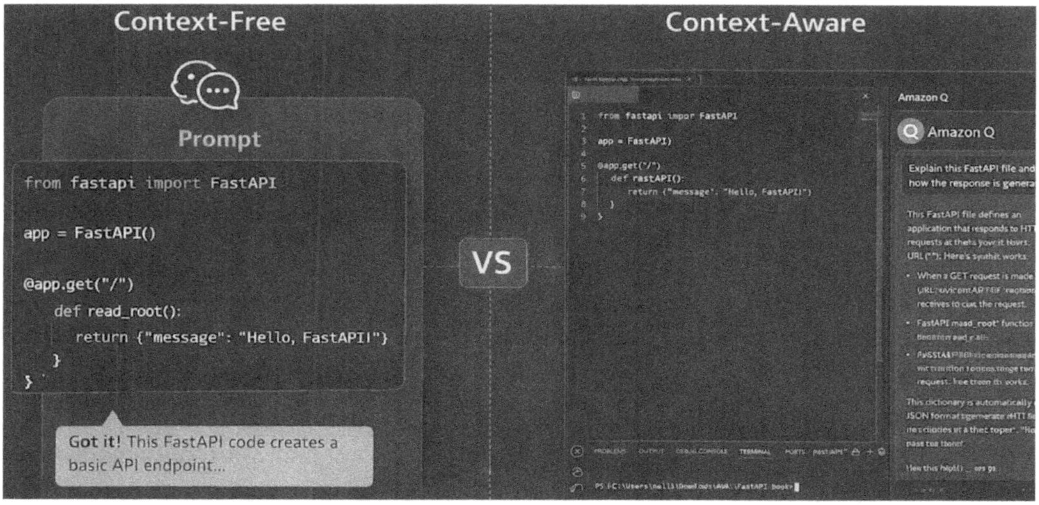

Figure 2.14: *Context-Aware versus Context-Free AI Interaction*

Once this distinction is clear, prompt writing becomes more efficient. Instead of pasting code by default, the developer first considers whether the assistant already sees the relevant context. Shorter prompts become possible, interruptions are reduced, and the cycle flows more naturally from execution to understanding.

With this clarified, we can now return to the development cycle itself and define the first concrete objective for the application—one that we can complete using the tools and interaction patterns that we have just established.

The First Concrete Objective

With the development cycle now clearly defined, the next step is not to design an application, but rather to choose the first objective that is small enough to be completed in a single iteration.

At this stage, the goal is explicitly not to build a complete backend, define a domain model, or make architectural decisions that will only make sense later. Attempting to do so would break the cycle before it even starts, replacing action with speculation.

The first objective is intentionally minimal: start FastAPI, make it respond to a request, and verify that the boundary described in *Chapter 1*, *From Zero to an API Using Prompts*, actually works.

This objective can be broken down into three concrete outcomes. First, the application must be able to start. Second, it must be reachable from the outside through an HTTP request. Third, it must return a response that can be directly observed.

None of these outcomes requires persistence, authentication, background tasks, or complex configuration. They only require that the FastAPI application exists, which is capable of receiving and answering a request. This is enough to complete the first cycle.

What matters here is not the usefulness of the response, but rather its existence. A trivial response is sufficient as long as it crosses the boundary: something from the external world enters the system, and something from the system comes back out.

By keeping the objective narrow, we make it possible to focus on the mechanics of the cycle itself. The reader can clearly see where the intention begins, how it is turned into a prompt, how code is produced, and how observation confirms that something real happened.

Once this objective is achieved, the application will still be extremely simple, but it will no longer be abstract. It will be a running system, however small, and that makes every subsequent step grounded in reality rather than theory.

With the objective defined, we can now move to the next step: turning this intention into a prompt that allows us to start a FastAPI project.

The First Prompt: Starting a FastAPI Project

With a clear objective in mind, the next step in the cycle is to turn that objective into a prompt. At this point, the intention is still very limited: we want to start a FastAPI project in a way that allows us to run it and observe a response.

The prompt does not attempt to define the entire project. It does not ask for best practices, advanced architecture, or long-term decisions. Its purpose is to unblock the first iteration, not to solve the whole problem.

A prompt that fits this intention might appear in the following manner:

Prompt

I want to start a new FastAPI application in Python.

I am using VS Code.

What is the simplest correct way to begin?

The preceding prompt is intentionally vague in some places and precise in others. It specifies the framework, the language, and the editor, but it does not impose constraints on structure or tooling. This is a deliberate choice. At the beginning of a project, asking for the best solution often leads to unnecessary complexity. Asking for a simple and correct starting point is usually more productive.

The response to this prompt will typically contain more information than is immediately needed.

Expected Response

A useful response will usually contain:

1. *Environment setup*

   - Python installation

   - Virtual environment creation

2. *Project dependencies*

   - FastAPI

   - Uvicorn

3. *Editor configuration*

   - VS Code Python extension

   - Interpreter selection

4. *Minimal application structure*

   - main.py

   - first endpoint

5. *Execution steps*

   - running the server

   - testing the API in the browser

The important point is not to memorize every step immediately, but rather to recognize the workflow and identify the next actionable task.

At this stage of the cycle, the goal is not to follow the response line-by-line. The goal is to extract just enough guidance to move from intention to code. In practice, this means identifying the minimal actions required to produce a running application.

From the response, we take three key ideas and deliberately ignore the rest for now. We need a project directory. We need a place where application code can live. We also need a single Python file that FastAPI can execute.

Everything else—testing, configuration, modularization, and environment management—can wait. Those concerns will naturally reappear in later cycles, when the application has grown enough to justify them.

With this filtered understanding of the response, the cycle is now ready to move forward. The next step is to translate this guidance into something concrete by creating the first files and folders in VS Code.

Translating the Prompt into Reality: VS Code

At this point in the cycle, the prompt has done its job. It has reduced uncertainty and provided enough direction to act. The next step is to translate that direction into something concrete by using a real editor and a real project structure.

We will open VS Code and create a new folder that will serve as the root of the project. The name is not important, but it should clearly identify the application. In this book, we will use the following folder:

```
fastapi_app/
```

This folder represents the boundary of the project itself. Everything related to the application will live inside it. For now, it is empty, and that is exactly what we want.

Inside the project root, we create a folder called "**app**." This folder will contain the application code.

```
fastapi_app/
└── app/
```

The choice to introduce the "**app**" folder at this stage is pragmatic rather than architectural. It gives us a clear place to put code without committing to a complex structure. Nothing more is implied yet. The structure is intentionally minimal. At this stage, the goal is not to design a complete architecture, but rather to create the smallest possible environment in which the application can run, evolve, and be understood step-by-step.

Inside the "app" folder, we will create a file named "**main.py**."

```
fastapi_app/
└── app/
    └── main.py
```

At this moment, the project consists of three elements: a root folder, a single subfolder, and a single Python file. There are no configuration files, no dependency declarations, and no supporting modules. This is intentional. The purpose of this step is not to anticipate future needs, but rather to create the minimum structure required to complete the first cycle.

It is worth noticing what we are not doing. We do not design architecture. We are not separating concerns. We are not choosing patterns. All those decisions depend on understanding how the application behaves, and that understanding does not exist yet.

The structure exists only to support execution. It is a temporary scaffold, and not a final design. Its correctness will be validated not by how elegant it looks, but rather by whether it allows FastAPI to start and respond.

With this minimal structure in place, the project is now ready for code. The next step in the cycle is to write the smallest possible FastAPI application inside the "main.py" file, and see what happens when it runs.

Writing the First Endpoint

With a minimal project structure in place, the next intention in the cycle is clear: write just enough code to verify that FastAPI can run and respond to a request.

At this stage, the code is not meant to be reusable, extensible, or elegant. It is only meant to be executable. The only requirement is that it allows the application to cross the boundary between the external world and the system, producing an observable response.

To do this, we return to "app/main.py" and write the smallest possible FastAPI application, which is as follows:

```
from fastapi import FastAPI

app = FastAPI()

@app.get("/")
def read_root():
    return {"message": "Hello, FastAPI"}
```

This file contains everything that is strictly necessary. A FastAPI application instance is created. A single HTTP endpoint is defined. The **`@app.get("/")`** line is called a "decorator." It tells FastAPI that the function below should handle HTTP "GET" requests sent to the root path (/). When that endpoint is called, it returns a Python dictionary.

At this point, it is important not to explain every line of this code. The purpose of this step is not understanding, but rather only execution. Explanation will come after we observe what the system does.

What matters is that the code expresses a clear intention: when a request reaches the root path, something should be returned. The details of how FastAPI turns this into an HTTP response are deliberately left opaque for now.

The cycle has now moved from intention to prompt, and then from prompt to code. The next step is to execute this code and observe what happens when the application runs.

Running the Application

Once the code exists, the cycle reaches a crucial point: execution. Until now, everything has been potential. Running the application turns that potential into observable behavior.

From the project root directory, "**fastapi_app/,**" we start the application using an Asynchronous Server Gateway Interface (ASGI) server. The command is executed in a terminal in the following way:

```
uvicorn app.main:app --reload
```

This command deserves brief attention because it connects the project structure to the running application, explained as follows:

- "`app.main`" refers to the Python file: **`app/main.py`**.
- "`:app`" refers to the FastAPI application object created inside that file.
- "`--reload`" tells Uvicorn to automatically restart the server whenever the code changes.

For now, it is enough to understand that this command allows FastAPI to locate and run the application.

If the application starts correctly, the terminal shows that a server is listening on a local address. By default, FastAPI runs on port 8000, which is why the browser address includes "`:8000`."

At this point, the application is active, waiting for requests.

To observe its behavior, we act from the outside. Using a browser, we navigate to the following:

```
http://127.0.0.1:8000/
```

The response is immediate and visible, which is as follows:

```
{"message":"Hello, FastAPI"}
```

This moment marks the observation phase of the cycle. A request originating outside the system reached the FastAPI application; it was handled by the code in "**`main.py`**," and resulted in a structured response. This is the reader's first real API: small, simple, and local, but already capable of receiving requests and returning JSON over HTTP. *Figure* 2.15 shows how a request sent from the browser crosses the FastAPI boundary and produces a JSON response generated by the application code.

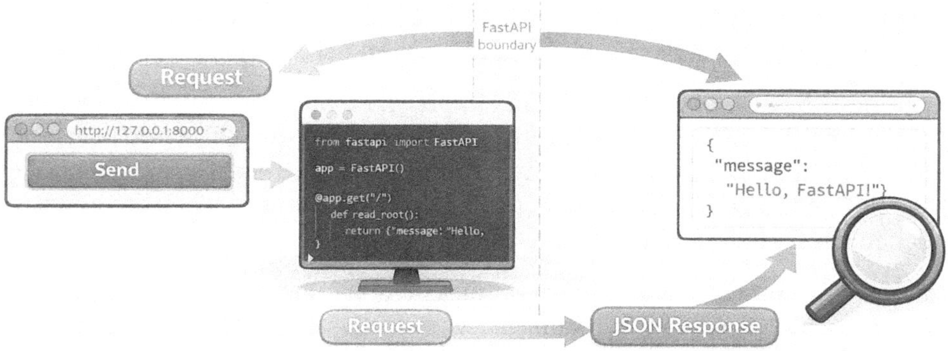

Figure 2.15: *First Observable Response from the FastAPI Application*

At this point, the application is still extremely simple, but something essential has happened. The boundary described in *Chapter 1, From Zero to an API Using Prompts*, is no longer an abstract concept. It has been exercised, and the system has responded.

The next step is not to add features or modify code, but rather to pause and reflect on what just happened. Understanding comes after observation, not before it.

Stopping to Understand What Happened

At this point, the temptation is to keep moving. The application runs, a response appears, and it feels natural to add more endpoints or change something. In this method, however, progress does not come from adding code, but rather from closing the cycle properly.

The system has responded, but the reasons for that response are not yet clear. This is intentional. Understanding is not assumed; it is constructed after observation.

A natural reaction at this stage is to ask what actually happened when the application was executed. That reaction becomes the next prompt.

Prompt

What happened when I ran this FastAPI application?

Why did it automatically return JSON,

and what role does uvicorn play in this process?

This prompt is different from the previous ones. It does not ask for new code. It asks for an explanation of behavior that has already been observed. The goal is not to change the system, but rather to refine the mental model.

The answer to this prompt connects several elements that were previously implicit. Uvicorn acted as the server that received the HTTP request. FastAPI acted as the boundary that translated that request into a function call. The function's return value was automatically converted into a JSON response. None of this required manual wiring, because FastAPI is designed to make these transitions explicit and predictable.

At this point, the concepts introduced in *Chapter 1: From Zero to an API Using Prompts* start to anchor themselves to concrete behavior. The "external world" is no longer an abstraction; it is the browser making a request. The "internal system" is no longer theoretical; it is the code inside "main.py." FastAPI is no longer just a framework; it is the mechanism that connects the two.

This marks the completion of the first full cycle, as shown in *Figure 2.16*. A clear intention led to a prompt. The prompt led to code. The code was executed. The execution produced observable behavior. That behavior led to understanding.

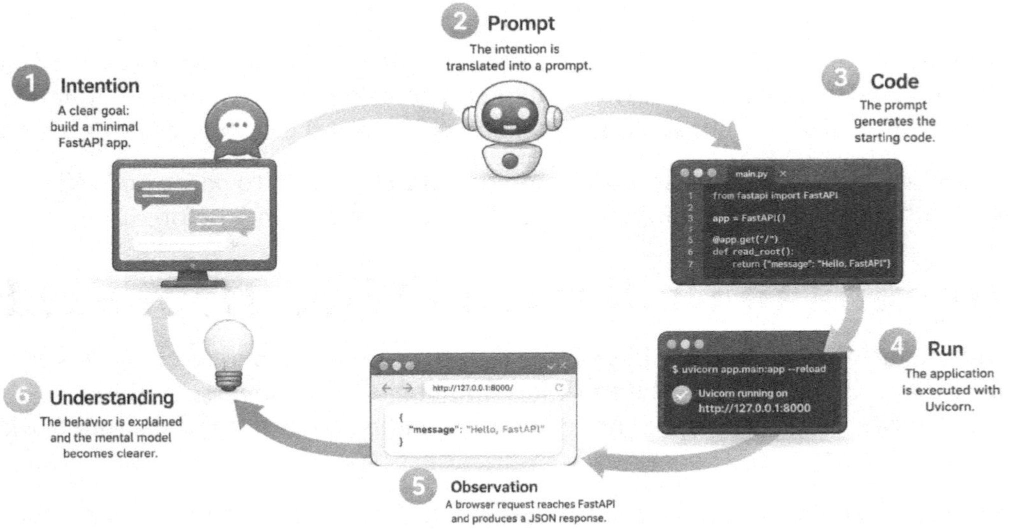

Figure 2.16: *First Observable Response from the FastAPI Application*

The application itself is still minimal, but it is real. More importantly, the reader now has a working reference point. From this point forward, every new feature and every new architectural decision will start from a known state rather than from abstraction.

In the next chapter, we will begin from this exact state of the project, make it explicit, and introduce the next intention that will drive the following cycle of development.

Completing Multiple Prompt Cycles

Up to this point, the prompt-driven development cycle has been explained and demonstrated once. In this guided lab, the goal is different: repeat the cycle several times, deliberately and consciously, using different AI tools for different purposes. Nothing new will be added to the application from a functional point of view. What grows here is the familiarity with the method.

The starting state is known. The project runs, FastAPI responds, and a minimal endpoint exists. From this stable reference point, we can iterate.

The first intention is purely explanatory. After running the application and seeing a JSON response, a beginner often has a vague understanding of what happened, but not a clear one. This is the right moment to use a chat-based AI, because the goal is reasoning, not writing.

Prompt

Explain in simple terms what happens when a FastAPI endpoint returns a Python dictionary.

Focus on the flow from the function return value to the HTTP response.

The value of this prompt is not the code that it might include, but rather the clarification it provides. It connects execution with the mental model, as introduced in *Chapter 1: From Zero to an API Using Prompts*: A function is called, a value is returned, and FastAPI turns that value into a structured HTTP response. Once this explanation makes sense, the cycle naturally generates a new intention.

The next intention is to change the system in a minimal yet concrete way. Not to refactor or to improve architecture, but simply to add something small and observable. This is the moment where writing happens, and where GitHub Copilot is the most appropriate tool.

The developer returns to "**`app/main.py`**" and writes a comment that expresses intent directly in the code in the following way:

```
# add a new GET endpoint at /health that returns a simple status message
```

Copilot reacts to this comment by suggesting an implementation inline in the following manner:

```
@app.get("/health")
def health_check():
    return {"status": "ok"}
```

The developer can accept it as-is, modify it, or reject it. What matters is not the exact code produced, but rather that the intent was expressed in the file itself and immediately translated into runnable code.

At this point, the code exists, but nothing has been observed yet. The next step is execution. The application is already running or has been restarted, and the new endpoint is accessed from the browser at "**`/health`**." A response appears. The system has changed, and that change is visible.

This brings us to the third intention, which is again explanatory. Something worked, but the internal path from request to response may still feel opaque. This is where an editor-aware assistant, such as Amazon Q, becomes useful.

Prompt

Explain how this new endpoint is connected to uvicorn,

and how an HTTP request reaches this function.

As the file is open in the editor, the assistant can reason about the existing code without any copy-paste. The explanation closes the cycle by linking behavior back to structure: the server receives the request, FastAPI routes it, the function executes, and the response is returned. *Figure 2.17* shows how each cycle uses a different assistant according to its strength: chat-based AI for reasoning, Copilot for writing, and Amazon Q for understanding existing code in context.

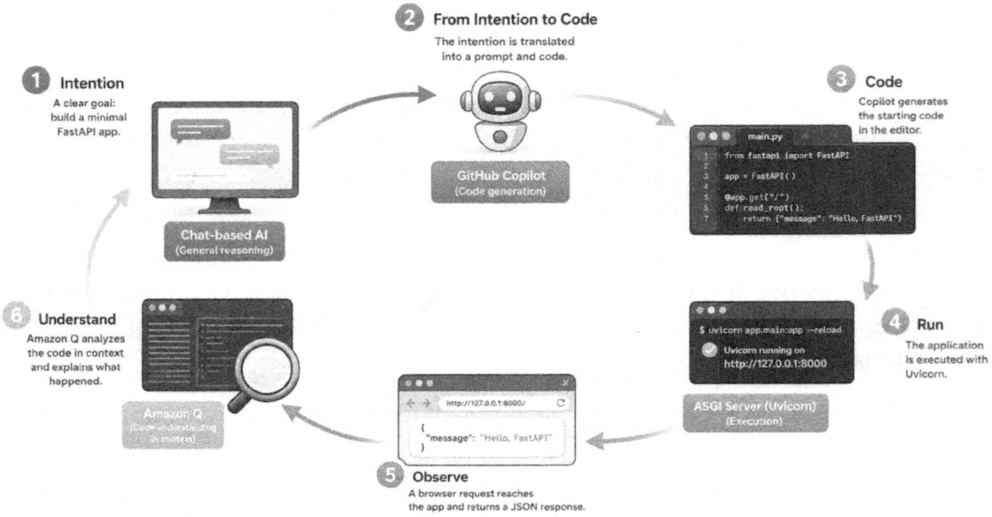

Figure 2.17: *Completing Multiple Prompt-Driven Cycles with Different AI Tools*

What matters in this lab is not the new endpoint itself. It is intentionally trivial. What matters is that the same cycle has now been completed multiple times—each time with a clearer sense of purpose and with more deliberate use of prompts.

The reader has now experienced how questions turn into prompts, how prompts lead to action, and how observation feeds understanding. This repetition transforms the method from an idea into a habit.

With this complete guided practice, the chapter can close. The workshop is ready, the cycle is familiar, and the reader is prepared to move forward—not by guessing what to do next, but rather by knowing how to ask the next right question.

Conclusion

In this chapter, we did not start by writing the application code. We started by asking questions.

We used those questions to set up a working environment, connect our tools, and apply the prompt-driven development cycle for the first time. The result is not a complex system, but rather something more important: a reliable workshop and a repeatable method for moving from intention to execution.

You now have a running FastAPI application, a configured development environment, and a clear way to proceed without guessing or over-planning. From here on, each chapter will build on this foundation, growing the application one step at a time through the same cycle you have just practiced.

In the next chapter, we will cover the transition from a minimal running server to a real Products API. Instead of focusing on theory first, we will generate working endpoints, run them, interact with them through Swagger UI, and observe how FastAPI exposes behavior as an HTTP contract.

We will also begin treating the API as something that can evolve through controlled iterations: generating an initial implementation, testing it as a client, intentionally breaking it, and improving it step-by-step.

Points to Remember

- Environment setup is part of development, and not just preparation.
- The cycle of Intention → Prompt → Code → Observation → Understanding also applies to setup and tooling.
- Early prompts should reduce uncertainty, not design the entire system.
- A minimal FastAPI app provides a real and observable starting point.
- VS Code, the terminal, the virtual environment, and AI assistants form the development workshop.
- AI assistants help during setup, but verification still belongs to the developer.
- Git provides simple checkpoints and visibility into project changes.
- Completing one full cycle before adding features builds confidence and clarity.

Multiple Choice Questions

1. What is the main objective of *Chapter 2, Setting up by Asking the Right Questions*?
    a. To design a complete FastAPI application
    b. To memorize FastAPI commands and configuration options
    c. To set up a working development environment using a prompt-driven approach
    d. To deploy an API to production

2. Why does this chapter treat environment setup as part of the development cycle?
    a. Because setup is optional in FastAPI
    b. Because setup decisions influence how code is written, run, and understood
    c. Because AI tools cannot work without setup
    d. Because FastAPI requires complex configuration
3. In the prompt-driven development cycle, what comes immediately after writing code?
    a. Refactoring
    b. Documentation
    c. Observation of the system's behavior
    d. Deployment
4. What is the purpose of keeping the first FastAPI application intentionally minimal?
    a. To avoid learning FastAPI features
    b. To reduce typing effort
    c. To allow the full development cycle to be completed quickly and clearly
    d. To prepare the app for production
5. How are AI assistants meant to be used during setup and early development?
    a. To automatically configure everything without user intervention
    b. To replace the developer's understanding
    c. To suggest steps and reduce uncertainty while the developer verifies outcomes
    d. To generate final architecture decisions
6. Why is VS Code presented as part of the "workshop" in this chapter?
    a. Because it is the only editor that supports FastAPI
    b. Because it integrates code editing, execution, and AI assistance in one place
    c. Because it replaces the terminal
    d. Because it automatically deploys applications

7. A beginner has created a FastAPI project folder but does not know what to do next. According to the method used in this chapter, what should happen first?
    a. Design the complete architecture
    b. Deploy the application immediately
    c. Ask a focused prompt to reduce uncertainty and identify the next action
    d. Memorize all FastAPI decorators

Answers

1. c
2. b
3. c
4. c
5. c
6. b
7. c

Questions

1. Why is it important to treat the environment setup as part of the development process rather than as a preliminary chore?
2. How does applying the Intention → Prompt → Code → Observation → Understanding cycle to the setup change the way you approach new tools and frameworks?
3. In what ways does starting from a working environment reduce uncertainty before writing application code?
4. How can prompts help you decide what not to do yet during the early stages of a project?
5. Why is it valuable to complete a full development cycle with a minimal FastAPI application instead of aiming for completeness from the start?
6. How does observing concrete outcomes (such as a running server, a response in the browser, an active assistant, and so on) influence understanding more effectively than reading setup instructions?
7. What risks arise if the setup steps suggested by AI tools are followed without verification?
8. Which decisions made during this chapter will most strongly influence how easily the application can evolve in later chapters?

Key Terms

- **Development Environment:** The complete workspace in which code is written, executed, and observed, including the editor, terminal, interpreter, dependencies, and supporting tools.
- **Virtual Environment:** An isolated Python environment that keeps a project's dependencies separate from the system-wide installation, ensuring reproducibility and avoiding conflicts.
- **Visual Studio (VS) Code:** A lightweight, extensible code editor used in this book as the central workspace for editing code, running commands, and interacting with AI assistants.
- **Integrated Terminal:** The terminal embedded in the editor, allowing commands to be executed in the same context as the code being edited.
- **Asynchronous Server Gateway Interface (ASGI) Server:** A server that implements the Asynchronous Server Gateway Interface, enabling non-blocking request handling; in this chapter, Uvicorn is used to run FastAPI applications.
- **Uvicorn:** A lightweight, high-performance ASGI server used to execute FastAPI applications and expose them to HTTP requests.
- **Prompt-Driven Development Cycle:** An iterative workflow consisting of intention, prompt, code, observation, and understanding, used throughout the book to guide learning and development.
- **Prompt:** A natural-language question or instruction given to an AI assistant to reduce uncertainty, explore options, or generate starting points for action.
- **Observation:** The act of inspecting concrete outcomes produced by running code or executing commands, such as server output, responses, or error messages.
- **Workshop:** The practical combination of tools, environment, and assistants prepared in this chapter serves as the space where all subsequent development takes place.
- **AI Assistant:** A generative AI tool (such as ChatGPT, GitHub Copilot, or Amazon Q Developer) used to support setup, exploration, and coding, while leaving decisions and validation to the developer.
- **Minimal Working Application:** A deliberately simple application that runs and responds, used to complete a full development cycle before adding complexity.

CHAPTER 3
Generating Your First Real API

Introduction

In the previous chapter, we established a way of working: starting from an intention, expressing it as a prompt, turning the result into running code, and observing what happens. This chapter will apply that method for the first time to something real. Here, we will build our first API. Instead of starting with a complete upfront design, we will begin with a working system, run it, and interact with it as a client. The goal is not completeness or elegance, but rather observable behavior.

The API introduced in this chapter is intentionally simple, but it is not a throwaway example. It will become the baseline that evolves throughout the book. For this reason, the focus is on execution, interaction through Swagger User Interface (UI), and small controlled improvements rather than the architecture or best practices.

By the end of this chapter, you will have a running Products API—with a clear picture of what it does and does not do, and a concrete reference point for everything that follows.

Structure

In this chapter, we will cover the following topics:

- From a Running Server to a Useful API
- Defining the First Real Objective
- Turning the Objective into a Prompt
- From Prompt to Code: Materializing the First Draft
- Running the Generated API
- First Contact with Swagger UI

- Exploring the API through Swagger (Hands-on)
- Breaking the API on Purpose
- Reading the API as a Client Contract
- Closing the First Cycle
- Understanding Where Behavior Comes from
- Second Cycle: A Targeted Improvement
- Observing the Improved Behavior
- Understanding Server Restarts
- Freezing the Current Mental Model
- Current progress and Next Steps

From a Running Server to a Useful API

At the end of the previous chapter, something important had happened. Not something complex or impressive, but rather something decisive: the environment stopped being theoretical. The editor was configured, the server could run, and FastAPI responded to a request. The workshop was no longer an idea; it was operational. Up to that point, everything revolved around possibility. Now, the focus shifts to production.

This chapter marks the first real transition of the book: from preparing the conditions for development to building something that behaves as a backend system. The tools are no longer the object of attention. They fade into the background where they belong. What matters now is what they allow us to produce.

It is worth making this transition explicit because many learning paths blur it. They move from setup directly into syntax, or from installation straight into architecture diagrams. This book deliberately avoids that jump. Instead, it introduces a clear threshold in the following way:

- Before this point, the goal was to make execution possible.
- After this point, the goal is to make behavior observable.

This chapter begins on the other side of that threshold. The question is no longer "Can FastAPI run?" The question becomes "What can this system actually do?" To answer that, we need to clarify what this book means by a real API. In this context, a real API is not defined by complexity, performance, or completeness. It is defined by behavior. A real API accepts structured input, applies rules to it, exposes a stable boundary, and responds in a predictable way—both when things go right and when they go wrong. It can be interacted with by a client, tested through requests, and reasoned about without reading its internal implementation line-by-line. *Table 3.1* summarizes the difference between a minimal "Hello World" endpoint and an API that already behaves as a real system boundary:

From "`Hello World`" to a Real API

Hello World Endpoint	Real API
Confirms the server is running	Handles structured domain data
Returns a static response	Applies validation and rules
No meaningful input	Accepts and processes requests
No observable failure cases	Returns both success and error responses
No real client contract	Exposes a predictable API boundary

Table 3.1: *Differences between a Minimal Endpoint and a Real API*

By that definition, a single endpoint returning "`Hello, world`" is not yet a real API. It proves that the server runs, but it does not establish a meaningful contract with the outside world. There is no domain, data, constraints, or failure modes to observe.

This chapter is where that changes. The objective is not to build a production-ready system or to introduce best practices or architecture patterns. Those concerns depend on experience, and experience comes from observing systems in motion. For now, the goal is simpler and more concrete: create an API that behaves as something a real client could use.

As in the previous chapter, we will not start with theory. We will not design the system up front. We will not explain FastAPI features exhaustively before touching the code. Instead, we will apply the same method again—this time to something larger than a single endpoint. We will define a clear objective, turn it into a prompt, materialize the result, run it, interact with it, and only then stop to understand what we have built. The difference is that this time, the result will not be disposable. The application created in this chapter will become the foundation for everything that follows. It will be extended, questioned, refined, and sometimes constrained—but it will not be thrown away and replaced with isolated examples. With that in mind, the next step is to decide what this first real API should actually do. Not in abstract terms, but in a way that is small enough to complete, yet realistic enough to behave as a backend system. That is the purpose of the next section.

Defining the First Real Objective

Before writing any code, we need to slow down again—however, just briefly. At the end of the previous chapter, we had a server that ran. That was an important milestone, but it is not yet a meaningful one from an application point of view. A running server proves that the environment works. It has not yet been proved that a system exists. This distinction matters. A server that starts successfully is infrastructure. An API begins only when there is something on the other side of the boundary that a client can use. So, the first question of this chapter is not "What framework features should we learn next?," but something much simpler and more practical: "What should this system do, so that interacting with it feels real?"

To answer that, we need the first objective. Not a long-term vision or a complete product, but rather a goal that satisfies three conditions. First, it must be small enough to complete in a single development cycle. If the goal requires multiple layers, external services, or advanced design decisions, it is too large for this stage. Second, it must be observable from the outside. We must be able to trigger behavior through HTTP requests and see clear and structured responses. If something goes wrong, the system should explicitly tell us. Third, it must resemble real backend behavior. Even if the implementation is simple, the interaction pattern should feel familiar to anyone who has worked with APIs before. With these criteria in mind, we will introduce the domain for this chapter: Products. Product data appears in many real systems, including e-commerce platforms, inventory management tools, warehouse systems, and internal business applications. This makes the domain simple enough for a first API, while still reflecting realistic backend behavior.

Products are intentionally simple and familiar, and that is a strength. Products are immediately understandable, even without domain knowledge. They have identifiers, attributes, and a natural lifecycle. More importantly, they map cleanly to the most common operations that APIs expose by creating resources, listing them, retrieving one by identifier, updating it, and deleting it. By choosing such a simple domain, we remove cognitive overhead. The reader does not need to learn a business model or interpret complex rules. All attention can stay on how the system behaves. At this stage, we also make a deliberate constraint: products will be stored in memory. This is not a shortcut. It is a teaching decision.

Persisting data introduces questions that are orthogonal to the goal of this chapter: database configuration, migrations, failure modes, and consistency. None of those are needed to observe how FastAPI handles requests, validation, routing, and responses. In-memory storage gives us the state while the server runs, without committing us to infrastructure we are not yet ready to explain.

This also allows us to observe an important limitation later: What happens when the server restarts? That limitation will become meaningful precisely because we chose it consciously.

It is just as important to state what we are not yet building, such as:

- We are not yet building authentication or authorization, because security concerns only become meaningful once the core API behavior is working correctly.
- We are not yet designing a project structure.
- We are not yet introducing routers, services, repositories, or dependency injections.

- We are not yet optimizing for performance or scalability.

All of the preceding concerns are real, but they only make sense once there is something real to protect, structure, or optimize. So, the objective for this chapter can be stated plainly: We want a FastAPI application that exposes a minimal yet functional REST API for managing products, using structured input and output, and responding predictably to both valid and invalid requests. Nothing more, nothing less.

With the objective now clearly defined, the next step is to do what this book insists on doing before touching the code: Turn that objective into a prompt. Not a description of implementation, but rather a request focused on behavior and execution. That is where we will go next.

Turning the Objective into a Prompt

At this point, the most tempting thing to do is to open "`main.py`" and start typing. The environment works, the goal feels clear, and writing the code seems as the natural next step. This is exactly the moment where the method of the book asks us to stop. Not to delay progress, but rather to prevent a common mistake: confusing intention with implementation. If we start writing code now, every decision—models, endpoints, and data structures—will be made implicitly without feedback. We would be designing in our heads instead of letting the system answer back. Hence, we pause and turn the objective into a prompt.

This requires a small yet important shift. We do not describe how the system should be built. We describe what it should do. The prompt is not a specification document or a list of best practices; rather, it is a request for observable behavior. A useful way to test a prompt at this stage is to ask a simple question: "If the assistant follows this prompt, will I be able to run the result and interact with it immediately?" If the answer is yes, then the prompt is probably focused enough.

A vague prompt at this stage usually produces a vague behavior.

Weak Prompt

Create a FastAPI app.

This request does not define the domain, the behavior, or the expected interactions. The generated result may run, but it will not necessarily support a meaningful learning cycle. A better prompt focuses on observable behavior and limits unnecessary complexity. Here is the prompt we will use for the first cycle of this chapter:

Good Prompt

Generate a simple FastAPI application that provides a REST API to manage products using in-memory storage.

The API must support creating products, listing all products, retrieving a product by id, updating a product, and deleting a product.

Use Pydantic models for input and output validation.

Keep the code minimal and runnable.

Explain only what is necessary.

Before moving on, it is worth reading this prompt carefully—not to memorize it, but rather to understand its shape.

Expected Output

A useful response will usually generate:

- a minimal FastAPI application

- Product models using Pydantic

- CRUD endpoints for products

- temporary in-memory storage

- instructions for running the server locally

The important point is not the exact implementation, but rather that the generated system can be executed and interacted with immediately. It explicitly names the framework and the goal: a FastAPI application that manages products. It constrains storage to memory, which avoids introducing infrastructure we are not ready to handle. It requires CRUD-style operations, which ensures that the API has enough surface area to feel real. It asks for Pydantic models, which guarantees structured input and output without requiring us to design validation logic manually.

Equally important is what the prompt does not ask for. It does not mention databases, authentication, async behavior, routers, or project structure. It does not ask for optimization, testing, or deployment. It does not ask for explanations of FastAPI concepts. These omissions are deliberate. Every extra requirement would either slow down execution or pull the generated code in a direction that we are not yet prepared to evaluate. One well-scoped prompt is enough for the first cycle. Adding more would not increase learning; it would only increase noise.

At this stage, we are not trying to get the best possible implementation. We are trying to get a working one that can run, respond, fail, and be observed. With the prompt defined, the cycle is ready to move forward. The next step is to let the assistant respond and to turn that response into something concrete inside our project. That is where suggestion becomes reality, and where the system starts to push back. That is what we do next.

From Prompt to Code: Materializing the First Draft

The prompt is now defined. Up to this point, everything has lived in the realm of intention and language. This is the moment when that changes. We submit the prompt to an AI assistant. Whether you use a chat-based tool, Amazon Q inside the editor, or a combination of tools, that does not matter here. What matters is how the result is treated.

The assistant responds with a complete and runnable FastAPI application. Following is a representative and deliberately didactic first draft—simple, explicit, and easy to reason about. This is the version we will use as the reference implementation for this chapter. Create or open the file "**`app/main.py`**" and replace its contents entirely with the following code:

```
from fastapi import FastAPI, HTTPException
from pydantic import BaseModel
from typing import List

app = FastAPI()
# In-memory storage
products = []
next_id = 1
class ProductCreate(BaseModel):
    name: str
    price: float
class Product(ProductCreate):
    id: int

@app.post("/products", response_model=Product)
def create_product(product: ProductCreate) -> Product:
    global next_id
    new_product = Product(id=next_id, **product.model_dump())
    products.append(new_product)
    next_id += 1
    return new_product

@app.get("/products", response_model=List[Product])
def list_products() -> List[Product]:
    return products

@app.get("/products/{product_id}", response_model=Product)
def get_product(product_id: int) -> Product:
    for product in products:
        if product.id == product_id:
```

```
            return product
    raise HTTPException(status_code=404, detail="Product not found")

@app.put("/products/{product_id}", response_model=Product)
def update_product(product_id: int, updated: ProductCreate) -> Product:
    for index, product in enumerate(products):
        if product.id == product_id:
            updated_product = Product(id=product_id, **updated.model_
dump())
            products[index] = updated_product
            return updated_product
    raise HTTPException(status_code=404, detail="Product not found")

@app.delete("/products/{product_id}")
def delete_product(product_id: int) -> dict:
    for index, product in enumerate(products):
        if product.id == product_id:
            products.pop(index)
            return {"message": "Product deleted"}
    raise HTTPException(status_code=404, detail="Product not found")
```

This implementation also makes deliberate trade-offs. Products are stored in a global in-memory state, which is sufficient for learning and experimentation, but not appropriate for production systems where concurrency, scalability, and persistence become important concerns. The implementation also uses simple linear searches through the product list. This is acceptable for a small in-memory dataset and keeps the behavior easy to observe.

At this stage, do not analyze the code line-by-line. That urge is natural, but it is premature. What matters right now is not whether this is the cleanest or most idiomatic FastAPI code. As it is not, and that is intentional. This is a first draft, which is optimized for clarity of behavior rather than elegance of design. Several important things have already happened, even before running the application.

The code defines a clear domain. There is a product with a name, a price, and an identifier. It defines a boundary through HTTP endpoints. It defines rules: products must have certain fields, IDs must exist, and invalid access produces errors. All of this exists now as executable reality, not as ideas. By pasting this code into "**app/main.py**," we cross a critical line in the method of this book. The AI's suggestion is no longer hypothetical. It is now part of your project. It can succeed, fail, or even surprise you, but it must now be dealt with as a real system.

Notice something else that is subtle yet important: We still have not designed anything. We did not decide where to store products, how to generate IDs, or how to handle errors in a sophisticated way. Those decisions were made implicitly by the assistant. That is acceptable at this stage, because the purpose of this cycle is not design mastery, but rather behavioral observation. The next step is, therefore, not reading the code or improving it. The next step is execution. Only once the system runs and responds do explanations become meaningful. That is where we will go next.

Running the Generated API

At this point, the code exists inside the project. That alone is not enough. Until it is executed, it is still only a possibility. From the root of the project, start the application exactly as you did in the previous chapter in the following way:

```
uvicorn app.main:app --reload
```

In this command:

- "**`app.main`**" refers to the file: **`app/main.py`**.
- "**`:app`**" refers to the FastAPI application instance created inside that file.
- "**`--reload`**" automatically restarts the server whenever the code changes.

The command itself is not new. What is new is what it activates. If everything is correct, the terminal will show that the server has started and is listening on a local address. *Figure* 3.1 shows the terminal output of the FastAPI application running with hot reload enabled, confirming that the system is active and reachable.

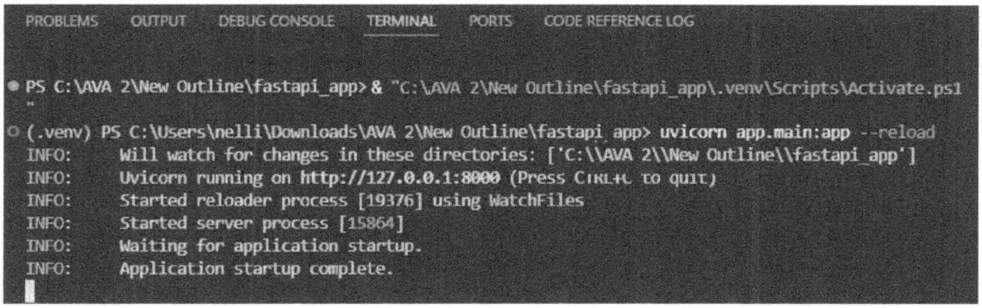

Figure 3.1: *Uvicorn Starts the Generated Products API*

This confirmation matters, but it is only the first signal. The running process does not yet tell us anything about behavior. What matters now is that the system is ready to receive requests. At this moment, the FastAPI application is no longer just a file. It is an active boundary between the outside world and the internal logic defined in "**`main.py`**." Requests can enter, responses can come out, and the state can change. This is the precise meaning of "It runs" in the context of this book.

"It runs" does not mean that:

- The code looks correct,
- There are no syntax errors, or
- The assistant generated something plausible.

Rather, "It runs" means that:

- The server is reachable at its local address (by default on port 8000),
- Endpoints can be called, or
- Behavior can be observed repeatedly.

Figure 3.2 shows a request sent to the running application returning an empty JSON list, demonstrating that the API boundary is active before any data is created.

***Figure* 3.2:** *First Observable JSON Response from the API*

Before interacting with the API, pause for a second and register what has already changed as compared to the end of *Chapter* 2, *Setting up by Asking the Right Questions*. In the previous chapter, running the server only proved that FastAPI was installed correctly. Now, running the server activates an entire domain, including products, identifiers, validation rules, and error conditions. The system has an internal state, even if that state is still very simple. Nothing has been tested yet. Nothing has been verified. Yet, the conditions for observation are now in place. The next step is to interact with the API from the outside, without touching the code. FastAPI gives us a built-in tool for exactly this purpose, and it is the first real "client" of the system. That is where we will go next.

First Contact with Swagger UI

With the server running, the system is alive, but we have not yet interacted with it. At this stage, touching the code again would be a mistake. The goal now is to understand the API strictly from the outside, exactly as a client would. FastAPI provides a built-in interface for this purpose, that is, Swagger UI. Open your browser and navigate to the following:

```
http://127.0.0.1:8000/docs
```

What you see is not static documentation. It is a live view of the running application. Every endpoint listed on this page is connected directly to the code that is currently executing. Every request you trigger here becomes a real HTTP request. Every response you see comes from the application, and not from examples or mocks. This distinction is crucial. Swagger UI is often described as "automatic documentation," but that description is misleading at this stage. For us, Swagger is the first real client of the API (see *Figure* 3.3).

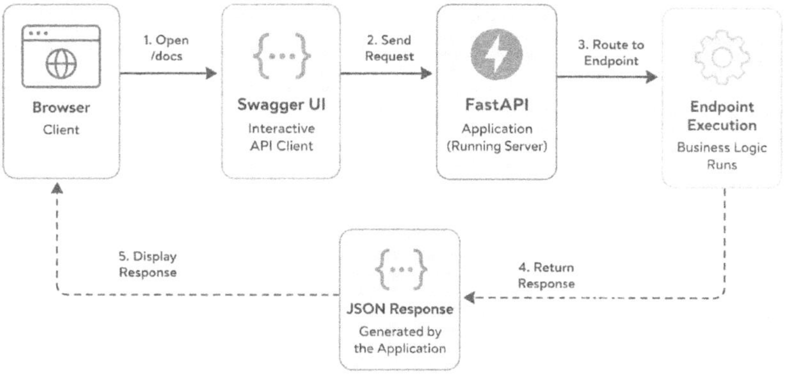

Figure 3.3: *Swagger UI as the First Client of the FastAPI Application*

This is how frontend developers interact. It is the place where the abstract idea of an endpoint turns into something concrete and testable. Before understanding anything, take a moment to simply look at the page. You should see a list of endpoints grouped by HTTP method and path (see *Figure* 3.4). You should see operations for creating products, listing them, retrieving a product by ID, updating it, and deleting it. Even without knowing how the code works, you can already infer something important: the shape of the system is visible.

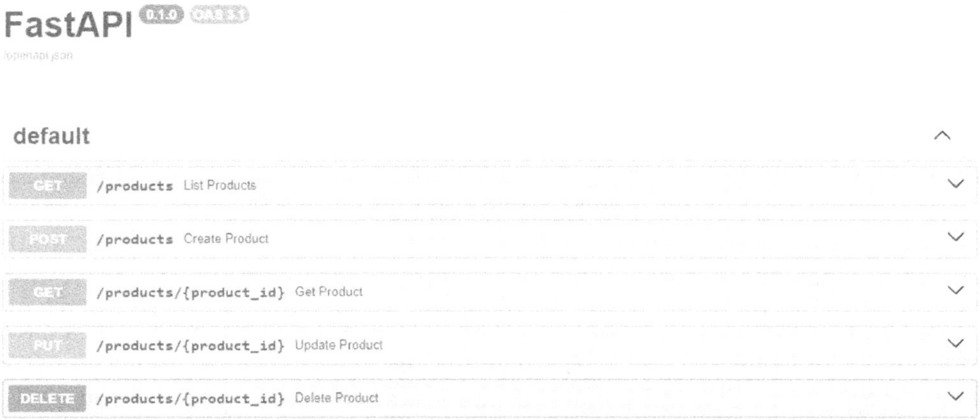

Figure 3.4: *Swagger UI as the Visible API Boundary*

Swagger displays the API boundary. By clicking on each endpoint, it expands to reveal a panel containing:

- The HTTP method,
- The path,
- The expected input, and
- The structure of the response.

Figure 3.5 shows the "`Try it out`" view displaying the JSON schema for product creation, including the required fields and their corresponding data types.

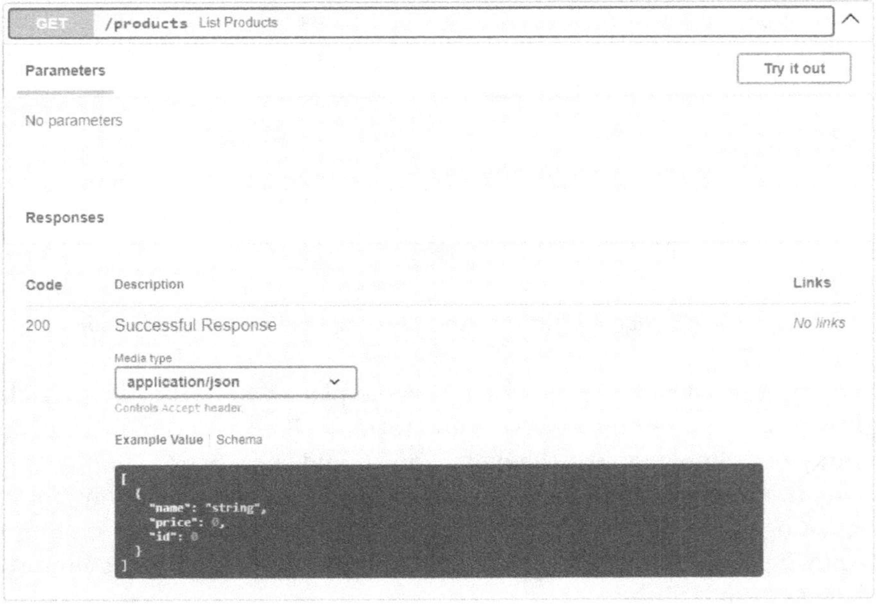

Figure 3.5: *Swagger UI Reveals Request Body Schema and Field Types*

All of this is derived automatically from the code that you have not yet read. That is not an accident. It is a direct consequence of FastAPI's design: types, models, and routes form an explicit contract. At this point, you are not expected to understand how FastAPI generated this interface. That explanation would be premature. What matters is that you can use it. Also Note, Swagger does not ask you to read the documentation before interacting. It invites you to try things. Every endpoint has a "Try it out" button. This is intentional. The API is meant to be explored through action, not description.

From the point of view of this book, Swagger UI plays a specific role. It sits exactly on the boundary as introduced in *Chapter 1, From Zero to an API Using Prompts*. It represents the external world looking at the system and asking: What can you do? What do you expect from me? What will you give back? In the next section, we will stop looking and start acting. We will use Swagger UI to send real requests, create real data, and observe how the system's state changes in response.

Exploring the API through Swagger (Hands-on)

At this point, the API is running and visible. Now, it needs to be exercised. Swagger UI is no longer something that we are observing passively. It has become an instrument.

Every interaction here is a real request sent to the application, and every response reflects the current internal state of the system. We start with the most basic and meaningful action: creating a product.

In Swagger UI, expand the endpoint that creates a product. It will typically be a "**`POST`**" request under "**`/products`**." Click "**`Try it out`**." Swagger now exposes the request body it expects. This is the first moment where the system communicates its rules to us. Enter a simple JSON payload, for example:

```
{
  "name": "Laptop",
  "price": 1200
}
```

Then, click "**`Execute`**" and carefully observe the response. If the request is valid, the API returns a structured JSON object containing the data that you provided along with an automatically generated identifier. This identifier did not exist before the request; it is only created by the system in response to your action. *Figure* 3.6 shows a screenshot of a "**`POST /products`**" request with a valid JSON body and the corresponding response, including the generated product ID.

Figure 3.6: *Creating a Product through Swagger UI*

This confirms several things at once. The API accepts structured input. It applies internal logic. It also produces a structured output that a client can rely on. Now, move to the endpoint that lists all products. Execute the "GET **/products**" request. The response should include the product you just created. This is an important observation: the system has a state. Even though there is no database, the application remembers what happened earlier while it is running. In this context, "state" simply means that data persists in memory during the lifetime of the application process. *Figure* 3.7 shows a screenshot of a "**GET /products**" response that includes the previously created product, demonstrating state persistence while the server is running.

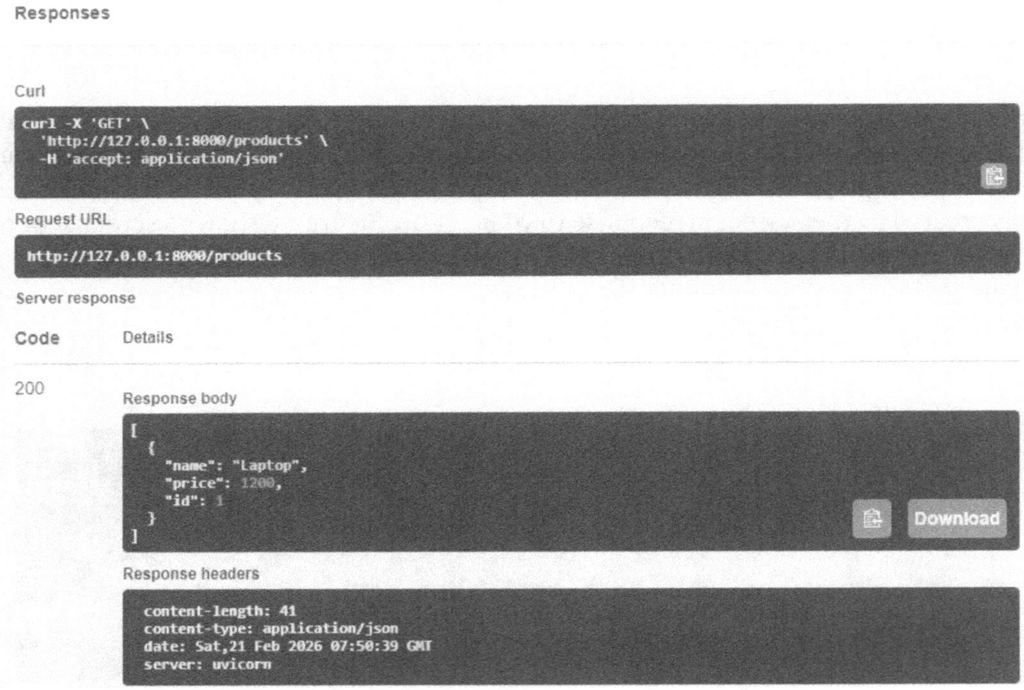

***Figure* 3.7:** *Listing Products Reveals Application State*

Use the ID returned when the product was created and call the corresponding "**GET /products/{product_id}**" endpoint (in this case, **id = 1**). As shown in *Figure* 3.7, focus on observing the behavior rather than explaining it. The API returns exactly one object, matching the structure that was previously observed. From the client's perspective, this confirms that identifiers are stable and meaningful within the lifetime of the application. You can then proceed by updating the product by using the "**PUT**" endpoint. Modify the name or the price, execute the request, and observe the response. Finally, retrieve the list of products again to verify that the changes are correctly reflected. *Figure* 3.8 shows a request to "GET **/products/{product_id}**," returning a single product object corresponding to the specified identifier.

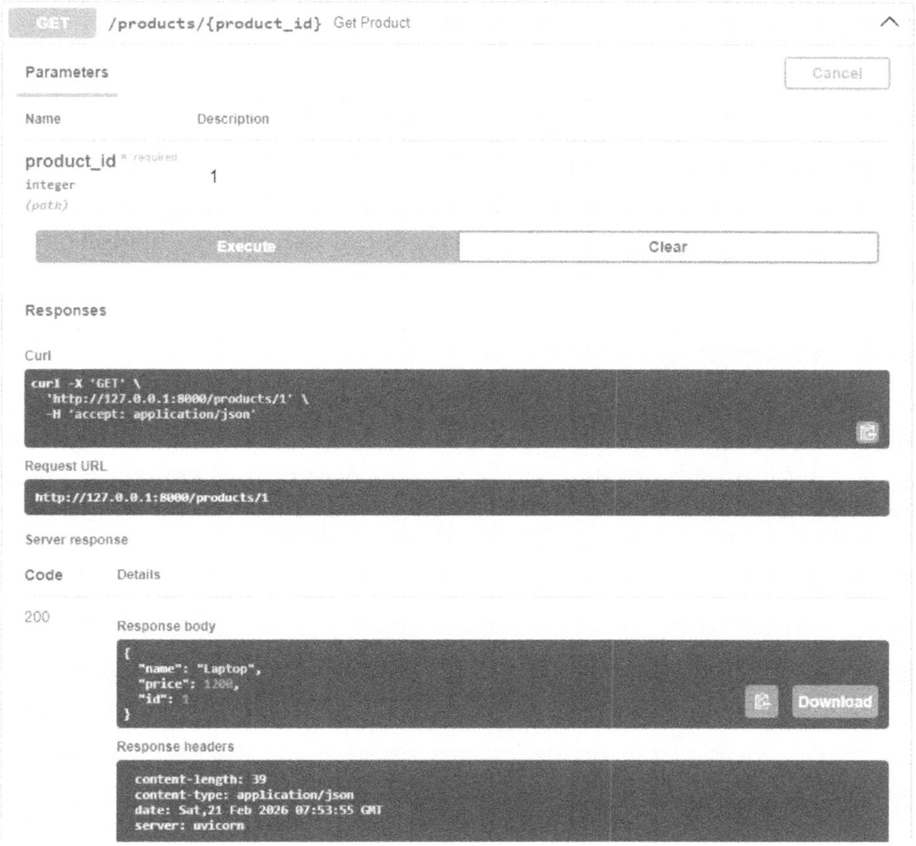

Figure 3.8: *Screenshot Showing a "GET /products/{id}" Request Followed by a "PUT" Update and the Updated Product Representation in the Response*

At this point, something subtle yet important has happened. You have interacted with the API multiple times without ever looking at the code. Yet, you already know quite a lot about the system. You know which operations exist, what data they expect, what data they return, and how the state evolves as you interact with it. This is exactly how a real client experiences an API. The client does not care how the data is stored or how IDs are generated. It only cares about what it can send and what it gets back. In the next section, we will deliberately do something uncomfortable, but also essential: we will break the API on purpose and observe how it fails.

Breaking the API on Purpose

Up to now, every interaction with the API has followed the rules. We sent valid data, used existing identifiers, and observed predictable results. This is only half of the picture. A real API is not defined by how it behaves when everything goes well, but rather by how it responds when things go wrong. So, in this section, we will deliberately stop being cooperative clients. We will send incorrect input, incomplete data, and invalid identifiers—not to test the system in a formal sense, but rather to observe how the boundary reacts when expectations are violated.

To better understand how the system handles invalid data, consider the case in which incomplete input is sent to the API. Return to the Swagger UI and open the endpoint which is responsible for creating a new product: **`POST /products`**. Click the "**`Try it out`**" button, but this time intentionally remove one of the required fields. For example, submit a JSON payload containing only the product name:

```
{
  "name": "Laptop"
}
```

Then, click "**`Execute`**." The request reaches the API, but it does not pass. Swagger displays a response with status code "**`422 Unprocessable Entity`**," along with a structured error body describing exactly what is missing (as shown in *Figure* 3.9). This validation happens automatically through the Pydantic models defined in the application.

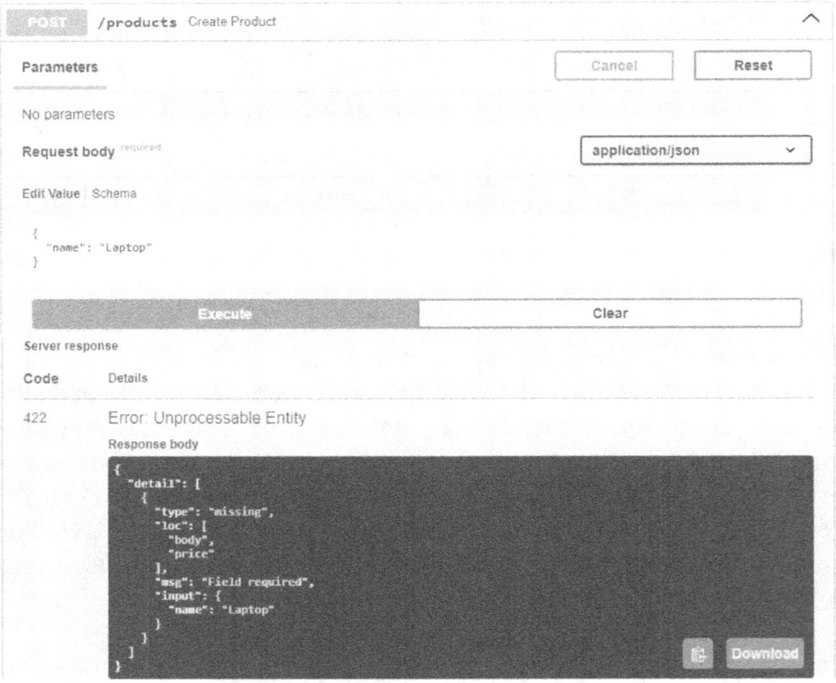

Figure 3.9: *Validation Error for Missing the Required Field*

This response is not something we coded explicitly. We did not write any if statements to check for missing fields. The system enforced these rules automatically. Pause and observe what this means from a client's perspective. The API clearly states that:

- The request was understood,
- The data was syntactically valid JSON, but
- It did not satisfy the contract.

The error message is not generic. It points to the exact field and explains the violation.

Now, try another variation. Send a value with the wrong type, demonstrated as follows:

```
{
  "name": "Laptop",
  "price": "expensive"
}
```

Execute the request again. The result is similar: a **422** response with a structured explanation (as shown in *Figure* 3.10). The API does not guess what you meant. It does not silently coerce values. It rejects the request and tells you why.

Figure 3.10: *Validation Error for Incorrect Data Type*

Now, let us try to use invalid identifiers, switching to the "**`GET /products/{product_id}`**" endpoint. Use an identifier that you know does not exist, such as a large number, for example, **`999. Execute the request`**. This time, the response is different. You receive a "**`404 Not Found`**" error with a clear message indicating that the product does not exist (see *Figure* 3.11). This error was explicitly defined in the code, but from the outside, that distinction does not matter. What matters is that the API communicates failure in a predictable and meaningful way. A useful distinction is given as follows:

- **`422`** Unprocessable Entity → The request data is invalid.
- **`404 Not Found`** → The requested resource does not exist.

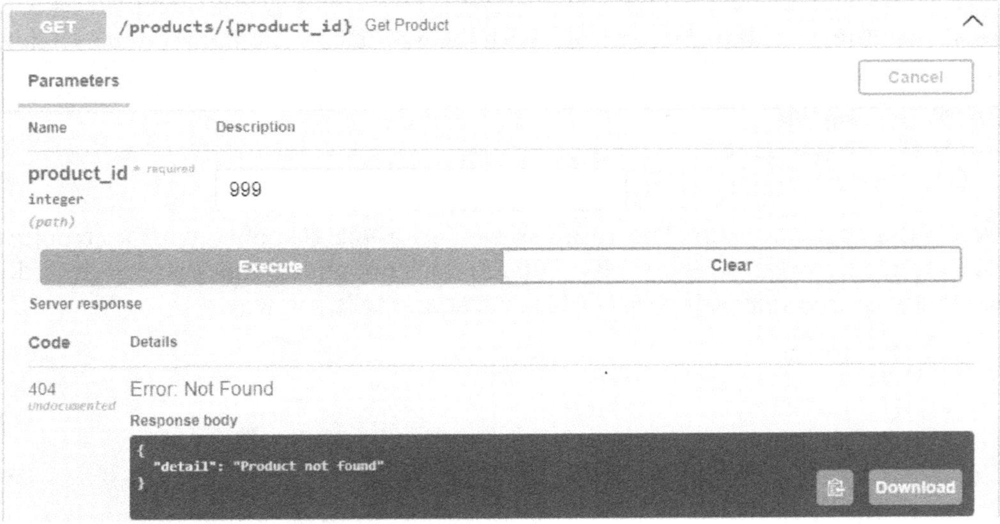

Figure 3.11: *Resource "Not Found" Error in Swagger UI*

Try the same with "**`update`**" and "**`delete`**" operations. Each time, the behavior is consistent. What you are observing here is the API acting as a boundary, not as a passive function. It enforces rules, rejects invalid input, and communicates problems in a structured form that clients can understand and handle. It is important to internalize this point before moving on. Errors are not signs that the system is broken. They are signals that the boundary is working. In the next section, we will take a step back and read the API purely as a client contract—without looking at the code at all—and articulate what a consumer of this API can know just by interacting with it.

Reading the API as a Client Contract

At this point, you have interacted with the API multiple times. You have created products, listed them, retrieved them, modified them, and deliberately broken requests to observe how the system reacts. All of this happened without reading "**`app/main.py`**." That is not an accident. It is the point. In this section, we will make that approach explicit. We will temporarily pretend that the code does not exist. We are acting as clients. The only thing we are allowed to see is what the API exposes through its boundary, primarily Swagger UI. This shift is important because it mirrors how real systems are consumed. Frontend developers, mobile applications, third-party integrations, and even other backend services interact with the API through its contract, and not through its internal implementation. An API contract defines what requests are accepted, what responses are returned, and how errors are communicated. So, the question we ask now is simple: "What can a client know about this system?" They care about API contracts. An API contract defines what clients can request, what responses they can expect, and how errors are communicated. So, the question we ask now is simple: "What can a client know about this system without looking at the code?" To answer it, we will ignore "main.py" completely and focus on what Swagger shows.

From Swagger UI alone, a client can clearly infer that the API manages a resource called "products." The available operations are visible and explicit. There is an endpoint to create a product, one to list all products, one to retrieve a product by ID, one to update it, and one to delete it. For each of these operations, Swagger reveals several crucial pieces of information. It shows which HTTP method must be used. It shows the path. It shows which parameters are required and where they must be provided. It shows the expected shape of the request body and the response structure. This is already a complete contract.

Without seeing any code, a client can know that:

- A product has a name and a price,
- The price must be a number,
- Products are identified by an integer ID,
- Invalid input is rejected with a structured error, and
- Missing resources result in a 404 response.

Equally important is what the client cannot know and is not supposed to know. The client cannot know how products are stored. It cannot know whether IDs are generated sequentially or randomly. It cannot know whether the data lives in memory or in a database. These details are intentionally hidden behind the boundary. This separation is not a limitation. It is the core strength of an API. To make this perspective concrete, we can turn it into a prompt—this time explicitly framed from the client's point of view.

Prompt

From the perspective of an API client, describe what this Products API does.

List the available endpoints, what each one expects as input, what it returns, and which errors a client should handle.

Do not explain how the API is implemented.

A good answer to this prompt reads almost as documentation, but notice the difference: it is grounded entirely in observable behavior. It does not speculate about internal structure. It does not mention FastAPI, Pydantic, or Python. It talks only about requests, responses, and rules. This is the mental model we want to establish before looking at the code. Once you can describe the system accurately in these terms, implementation details become easier to place. Instead of trying to understand code in isolation, you will be able to ask a much more precise question: Where does this observed behavior come from? That is exactly the transition we will make next.

Closing the First Cycle

At this point, the first development cycle is complete. We started with an intention, turned it into a prompt, materialized the result as code, executed it, and interacted with the system from the outside. Only now do we stop consolidating what we have built. This pause is essential. Without it, development turns into accumulation: more code, more features, more complexity, yet no stable understanding. So, we freeze the picture. From the outside, the system we have built is a Products API. It exposes a clear and limited set of behaviors. A client can create products by sending structured data. The system assigns identifiers. Products can be listed, retrieved individually, updated, and deleted. Invalid input is rejected with structured validation errors. Requests for missing resources return a clear 404 response. Nothing else is visible, and nothing else needs to be.

It is important to notice what this summary does not include. It does not mention how products are stored. It does not mention which libraries are used. It does not describe control flow or data structures. All of that belongs to the implementation, and not to the behavior. This distinction is deliberate. At this stage of the book, the goal is not to master FastAPI internals. The goal is to be able to say, with confidence, what the system does. A useful way to reinforce this snapshot is to ask the AI for a synthesis that is explicitly behavior-oriented.

Prompt

Summarize the behavior of the current Products API in terms of endpoints, inputs, outputs, and error cases.

Do not describe implementation details. Focus only on what a client can observe.

An expected output to this prompt could be as follows:

Expected Output

The API allows clients to create, retrieve, update,

and delete products through HTTP requests.

Each product contains structured fields such as

name, price, and availability.

Invalid input automatically produces validation errors,

while requests for missing products return clear

"not found" responses.

The API exposes a predictable contract that clients

can explore and interact with through Swagger UI.

A good answer to this prompt acts as a verbal contract. It should match what you have already seen through Swagger UI and interaction. If it does not, that mismatch is a signal that something was misunderstood or not fully observed. Once you can read that summary and recognize the system you interacted with, the first cycle is truly closed. Only now does it make sense to look inward. In the next section, we will turn our attention to the code—not to refactor it or improve it, but rather to answer a specific question: Where does the behavior we observed actually come from?

Understanding Where Behavior Comes From

Up to this point, the code has intentionally stayed in the background. We interacted with the API, observed its behavior, and described it from the client's point of view. Only now does it make sense to bring the code back into focus. The purpose of this section is neither to improve the implementation, nor to judge its quality. It is to connect specific, observable behaviors to specific parts of the file that produced them. We are not looking for abstractions or patterns yet. We are answering a much simpler question: Where does what we observed actually come from?

Open "**`app/main.py`**" again, but do not read it line-by-line from top to bottom. Instead, keep in mind the behaviors you have already seen through Swagger UI and move through the file looking for their origins.

Earlier, you observed that sending incomplete or invalid input resulted in a 422 error with a detailed and structured response. That behavior does not come from explicit checks written by the developer. There are no conditional statements that manually inspect the request body. Instead, the rules are declared through Pydantic models attached to the endpoint parameters. Those models define which fields are required and which types are expected. FastAPI uses that information to validate incoming requests before the endpoint logic runs. This means that the API boundary is enforcing the contract. If required fields are missing or types are invalid, FastAPI intercepts the request immediately and returns a structured **`422 validation error`** before the application code executes.

You also observed that every product receives an identifier automatically when it is created, and that the identifier remains stable while the application is running. Looking at the code, this behavior comes from a simple mechanism: a counter defined at the module level and incremented each time a new product is added. There is nothing hidden or implicit about it. The code makes the decision directly, and the effect is immediately visible in the responses you saw earlier. This simplicity is intentional at this stage, because it makes the connection between cause and effect easy to trace.

Another behavior you observed was statefulness. After creating a product, listing all products returned the newly-created item. That behavior is explained by the presence of an in-memory data structure shared by all endpoints. The list that holds products exists as long as the process runs, and every request operates on that same object. This is why the system remembers previous interactions, and why that memory disappears when the server restarts. The limitation you observed later is not an accident; it is a direct consequence of this design choice.

Finally, you observed that requesting a product with an identifier that does not exist produces a 404 response with a readable message. Unlike validation errors, this behavior is defined explicitly. The code checks whether a product can be found and raises an exception when it cannot. FastAPI then translates that exception into an HTTP response. Seeing this side-by-side with automatic validation is useful: some behaviors emerge from declared rules, others from explicit decisions in endpoint logic.

At this point, something important should be happening cognitively. You are no longer reading the code in isolation, and you are no longer interpreting the behavior as magic. You can move back and forth between the two and explain, in simple terms, why the system behaves the way it does. This is exactly the level of understanding we want before making any changes. With this connection established, we are ready to begin a second cycle. This time, we will deliberately change the behavior of the API in a small yet meaningful way, then observe the difference from the client's perspective.

Second Cycle: A Targeted Improvement

At this point, the system works. That statement is important because it gives us permission to change it. Until now, every action has been about making something exist and understanding how it behaves. Only once a system is real and observable does it make sense to improve it. Improving something that does not yet exist is speculation; improving something that already runs is learning. The key constraint for this second cycle is restraint. We are not refactoring the codebase. We are not reorganizing files. We are not introducing new concepts or expanding the domain. The goal is to make a small and targeted improvement that changes observable behavior in a meaningful way for a client.

Looking back at the interactions through Swagger UI, two aspects stand out. When a product is created, the API returns a valid response, but the status code does not clearly communicate what happened. When a product is not found, the error message works, but it could be more explicit and consistent across endpoints. These are not internal concerns; they are a part of the API contract.

So, the intention for this cycle is simple: improve how the API communicates outcomes to its clients, without changing what the API fundamentally does. As always, we do not start by editing code. We start by expressing the intention as a prompt.

Prompt

Update the existing FastAPI Products API with the following changes:

- When creating a product, return HTTP status code 201 Created.

- When updating a product, explicitly return HTTP 200 OK.

- For any case where a product is not found, return HTTP 404 with a clear message that includes the product id.

Do not add new features, files, or abstractions.

Keep the code minimal and fully contained in app/main.py.

Return the full updated file.

The important part of this prompt is not the list of changes, but rather the constraints. We explicitly forbid architectural expansion. We are asking for behavior refinement, not redesign. Following is a representative response that satisfies the prompt and will serve as the new reference implementation for this chapter. Replace the contents of "**app/main.py**" with the following code:

```
from fastapi import FastAPI, HTTPException, status
from pydantic import BaseModel
from typing import List

app = FastAPI()

# In-memory storage
products: List["Product"] = []
next_id = 1


class ProductCreate(BaseModel):
    name: str
    price: float


class Product(ProductCreate):
    id: int


@app.post(
    "/products",
    response_model=Product,
    status_code=status.HTTP_201_CREATED
)
def create_product(product: ProductCreate) -> Product:
    global next_id
    new_product = Product(id=next_id, **product.model_dump())
    products.append(new_product)
    next_id += 1
```

```
    return new_product

@app.get("/products", response_model=List[Product])
def list_products() -> List[Product]:
    return products

@app.get("/products/{product_id}", response_model=Product)
def get_product(product_id: int) -> Product:
    for product in products:
        if product.id == product_id:
            return product

    raise HTTPException(
        status_code=status.HTTP_404_NOT_FOUND,
        detail=f"Product {product_id} not found",
    )

@app.put(
    "/products/{product_id}",
    response_model=Product,
    status_code=status.HTTP_200_OK,
)
def update_product(
    product_id: int,
    updated: ProductCreate
) -> Product:
    for index, product in enumerate(products):
        if product.id == product_id:
            updated_product = Product(
                id=product_id,
                **updated.model_dump()
            )
            products[index] = updated_product
            return updated_product

    raise HTTPException(
        status_code=status.HTTP_404_NOT_FOUND,
        detail=f"Product {product_id} not found",
    )

@app.delete("/products/{product_id}")
def delete_product(product_id: int) -> dict:
    for index, product in enumerate(products):
        if product.id == product_id:
```

```
            products.pop(index)
            return {"message": f"Product {product_id} deleted"}

    raise HTTPException(
        status_code=status.HTTP_404_NOT_FOUND,
        detail=f"Product {product_id} not found",
    )
```

At this stage, do not analyze the differences line-by-line. What matters is that the intention has been translated into concrete behavior changes, and those changes are now part of the running system. Save the file and let the server reload, or restart it manually, if needed. The system is ready to be observed again. In the next section, we will return to Swagger UI and verify that these improvements are visible from the client's point of view, without relying on code inspection.

Observing the Improved Behavior

The server is running again, but the most important thing to notice is that nothing looks different at first glance. The same endpoints are listed in Swagger UI. The same paths are available. The API still manages products in memory, exactly as before. What changed is not the visible structure of the API, but its behavior when handling requests and responses.

This is expected. Improvements in a real API often do not announce themselves through new features, but through clearer signals. To see those signals, we must interact with the system again, deliberately repeating the same actions we performed in the first cycle. Open the browser and navigate once more to the following:

```
http://127.0.0.1:8000/docs
```

Start by creating a new product. Use the "**`POST /products`**" endpoint and submit a valid request body, such as:

```
{
  "name": "Keyboard",
  "price": 99.99
}
```

This time, pay attention not only to the response body, but also to the metadata surrounding it. Swagger clearly shows that the response status code is now "**`201 Created`**" (as shown in *Figure* 3.12). This single number carries meaning. It tells a client, unambiguously, that a new resource has been created because of this request.

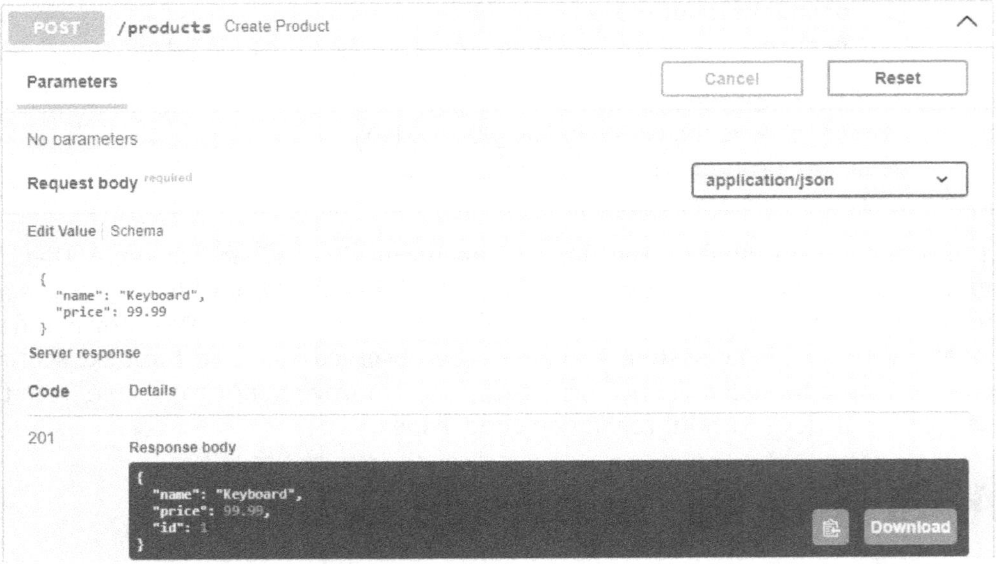

Figure 3.12: *Product Creation with Explicit 201 Created Status*

The response body itself contains the full product representation, including the assigned identifier. From the client's point of view, this interaction now feels complete: the request created something, and the API confirmed it using both structure and protocol semantics. Next, try updating an existing product. Use the "**`PUT /products/{product_id}`**" endpoint with a valid identifier (in our case, **`id=1`**) and a modified payload, as follows:

```
{
  "name": "Keyboard",
  "price": 100.01
}
```

Once again, observe the status code. The API explicitly returns "**`200 OK`**," confirming that an existing resource was successfully modified. The response body reflects the updated state. Nothing about this interaction required reading the code. Everything the client needs to know is visible at the boundary. Now, trigger a failure on purpose. Request a product using an identifier that does not exist. For example:

```
GET /products/999
```

The response is immediate and clear. The status code is **`404 Not Found`**, and the response body includes a human-readable message that names the missing resource (as shown in *Figure* 3.13). This is not just an error; it is a signal that the client can act upon. A frontend can display it. A test can assert it. A developer can reason about it.

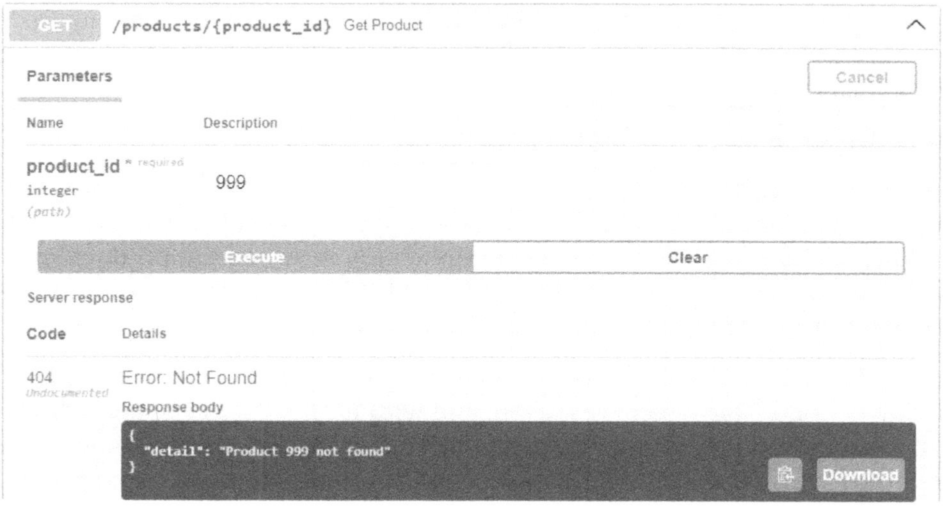

Figure 3.13: *Clear 404 Response after Second Iteration*

Compare this behavior to the first iteration. The functionality is the same. The difference lies entirely in communication. At this point, it becomes clear why the book insists on small and controlled improvements. The API did not become more complex, but it became more precise. From the outside, it now behaves more as a system that was designed intentionally, even though it was generated and refined through prompts. This completes the second full cycle. We defined an intention, expressed it as a prompt, applied the result, and then verified—through observation—that the system's behavior changed in the exact way we expected. In the next section, we will explore a different kind of observation, one that reveals a limitation of the current design and prepares the ground for the next conceptual step, without solving it yet.

Understanding Server Restarts

Up to now, every interaction with the API has happened within a single uninterrupted server session. Products were created, listed, updated, and retrieved, and the system behaved consistently. This continuity makes the API feel stable and reliable.

In Swagger UI, we execute the "**`GET /products`**" endpoint and receive the list of products we have created so far. In our case, it contains only the following:

```
[
  {
    "name": "Keyboard",
    "price": 100.01,
    "id": 1
  }
]
```

Now, we will deliberately break that continuity. Stop the server by pressing *Ctrl+C* in the terminal. Wait until the process is fully terminated. Then, start it again by using the same command as before, which is as follows:

```
uvicorn app.main:app --reload
```

Nothing in the code has changed. The application starts without errors. Swagger UI is still available at "**/docs**." From the outside, everything appears identical. Now, try to list the products. Use the "**GET**" endpoint that previously returned the products that you created. This time, the response is different. The list is empty. The products are gone. This moment is not a bug, and it is not a mistake. It is a signal.

What just happened is entirely observable from the outside, without inspecting a single line of code. The system restarted, and with it, the state disappeared. The API did not crash, it did not corrupt data, and it did not behave unpredictably. It simply started fresh. This observation reveals an important property of the current system: its data exists only in memory. As shown in *Figure* 3.14, this observation reveals an important property of the current system: its data exists only in memory. In other words, the current API is temporarily stateful while the server process is running, but effectively stateless across restarts because no persistent storage exists. As long as the server process is alive, the data is available. When the process stops, the data is lost.

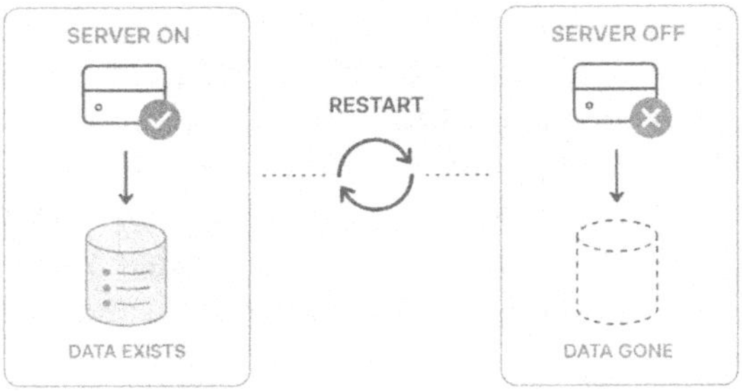

***Figure 3.14**: Server Restart Resets the Application State*

From a client's point of view, this behavior is perfectly coherent. The API never promised persistence. There was no indication that data would survive a restart. The contract, as observed through Swagger and HTTP behavior, was respected. This is why this chapter does not rush to introduce a database. Before adding persistence, it is essential to feel its absence. By restarting the server and seeing the data disappear, the reader experiences the limitation directly, instead of being told about it abstractly. The need for persistence emerges naturally from observation, not from theory.

At this stage, the correct reaction is not to fix the problem, but rather to name it. The system currently behaves as a volatile component. It is suitable for experimentation, prototyping, and understanding behavior, but not for long-term storage. A useful way to consolidate this understanding is to ask a question that explains the limitation without proposing solutions.

Prompt

Why does this FastAPI application lose all products when the server restarts?

Explain the behavior without suggesting databases or persistence solutions yet.

A good answer will reinforce what you already observed: data is stored in memory structures that live only as long as the process itself. When the process ends, the memory is released, and the state is reset. This realization completes another learning loop. You have not only seen what the system can do, but also what it cannot do and why. That boundary is now part of your mental model. In the next section, we will deliberately freeze this model. Before adding more features or infrastructure, we will summarize what this API is, what it guarantees, and what it intentionally does not.

Freezing the Current Mental Model

At this point, the temptation to continue is strong. You can feel where the application is going. You have already identified its main limitation, and you can probably imagine several ways to address it. That is precisely why this is the right moment to stop and freeze the current mental model. Freezing does not mean declaring the system finished. It means taking a clear snapshot of what the system is right now, before adding anything else. Forget the code for a moment. Imagine explaining this API to someone who will never see "**`app/main.py`**." What can you say with confidence, based only on what you have observed?

You can say that the system exposes a REST API for managing products. You can say that clients can create products, retrieve them, update them, and delete them. You can say that all interactions use structured JSON input and output. You can say that invalid input is rejected with clear validation errors, and that missing resources produce explicit 404 responses. You can also say something equally important: data exists only while the server is running. Restarting the application resets the state. This is not a hidden detail; it is a defining characteristic of the system at this stage. This description fits in a few sentences, and that is exactly the point. A good mental model is compact. It does not list implementation details, and it does not speculate about the future. It describes behavior that has been observed and verified.

The current state of the system can now be summarized explicitly. This checkpoint captures the mental model we have constructed through execution, observation, and interaction with the API.

Current Mental Model—Products API (Checkpoint)

What Does the API do?

- Exposes REST endpoints for managing products.
- Accepts and returns structured JSON data.

- Validates requests automatically through Pydantic models.
- Returns predictable HTTP responses and errors.
- Maintains a temporary in-memory state while the server runs.

What Does the API Do Not Do (Yet)?

- Does not persist data across restarts.
- Does not use a database.
- Does not include authentication or authorization.
- Does not use advanced project structure or architectural layers.

What Have You Understood Now?

- How requests flow through FastAPI,
- How validation and error handling appear at the API boundary,
- How Swagger UI acts as a real API client, and
- How the cycle **Prompt → Code → Execution → Observation** works in practice.

At this stage, you know how to do several things that you could not do before. You know how to turn a vague goal into a concrete prompt. You know how to accept generated code without losing control. You know how to interrogate a running API through Swagger UI and reason about it from the client's point of view. You know how to improve behavior in small and targeted steps and verify the result through execution. At the same time, there are things you deliberately do not know yet. You do not know how this code should be structured for scale. You do not know how persistence should be introduced. You have not discussed dependency injections, routers, background tasks, or authentication. This is not a gap; rather, it is a boundary.

By freezing the model here, you prevent a common learning failure: blurring together what the system does now with what you assume it should eventually do. Everything beyond this point will be built on top of a system you already understand, not on top of abstractions. This frozen snapshot is the reference point for the next chapters. When we introduce new concepts, they will not appear in isolation. They will attach themselves to this exact API, modifying its behavior in observable ways.

In the next and final section of this chapter, we will make explicit why stopping here is not a limitation, but rather a deliberate design choice—and why moving forward without this pause would weaken rather than strengthen your understanding.

Current Progress and Next Steps

This is the right place to stop. Not because there is nothing more to do, but rather because doing more now would break the method that this book is deliberately enforcing. Look at the state of the project at this moment. You have a FastAPI application that runs locally without friction. It exposes a real REST API, not a demo endpoint. It manages data, even if only in memory. It accepts structured input, returns structured output, and communicates failure explicitly through HTTP status codes and error bodies. You have interacted with it as a client, not as an implementer. You have seen it succeed, fail, improve, and reset.

Most importantly, the system talks back. Every request produces feedback. Every invalid input produces a signal. Every change you make can be observed immediately at the boundary. This is the minimum condition that is required for meaningful backend development. It would be easy to continue from here. You could reorganize the code into routers. You could introduce persistence. You could refactor models, add configuration files, or clean things up. All of those steps are legitimate—but taking them now would collapse too many concerns into a single moment.

This chapter was not about writing better code. It was about building something real before understanding everything about it, including:

- You trusted execution before theory.
- You accepted a first draft before judging it.
- You used prompts to move forward and observation to anchor understanding.

That inversion is intentional, and it only works if you respect its stopping points. By stopping here, you preserve a clean reference state. The application is simple, but it is stable. The behavior is clear. The limitations are visible. Nothing is hidden behind abstraction or premature architecture. Before moving on, ensure that the following statements are true for your project:

- The server starts without errors.
- The "`/docs`" page loads correctly.
- Products can be created, listed, updated, and deleted.
- Invalid input produces structured validation errors.
- Missing products return a clear 404 response.
- Restarting the server resets the data.

If all of these are true, you are exactly where you need to be.

In the next chapter, the direction will change. Instead of generating more functionality, we will slow down and turn our attention inward. We will learn how to read the code we already have, how to interrogate it with better prompts, and how to connect its structure to the behavior you have already observed. This chapter taught you how to create. The next one will teach you how to understand. From that point on, the application will stop feeling as something that just works and start feeling as something you actually control.

Conclusion

In this chapter, you moved from a prepared environment to a working API that behaves as a real backend system. By defining a clear objective, translating it into focused prompts, and observing the system through execution and interaction, you completed multiple prompt-driven development cycles. The "Products" API you built is intentionally simple but it is concrete, observable, and functional. It responds to valid requests, rejects invalid ones, and exposes its behavior clearly through HTTP and Swagger UI. This makes it a reliable reference point for the chapters that will follow. With a real system now in place, the next step is not to add more features, but to deepen understanding—learning how to read, question, and reason about the code that produced the behavior you observed.

In the next chapter, we will shift focus from interacting with the API to understanding the code that produces its behavior. Instead of adding new features, we will learn how to use prompts to explain, predict, and verify what happens inside the application when requests cross the FastAPI boundary.

By repeatedly connecting small code changes to observable effects in Swagger UI, the goal will no longer be simply that "the API works," but also that "the behavior is understandable and predictable."

Points to Remember

- A running server is not automatically a real API.
- A real API exposes clear requests, responses, and behavior.
- Small objectives reduce premature complexity.
- Good prompts describe behavior, not implementation details.
- AI-generated code should be executed and observed before being trusted.
- Swagger UI acts as the first real client of the API.
- Validation errors help define the API boundary.
- Small prompt-driven cycles build understanding progressively.
- A minimal working system creates a stable reference point for future improvements.

Multiple Choice Questions

1. What is the main objective of *Chapter 3, Generating Your First Real API*?
    a. To optimize performance and scalability
    b. To generate and observe a first real, functional API using a prompt-driven cycle

   c. To refactor a FastAPI project following best practices
   d. To introduce database persistence and migrations

2. Why does the chapter emphasize starting from a concrete objective instead of architecture or theory?
   a. Because observable behavior provides a stable foundation for understanding
   b. Because FastAPI discourages architectural design
   c. Because AI cannot generate architectural code
   d. Because architecture is irrelevant for small projects

3. What defines a "real API" in the context of this chapter?
   a. An API written entirely by hand
   b. An API deployed to production
   c. An API that exposes meaningful endpoints and predictable behavior to clients
   d. An API with authentication and persistence

4. Why is in-memory storage used for the Products API?
   a. Because FastAPI does not support databases
   b. Because it allows focusing on API behavior without infrastructure complexity
   c. Because it is faster than databases
   d. Because it is required by Swagger UI

5. Why does the chapter recommend running the generated code before reading it in detail?
   a. To save time during development
   b. To ensure the AI-generated code is optimal
   c. To avoid understanding FastAPI internals
   d. To anchor understanding in observable behavior rather than assumptions

6. What role does Swagger UI play in this chapter?
   a. It generates database schemas.
   b. It acts as the first real client of the API, making behavior visible.
   c. It serves as static documentation.
   d. It replaces automated testing.

7. You create a product using the API and then restart the server. What will happen when you call `GET` /products?
   a. The API duplicates the product.
   b. The product list is empty.
   c. The API returns an error.
   d. The previously created product is still available.
8. A frontend developer uses your API but does not have access to the code. What information can they reliably obtain?
   a. API endpoints, inputs, outputs, and error responses
   b. Internal data structures
   c. Python implementation details
   d. Database schema

Answers

1. b
2. a
3. c
4. b
5. d
6. b
7. b
8. a

Questions

1. Why is it important to define a concrete objective for an API before writing or generating any code?
2. How does starting from observable behavior change the way you evaluate AI-generated code compared to reading it first?
3. In what sense does interacting with the API through Swagger UI help you understand the system without looking at its implementation?
4. Why are errors such as validation failures and "not found" responses essential parts of an API contract rather than signs of failure?
5. What risks arise if you keep expanding features before completing a full Intention → Prompt → Execution → Observation cycle?

6. How does using in-memory storage support learning at this stage, even though it is not suitable for real persistence?
7. Why is it useful to perform a small, controlled improvement iteration instead of refactoring or redesigning the API?
8. Which responsibilities remain entirely human when using AI to generate and modify a backend API?

Key Terms

- **Real API:** An API that exposes meaningful behavior through clear endpoints, structured input and output, and predictable error responses, allowing clients to interact with it as a true backend system rather than a demo.
- **Objective:** A concrete, narrowly defined goal that guides a development cycle and can be completed, executed, and observed within a short iteration.
- **In-Memory Storage:** A data storage approach where information exists only while the application is running, used here to focus on API behavior without introducing persistence complexity.
- **Prompt-Driven Development Cycle:** An iterative workflow in which an intention is expressed as a prompt, translated into code, executed to produce observable behavior, and consolidated into understanding before the next iteration.
- **First Draft Code:** AI-generated or rapidly written code that prioritizes executability and observable behavior over elegance, optimization, or long-term structure.
- **Observable Behavior:** The concrete responses produced by an API when it receives requests, including successful outputs, error messages, and HTTP status codes.
- **Swagger UI:** The interactive web interface automatically generated by FastAPI that allows developers to explore, test, and understand an API through live HTTP interactions.
- **API Contract:** The set of guarantees an API makes to its clients, defined by its endpoints, expected inputs, outputs, and error responses, independent of internal implementation details.
- **Iteration:** A single pass through the development cycle, resulting in a working change that can be observed and understood before proceeding further.
- **Client Perspective:** Viewing the API strictly from the outside, focusing on what requests can be made and what responses are returned, without relying on knowledge of the underlying code.

CHAPTER 4
Understanding Code through Better Prompts

Introduction

In the previous chapter, you built a Products API that runs, responds, and fails in predictable ways. That gave you something real: a working boundary that you can test through Swagger UI. However, a working boundary is not the same as understanding. This chapter is about closing that gap. You will not add new features. You will not reorganize the project. Instead, you will take the application you already have in "**`app/main.py`**" and learn to interrogate it with prompts that produce control: prompts that explain observed behavior, predict the impact of a change, and zoom into a single line until its effect becomes obvious at the boundary. The method is simple and strict. You ask a targeted question, make a prediction, apply a minimal edit, and verify the result in Swagger UI. Over and over, until "It works" becomes "I know what will happen if I touch this."

By the end of this chapter, you will have two outcomes. First, a compact mental model of what happens from request to response in this specific application. Second, a clean reference version of "**`app/main.py`**" that you can carry forward into the next chapters—no longer as generated code, but rather as behavior you can understand and deliberately reshape.

Structure

In this chapter, we will cover the following topics:

- From "It Works" to "I Control It"
- From Black Box to Flow
- Choosing the Right Assistant for the Job
- Freeze the Reference Code before You Touch Anything

- From API Contract to Code
- Explain This Line Like I Am New
- The Effect of Changing X
- Debugging With Prompts: Reading Errors as Signals
- Request to Response in One Page
- Annotated Reference File: Making Behavior Explicit
- From Annotated to Clean
- Practice: Applying the Method without Guidance
- Chapter Checkpoint
- The Importance of This Step before Architecture

From "It Works" to "I Control It"

At the end of the previous chapter, something important had happened. You built a working API. You can now create, retrieve, update, and delete products while observing clear validation and error behavior through Swagger UI. The system runs. It responds. It fails predictably. However, there is a subtle difference between "It works" and "I control it." Right now, your Products API works because you generated it, ran it, and improved it. You have observed its behavior from the outside. You know what it does. What you do not yet fully know is why it behaves the way it does and how confident you can be when modifying it. That gap is what this chapter is about.

A real developer encounters this situation constantly. Imagine changing a route decorator from "`@app.get("/products/{product_id}")`" to a different path while experimenting. The application may still start correctly, but the endpoint can disappear from the location where Swagger UI expects it. The question is no longer "Does the code run?", but rather "Why did the behavior change?" Understanding that connection is what transforms execution into control.

This chapter does not introduce new features. It does not add persistence. It does not reorganize the project. Instead, it changes the direction. In the previous chapter, you moved forward by generating behavior. In this chapter, you will move inward by interrogating behavior. A visual representation of the conceptual transition introduced in this chapter is shown in *Figure* 4.1. A working API becomes a controlled system through targeted, structured questioning, small experiments, and observable verification. *Figure* 4.1 illustrates the shift from "It works" to "I understand why it works."

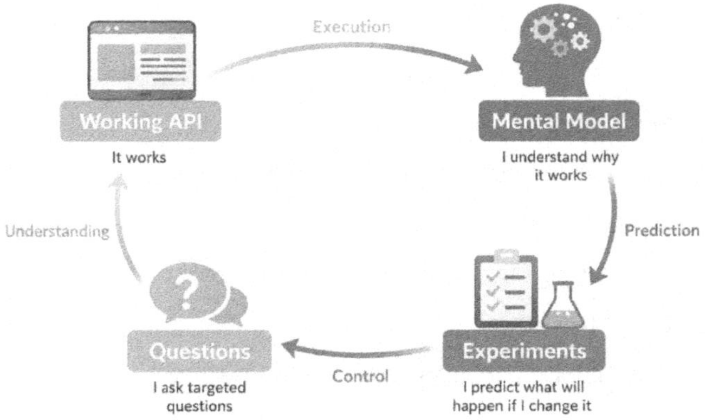

Figure 4.1: *From Execution to Control*

The goal is not to memorize FastAPI internals. The goal is to build a mental model that is strong enough to let you ask three questions, and to trust the answers: why this works, what will happen if you change something, and what a specific line means in the behavior you observe. *Figure* 4.2 summarizes these three prompt patterns as a simple toolbox:

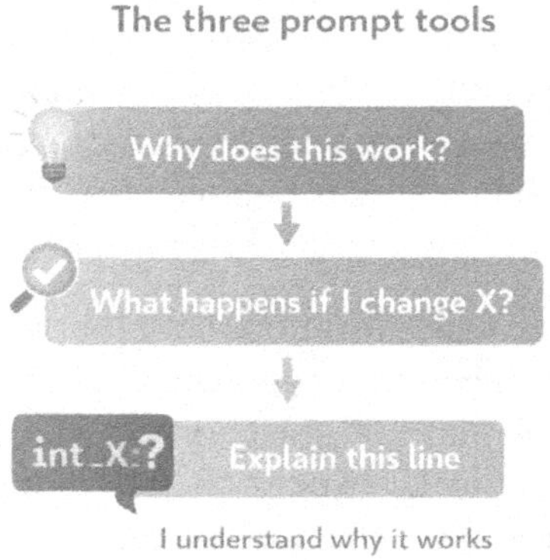

Figure 4.2: *The Three Core Prompt Patterns Used in This Chapter*

Figure 4.2 shows a visual summary of the three question types that replace passive reading: explaining observed behavior ("Why does this work?"), predicting change ("What happens if I modify X?"), and zooming into a single declaration ("Explain this line like I am new."). Together, they form the operational method of this chapter.

Before going further, pause and consider your current position. You have a file called "**`app/main.py`**." It defines routes, models, and in-memory storage. When you send a "POST **`/products`**" request, you receive a structured JSON response. When you send invalid data, you receive a 422 error. When you request a missing product, you receive a 404. You can describe these behaviors from the outside. However, can you trace them precisely inside the file? Can you predict what will happen if you make a small change? Can you explain to someone else why validation happens before your endpoint logic runs? If the answer is "not yet," that is not a problem. It is exactly why this chapter exists. To make this transition concrete, we will begin with the first core prompt of the chapter:

Prompt

Why does this Products API work at all? Explain, at a high level, what happens between sending an HTTP request in Swagger UI and receiving a JSON response.

A clear answer should describe a flow, not a list of definitions. It should connect the request, the route, model validation, function execution, and the final response, staying grounded in the behavior you already observed in the previous chapter. As you read it, keep Swagger open and mentally match each step to something you can actually see: the selected endpoint, the request schema, and the difference between a 422 validation failure and a 404 not-found error. Notice what we are not doing. We are not opening documentation. We are not reading an API reference. We are not scanning the file line-by-line. We are asking a targeted question about behavior. This is the method of the chapter. Throughout the next sections, every piece of understanding will be anchored to a prompt. When something is unclear, we will ask. When we modify, we will first form a hypothesis and then verify it against the running application. When a line looks cryptic, we will zoom in with a focused explanation request. By the end of this chapter, you will have two concrete outcomes: an annotated version of "**`app/main.py`**" that explains essential behaviors without becoming a wall of comments, and a compact mental model of how FastAPI handles requests in this application—routing, validation, execution, and response generation. From that point forward, the code will no longer feel like something that just works. It will feel like something that behaves according to the rules that you can understand, test, and deliberately modify. That is the shift from execution to control—it is what makes the refactoring in the next chapter possible.

From Black Box to Flow

In the previous chapter, you deliberately treated the API as a black box. You sent requests, observed responses, and refined behavior. That was the right move at that stage. You needed something real before you could understand it. Now, we can open the box. Not by dissecting every line, or by reading documentation. We open it by tracing a single, concrete event that you have already experienced many times. Think about what happens when you click "Execute" in Swagger UI for a "POST **`/products`**" request. You provide valid JSON. You receive a "201 Created" response containing a product with an automatically assigned ID. You have seen this happen repeatedly. The behavior is stable. Instead of asking "What is FastAPI?", we ask something much narrower and much more useful: "What actually happens between clicking 'Execute' and receiving that JSON response?" Turn that into a prompt in the following way:

Prompt

In this FastAPI Products API, describe step-by-step what happens internally when a client sends a POST /products request with valid JSON data. Focus on the flow of execution, from request arrival to JSON response.

A strong answer will describe a sequence of events. The HTTP request reaches the FastAPI application. FastAPI examines the method and the path, matching them to the "**create_product**" route. The request body is parsed as JSON and validated against the "**ProductCreate**" model. If validation succeeds, the endpoint function is executed. Inside that function, a new Product instance is created and appended to the in-memory list. The function returns that object. FastAPI then serializes the returned value according to the declared **response_model,** applies the specified status code, and sends a JSON response back to the client. Notice the structure of this explanation. It is not a list of definitions, but rather a pipeline. A request enters, which is then routed, validated, executed, serialized, and returned. That is your first internal mental model of this application.

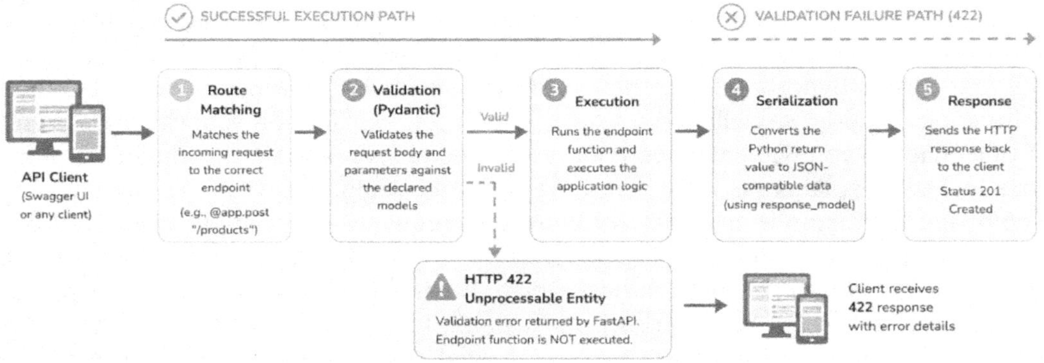

Figure 4.3: *Request Lifecycle in the Products API*

Figure 4.3 shows a simplified execution flow of a "**POST /products**" request: request arrival, route matching, input validation, function execution, serialization according to **response_model**, and HTTP response generation. Now, make it concrete. Open "**app/main.py**" and look at the "**create_product**" endpoint in the following manner:

```
@app.post("/products", response_model=Product, status_code=status.
HTTP_201_CREATED)
def create_product(product: ProductCreate) -> Product:
    global next_id
    new_product = Product(id=next_id, **product.model_dump())
    products.append(new_product)
    next_id += 1
    return new_product
```

Now, do not read it top to bottom. Instead, interrogate it in the following way:

Prompt

In this endpoint definition, which parts are responsible for routing, which part triggers input validation, which part defines the response structure, and which part sets the HTTP status code? Refer directly to the code elements.

A precise answer will map behavior to the structure. The "**`@app.post("/products", ...)`**" decorator binds the HTTP method and path to this function. The parameter annotation "**`product: ProductCreate`**" tells FastAPI to parse and validate the request body against that model. The "**`response_model=Product`**" declaration defines the output shape and enforces output filtering. The "**`status_code=...`**" argument sets the HTTP semantics of the response. The function body itself contains the business logic that manipulates the in-memory state. Without this mapping, decorators and type hints look like syntax. With it, they become behavior declarations. *Figure* 4.4 shows a diagram linking routing declarations, type annotations, **`response_model`**, and HTTP status codes to the behaviors observed in Swagger UI.

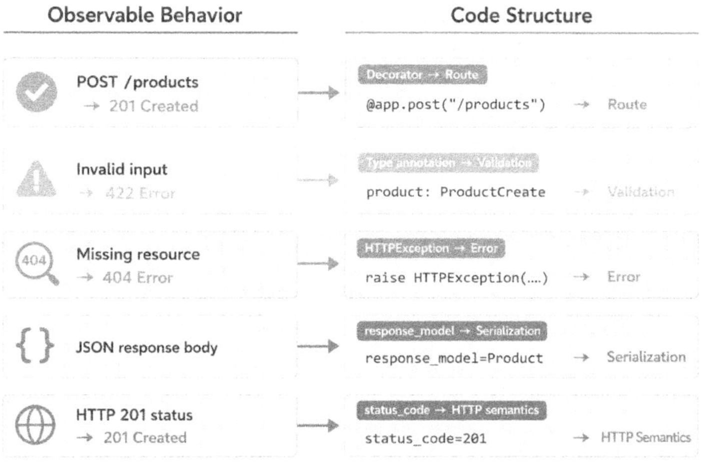

Figure 4.4: *Mapping API Behavior to Code Structure*

Now, we will move from explanation to prediction. Before touching the code, ask a focused question:

Prompt

What would happen if I remove the response_model parameter from the POST /products endpoint? Describe how the observable behavior in Swagger UI and in the response body would change.

Pause and predict before you modify anything.

A careful answer should mention two visible effects. First, the generated API documentation will show a different response schema because FastAPI no longer has an explicit output model to expose. Second, FastAPI will no longer enforce that the returned object conforms to the Product structure, even though in this specific case, the object may still serialize correctly.

Now, test it. Remove "**`response_model=Product`**" from the decorator, save the file, and let the server reload. Open the documentation page again and inspect the "**`POST /products`**" endpoint. Compare the response schema with the previous version, then create a product and inspect the returned JSON.

Then, restore the original line. You have just completed a full control cycle: you asked a precise question, predicted the effect, changed the code, observed the boundary, and compared reality to expectation. That movement—from black box to traced flow, from explanation to experiment—is the core of this chapter. At this point, you should be able to describe the request lifecycle in your own words. When a request arrives, FastAPI matches it to a route based on method and path, validates the input using declared models, executes the endpoint function, serializes the return value according to the response model, and sends an HTTP response.

That sentence is not a theory. It is a compressed description of behavior you have already observed and tested. In the next section, we will narrow the focus even further. Instead of tracing the entire request flow, we will take a single line of code and interrogate it with the simplest and most powerful prompt in this chapter: "Explain this line like I am new."

Choosing the Right Assistant for the Job

By now, prompts are no longer occasional tools; rather, they are becoming instruments. However, not every instrument is suited for the same task. In the previous chapter, you primarily used AI to generate the working code. In the previous section of this chapter, you used it to explain flow and map behavior to structure. These are different cognitive operations: One is generative, and the other is analytical.

If you treat every question as the same kind of request, you will get answers that feel misaligned, long explanations when you wanted a quick change, large rewrites when you only needed clarity on one line, or worse, confident yet shallow reasoning. So before moving further, we make something explicit: different prompt intentions benefit from different interaction styles. *Figure* 4.5 visualizes how different prompt intentions align with different assistant behaviors:

Figure 4.5: *Matching Prompt Intention to Assistant Behavior*

It is a conceptual mapping between reasoning prompts, modification prompts, and context-aware explanations, showing how each interaction style supports a different stage of controlled development. When your goal is reasoning—understanding why validation runs before your function body, or how routing selects an endpoint—a conversational, chat-based assistant is often the most effective. It can walk through flow, rephrase explanations, and adapt to follow-up questions.

When your goal is modification—changing a model, adjusting a decorator, or rewriting a function body—a code-aware assistant integrated into the editor is usually more precise. It can see the file in context and propose minimal edits rather than conceptual summaries.

When your goal is the explanation of existing code without copy-paste—that is, asking "what does this file do?" directly from within the editor—an assistant with direct access to the file context reduces friction and avoids errors introduced by manual copying. This distinction is not theoretical. It affects the outcome of your experiments. Let us make this concrete. Imagine that you want to explore what happens if you make the price field optional. You could ask a reasoning-style question in the following manner:

Prompt

What would happen if I make the price field optional in the ProductCreate model? Predict how this would affect validation and Swagger UI.

A chat-based assistant will likely respond with a conceptual explanation: the field would no longer be required, validation rules would change, Swagger would reflect the updated schema, and clients could omit the field. That is useful for prediction. Now, you need to implement the change. Instead of asking for a full rewrite of the file, you can ask a more surgical prompt inside your editor in the following way:

Prompt

Modify the ProductCreate model so that price is optional, without changing any other part of the file. Show only the updated model definition.

A context-aware assistant will typically respond in the following manner:

```
from typing import Optional

class ProductCreate(BaseModel):
    name: str
    price: Optional[float] = None
```

At this point, you should not blindly trust either explanation or modification. Replace the original "**`ProductCreate`**" definition with this updated version in **`app/main.py`**. Ensure that the necessary import is present at the top of the file in the following way:

```
from typing import List, Optional
```

Save the file and let the server reload. Now, go back to Swagger UI. Expand the "POST /products" endpoint. Look at the request body schema. You should observe that the price is no longer marked as required. Try sending a request without a price in the following manner:

```
{
  "name": "NoPriceProduct"
}
```

Now, observe what happens. Does the request succeed? What does the returned object look like? Does price appear as null? Does anything break in the response model? You have now combined three distinct operations: reasoning about change, implementing change, and verifying change at the boundary. The assistant did not do the work; rather, it supported different stages of the work. One tool helped you predict, while another helped you modify. Swagger helped you to verify. This separation matters. If you use a generative prompt when you need precision, you may receive more code than necessary. If you use a modification prompt when you need reasoning, you may get changes without understanding. Control comes from matching the tool to the question.

Now, restore the original "**`ProductCreate`**" model, so that price is required again. Save the file. Confirm that Swagger marks price as required once more and that sending a request without it produces a 422 validation error. You have just practiced something subtle yet essential: not only how to ask better prompts, but rather how to choose the right assistant behavior for the stage you are in. In the next section, we will establish a discipline that will anchor every future modification. Before changing anything else, we will freeze a behavioral baseline and make it explicit.

Freeze the Reference Code before You Touch Anything

At this point, you have already modified the code once and restored it. The system behaved predictably. Swagger reflected the change. Validation rules shifted and then returned to their original state. That small exercise reveals something important. You are now capable of changing the system. Yet, capability without discipline becomes chaos quickly. If you continue experimenting without a stable reference, you will eventually lose track of what "correct" actually means. So before going further, we will freeze the baseline.

Freezing a baseline is not about preserving a copy of the file. It is about identifying the behaviors that define a known-good version of the application and treating them as reference points for future experiments. These are the behaviors a client can observe through the API. They are not internal implementation details. They are what a client can see and rely on. Ensure that your **`app/main.py`** is back to the final version from the previous chapter, where price is required, and the "POST **`/products`**" endpoint declares **`response_model=Product`** and **`status_code=status.HTTP_201_CREATED`**. Run the server. Open Swagger UI. Now, instead of manually listing what you think should work, let us anchor this baseline through a prompt in the following way:

Prompt

Before we start modifying anything, list the baseline checks I should perform in Swagger UI to confirm that the Products API is working correctly. Keep them concrete and testable. Refer to specific endpoints and status codes.

A strong answer should not talk about models or decorators. It should describe actions and results. Creating a product should return a 201 status code and include an ID in the response body. Listing products should return a JSON array containing previously created items. Requesting a non-existent product ID should return a 404 with a message that includes the ID. Sending invalid input, such as a missing price or a wrong type, should return a 422 validation error before any business logic runs. Do not copy the assistant's answer mechanically; rather, use it as a checklist. Now, verify each behavior manually. *Figure* 4.6 captures the baseline behaviors that should remain stable throughout the experiments in this chapter:

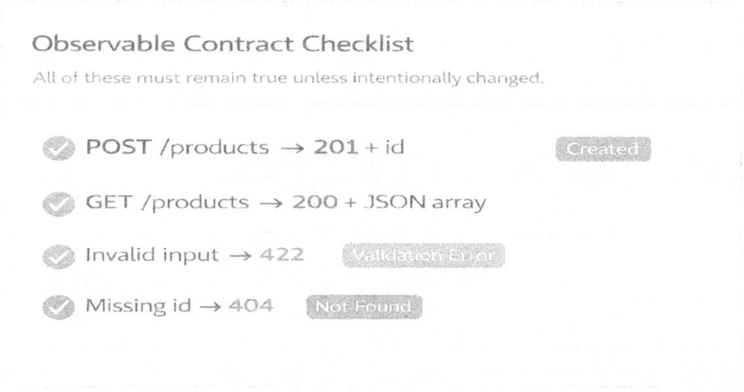

Figure 4.6: *Baseline Verification of the Products API in Swagger UI*

This is a representative view of the stable contract (see *Figure* 4.6): successful creation returns 201 with an ID, listing returns a JSON array, invalid input produces a 422 validation error, and requesting a non-existent resource returns 404. These behaviors define the frozen baseline. Create a product. Confirm that the response status is 201 and that the body includes the generated ID. Retrieve the product by ID and confirm a 200 response with the same data. Send a malformed request and confirm that a 422 error appears with a structured validation message. Request a product ID that does not exist and confirm a 404 with the expected detail message.

If any of these behaviors do not match expectations, stop and correct the file before continuing. The baseline must be stable. This step may feel redundant. After all, you have already seen these behaviors in the previous chapter. However, repetition here is not about memory. It is about anchoring control. From this point forward, every experiment will be evaluated against this baseline. If a change alters the documented response schema in Swagger, you will notice. If validation stops triggering where it should, you will notice. If a status code shifts from 201 to 200, you will notice.

Without a baseline, changes feel ambiguous. With a baseline, changes become measurable. To make this discipline even more concrete, ask one more prompt in the following way:

Prompt

Summarize the current Products API strictly in terms of observable behavior. Describe what a client can do, what responses it receives, and which error cases exist. Do not mention internal implementation details.

Read the summary carefully. It should match exactly what you just verified in Swagger. If it mentions things you cannot observe directly, it is drifting into implementation. If it misses something you can see at the boundary, your understanding is incomplete. This summary is not documentation for others. It is a checkpoint for you. At this moment, the system is frozen in a known-good state. The code runs. The behavior is verified. The contract is clear. Now, experimentation becomes safe. In the next section, we will use that baseline to perform controlled, small changes—predicting their effects before touching the code, then observing how the boundary responds.

From API Contract to Code

Up to this point, you have done two things deliberately. First, you have explored the API from the outside. Then, you have established a baseline of expected behaviors. You can now describe what the system does without reading the file. Now, we reverse the direction. Instead of starting from code and trying to guess what it does, we will start from the contract—the behaviors that you verified in Swagger—and map each one back to the specific structure in `app/main.py` that produces it. This is the moment where control begins to solidify.

Open Swagger UI and look again at the "**`POST /products`**" endpoint. You know that it accepts a JSON body with name and price. You know that it returns a JSON object with ID, name, and price. You know that invalid input triggers a 422 before the function body runs. You know that a successful creation returns a 201 status code. All of this can be verified from the API boundary. *Figure* 4.7 illustrates how the external contract maps to the internal structure that implements it:

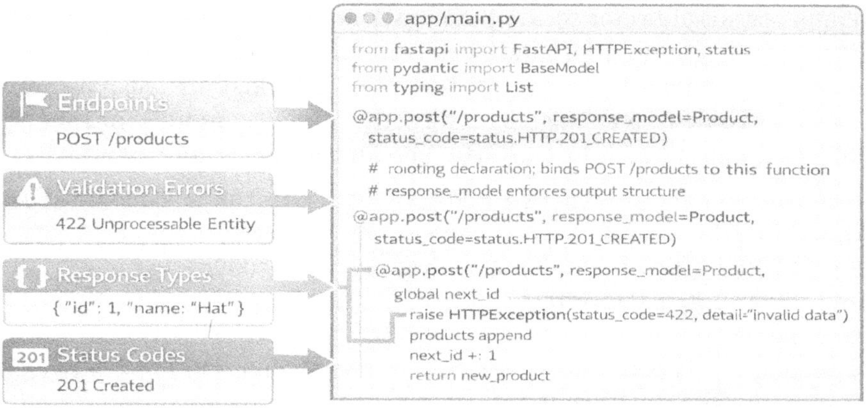

Figure 4.7: *Mapping Observable API Contract to Code Structure*

Figure 4.7 links client-visible behavior (such as endpoints, validation errors, status codes, and more) to the corresponding elements in **`app/main.py`**, including decorators, type annotations, **`response_model`** declarations, and explicit **`HTTPException`** calls.

Now, open **`app/main.py`**.

Instead of reading from the top, ask a focused question in the following way:

Prompt

Given this FastAPI app, map each endpoint to:

(1) the request data it receives,

(2) how that data is validated,

(3) where the response structure is defined,

(4) where errors are raised.

Keep the explanation concrete and refer directly to the code.

A strong answer will not explain FastAPI in general. It will point to specific elements in your file. It will identify the decorator as the routing declaration. It will point to the type annotation product: "**`ProductCreate`**" as the validation trigger. It will identify **`response_model=Product`** as the output contract. It will raise **`HTTPException(...)`** as the explicit source of 404 behavior. Read that mapping slowly. Then, verify it yourself. For example, you know that a 404 response appears when you request a non-existent product ID. Search for the string "Product **`{product_id}`** not found" in your file. You will find it inside the "**`get_product`**," "**`update_product`**," and "**`delete_product`**" functions, inside a raise "**`HTTPException(...)`**" call. Now, ask a sharper question.

Prompt

*Why does a 422 validation error occur before the **`create_product`** function body runs? Point to the specific code element responsible for that behavior.*

A precise answer should refer to the parameter annotation product: **`ProductCreate`**. FastAPI inspects this annotation and uses the Pydantic model to parse and validate the request body before invoking the function. If validation fails, the function is never executed. You can test this claim directly. Add a temporary **`print("FUNCTION EXECUTED")`** as the first line inside **`create_product`** in the following way:

```
@app.post("/products", response_model=Product, status_code=status.
HTTP_201_CREATED)
def create_product(product: ProductCreate) -> Product:
    print("FUNCTION EXECUTED")
    global next_id
    new_product = Product(id=next_id, **model_dump())
    products.append(new_product)
    next_id += 1
    return new_product
```

Save the file. Reload the server.

Now, send an invalid request in Swagger UI, for example:

```
{
  "name": "Invalid"
}
```

Observe two things. Swagger returns a 422 error. The terminal does not print "**`FUNCTION EXECUTED`**". That absence is evidence. The missing print statement confirms that the endpoint function was never executed. Validation intercepted the request and returned the error before the application logic could run. This request flow boundary between validation and execution is visualized in *Figure* 4.8:

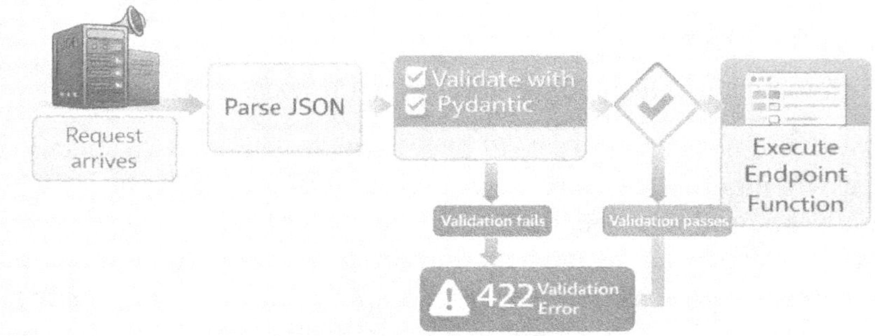

Figure 4.8: *Validation Occurs before Endpoint Execution*

In *Figure* 4.8, a flow diagram shows request arrival, JSON parsing, Pydantic validation, and the conditional path, where either a 422 response is returned immediately or the endpoint function is executed. You did not need to read the documentation to prove it. You tested it. Remove the temporary print statement before continuing. Now, perform another mapping exercise, focusing on routing in the following way:

Prompt

Why does GET /products/3 call the get_product function with product_id equal to 3? Explain how method and path are matched to the function and how the path segment becomes an integer parameter.

A clear answer should mention the decorator **`@app.get("/products/{product_id}")`**. The string inside the decorator declares a path template. The "**`{product_id}`**" segment tells FastAPI to extract that part of the URL and pass it as an argument to the function. The type annotation **`product_id`**: int tells FastAPI to convert that path segment into an integer before passing it in. Again, do not trust the explanation blindly. Add to the "POST **`/products`**" endpoint a product in the following way:

```
{
  "name": "Keyboard",
  "price": 99.9
}
```

Change the route temporarily in the following manner:

```
@app.get("/products/{id}", response_model=Product)
def get_product(product_id: int):
```

Save the file and reload. Now, try calling "GET **`/products/1`**" in Swagger. You should encounter a **`422 Error: Unprocessable Entity`** because the path parameter name "**`{id}`**" no longer matches the function parameter name product_id. FastAPI uses path parameter binding to connect values extracted from the URL to the corresponding function parameters. Since the names no longer match, FastAPI cannot bind the extracted path segment correctly. Restore the original version in the following way:

```
@app.get("/products/{product_id}", response_model=Product)
def get_product(product_id: int) -> Product:
```

What just happened? You moved from observing behavior to mapping it to code, breaking the mapping deliberately, and restoring it. That cycle transforms decorators and type hints from the "syntax you accept" into the "declarations you understand." This is the shift from reading code as text to reading code as contract. After this experiment, the API should feel less mysterious. You can look at a decorator and predict what it declares. You can look at a type annotation and predict how validation behaves. You can locate exactly where 404 errors originate. In the next section, we will narrow the focus even further. Instead of tracing entire flows or mapping endpoints, we zoom in on individual lines that often confuse beginners and interrogate them with the simplest prompt in this chapter: "Explain this line like I am new."

Explain This Line Like I am New

So far, you have traced entire flows and mapped observable behavior to structural elements in the file. That gives you a global mental model. Now, we narrow the lens. Most confusion does not come from entire functions. It comes from single lines that look simple but hide behavior. A decorator. A type annotation. A parameter you did not explicitly use. A variable defined outside a function. Instead of reading documentation or guessing, we apply the most focused prompt in this chapter: "Explain this line like I am new."

Open **app/main.py** and look at the following line:

```
@app.post("/products", response_model=Product, status_code=status.
HTTP_201_CREATED)
```

Figure 4.9 shows what this kind of zoom-in appear on a real line of code as follows:

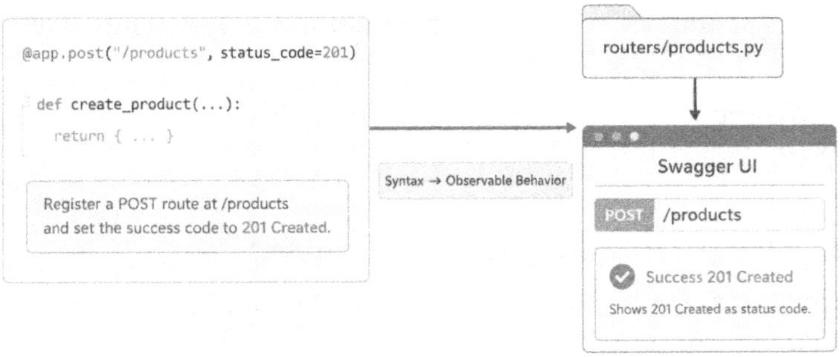

***Figure 4.9**: Zooming into a Single Line*

An annotated code callout shows one high-impact line (such as a decorator or type annotation) and the specific behavior it controls in Swagger UI (as shown in *Figure* 4.9). *Figure* 4.9 illustrates how the prompt "Explain this line like I am new" turns syntax into an observable effect. You have already seen what this endpoint does. You have observed its behavior in Swagger. However, now we can isolate the declaration.

Prompt

Explain this line like I am new:

@app.post("/products", response_model=Product, status_code=status.HTTP_201_CREATED)

What does each part change in the behavior I observe in Swagger UI?

A strong answer should not drift into abstract framework explanations. It should connect each argument to something you can see. The string **"/products"** defines the path that appears in Swagger. The post method determines which HTTP method is accepted. The **response_model=Product** shapes the documented response schema and enforces output filtering. The **status_code=status.HTTP_201_CREATED** ensures that successful creation returns 201 instead of the default 200. Now, test that understanding. Temporarily remove the status_code argument in the following way:

```
@app.post("/products", response_model=Product)
```

Save and reload. Create a product in Swagger. Observe the status code. It should now return 200 instead of 201. Restore the original declaration. You just confirmed that a single keyword argument changes protocol semantics at the boundary. Now, move to a different kind of line in the following manner:

```
def create_product(product: ProductCreate) -> Product:
```

Prompt

Explain this line like I am new:

def create_product(product: ProductCreate) -> Product:

Why is product typed as ProductCreate, and what would change if I removed the type annotation?

A precise answer should connect the type annotation to request parsing and validation. FastAPI inspects the parameter type. As it is a Pydantic model, it expects a JSON body and validates it accordingly. If you remove the type annotation entirely, FastAPI will no longer know how to parse structured input for that parameter. Test it. Temporarily change the function signature to:

```
def create_product(product) -> Product:
```

Save and reload. Open Swagger. Inspect the "**`POST /products`**" endpoint. You should notice that the request body schema disappears or becomes undefined. Try sending a JSON payload. The behavior will no longer match the structured validation you previously relied on. Restore the original signature with product: **`ProductCreate`**. This experiment makes something clear. The type annotation is not documentation. It is behavior. Now, examine a line that does not involve FastAPI at all:

```
products = []
```

At first glance, it looks trivial. It is just a list.

Prompt

Explain this line like I am new:

products = []

Why does this list persist across multiple requests, and why does it reset when the server restarts?

The correct explanation should connect this line to process memory. The list is defined at the module level. As long as the Python process is running, that list object exists which is shared across all requests handled by that process. When you stop the server, the process ends, memory is released, and the list disappears. You have already observed this in the previous chapter when restarting the server erased all products. Now, you can tie that observation directly to a specific line. Finally, look at this line inside **`create_product: global next_id`**.

Prompt

Explain this line like I am new:

global next_id

Why is this needed here, and what would happen if it were removed?

A clear explanation should state that, without the global declaration, assigning to **next_id** inside the function would create a new local variable rather than modifying the module-level counter. Removing it would likely produce an error or incorrect behavior when incrementing the ID. Test it if you want to verify the claim. Remove **global next_id**, reload, and try creating a product. Observe the error in the terminal. Then, restore the original code. What you are doing in this section is not memorizing syntax. You are converting lines into behavior statements. Every line that once looked like "just code" is now tied to something observable: a schema in Swagger, a status code, a validation error, a persistent list, or a runtime failure. This zoomed-in interrogation is essential. Global flow gives you direction. Line-level clarity gives you confidence. In the next section, we will return to a broader view— this time with a different angle. Instead of asking why something works, we will deliberately break assumptions and ask a predictive question: "What happens if I change X?"

The Effect of Changing X

Until now, you have traced behavior and clarified individual lines. You have asked why something works while mapping declarations to effects. That builds understanding. However, understanding becomes control only when you can predict change. This section will introduce the most powerful question in this chapter: "What happens if I change X?"

The structure is always the same. First, you predict. Then, you modify. Then, you run the system. Finally, you observe the boundary and compare it to your prediction. This loop that we will repeat in each experiment is shown in *Figure* 4.10:

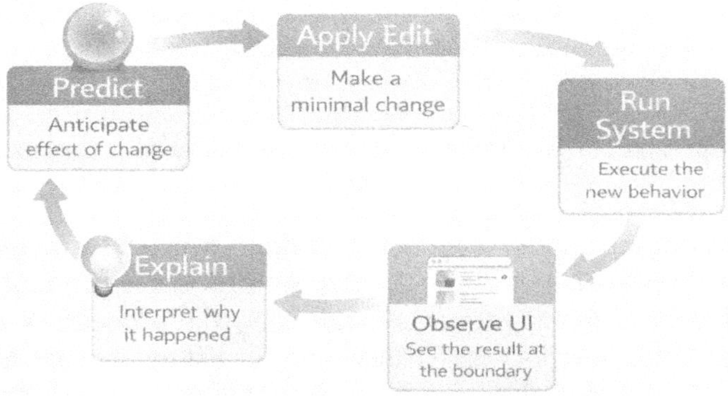

Figure 4.10: *The Experiment Loop Used in This Chapter*

Figure 4.10 shows a reusable template for controlled change: predict the effect, apply a minimal edit, run the system, observe the boundary in Swagger UI, and explain the result. This loop turns modifications into learning instead of trial-and-error.

We begin with a small change that affects validation and documentation at the same time. Look at the following "**ProductCreate**" model:

```
class ProductCreate(BaseModel):
    name: str
    price: float
```

Right now, the name field accepts any non-empty string. Swagger documents it simply as a required string. If you send "name": "A", the request succeeds as long as the price is valid. Before touching the file, ask a precise question in the following way:

Prompt

What happens if I require that the product name must contain at least 3 characters? Predict how this will affect validation behavior and the request schema shown in Swagger UI.

Pause and predict. A careful answer should mention two visible effects. First, Swagger will reflect the new constraint in the request body schema, typically by showing a "**minLength: 3**" rule for the name field. Second, sending a request with a name shorter than three characters will now produce a 422 validation error before the endpoint function executes. Now, implement the change. Modify the model to:

```
from pydantic import BaseModel, Field

class ProductCreate(BaseModel):
    name: str = Field(..., min_length=3)
    price: float
```

Save the file and let the server reload. Go to Swagger. Expand **POST /products**. Inspect the schema. You should now see that the **name** field includes a minimum length constraint. Now, send the following request:

```
{
  "name": "AB",
  "price": 10.0
}
```

Observe the response. Does it succeed? Does the returned object include "price": null? Does anything else change? Compare what you see to your prediction. Now, restore the original model with **price**: float and confirm that Swagger once again marks the field as required and that omitting it produces a 422 error. You have just completed a full experiment cycle.

Now, try a different kind of change that affects the response contract rather than the request. Look again at the "**POST /products**" decorator:

```
@app.post("/products", response_model=Product, status_code=status.
HTTP_201_CREATED)
```

You already tested removing status_code. Now, test something subtler. The "`response_model`" parameter is responsible for output validation. FastAPI uses it to verify that the returned data matches the declared response schema before generating the final JSON response.

Prompt

What would happen if I remove response_model=Product from the POST /products endpoint? Predict the changes in Swagger documentation and in runtime response behavior.

Think before editing. A precise answer should mention that removing **`response_model=Product`** does not necessarily change the visible response immediately. The endpoint may still return the same JSON structure if the function returns a Product instance. The difference is not in what you see first; rather, it is in what is enforced. With **`response_model=Product`,** FastAPI validates and filters the output according to the declared model. Without it, FastAPI serializes whatever the function returns. Now, modify the decorator in the following way:

```
@app.post("/products", status_code=status.HTTP_201_CREATED)
```

Save and reload. Create a product. You may notice that the response body looks identical. To expose the difference, temporarily modify the return statement in the following manner:

```
return {"id": new_product.id, "name": new_product.name}
```

Now, test the endpoint again. Without response_model, the request succeeds and returns the incomplete structure. Restore **`response_model=Product`** and then test. This time, FastAPI raises an error because the returned object does not satisfy the declared response contract. This is what "weaker contract" means. The structure of the response is no longer enforced at runtime. It works until something drifts. Now, modify the decorator again in the following way:

```
@app.post("/items", response_model=Product, status_code=status.HTTP_201_
CREATED)
```

Save and reload. Open Swagger. Observe that "**`POST /products`**" has disappeared and "POST **`/items`**" has appeared. Try calling the old path manually in the browser. It should return a 404. Restore the original path. Each of these changes is small. None of them required new concepts. However, each strengthens your predictive model. You are no longer reading about routing, validation, and serialization.

You are manipulating them and observing their effects at the boundary. This is the lab core of the chapter. The pattern should now feel familiar. You do not modify code casually. You ask a question. You predict the effect. You apply a minimal change. You observe Swagger and the HTTP response. You compare reality to expectation. Then, you restore the baseline. The system remains simple. The file remains short. However, your relationship with it has changed. In the next section, we will take this experimental mindset into a more realistic scenario: debugging. Instead of asking what happens if we change something intentionally, we will analyze what happens when something breaks, and how to use prompts to move from error message to minimal fix.

Debugging with Prompts: Reading Errors as Signals

So far, every change has been deliberate: you predicted the outcome, modified the code, and verified the result. Debugging feels different. Something breaks, and the instinct is to fix it immediately. Instead, we slow down. An error is not noise; it is diagnostic information. Let us create a realistic failure. Open the "**`create_product`**" endpoint and remove the global "**`next_id`**" declaration. Before making the change, it is useful to recall a basic Python rule about variable scope. A variable defined outside a function is global, but assigning to that variable inside a function creates a new local variable unless it is explicitly declared with global. The "**`next_id`**" counter lives outside the endpoint function, so that FastAPI can read it, but updating it requires Python to know that we intend to modify the global variable rather than create a local one.

```
def create_product(product: ProductCreate) -> Product:
    new_product = Product(id=next_id, ** .model_dump())
    products.append(new_product)
    next_id += 1
    return new_product
```

Save the file and reload the server. Now, send a "**`POST /products`**" request in Swagger. In Swagger UI, you will see a "**`500 Internal Server Error`**." This is the client-visible symptom: something failed while the server was handling the request. A 500 error does not tell you what went wrong; it only tells you that the failure happened inside the application. When you encounter a 500 error, do not stop at Swagger. Look at the terminal where the FastAPI server is running. There, you should see a Python exception similar to the following:

```
UnboundLocalError: local variable 'next_id' referenced before assignment
```

Swagger shows the symptom. The terminal shows the cause. Instead of immediately restoring the missing line, ask a structured prompt in the following way:

Prompt

I removed the global next_id declaration and now POST /products returns 500 Internal Server Error. The server logs show an UnboundLocalError about next_id. Explain why this happens and provide the minimal fix. Do not refactor the design.

A strong answer should explain that assigning to **`next_id`** inside the function makes it a local variable according to Python's scope rules. As the function both reads and modifies **next_id**, Python treats it as local. However, it has not been initialized within the function, which leads to the **UnboundLocalError.** The global **next_id** declaration tells Python to use the module-level variable instead of creating a new local one. The minimal fix is to add the global **next_id** declaration inside the "**create_product**" endpoint, so that Python uses the module-level variable instead of treating it as local in the following way:

```
def create_product(product: ProductCreate):
    global next_id
    new_product = Product(id=next_id, **product.dict())
    products.append(new_product)
    next_id += 1
    return new_product
```

This ensures that "**next_id**" refers to the shared counter defined at module level and prevents the "**UnboundLocalError**." Reload the server and confirm that the endpoint works again. Notice the pattern. The prompt was not "fix my code." It was "explain why this happens and provide the minimal fix." That phrasing protects the structure of the application while restoring behavior. Debugging, in this chapter, is not about reacting quickly. It is about extracting information from failure and making the smallest possible correction.

This small debugging cycle reinforces a core idea. An error message is not a failure of the system; rather, it is the system telling you which assumption you broke. A visual representation of the debugging loop used in this chapter is shown in *Figure 4.11*:

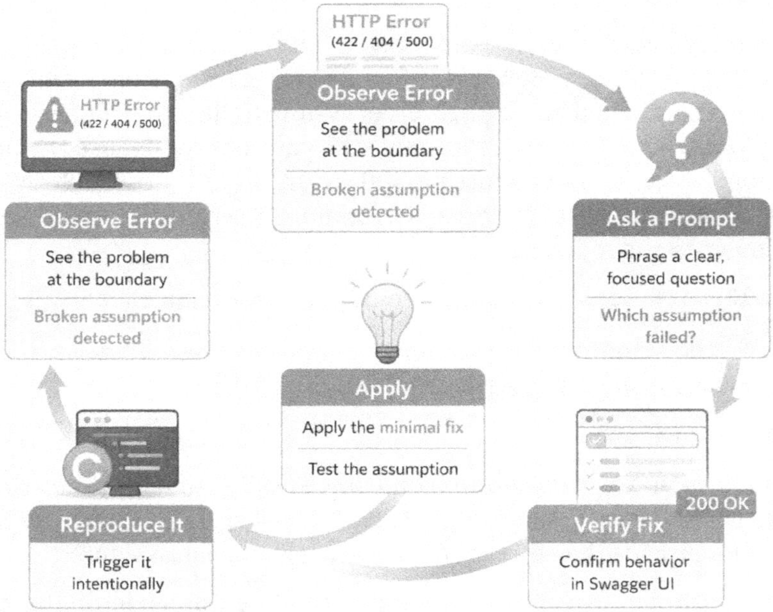

Figure 4.11: *Debugging as Structured Interrogation*

The prompt is not there to repair blindly. It is there to clarify the broken assumption and suggest the smallest change that restores the contract. If you follow this pattern consistently, debugging becomes structured rather than reactive. You identify the observable symptom at the boundary. You reproduce it. You ask a precise question. You request a minimal fix. You apply it. You verify in Swagger. Then, you stop. In the next section, we will step back from individual experiments and debugging cases and consolidate everything into a compact mental model of the request lifecycle in this application.

Request to Response in One Page

Up to this point, you have traced flows, mapped decorators to behavior, modified models, broken routing on purpose, and restored scope errors. You have predicted changes and verified them at the boundary. You have seen validation stop execution before your function runs. You have seen serialization shape responses. You have seen how a single parameter in a decorator changes protocol semantics. Now, we will compress all of that into a single, teachable model.

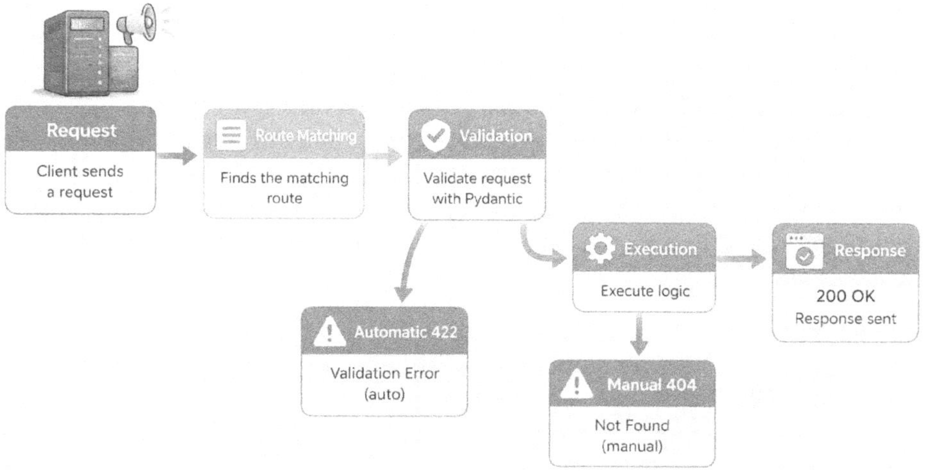

Figure 4.12: *Request-to-Response Lifecycle in the Products API*

Condensed mental model of this specific application (as shown in *Figure 4.12*): request arrival via Uvicorn, route matching through decorators, path parameter extraction, Pydantic validation, endpoint execution, optional **`HTTPException`** handling, response serialization via **`response_model`**, and final JSON response with status code.

This is not documentation. It is not a theory. It is a representation of behavior that you can hold in your head and use to predict outcomes.

Before writing it yourself, ask the assistant for a structured synthesis in the following way:

Prompt

Write a one-page mental model of this FastAPI Products API. Describe what happens from the moment a request reaches the server to the moment a JSON response is sent. Keep it concrete and tied to this specific app. Do not describe generic FastAPI features. Focus only on what actually happens here.

A strong answer should describe a sequence. A request reaches the FastAPI application through Uvicorn. FastAPI examines the HTTP method and path, and selects the matching endpoint based on the decorator declarations. If the route includes path parameters, those segments are extracted and converted according to their declared types. If the endpoint expects a request body typed as a Pydantic model, the incoming JSON is parsed and validated before the function body executes. If validation fails, FastAPI immediately returns a 422 response, and the function is never called. If validation succeeds, the endpoint function runs. Inside that function, business logic manipulates the in-memory state and may explicitly raise **`HTTPException`** for error cases such as missing resources. When the function returns a value, FastAPI serializes it according to the declared **`response_model`** and attaches the specified status code. The final JSON response is then sent back to the client.

Read that description carefully. Now, close the assistant and write the same explanation in your own words. Keep it under ten sentences. If you cannot explain it clearly without looking at the file, revisit the earlier sections. This mental model has a clear structure. A request enters. Routing selects an endpoint. Parsing and validation occur. The function executes. A return value is serialized. A response is sent. Errors can be generated either automatically by validation or explicitly inside the function. Notice something important. Every stage in this model corresponds to something you have directly observed.

Routing was visible when you changed the path and saw the Swagger update. Validation was visible when 422 errors appeared, without your function printing anything. Execution was visible when you inserted a temporary print statement. Serialization was visible when removing the "**`response_model`**" changed the documented schema. Explicit errors were visible when 404 responses included your custom message. Nothing in this model is abstract. This compression step matters because the next chapters will add structure, persistence, concurrency, and security. If your model of request-handling is vague, those additions will feel like layers of complexity. If your model is stable, those additions will feel like extensions of something you already understand.

Before moving on, perform one last verification. Ask yourself: if I add a new endpoint tomorrow, can I predict how FastAPI will route it, validate it, execute it, and serialize it? If I change a model, can I predict how Swagger reflects that change? If I see a 422 error, can I immediately identify which stage of the flow produced it?

If the answer is yes, the code no longer feels like something that "just works." It behaves according to the rules you can articulate. In the next section, we will apply this mental model one more time, not by adding complexity, but rather by refining the file itself—first through an annotated version that makes behavior explicit, and then through a cleaner version that removes scaffolding while preserving clarity.

Annotated Reference File: Making Behavior Explicit

You now have a mental model of the request lifecycle. You can trace routing, validation, execution, and serialization. The next step is not to change the architecture, but rather to make the behavior visible directly in the file. Instead of printing the entire annotated file here, we will focus on the most important parts. The complete annotated version of **`app/main.py`** is available in the companion GitHub repository. This keeps the chapter readable, while still giving you a full reference when you need it.

The first excerpt shows where validation, HTTP semantics, and serialization are declared in the following way:

```
@app.post(
    "/products",
    response_model=Product,
    status_code=status.HTTP_201_CREATED,
)
def create_product(product: ProductCreate) -> Product:
    # Validation already happened before this line runs.
    global next_id

    new_product = Product(
        id=next_id,
        **product.model_dump()
    )

    products.append(new_product)
    next_id += 1

    return new_product
```

Here, three behaviors are declared in a small amount of code: the decorator registers the route, **`ProductCreate`** triggers input validation, and **`response_model=Product`** controls the output shape.

A second excerpt shows explicit error-handling in the following way:

```
raise HTTPException(
    status_code=status.HTTP_404_NOT_FOUND,
    detail=f"Product {product_id} not found",
)
```

This is different from automatic validation errors. A 422 response is produced by FastAPI and Pydantic before the endpoint runs. A 404 response is produced manually by our application logic when a requested product does not exist.

Run the server and verify that everything still behaves like the baseline. *Figure* 4.13 makes the mental model concrete by showing where routing, validation, execution, serialization, and error handling appear inside the actual file:

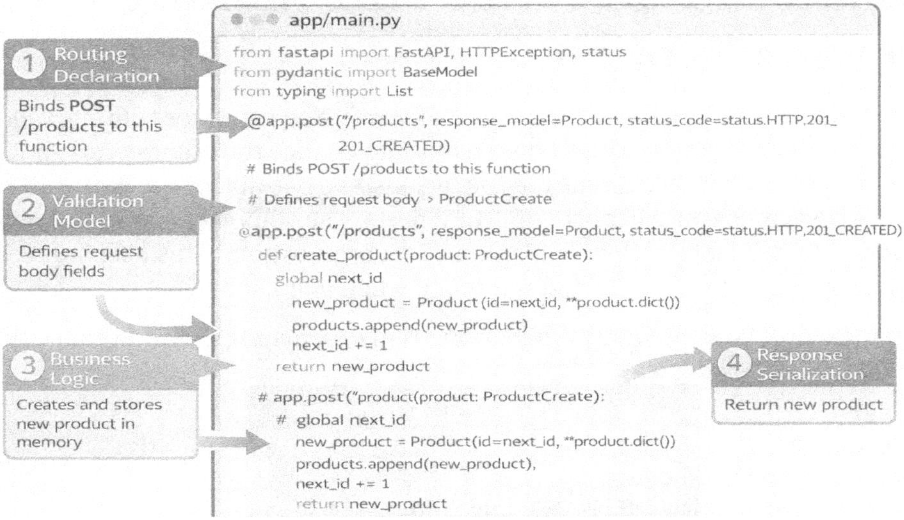

Figure 4.13: *Annotated Reference File Aligned to the Request Lifecycle*

Notice, in *Figure* 4.13, how the routing declaration appears directly in the decorator. The validation stage is anchored to the "**`ProductCreate`**" model and the typed function parameter. The business logic is confined to the body of the endpoint function, where the in-memory state is modified. Finally, response serialization is controlled by **`response_model`**, which determines the structure of the returned JSON. This visualization is not adding new concepts; rather, it is aligning the mental model from the previous section with specific lines in **`app/main.py`**. Each numbered block corresponds to a stage in the request-to-response flow you have already traced: route selection, input validation, function execution, and output serialization. The purpose of this annotated version is clarity. It allows you to see, at a glance, how the API behavior you observe in Swagger UI connects to specific declarations in the file. The comments do not change the behavior of the application. They simply make the structure explicit before we remove the scaffolding in the next section.

Now, ask a reflective prompt in the following manner:

Prompt

Review this annotated FastAPI file and explain which comments describe routing, which describe validation, which describe business logic, and which describe response serialization. Confirm whether each comment matches actual observable behavior in Swagger UI.

A good answer will not invent new concepts. It will confirm that the comment above "`@app.post`" relates to routing and HTTP semantics. It will identify the "`ProductCreate`" model as the validation trigger. It will describe the in-memory list as a state tied to the process lifetime. It will connect `response_model` to the documented schema in Swagger. If any comment feels inaccurate or vague, adjust it. Do not add more comments. Refine the ones that matter. The purpose of this version is didactic clarity. It makes the mental model explicit. Yet, it is not the version you want to keep forever. Too many comments eventually become noise. The next step is to remove the scaffolding while preserving clarity. That is where we will go next.

From Annotated to Clean

The annotated version of the file served a specific purpose. It made behavior explicit. It connected routing, validation, execution, and serialization directly to concrete lines. It turned implicit knowledge into a visible structure. However, that version is not the one you want to carry forward. A production-ready file does not explain itself in full sentences. Comments that restate what the code already communicates eventually become noise. The goal now is not to remove understanding, but rather to remove scaffolding. Comments are scaffolding, not architecture. They build understanding while the mental model is forming, but they are not part of the application's behavior. Once the concepts are understood, the code itself should communicate its intent through structure, naming, and clear design.

This is an important transition. If removing comments makes you feel less confident, your understanding was still attached to the comments. If removing them feels natural, your understanding has moved into your mental model. Replace your annotated file with the clean reference version by removing the explanatory comments. The structure and behavior must remain identical. The clean file is the same implementation you have just verified, without the didactic comments. No logic has changed. Run the server. Open Swagger. Create, retrieve, update, and delete. Trigger validation errors. Request a missing ID. Nothing should behave differently. The behavior remains identical, but explanatory comments are removed once the mental model is internalized.

Now, ask a different kind of prompt in the following way:

Prompt

Review this clean version of the Products API as a senior engineer. Without rewriting the architecture, confirm whether the behavior matches the intended contract and identify any lines that are critical to routing, validation, or response semantics.

Notice the difference from earlier prompts. You are no longer asking "what does this line do?" You are now asking for confirmation of alignment between the structure and the contract.

A good answer should highlight the decorators as routing declarations, the type annotations as validation triggers, the "**response_model**" and "**status_code**" parameters as response semantics, and the **HTTPException** raises as explicit boundary errors. It should not propose adding layers, routers, or services. That is not the objective of this chapter. At this stage, the file is clean. It contains no didactic comments. Yet, you should still be able to explain the request lifecycle, predict the impact of a small change, and debug mismatches between path parameters and function signatures. This is the real test of control. The annotated version was training wheels. The clean version is the reference that you carry into the next chapters. It is the stable core that will later be modularized, extended with persistence, secured, tested, and optimized. If you can read this file now and mentally simulate what happens when a request arrives, the chapter has done its job. In the next section, we will consolidate everything through hands-on practice tasks that force you to apply the method without guided explanations.

Practice: Applying the Method without Guidance

Up to this point, every experiment was guided. You were told what to change, what to observe, and when to restore the baseline. That support now recedes. The objective of this section is not to add features randomly, but rather to make you apply the method on your own: define a goal, write a precise prompt, predict the outcome, make a minimal edit, verify the result in Swagger UI, and confirm that your mental model still holds.

Figure 4.14 summarizes the practice loop: define a concrete intention, write a precise prompt, predict what will change at the boundary, apply a minimal edit in **app/main.py**, verify the behavior in Swagger, and compare the result to the prediction. In the following exercises, the "success condition" is not always a 200 or 201 response. Often, the correct outcome is a 422 validation error. That is not something to fix. It is evidence that validation is enforcing the contract before your endpoint logic runs.

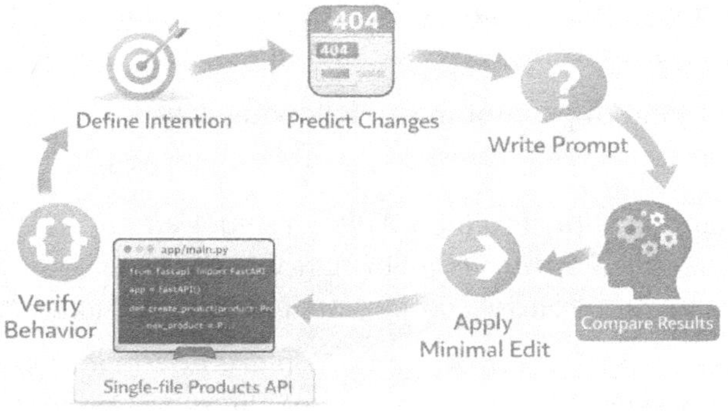

Figure 4.14: *Practice Loop—Applying the Method without Guidance*

Begin with a small contract extension. Imagine that products should include a description field. This is not optional documentation in comments; it is part of the API contract. Before touching the code, formulate the question clearly in the following way:

Prompt

Modify the current Products API so that products include a description field of type string. Update both input and output models. Do not introduce new files or architectural changes. Keep everything in app/main.py.

Pause and predict. Adding a field to "**`ProductCreate`**" should change validation behavior and the request schema in Swagger. As "**`Product`**" inherits from "**`ProductCreate`**," the new field should also appear in responses automatically. If the field is required, Swagger should mark it as required, and omitting it should produce a 422 response.

Now, implement the change by updating the model in the following way:

```
class ProductCreate(BaseModel):
    name: str
    price: float
    description: str
```

Do not modify anything else. Save the file and reload the server. Open Swagger UI and expand **`POST /products`**. Observe the updated schema: the request body should now require a description. Try creating a product without it. You should receive a 422 validation error, which confirms that the contract is being enforced at the boundary.

Now, send a complete request in the following manner:

```
{
  "name": "Laptop",
  "price": 1200,
  "description": "High-end machine"
}
```

Observe the response. The returned object should include the description field. You have extended the contract without altering routing, business logic structure, or error semantics.

Next, move from extending the contract to strengthening it. Suppose negative prices should be rejected. Do not implement this with manual if statements inside the endpoint. Enforce it through validation rules so the rejection happens before execution.

Prompt

Update the ProductCreate model so that price must be greater than 0. Use Pydantic validation features. Do not modify endpoint logic.

Pause and predict. If validation is enforced at the model level, Swagger should reflect the constraint, and sending a negative price should produce a 422 response before the function body executes. One possible implementation is as follows:

```
from pydantic import BaseModel, Field

class ProductCreate(BaseModel):
    name: str
    price: float = Field(..., gt=0)
    description: str
```

Observe the response. You should receive a 422 validation error indicating that the value violates the constraint. Again, this is the expected outcome: it confirms that validation still occurs before execution. If you want to prove that the endpoint did not run, you can temporarily insert a "**`print()`**" at the start of "**`create_product`**" and confirm that it does not trigger for invalid input.

Now, try a change that should not affect models at all. Add a simple health endpoint that returns a static status object. This endpoint is not about business functionality; it exists to confirm routing isolation: adding a new route should not alter existing behavior.

Prompt

Add a new GET /health endpoint that returns {"status": "ok"} with HTTP 200. Do not change existing endpoints.

Implement it directly below the existing route.

Implement it directly below the existing routes in the following way:

```
@app.get("/health")
def health():
    return {"status": "ok"}
```

Reload and verify in Swagger UI that a new endpoint appears. Call it and confirm the response. Then, re-test the existing endpoints. They should behave exactly as before. Your baseline still holds.

Finally, reflect on a subtle contract detail that is already present in your current design: the client provides name, price, and description when creating a product, while ID remains output-only. Ask yourself why Swagger does not expect an ID in the "**`POST / products`**" request body. Which model controls the input? Which controls the output? If you can answer that without looking up documentation, the method is working.

These exercises are not about expanding the API significantly. They are about reinforcing the cycle. Every modification must pass through the same filter: define the intention, phrase a precise prompt, predict observable changes, implement minimal code, verify in Swagger UI, and confirm alignment with your mental model. If something behaves differently than predicted, that is not a failure. It is an opportunity to refine the model. In the next section, we will pause once more and define exactly what your project should look like at this stage—before moving into structural reorganization in the following chapter.

Chapter Checkpoint

Before moving forward, we stop here again. Not because the application is finished, but rather because it is stable. At this point, your "**`app/main.py`**" should still be a single-file FastAPI application. It should expose a small yet complete Products API.

Figure 4.15 shows a compact snapshot of what should be true at the end of this chapter: a single-file Products API in "**`app/main.py`**," stable endpoints visible in Swagger UI, predictable status codes, validation producing 422 errors, missing resources producing 404 errors, and in-memory state resetting on server restart.

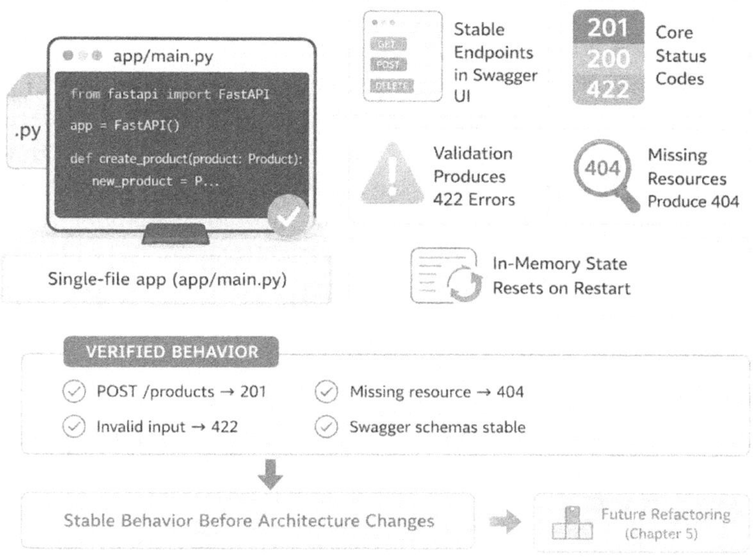

Figure 4.15: *Verified Behavior before Architecture Changes*

It may now include an additional field such as description, a validation constraint on price, and possibly a simple "**`/health`**" endpoint. Structurally, nothing fundamental has changed. The system still behaves according to the same request lifecycle model that you consolidated earlier. A request arrives. FastAPI matches it to a route through decorators. If the route declares path parameters, they are extracted and converted according to their types. If the endpoint expects a request body typed as a Pydantic model, that body is parsed and validated before the function runs. If validation fails, a 422 error is returned automatically. If validation succeeds, the function executes. It manipulates the in-memory state. It may raise explicit "**`HTTPException`**" instances for error cases such as missing resources. The return value is serialized according to the declared **response_model**, and the HTTP response is sent with the appropriate status code.

This model should now feel natural. Open your file and scan it from top to bottom. You should recognize immediately which lines define routing, validation, response semantics, and contain business logic. Nothing in the file should feel mysterious. Run the server one more time. Interact with Swagger. Create a product. Trigger a validation error. Request a non-existent ID. Call the health endpoint if you added it. Restart the server and confirm that the in-memory state resets. Everything should behave exactly as you expect. If something surprises you, stop and investigate before continuing. Surprises are signals that your mental model is incomplete. Now, consider what has not changed.

You have not reorganized the project into routers or modules. You have not introduced dependency injection. You have not added persistence. You have not implemented authentication or background tasks. You have not optimized performance.

Those concerns are real, but they depend on something more fundamental: understanding the behavior of the core system. At this stage, your project should satisfy three conditions. First, it must run without errors and expose its endpoints clearly through Swagger. Second, every observable behavior at the boundary must be explainable in terms of specific lines in the file. Third, small modifications should feel predictable rather than risky. If those conditions are met, this chapter has achieved its purpose. In the next chapter, the direction will shift again. We will not add features for their own sake. We will reorganize the project structure. This time, you will not be moving files blindly. You will be restructuring something whose behavior you already control. That difference changes everything.

The Importance of This Step before Architecture

It is tempting, at this stage, to think that the next logical step is structural improvement. Separate files. Routers. Services. Clearer layering. A more professional layout. That instinct is correct—but only if it comes after control. Architecture organizes behavior. It does not create it. A common anti-pattern is to start moving files, creating packages, and introducing layers before understanding how the application actually behaves. For example, a developer might split routes into separate modules, introduce service classes, and reorganize the project structure, only to discover later that they do not fully understand why validation produces a 422 error or where a 404 response originates. The code looks more professional, but understanding has not improved. *Figure* 4.16 shows the conceptual transition showing that architecture organizes existing behavior rather than creating it. A clear understanding of the request lifecycle and a verified API contract provide the foundation for refactoring. Structural changes can then be introduced without affecting the behavior as experienced by clients.

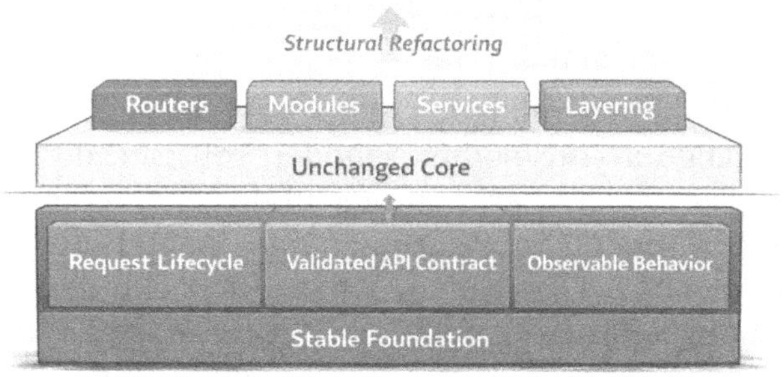

Figure 4.16: *Architecture Builds on Stable and Verified Behavior without Altering the Boundary Contract*

If you reorganize code without understanding how routing binds paths to functions, how validation precedes execution, or how response models enforce output contracts, then structure becomes cosmetic. Files move, and imports change. The system still works, but your mental model remains fragile. This chapter was designed to prevent that fragility. You did not learn FastAPI features in isolation. You did not memorize decorators. You did not read an API reference. You learned to ask three disciplined questions and to test the answers against a running system. When you asked why something works, you traced the behavior to structure. When you asked what happens if you change something, you predicted before modifying. When you asked to explain a single line, you connected syntax to behavior. That method is transferable.

In the next chapter, when we reorganize the project, you will still rely on the same flow. You will predict how routing behaves after moving endpoints into routers. You will verify that validation still occurs before execution. You will confirm that Swagger reflects the new structure correctly. You will treat refactoring not as decoration, but rather as a controlled transformation. The code itself has not grown dramatically in this chapter. It is still small, readable, and contained in a single file. What has changed is your relationship to it. It no longer feels like something that "just works." It behaves according to the rules you can articulate, test, and manipulate deliberately. That shift—from execution to control—is what makes architecture meaningful rather than ornamental.

In the next chapter, we will begin restructuring the application. This time, every move will rest on a stable understanding of what must remain true at the boundary. You are no longer generating an API; rather, you are shaping one.

Conclusion

In this chapter, you did not add complexity to the system—you deepened your control over it. Instead of expanding features or reorganizing files, you slowed down and examined behavior with discipline. You traced requests from arrival to response, mapped observable effects to specific lines of code, predicted the outcome of small changes, and treated errors as signals rather than setbacks.

The Products API is still small. It still fits in a single file. Yet, it no longer feels like a black box. You can explain why validation happens before execution. You can predict how Swagger will change if you modify a model. You can identify exactly where a 404 originates. That clarity is the real outcome of this chapter. By freezing a baseline, running controlled experiments, and refining your mental model, you transformed "It works" into "I control it." That shift is what makes the next step—architectural refactoring—meaningful. You are not about to reorganize code you barely understand. You are about to reshape a system whose behavior you can already articulate, test, and preserve. From this point forward, structure will serve understanding, not replace it.

In the next chapter, that understanding becomes the foundation for refactoring. You will take the current single-file application and reorganize it into a modular project structure with separate layers for application assembly, routing, schemas, and business logic. The challenge will not be making the API do something new, but proving that it behaves the same after every structural change. The endpoints, validation rules, status codes, and error responses must remain unchanged. By approaching refactoring as a controlled transformation rather than a redesign, you will learn how architecture can improve maintainability while preserving a verified, well-understood API contract.

Points to Remember

- A working API becomes a controlled API when you can explain its behavior and predict the impact of changes.
- Understanding grows through three questions: Why does it work? What happens if I change it? What does this line do?
- The core FastAPI flow is: Routing → Validation → Execution → Serialization → Response.
- Pydantic validation runs before endpoint execution and can produce automatic 422 errors.
- Decorators, type annotations, response_model, and status_code declare observable API behavior.
- Freeze a baseline before experimenting so that changes can be verified safely.
- Learn through a simple loop: Predict → Change → Run → Observe → Explain.
- Errors are signals of broken assumptions, not just problems to fix.
- Comments help learning, but long-term understanding comes from a mental model.
- Refactor only after behavior is understood and verified.

Multiple Choice Questions

1. What is the primary objective of *Chapter 4, Understanding Code through Better Prompts*?
    a. To add database persistence to the Products API
    b. To reorganize the project into multiple modules
    c. To move from "It works" to "I control it" by building a reliable mental model of behavior
    d. To optimize the performance of FastAPI endpoints
2. What is the purpose of freezing a baseline before making further changes?
    a. To create a backup copy of the project files
    b. To prevent any future refactoring
    c. To define stable, observable behaviors against which experiments can be measured
    d. To improve Swagger documentation automatically
3. Why is the question "What happens if I change X?" central to this chapter?
    a. It generates more complex features.
    b. It forces prediction before modification, strengthening control over behavior.
    c. It replaces the need for testing.
    d. It avoids reading the code entirely.
4. Why does a 422 validation error occur before the endpoint function body runs?
    a. Because HTTP errors are generated randomly by FastAPI
    b. Because the decorator intercepts all requests
    c. Because Pydantic validation is triggered by the type annotation in the function signature
    d. Because Swagger UI performs validation before sending the request
5. In the context of this chapter, what is the role of the `response_model` parameter?
    a. It improves the performance of JSON serialization.
    b. It defines and enforces the structure of the response visible at the API boundary.
    c. It automatically stores data in memory.
    d. It replaces the need for HTTP status codes.

6. What distinguishes structured debugging from reactive debugging in this chapter?
    a. Structured debugging avoids error messages
    b. Structured debugging focuses only on rewriting code
    c. Structured debugging treats errors as signals, asks precise questions, and applies minimal fixes
    d. Structured debugging requires advanced logging frameworks
7. Why does the chapter include an annotated version of app/main.py?
    a. To prepare the code for production deployment
    b. To add permanent documentation for future maintainers
    c. To make the mental model explicit by linking comments to observable behavior
    d. To increase the file size for clarity
8. What is the key risk of refactoring before fully understanding behavior?
    a. Slower server startup time
    b. Cosmetic structural changes without strengthening the mental model
    c. Automatic validation failures
    d. Loss of Swagger UI support
9. What is the core structure of the experiment loop introduced in this chapter?
    a. Read documentation → refactor → deploy → optimize
    b. Predict → apply minimal edit → run → observe → explain
    c. Generate code → copy-paste → trust → move on
    d. Test → delete → rewrite → repeat
10. Why is architecture introduced only after behavioral control is established?
    a. Because FastAPI requires a single-file application
    b. Because architecture creates behavior from scratch
    c. Because architecture should organize behavior that is already understood and verified
    d. Because architectural patterns are incompatible with Swagger UI
11. What change is most likely to appear first in Swagger UI?
    a. The route disappears from the documentation
    b. The request body schema is no longer defined correctly, and automatic validation is lost

c. The endpoint status code changes from 201 to 200
d. Product IDs stop incrementing

Answers

1. c
2. c
3. b
4. c
5. b
6. c
7. c
8. b
9. b
10. c
11. b

Questions

1. What is the difference between "It works" and "I control it" in the context of this chapter, and how can you tell when you have truly moved to control?
2. Why is freezing a behavioral baseline before experimenting essential for developing a reliable mental model?
3. How does asking "Why does this work?" differ from asking "What happens if I change X?" in terms of the type of understanding it produces?
4. In what way does the prompt "Explain this line like I am new" transform isolated syntax into observable behavior?
5. Why is prediction before modification a critical discipline, rather than simply editing the code and observing what happens?
6. How does treating errors as signals about broken assumptions change your approach to debugging?
7. Why is it important to distinguish between routing declarations, validation triggers, business logic, and response semantics when reading a FastAPI file?
8. What risks arise if you refactor or reorganize code before fully understanding how request handling, validation, and serialization interact?
9. How does writing a one-page mental model of the request lifecycle strengthen your ability to extend or restructure the application later?

10. Which parts of the control cycle (including prediction, modification, verification, and interpretation) remain entirely your responsibility, even when using AI assistants?

Key Terms

- **Behavioral Baseline:** The verified set of observable behaviors (such as status codes, response bodies, validation errors, and so on) that define the stable contract of the API before any modification is attempted.
- **Control Cycle:** The disciplined sequence of predicting a change, applying a minimal edit, running the system, observing the boundary, and comparing the result to the prediction.
- **Observable Boundary:** The external surface of the API as seen by a client, including endpoints, request schemas, responses, and HTTP status codes, independent of internal implementation.
- **Request Lifecycle Model:** The mental representation of how a request moves through the system: routing, parameter extraction, validation, endpoint execution, optional error raising, serialization, and response generation.
- **Routing Declaration:** The decorator-based binding between an HTTP method and path (for example, `@app.post("/products")`) and the function that handles that request.
- **Validation Trigger:** A type annotation (such as product: `ProductCreate`) that instructs FastAPI to parse and validate incoming data before the endpoint function executes.
- **Response Contract:** The explicitly declared output structure and status semantics (via `response_model` and `status_code`) that shape and constrain what the client receives.
- **Structured Debugging:** A method of treating errors as signals about broken assumptions, using precise prompts to explain causes and apply minimal fixes instead of making reactive changes.
- **Line-Level Interrogation:** The practice of isolating a single line of code and asking "Explain this line like I am new" to connect syntax directly to observable behavior.
- **Scaffolding versus Clean Reference:** The transition from an annotated, didactic version of a file used to clarify behavior, to a clean production-ready version where understanding resides in the developer's mental model rather than in comments.

CHAPTER 5
Structuring an API Project with AI Guidance

Introduction

At the end of the previous chapter, you achieved something more important than a working Application Programming Interface (API): you achieved control. You could trace a request from arrival to response, predict the effect of small changes, and explain which lines defined routing, validation, and response semantics. Now, a new question emerges. If the behavior is clear and stable, how should the project be structured?

This chapter is not about adding features. It is about reorganizing what already works. The goal is to move from a single-file implementation to a modular project layout—without changing a single observable behavior at the API boundary. Same endpoints. Same status codes. Same validation. Same errors. Refactoring here is treated as a controlled transformation, and not as a redesign. After every structural change, you will verify in the Swagger User Interface (UI) that the contract remains identical. If behavior changes, the refactor failed.

By the end of this chapter, the application will be split into clearly defined responsibility layers—application assembly, routing, schemas, and domain logic—while remaining functionally indistinguishable from its original version. Structure will not replace understanding.

It will rest on it.

Structure

In this chapter, we will discuss the following topics:

- The Role of Structure after Understanding
- Freezing the Behavioral Baseline
- Extracting Endpoints into a Router

- Understanding include_router Runtime Behavior
- Extracting Models into a Dedicated Module
- Extracting State and Domain Logic into a Service Module
- Verifying Behavioral Equivalence
- Using AI as a Pair Programmer, Not an Architect
- Freezing the Structured Version as the New Baseline

The Role of Structure after Understanding

At this point, the temptation is strong. You have a working API. You understand how requests are routed, how validation happens before execution, and how responses are shaped by declared models. You can explain why a 422 appears, why a decorator changes Swagger, and why removing a type annotation alters behavior. The natural next thought is: this file is getting crowded. That thought is not wrong. Yet, it is dangerous if acted on too early. Structure is not the first step toward quality, but understanding is. Many beginners refactor too soon. They split files, introduce folders, and adopt patterns they have seen elsewhere. For example, a simple application that was previously easy to follow in a single main.py file may suddenly be divided into routers, services, repositories, and utility modules. The structure looks more professional, but the request flow becomes harder to trace. A developer who could previously follow a request from route to response in one file must now jump across multiple layers to understand the same behavior.

The code looks more professional, but their control over it actually decreases. When something breaks, they no longer know where behavior comes from. Routing feels indirect. Validation feels magical again. Debugging becomes guesswork.

They split files, introduce folders, and adopt patterns they have seen elsewhere. The code looks more professional, but their control over it actually decreases. When something breaks, they no longer know where behavior comes from. Routing feels indirect. Validation feels magical again. Debugging becomes guesswork.

This chapter exists to prevent that outcome. The goal here is not to make the project look bigger, but rather to make it easier to reason about without changing what it does. Everything you built in *Chapter 4: Understanding Code through Better Prompts* still applies. The request lifecycle does not change. The validation boundary does not move. Swagger should still describe the same contract. If any observable behavior changes, the refactoring failed. That constraint defines the entire chapter. Before touching the code, we will start with a prompt that sets the tone for everything that follows, which is as follows:

Prompt

How can I refactor this FastAPI application into a clearer project structure without changing any observable behavior at the API boundary?

This is not a request for patterns. It is not a request for "best practices," but rather it is a request for a controlled transformation. A good answer does not start by listing folders. It starts by acknowledging the constraint: behavior must remain identical. That constraint changes how you think about structure. Structure is no longer about elegance. It is about responsibility. Routing logic should live where routing is declared. Data models should live where schemas are defined. Business logic should not be mixed with HTTP concerns. However, none of these separations are allowed to alter the contract that your API already exposes.

This is why *Chapter 4, Understanding Code through Better Prompts* had to come first. You now know where behavior comes from. You know which lines affect routing, validation, and responses. That knowledge allows you to move the code without losing meaning. In this chapter, we will reorganize the application in small, verifiable steps. After each step, you will return to Swagger UI and confirm that the observable behavior at the API boundary is identical. Refactoring will be treated as an experiment, not as a leap of faith. If something breaks, you will not guess. You will interrogate it using the same prompt-driven method you have already practiced. By the end of this chapter, the code will be spread across multiple files. Yet, it will feel more controlled than the single-file version. You will know where to look when something changes. You will know which file owns which responsibility. Most importantly, you will trust that the structure is helping you think, not hiding behavior from you. That is the only reason structure is worth introducing.

Figure 5.1 provides a visual overview of the transition from a single-file FastAPI application to a modular project layout. It emphasizes that observable API behavior remains identical while internal responsibilities are reorganized.

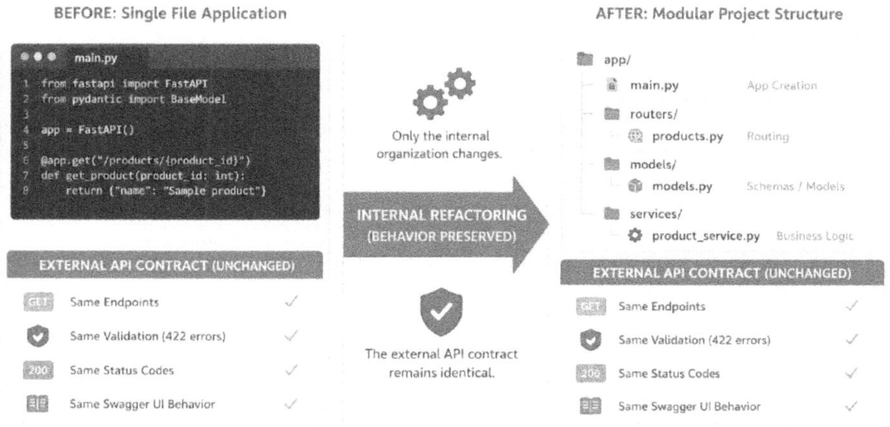

Figure 5.1: *From Single-File to Structured Project*

In the next section, before we move a single line of code, we will freeze the current behavior one last time. Refactoring is only safe when you know exactly what must remain true.

Freezing the Behavioral Baseline

Before restructuring the project, you must freeze its external behavior. Refactoring changes the internal structure of a system while requiring that its observable behavior remains identical. If behavior changes, the operation is no longer refactoring—it is a functional modification. At this point, the entire application still lives in a single file: **`app/main.py`**. Routes, models, storage, and business logic are defined together. The application works correctly. Swagger exposes the endpoints, validation behaves as expected, and the API returns consistent status codes. If you split this file into multiple modules and something subtle changes, how will you detect it? As shown in *Figure* 5.1, the goal of the refactor is to reorganize the internal structure while preserving the same observable behavior at the API boundary. The endpoints, validation behavior, status codes, and Swagger contract must remain unchanged.

Consider a simple example. During a refactor, you will move the route definitions into a separate module and accidentally remove "**`status_code=status.HTTP_201_CREATED`**" from the "POST **`/products`**" endpoint. The application still starts, requests still succeed, and the endpoint still creates products. However, the API now returns "200 OK" instead of "201 Created." Without a frozen baseline, this change can easily go unnoticed because the functionality appears to work. The behavior has changed, even though the intent of the refactor was only structural.

You detect it by defining the behavioral contract before you refactor. This means describing the API strictly in terms of observable behavior at its boundary—that is, the HTTP interface. Internal modules, file names, and implementation details are irrelevant. What matters is what a client can observe. The following prompt captures that idea:

Prompt

List the observable behaviors of this FastAPI Products API *that must remain identical after refactoring the project into multiple files.*

A strong answer focuses on testable invariants. For example:

- POST **`/products`** must return "201 Created" and include an automatically generated ID.
- Invalid input must still produce "422 Unprocessable Entity" before endpoint logic executes.
- Requesting a non-existent product must return "404 Not Found" with the same error structure.

- GET **`/products`** must return the current in-memory collection.
- Swagger must document the same request and response schemas.

These invariants describe the external contract of the system. *Figure* 5.2 summarizes these behavioral invariants from the perspective of an API client. It intentionally ignores internal implementation details and focuses only on what is observable at the HTTP boundary: endpoints, status codes, validation behavior, and response structures. These invariants represent the behavioral contract that must remain unchanged throughout the refactoring process.

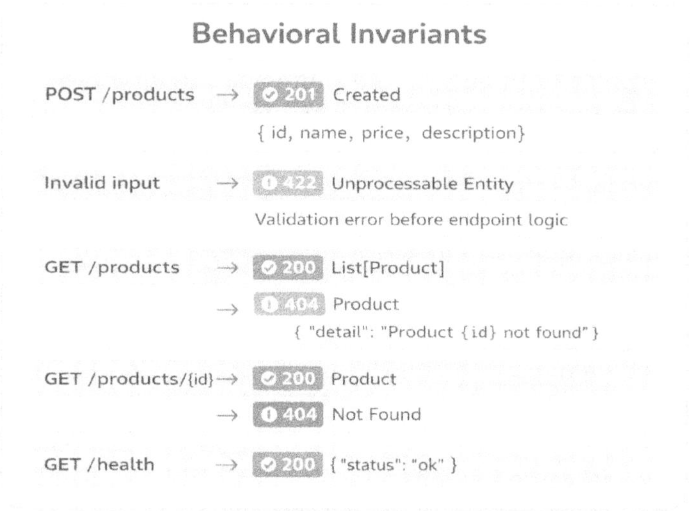

Figure 5.2: *Behavioral Invariants That Must Remain Unchanged during Refactoring*

To confirm this contract, run the application and verify the behaviors through Swagger with the following steps:

1. Create a product with valid data and confirm the 201 response.
2. Submit invalid input and confirm a 422 validation error.
3. Request a non-existent product and confirm a 404 response.
4. List products and confirm previously created items are returned.

You are not testing new functionality. You are capturing a behavioral snapshot of the system. This snapshot becomes your safety net. If any of these behaviors change after refactoring—whether a status code, response schema, validation error, or Swagger documentation—you will detect it immediately. Refactoring without a behavioral baseline is similar to rearranging machinery while the system is running and hoping that nothing breaks. Refactoring with a frozen contract is controlled surgery.

Extracting Endpoints into a Router

Up to this point, the entire application has lived inside **`app/main.py`**. Routes, data models, in-memory storage, and business logic all coexist in a single file. For a small example, this is perfectly acceptable. However, as an application grows, this structure becomes difficult to reason about and maintain. The objective here is not to redesign the system or introduce new abstractions, but rather to reorganize responsibilities incrementally. Rather than restructuring everything at once, we will practice incremental refactoring: making small and controlled structural changes and verifying after each step that the observable behavior remains unchanged. The first responsibility to isolate is routing. In the current version, decorators such as **`@app.post("/products")`** both declare the route and attach it directly to the FastAPI application instance. FastAPI provides a more modular mechanism for organizing endpoints through **`APIRouter`**. Instead of registering endpoints directly on the main application object, related routes can be grouped inside a router and then registered with the application. This separation improves structural clarity without altering how requests are handled or how responses are produced.

Figure 5.3 presents a side-by-side comparison between the original single-file application and the refactored router-based structure. On the left, all endpoint declarations are defined directly inside **`app/main.py`**. On the right, those same endpoint decorators have been moved into **`app/routers/products.py`**, while **`app/main.py`** is reduced to application initialization and router registration through **`include_router`**. *Figure* 5.3 highlights that, although routing responsibility has been relocated internally, the external API contract—paths, status codes, and response behavior—remains the same.

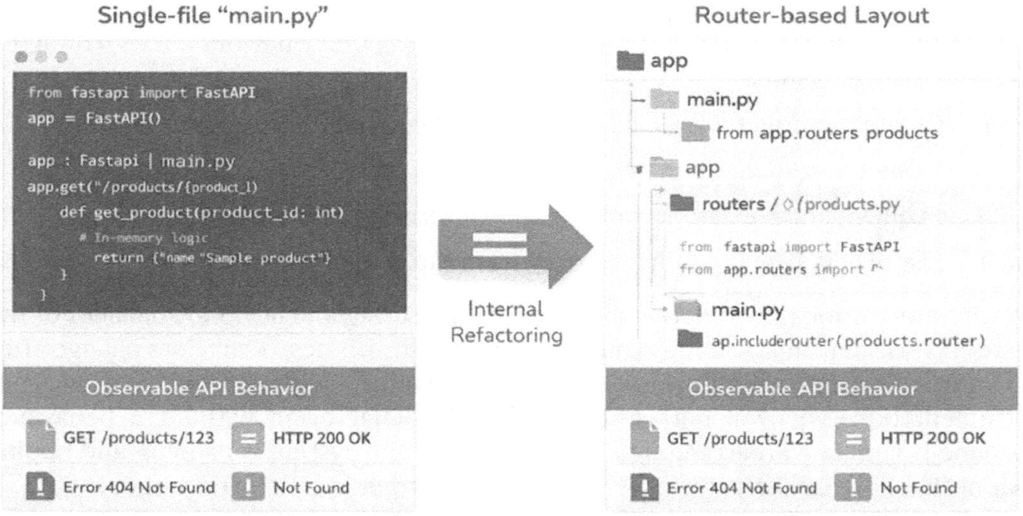

Figure 5.3: *Extracting Routing Responsibility into a Dedicated Module*

The central constraint remains unchanged: observable behavior at the API boundary must remain identical. The purpose of this refactor is structural clarity, not functional modification.

To make that constraint explicit, formulate a precise prompt that describes both the intended structural change and the behavioral invariants that must be preserved, which is as follows:

Prompt

Refactor this FastAPI Products API so that all product-related endpoints are moved into an APIRouter inside app/routers/products.py. The main application should include the router. Do not change any endpoint paths, status codes, models, or response behavior.

A correct response should introduce a dedicated router module and update the main application file accordingly. Begin by creating a new directory called "**`app/routers/`**," and inside it, a file named "**`products.py`**," which will contain the route declarations as previously defined in **`app/main.py`**. The resulting router module should resemble the following structure:

```
# app/routers/products.py
# products.py → HTTP routes only

from fastapi import APIRouter, HTTPException, status
from pydantic import BaseModel
from typing import List

router = APIRouter()
# In-memory storage
products: List["Product"] = []
next_id = 1

class ProductCreate(BaseModel):
    name: str
    price: float = Field(..., gt=0)
    description: str

class Product(ProductCreate):
    id: int

@router.post("/products", response_model=Product, status_code=status.
HTTP_201_CREATED)
def create_product(product: ProductCreate) -> Product:
    global next_id
    new_product = Product(id=next_id, **product.model_dump())
    products.append(new_product)
    next_id += 1
    return new_product
```

```
@router.get("/products", response_model=List[Product])
def list_products() -> List[Product]:
    return products

@router.get("/products/{product_id}", response_model=Product)
def get_product(product_id: int) -> Product:
    for product in products:
        if product.id == product_id:
            return product
    raise HTTPException(
        status_code=status.HTTP_404_NOT_FOUND,
        detail=f"Product {product_id} not found",
    )

@router.put("/products/{product_id}",response_model=Product, status_
code=status.HTTP_200_OK)
def update_product(product_id: int, updated: ProductCreate) -> Product:
    for index, product in enumerate(products):
        if product.id == product_id:
            updated_product = Product(id=product_id, **updated.model_dump())
            products[index] = updated_product
            return updated_product
    raise HTTPException(
        status_code=status.HTTP_404_NOT_FOUND,
        detail=f"Product {product_id} not found",
    )
@router.delete("/products/{product_id}")
def delete_product(product_id: int) -> dict:
    for index, product in enumerate(products):
        if product.id == product_id:
            products.pop(index)
            return {"message": f"Product {product_id} deleted"}
    raise HTTPException(
        status_code=status.HTTP_404_NOT_FOUND,
        detail=f"Product {product_id} not found",
    )
```

Before the router can be imported, the new "**app/routers/**" directory must be created as a Python package. Add an empty "**__init__.py**" file inside it. This makes the package structure explicit and allows the router module to be imported from main.py.

At this point, **app/main.py** must also be updated. It no longer contains the product endpoint declarations directly. Instead, it creates the FastAPI application instance, imports the router from **app.routers.products**, and registers it through **include_router**.

For example:

```
# app/main.py
from fastapi import FastAPI
from app.routers.products import router as products_router

app = FastAPI()
app.include_router(products_router)

@app.get("/health")
def health() -> dict:
  return {"status": "ok"}
```

If the "**/health**" endpoint is not being extracted yet, it should remain in main.py for now. This makes the scope of the refactor explicit: only the product-related routes are moved, while the external API behavior remains unchanged.

Now, the route declarations live in **app/routers/products.py**, while the main application file initializes the FastAPI application and attaches the router to it. This is the structural change introduced in this step.

At this stage, resist the temptation to introduce further improvements. Do not rename routes, add prefixes, or reorganize models yet. The purpose of this step is deliberately narrow: relocate routing declarations into a dedicated router module while preserving identical observable behavior at the API boundary. Once the extraction is complete, restart the server and verify the system through Swagger UI. Create a product and confirm that the response still returns "HTTP 201." Submit invalid input and ensure that validation continues to produce a 422 error. Request a non-existent product and confirm that the API returns a 404 response. Finally, list products and verify that the collection behaves exactly as before. If every observable behavior remains unchanged, the refactoring has succeeded.

While the internal structure of the project has changed significantly—endpoints no longer reside in the main application file but in a router module—the external contract remains intact. The main file now initializes the FastAPI application and registers the router, while the router groups route declarations in a modular form. The key insight of this section is that routing registration is structural, whereas routing behavior is declarative. The decorator still defines the HTTP method, path, response model, and status code. The router simply aggregates these declarations and attaches them to the application instance. The request lifecycle has not changed. Only the location of routing declarations has changed. This is a controlled example of structural refactoring without behavioral drift.

Figure 5.4 shows how routing declarations are moved from the main application file into a dedicated router module, while the observable API contract remains unchanged. It contrasts the internal structural refactor with the external boundary exposed through Swagger UI.

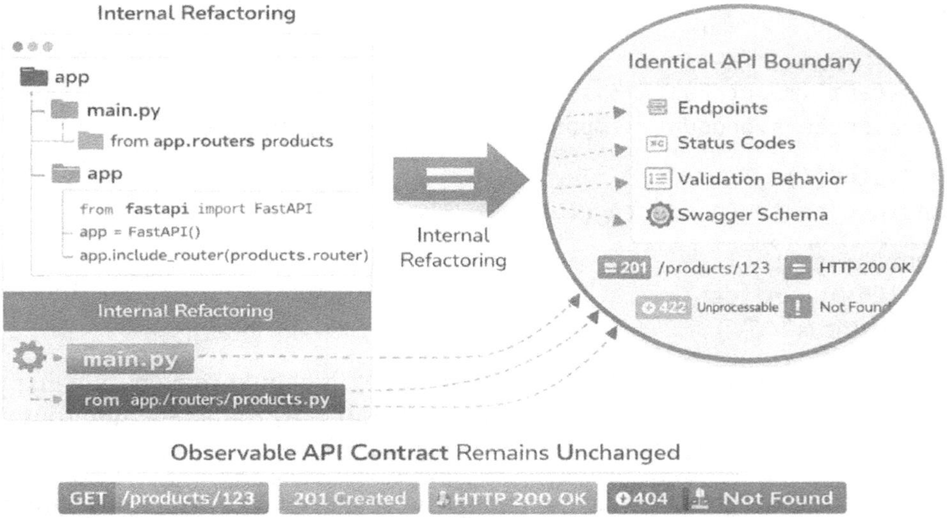

***Figure 5.4**: Structural Change with an Identical API Contract*

Even though endpoint decorators are relocated, and the project layout becomes modular, the visible behavior—endpoints, HTTP status codes, validation responses, and generated schema—stays identical. *Figure* 5.4 makes explicit that the refactor only affects internal organization, not the API contract presented to clients.

In the next section, you will interrogate a single line that now appears in **main.py** and looks deceptively simple, which is as follows:

```
app.include_router(products_router)
```

Understanding what that line actually does will prevent the router from becoming another black box.Fine modulo

Understanding include_router Runtime Behavior

After the previous section, your **app/main.py** became almost empty. It creates the FastAPI app, imports a router, and includes it in the following way:

```
app.include_router(products_router)
```

That line looks harmless. It appears as a configuration setting. In practice, however, it determines whether the router's endpoints become a part of the API. If you treat it as magic, you will lose control again. So, we will interrogate it in the same way as we interrogated decorators and type annotations in *Chapter* 4, *Understanding Code Through Better Prompts*. Before reading the documentation, ask a prompt that is specific to your project, which is as follows:

Prompt

In this project, what does app.include_router(products_router) actually do at runtime? Explain what changes inside the FastAPI application when this line runs, and connect the explanation to what I observe in Swagger UI.

A good answer should describe a concrete effect: When the application starts, FastAPI builds an internal routing table. Without the router, the application routing table contains only the routes registered directly on the application, such as the default documentation endpoints and any routes that remain in **`main.py`**. When you call **`include_router`**, the routes declared in the router module—those created by **`@router.get`**, **`@router.post`**, and so on—are registered into the application's route table. Swagger UI is generated from that route table.

Figure 5.5 illustrates the runtime flow that connects route declarations to their visibility at the API boundary. On one side, routes are defined inside an APIRouter through decorators such as **`@router.get`** and **`@router.post`**. These declarations, however, do not automatically become part of the running application. *Figure* 5.5 shows that when **`app.include_router`** is executed in the main module, FastAPI registers those router-defined endpoints into its internal routing table. It is this registration step that makes the routes active and subsequently visible in Swagger UI. *Figure* 5.5 emphasizes that **`include_router`** is not a passive configuration detail, but rather the precise moment when declared routes are attached to the application and become part of the exposed API contract.

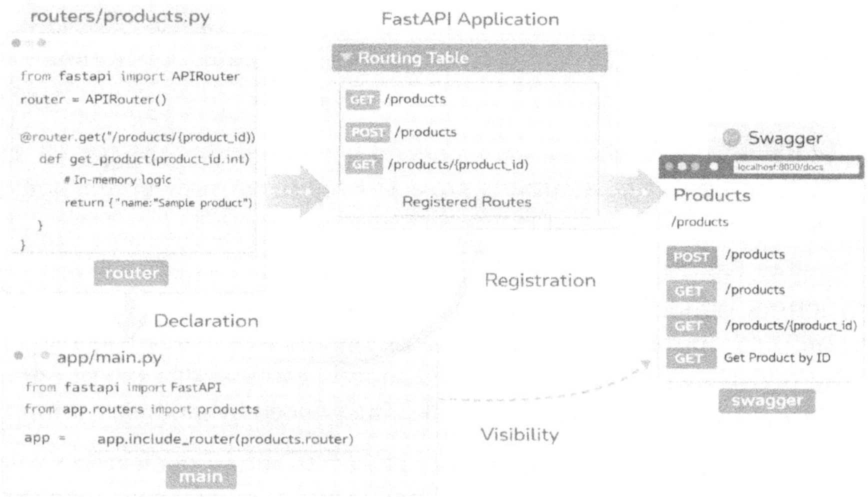

Figure 5.5: *Route Registration through include_router*

So, if the router is not included, Swagger will not show "**`/products`**" endpoints because they are not a part of the application's registered routes. Now, verify this claim through an experiment. Comment out the line in the following manner:

```
# app.include_router(products_router)
```

After commenting out the "**include_router**" call and reloading the application, Swagger UI no longer displays the "**/products**" endpoints. The application process still runs, but the API contract effectively disappears from the boundary. Restoring the line and reloading the server immediately brings the endpoints back into the documented interface.

This experiment makes the registration step visible. Route decorators inside an **APIRouter** define routes, but those routes do not become part of the running application until the router is included. **app.include_router(products_router)** is the moment when those declarations are attached to the FastAPI application and become visible in Swagger UI. Swagger UI is generated from that routing table. If a router is not included, its endpoints do not exist from the perspective of the running application.

In the original single-file version, route decorators were attached directly to the app instance. In the refactored version, they are attached to an APIRouter, and the application only exposes them once **include_router** executes. The lifecycle of the API, therefore, depends on this registration step.

This structural improvement introduces a new failure mode: it is now possible to define correct endpoints in products.py while still exposing no API at all if the router is not included or imported incorrectly. Recognizing this dependency is part of maintaining control over a modular structure.

At this point, the relevant question is no longer how routers work in general, but rather how this specific project behaves at the boundary when route registration is altered.

Prompt

If my router file is correct but the endpoints do not appear in Swagger UI, what are the most likely structural causes in this project? Keep the answer minimal and tied to `include_router` and imports.

When endpoints fail to appear in Swagger UI after refactoring, the cause is almost always structural rather than functional. The router may not have been imported correctly, **include_router** may be missing, the import path may be incorrect, or the object being registered is not the expected router instance. These are not abstract concerns; they are the practical failure modes introduced by modularization.

At this stage, routing has been successfully extracted into a dedicated module, and observable behavior at the API boundary should remain unchanged. Swagger should continue to display the same endpoints, schemas, and status codes.

However, the router module still combines multiple responsibilities. It declares routes, defines models, and owns in-memory state. While this is functionally correct, it does not yet reflect a stable separation of concerns. The routing layer should ideally focus on HTTP translation, leaving schema definitions and domain logic to dedicated modules.

Therefore, the next step is to extract the Pydantic models into a separate module. This move will not alter behavior, but it will clarify responsibility boundaries and reduce coupling between schema definitions and routing logic.

Extracting Models into a Dedicated Module

At this stage, the router module still carries multiple responsibilities. It declares HTTP routes, defines the data models used for validation and serialization, and maintains the in-memory state. This is acceptable immediately after the first structural extraction, but it does not represent a stable design for a growing application.

The next responsibility to isolate is the definition of data shapes. Pydantic models are part of the API contract. They define request parsing, validation rules, response serialization, and the schemas exposed in Swagger UI. They define what clients are allowed to send, what they can expect to receive, and how validation is enforced. For that reason, they deserve a dedicated location in the project structure.

As shown in *Figure* 5.6, the "ProductCreate" and "Product" models are moved into **`app/models.py`** and then imported by **`app/routers/products.py`**, separating schema definitions from routing logic. While their location changes, the router preserves the same endpoint signatures and "**`response_model`**" references, ensuring that Swagger documentation, request validation, and response schemas remain the same at the API boundary.

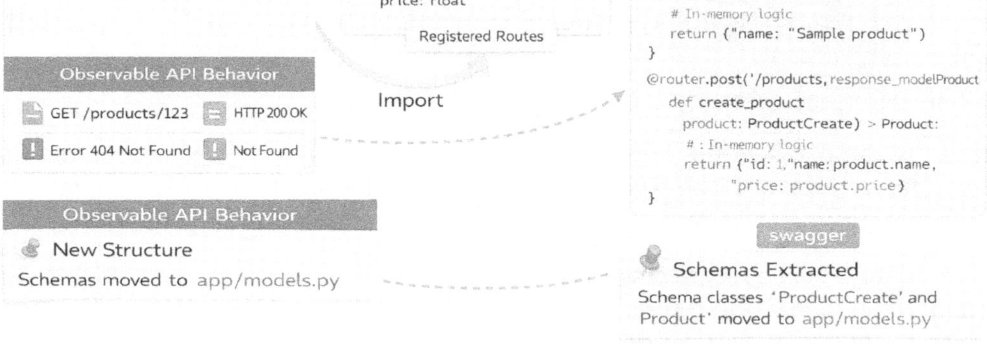

Figure 5.6: *Separating Schema Definitions from Routing Logic*

They define what clients send and receive. They also drive Swagger documentation and validation behavior. Keeping them embedded inside a router file makes them harder to reuse and harder to reason about as the application grows. So, we will extract them. As always, we do not start by moving the code manually. We will start by stating the intention precisely, demonstrated in the following prompt:

Prompt

Move the Product and ProductCreate Pydantic models into app/models.py, and update the router imports accordingly. Preserve the existing request fields, validation rules, response schemas, endpoint paths, and status codes. Keep the application runnable.

A good response should produce one new file and update the router file. Create **app/models.py** with the models in the following way:

```
from pydantic import BaseModel, Field

class ProductCreate(BaseModel):
   name: str
   price: float = Field(..., gt=0)
   description: str

class Product(ProductCreate):
   id: int
```

The validation rule "**Field(..., gt=0)**" deserves a brief explanation. The "**...**" indicates that the field is required, while "**gt=0**" means that the value must be greater than zero. These constraints are used not only for validation, but also to enrich the schema automatically generated in Swagger UI.

For example, the following request body is invalid:

```
{
  "name": "Keyboard",
  "price": 0,
  "description": "Mechanical keyboard"
}
```

The request never reaches the endpoint function. Instead, FastAPI and Pydantic automatically return:

```
422 Unprocessable Entity
```

This is the same validation behavior you observed in *Chapter 4, Understanding Code through Better Prompts*. The schema declaration defines both the API contract visible in Swagger and the validation rules enforced at runtime.

Now, update **app/routers/products.py,** so that it imports models rather than defining them inline. The router code itself does not change. The only modification is that the models are no longer defined inline. Instead, they are imported from the new module in the following way:

```
# app/routers/products.py

from fastapi import APIRouter, HTTPException, status
from typing import List

from app.models import Product, ProductCreate
```

No other changes are required. The endpoint paths, function signatures, response models, and validation behavior remain the same.

It is important to observe what remained unchanged during this refactor. The endpoint paths are identical, the HTTP status codes are the same, and both request and response schemas are preserved. From the perspective of a client interacting through Swagger UI, the API contract has not shifted in any way. The only structural change introduced in this step concerns the location of the Pydantic model definitions. The router now imports "**Product**" and "**ProductCreate**" from **app/models.py** instead of defining them inline. As the same model classes are still referenced in endpoint signatures and "**response_model**" declarations, FastAPI continues to generate the same validation rules and Swagger documentation. In other words, the behavior of the system is determined by the model objects themselves, not by the files in which they are defined. Moving models changes import paths, not semantics.

Restart the server and inspect the application again through Swagger UI. If the server is not already running, start it from the project root using:

```
uvicorn app.main:app --reload
```

Then, open **http://127.0.0.1:8000/docs** in your browser.

The endpoints should appear exactly as before. The request body schema for "**POST**" and "**PUT**" must require the same fields, and the response schema should still expose ID, name, price, and description. Validation errors should continue to produce a 422 response when the price is less than or equal to zero, and requests for missing resources should still return the same 404 structure.

If any of these observable elements differ, the refactor has altered behavior and must be corrected.

Prompt

In this refactor, why did moving Pydantic models into app/models.py not change behavior? Explain which parts of FastAPI depend on the model definitions and which depend on where they are located.

A good answer should make a key point: FastAPI depends on the model types themselves and on how they are referenced in endpoint signatures, not on which file they live in. Moving models changes import paths, not semantics, as long as the same model classes are used in the same places. The runtime does not care about file boundaries. It cares about objects. At this point, the router file is cleaner. It declares routes and imports models from a dedicated module. However, it still contains in-memory storage and business logic. Routing is still mixed with the mechanics of storing and retrieving products. That is the next responsibility to extract.

In the next section, we will move in-memory storage and product manipulation logic into a small service module, so that the router becomes a thin HTTP boundary rather than the place where state is managed.

Extracting State and Domain Logic into a Service Module

At this stage, the router file is noticeably cleaner than in the initial extraction. It now declares endpoints and imports models from **`app/models.py`**, which already clarifies the separation between HTTP boundary and schema definition. However, it still combines multiple responsibilities: it maintains in-memory state, performs product manipulation, and determines how "not found" situations are handled.

This concentration of responsibilities is common after an initial refactor, but it is not a stable structure to carry forward. The goal is not to introduce architectural complexity, but rather to refine responsibility boundaries. The router should act strictly as a boundary layer: it should translate HTTP requests into service calls and translate service outcomes into HTTP responses. State management and product manipulation logic—even if still implemented in memory—belong elsewhere. For this reason, the next step is to extract a small service module that owns storage and domain operations, leaving the router focused exclusively on HTTP semantics.

Figure 5.7 illustrates the separation introduced by extracting state and application logic into a service module. The router is shown acting purely as an HTTP boundary: it declares endpoints, assigns status codes, references response models, and translates internal outcomes into HTTP responses. Instead of directly manipulating in-memory data, the router delegates product operations to the service layer, which owns the application state and performs the underlying product operations.

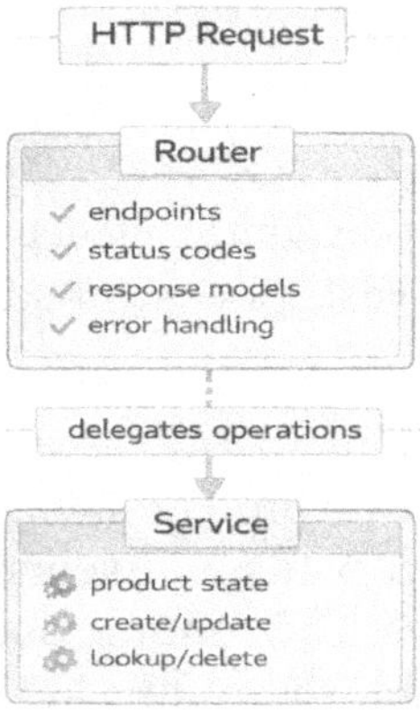

Figure 5.7: *Moving State and Domain Operations into a Service Module*

The service module, in turn, owns the in-memory state and implements the core domain operations such as creation, lookup, update, and deletion of products. This visual separation makes clear that HTTP concerns remain in the router layer, while business logic and state management are isolated in the service layer. Despite this structural change, the observable API behavior—status codes, validation rules, and Swagger documentation—remains identical.

Thus, before moving code, make the intention explicit, as demonstrated in the following prompt:

Prompt

Extract the in-memory storage and product manipulation logic into a separate module app/services/product_service.py. The router should call this service. Keep all endpoint paths, status codes, validation rules, and response structures unchanged. Do not add new abstractions beyond what is necessary.

A good answer produces a small service file and updates the router accordingly. Create the "**app/services/**" directory and add an empty "**__init__.py**" file, so that the service module can be imported cleanly from the router.

The complete implementation of **app/services/product_service.py** is available in the companion GitHub repository. In the book, we focus only on the essential idea: the router no longer owns the list, the counter, or the CRUD logic. It delegates that responsibility to the service layer in the following manner:

```
# app/services/product_service.py

from typing import List, Optional
from app.models import Product, ProductCreate

products: List[Product] = [] #"Not safe for concurrent production
access"
next_id = 1

def create_product(data: ProductCreate) -> Product:
    global next_id
    product = Product(id=next_id, **data.dict())
    products.append(product)
    next_id += 1
    return product
```

The important change is not the algorithm itself, but rather the responsibility boundary: the service owns product-related operations, while the router remains focused on HTTP behavior.

Note: *This in-memory list is useful for learning, but it is not safe for concurrent production access. In a real system, shared state should be handled by a database or another persistent storage mechanism.*

Now, update **app/routers/products.py** so that the router delegates to the service instead of owning the list and counter in the following way:

```
@router.post("/products", response_model=Product, status_code=status.
HTTP_201_CREATED)
def create_product(product: ProductCreate):
    return product_service.create_product(product)
```

At this point, restart the server and open Swagger UI to verify that the structured version of the project behaves exactly like the original. Repeat the same baseline checks you defined earlier: create a product, list all products, retrieve a specific item, update it, and delete it.

To confirm that the refactor preserved the API contract, perform a simple end-to-end test using the same data shape as defined by the models. For example, create a product with the fields name, price, and description. Then, deliberately trigger error conditions by sending invalid data to produce a 422 validation response and by requesting a non-existent identifier to produce a 404 error.

Every observable behavior should remain identical to the pre-refactoring version. Status codes, response bodies, validation rules, and error structures must not drift. If you detect any difference, it is a signal that responsibility boundaries were altered incorrectly during the refactor. This is precisely why verification follows every structural change: refactoring is successful only when structure evolves, and behavior does not.

Before proceeding further, pause and analyze the transformation you just performed through a focused prompt, demonstrated as follows:

Prompt

In this refactor, what responsibilities moved from the router into the service, and what responsibilities intentionally stayed inside the router? Explain the boundary between HTTP concerns and business logic in this project.

Figure 5.8 illustrates the responsibility split introduced by the refactoring. The router represents the HTTP layer: it declares endpoints, assigns status codes, references response models, and translates internal outcomes into HTTPException responses when necessary. The service module, by contrast, contains the internal application logic. It manages in-memory state and performs the core product operations such as creation, lookup, update, and deletion.

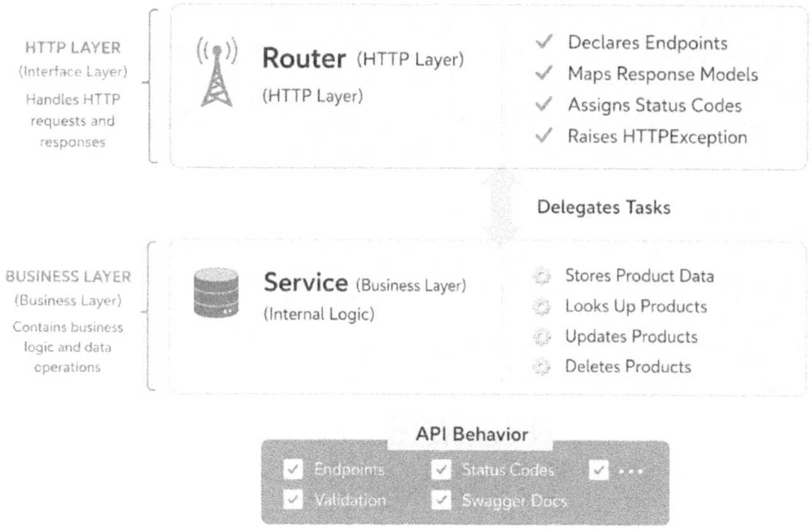

Figure 5.8: *Clear Responsibility Split—HTTP Layer versus Internal Logic*

The key point illustrated in *Figure* 5.8 is that this separation affects only internal organization. From the client's perspective, the API boundary remains unchanged. Endpoints, validation behavior, response schemas, and status codes continue to behave exactly as before, even though responsibilities are now divided between the HTTP layer and the internal application logic. The router owns HTTP semantics: endpoint declarations, status codes, response models, and error translation into HTTPException. The service owns state and product operations. The router remains the boundary through which requests enter the system, while the service performs the underlying work. This structure creates a stable foundation for future changes. Persistence can replace the service internals without modifying routes, and concurrency concerns can be addressed where state is managed. In the next section, we will verify that this structured version still matches the original single-file application in terms of observable behavior.

Verifying Behavioral Equivalence

At this stage, the internal structure of your project has changed significantly. The application is now composed of a main module that is responsible for assembling the app, a router module that declares HTTP endpoints, a models module that defines request and response schemas, and a service module that encapsulates in-memory state and product operations. Before proceeding, perform a simple regression check. Run the application and verify that the key behaviors remain unchanged: creating a product still returns "**`201 Created`**," invalid input still produces "**`422 Unprocessable Entity`**," missing products still return "**`404 Not Found`**," and Swagger UI exposes the same endpoints and schemas as before.

However, structural change alone is not the success criterion. The real measure of a correct refactor is behavioral equivalence. From the perspective of a client interacting with the API, nothing should have changed. Swagger UI must display the same endpoints, requests must return the same status codes, validation must follow the same rules, and error responses must preserve their structure.

To verify that this equivalence truly holds, perform a concrete test against the running application. Start the development server from the project root in the following way:

```
uvicorn app.main:app --reload
```

Then, open Swagger UI in your browser through the following:

```
http://127.0.0.1:8000/docs
```

Now, run the following checks to confirm that the API contract is unchanged. Begin by creating a product with **`POST /products`** using the same request structure defined by the models:

```
{
  "name": "Mechanical Keyboard",
  "price": 120,
  "description": "Compact keyboard with tactile switches"
}
```

The API should respond with "**`201 Created`**," returning a representation that includes the automatically generated ID together with the original fields in the following way:

```
{
  "id": 1,
  "name": "Mechanical Keyboard",
  "price": 120,
  "description": "Compact keyboard with tactile switches"
}
```

Listing products by **`GET /products`** should now return a collection containing the newly created item, and retrieving the product by its identifier should produce the same representation. Updating the product through the "**`PUT /products/{product_id}`**" endpoint should return "**`200 OK`**" while preserving the same schema, and deleting it should produce the same confirmation message as defined in the original contract.

Equally important is verifying the failure paths. Submitting invalid input—for example, a request where the price is 0—should still trigger FastAPI's validation mechanism and return "**`422 Unprocessable Entity`**," confirming that the rule "**`price > 0`**" remains enforced. Requesting a non-existent identifier such as **`/products/999`** should still return "**`404 Not Found`**" with the same error structure as before.

If all of these observations match the behavior of the original single-file application, the refactoring has preserved the API contract. The internal organization of the project has evolved, but the observable behavior at the API boundary has not changed.

In other words, the behavioral invariants defined at the beginning of this chapter still hold. The endpoints, validation rules, status codes, and response structures remain unchanged. The refactor reorganized responsibilities inside the codebase, but it did not alter the contract exposed to clients.

Prompt

Compare the refactored multi-file version of this Products API with the original single-file version. In terms of observable behavior at the API boundary, what must remain identical?

A correct answer for the preceding prompt should highlight a key principle: FastAPI's behavior depends on the objects used in endpoint declarations, not on the files in which those objects are defined. Routes are still declared through decorators, models still define validation and schema generation, and responses are still controlled by **`response_model`** and **`status_code`**. The refactor changed module boundaries, but the request-response lifecycle remains the same.

This confirmation closes the refactoring sequence. The project is now structurally clearer while preserving the same observable behavior at the API boundary. In the next section, the assistant will be used in a different role: not to generate code, but rather to evaluate whether the new structure improves clarity without introducing unnecessary complexity.

Using AI as a Pair Programmer, Not an Architect

At this stage, the risk is no longer misunderstanding behavior but rather overengineering the structure. Once an application has been split into multiple modules, the natural temptation is to continue adding layers, including repositories, interfaces, dependency injection mechanisms, or architectural patterns borrowed from larger systems.

While these elements may be appropriate in more complex environments, introducing them prematurely often increases conceptual overhead without improving clarity. The result is a system that appears sophisticated, yet it becomes harder to reason about.

Artificial Intelligence (AI) assistants can unintentionally amplify this tendency when given vague architectural prompts. If asked to "improve the architecture" or "make the project production-ready," they will often suggest additional layers, abstractions, and patterns based on common industry examples. The recommendations are not necessarily wrong, but they may be inappropriate for the current stage of the project. Without clear constraints, a simple application can quickly accumulate repositories, interfaces, service hierarchies, and dependency injection mechanisms that solve problems the project does not yet have.

The objective of this chapter is deliberately narrower. The goal is not to design a fully layered architecture, but rather to separate responsibilities just enough to improve clarity, while preserving identical observable behavior.

For this reason, the assistant is used here in a constrained role—not as an architect proposing abstractions, but rather as a pair programmer or reviewer operating within clearly defined limits. The quality of the outcome depends largely on how those limits are expressed in the prompt.

Figure 5.9 illustrates two different ways of using AI during structural evolution. On one side, an open-ended architectural prompt invites the assistant to expand the system by introducing layers and abstractions. On the other side, a constrained structural review keeps the assistant focused on evaluating the existing structure under explicit behavioral constraints.

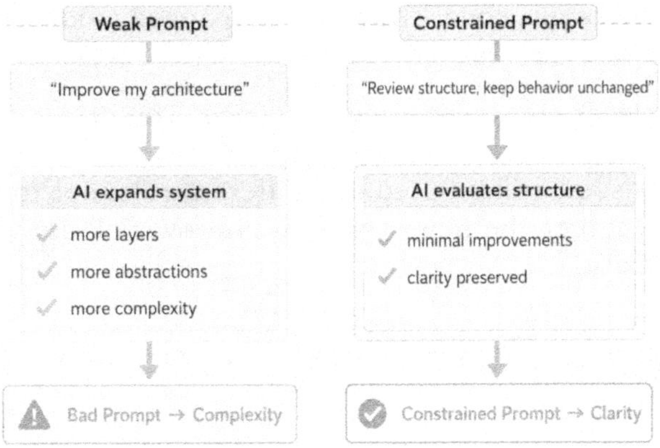

Figure 5.9: *Using AI under Structural Constraints*

The difference lies not in the tool, but rather in the framing of the prompt. When instructions are precise and anchored to behavioral invariants, AI becomes a disciplined reviewer rather than an engine of architectural expansion.

A weak prompt at this stage appears as follows:

Prompt

Improve my architecture.

Such a request invites additional abstraction and unnecessary complexity. A good prompt is narrow and anchored to the current objective of the chapter, demonstrated as follows:

A useful review should evaluate whether the responsibilities introduced so far are coherent: the main module assembling the application, the router defining the HTTP boundary, the models expressing the schema contract, and the service encapsulating application logic and state.

Prompt

Review this refactored FastAPI project structure as a senior engineer. Is anything unnecessarily complex for this stage? Suggest only minimal improvements that increase clarity without adding new layers or changing behavior.

At this stage, improvements should remain small and local. They typically involve naming consistency, import organization, or the removal of minor duplication rather than the introduction of additional architectural layers.

Prompt

Keep the current structure. Do not introduce new layers such as repositories or dependency injection. Suggest only improvements that reduce duplication or make the flow easier to read, while preserving identical Swagger behavior.

One concrete example is the repeated construction of identical 404 errors in the router. In the current design, the service returns "**`None`**" or "**`False`**" when a resource is not found, and the router translates that outcome into an **`HTTPException`**. This repetition is not incorrect, but it can be simplified slightly without altering behavior.

Prompt

In the router file only, remove duplication in the 404 error-raising logic without changing any endpoint behavior or response detail strings. Show the minimal edit.

After applying such a small improvement, verification remains essential. The observable contract exposed through Swagger UI must remain unchanged.

The purpose of involving AI at this stage is not to delegate architectural decisions, but rather to reduce friction and surface small clarity improvements. Architectural direction remains a human responsibility. Without explicit constraints, the assistant will naturally tend toward additional abstraction.

The structure introduced in this chapter intentionally remains minimal: a router defining the HTTP boundary, models defining the schema contract, and a service module containing application logic and state. This separation is sufficient to support future extensions—such as persistence, concurrency, security, and testing—without introducing unnecessary complexity.

In the next section, this structured version will become the new baseline for the chapters that follow.

Freezing the Structured Version as the New Baseline

At this stage, the transformation you performed is more significant than it may initially appear. From the outside, the API behaves exactly as it did in *Chapter 3: Generating*

Your First Real API. The same endpoints are exposed, the same status codes are returned, validation rules operate in the same way, and error messages follow the same structure. A client interacting through Swagger UI cannot detect any difference.

Yet, internally, the organization of the system has changed substantially. Routing responsibilities are now isolated in a router module. Schema definitions reside in a models module. In-memory state and application logic are encapsulated inside a service module. The main file has been reduced to its essential role: assembling the FastAPI application and registering its components.

What remains constant is the observable behavior; what has evolved are the responsibility boundaries. This distinction defines the new baseline for the project.

The current structure of the application now appears as follows:

```
app/
    main.py
    models.py
    routers/
        products.py
    services/
        product_service.py
```

This modular version will become the stable reference point for the chapters that follow.

Figure 5.10 presents the structured project layout after refactoring. It highlights the separation of responsibilities introduced in this chapter: the main module assembles the application, the router layer defines the HTTP boundary, the models module defines the API schemas, and the service layer contains the application logic and in-memory state.

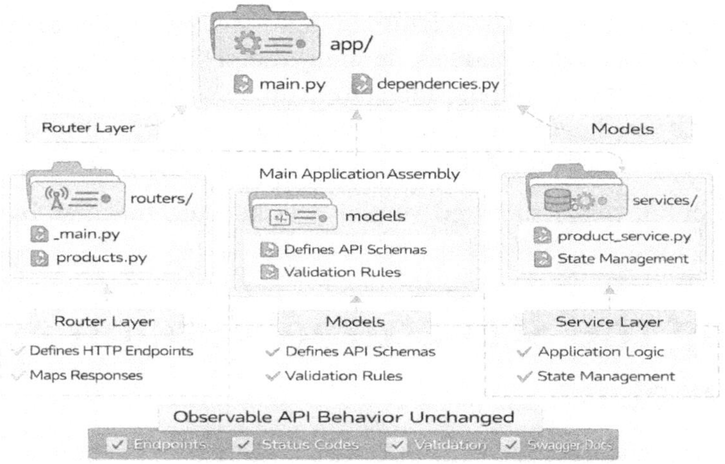

Figure 5.10: *Structured FastAPI Project as the New Behavioral Baseline*

While responsibilities are now distributed across multiple modules, the external API contract remains unchanged. Endpoints, validation behavior, status codes, and Swagger documentation are identical to the single-file version. The refactor altered the internal organization of the codebase, not the observable behavior of the API.

Before considering the chapter complete, run the application one final time and verify its behavior from the outside. Start the server and interact with the API through Swagger UI exactly as you did earlier in the chapter: create a product, retrieve it, update it, and delete it. Intentionally trigger both validation errors and not-found scenarios. This final verification confirms that the modular version preserves the same external contract as the original single-file implementation.

While the observable behavior has not changed, the internal structure now reflects clear responsibility boundaries. The main module assembles the application. The router owns HTTP semantics and translates internal outcomes into responses. The models module defines the schema contract used for validation and serialization. The service module encapsulates application logic together with in-memory state.

To consolidate that understanding, ask the assistant to describe the architecture you have created in the following manner:

Prompt

Describe the current architecture of this FastAPI project in terms of responsibility boundaries. Explain what each module owns and why this separation makes future changes safer.

A correct description should identify the main module as responsible for application composition, the router as the HTTP boundary, the models module as the definition of API schemas, and the service module as the owner of application logic and state.

This description becomes the reference map for the chapters that follow. When persistence is introduced later, the in-memory service implementation can be replaced without rewriting routes. When authentication is added, security concerns can be applied at the HTTP boundary. When concurrency is explored, endpoint definitions and service internals can evolve independently without requiring another structural reorganization.

Ask the assistant to summarize the transformation performed throughout this chapter in the following manner:

Prompt

Summarize how this FastAPI project evolved from a single-file working API to a structured multi-module project, without changing observable behavior. Focus on the reasoning process rather than the code details.

If the assistant's summary highlights controlled refactoring, clear responsibility boundaries, and strict preservation of observable behavior, then the objective of this chapter has been achieved.

The goal was never to make the system appear more sophisticated by increasing its architectural complexity. The goal was to make it more stable by organizing responsibilities while preserving behavior. No new features were introduced, and no additional architectural layers were added. Instead, the existing functionality was preserved while the internal structure was clarified.

The result is not a more complex system, but rather a more controlled one.

This structured version of the project now becomes the foundation for everything that follows.

Conclusion

In this chapter, you reorganized a working FastAPI application without changing a single observable behavior. By extracting routing into a router module, schemas into a models module, and domain logic into a service layer, you clarified responsibility boundaries while preserving the API contract. At every step, the API contract remained unchanged. What changed was the structure; what did not change was the behavior observed at the boundary. What changed was the structure; what did not change was the boundary. The result is not a more complex system, but a more stable one—ready to support future extensions without losing control.

In the next chapter, the focus will shift from reorganizing code to extending the system's capabilities, including concurrency, background tasks, and real-time behavior. As responsibility boundaries are now explicit and behavior has been carefully preserved, those extensions will build incrementally on a stable base.

If this chapter were about discipline in structural change, the next one would be about controlled expansion of capability. The modular structure created in this chapter becomes the foundation for everything that follows. In the next chapter, we will build on that foundation by introducing concurrency, background tasks, and real-time interactions while preserving the same disciplined approach to observable behavior.

Points to Remember

- Refactoring changes structure, not behavior.
- Freeze the API contract before changing the code.
- Endpoints, status codes, validation, and errors must remain unchanged.
- Separate responsibilities: routing, schemas, and business logic.
- include_router() makes routes part of the running API.
- Moving code between files should not change observable behavior.
- Verify behavior after every refactoring step.

- Constrained prompts reduce overengineering and preserve clarity.
- Prefer clear responsibilities over unnecessary architectural complexity.

Multiple Choice Questions

1. What is the main objective of *Chapter 5: Structuring an API Project with AI Guidance*?
   a. To add new business features to the Products API
   b. To introduce database persistence
   c. To reorganize the project into a modular structure without changing observable behavior
   d. To optimize performance and scalability
2. Why must observable API behavior remain identical during refactoring?
   a. Because FastAPI does not allow behavior changes
   b. Because refactoring is about structural clarity, not functional modification
   c. Because Swagger UI cannot detect changes
   d. Because AI-generated code is unreliable
3. What is the purpose of freezing the behavioral baseline before refactoring?
   a. To prevent the server from restarting
   b. To create a checklist of invariants that must remain true
   c. To simplify file imports
   d. To improve performance benchmarks
4. What does include_router actually do at runtime?
   a. It generates database tables.
   b. It validates Pydantic models.
   c. It registers router-defined endpoints into the application's routing table.
   d. It optimizes HTTP performance.
5. Why does moving Pydantic models into app/models.py not change API behavior?
   a. Because FastAPI ignores models in separate files
   b. Because model location determines routing behavior

   c. Because FastAPI depends on model objects and how they are referenced, not on their file location
   d. Because Swagger UI caches schemas

6. After extracting a service module, what responsibility remains in the router?
   a. Managing in-memory state directly
   b. Translating HTTP requests and responses, including error mapping
   c. Performing database migrations
   d. Handling background tasks
7. What is the primary risk when using AI with open-ended architectural prompts during refactoring?
   a. The code will not compile.
   b. The assistant will remove existing endpoints.
   c. The system may become unnecessarily complex.
   d. Validation errors will disappear.
8. What defines successful structural refactoring in this chapter?
   a. The number of modules created
   b. The introduction of design patterns
   c. Identical external API behavior with clearer internal responsibility boundaries
   d. Reduced file size
9. After refactoring, Swagger UI no longer shows the /products endpoints. What is the most likely cause?
   a. Validation failed during application startup.
   b. The router was not included in the FastAPI application.
   c. The service layer raised an exception.
   d. The Pydantic models were moved to a different file.

Answers

1. c
2. b
3. b
4. c

5. c
6. b
7. c
8. c
9. b

Questions

1. Why must observable API behavior be frozen before performing structural refactoring, and what risks arise if you skip this step?
2. In what ways does separating routing, models, and service logic improve reasoning about the system without changing its external contract?
3. How does include_router change the internal structure of the application, while leaving the request-response lifecycle intact?
4. Why does moving Pydantic models into a dedicated module not alter validation behavior or Swagger documentation?
5. What is the conceptual boundary between HTTP concerns and domain logic in the refactored version of the project?
6. How does verifying behavior in Swagger UI after every structural change prevent refactoring from turning into unintended redesign?
7. What are the risks of using open-ended architectural prompts with AI during refactoring, and how do constrained prompts reduce overengineering?
8. Why is the modular multi-file structure introduced in this chapter a more stable foundation for future changes, such as persistence, security, or concurrency?

Key Terms

- **Structural Refactoring**: The process of reorganizing code across modules and layers without altering the observable behavior of the system at the API boundary.
- **Behavioral Baseline**: The explicit snapshot of observable API behavior (such as endpoints, status codes, validation rules, error formats, and schemas) that must remain unchanged during refactoring.
- **Responsibility Boundary**: A clear separation of concerns between different parts of the system, such as application assembly, HTTP routing, schema definition, and domain logic.

- **Router (APIRouter)**: A FastAPI component used to group related endpoint declarations and register them with the main application through include_router, improving structural organization without changing behavior.
- **Route Registration**: The runtime process by which endpoints declared in a router are attached to the FastAPI application's internal routing table, making them visible in Swagger UI.
- **Schema Module**: A dedicated module (for example, app/models.py) that contains Pydantic models defining request and response shapes, independent of routing logic.
- **Service Layer**: A module responsible for domain operations and state management (such as in-memory storage), isolated from HTTP concerns handled by the router.
- **Behavioral Invariants**: Observable characteristics of the API contract (such as paths, status codes, validation behavior, and response structures) that must remain identical during structural change.
- **HTTP Boundary**: The layer of the application that translates incoming requests into domain calls and converts domain outcomes into HTTP responses, including status codes and exceptions.
- **Constrained Prompting**: A prompt strategy that explicitly limits architectural scope and preserves behavioral invariants, preventing unnecessary complexity or overengineering during AI-assisted refactoring.

CHAPTER 6
Handling Concurrency and Real-Time Workflows

Introduction

In the previous chapter, the Products Application Programming Interface (API) gained a clear internal structure. Routing logic, schema definitions, and domain operations were separated into distinct modules, allowing the application to grow without losing clarity or control. With that structure in place, the next step is not to reorganize the code again, but rather to expand what the system can do.

Real APIs rarely operate in a strictly instantaneous request–response model. Some operations take time. Consider a few common examples. A user uploads a large file and expects processing to continue in the background. A manager requests a monthly sales report that may take several seconds to generate. A client application monitors a long-running operation and benefits from receiving progress updates rather than waiting for a final result. These scenarios introduce a new dimension to API design: how the system represents time and the ongoing work.

This chapter explores three practical ways of handling such workflows in FastAPI: asynchronous endpoints, background tasks, and streaming responses. Each mechanism is introduced through a concrete need inside the existing Products API and implemented using the same prompt-driven approach, which is used throughout the book. Rather than starting with theory, we will begin with observable behavior and ask how an API should respond when work cannot or should not be completed immediately.

By the end of the chapter, the application will support three distinct timing patterns while preserving the same structured architecture that was introduced earlier. The goal is not to introduce complexity, but rather to make the API capable of expressing realistic workflows without losing clarity or control.

Structure

In this chapter, we will cover the following sections:

- Starting Point: The Structured Products API
- Concurrency Matters Only When Behavior Requires It
- Identifying the First Real Need: A Slow but Observable Operation
- First Async Endpoint: Making a Slow Operation Non-Blocking
- Observing What Changed When the Endpoint Became Async
- Background Tasks: Work That Continues after the Response
- Adding a Background Task to the Products API
- Streaming Responses: Returning Output Gradually
- Adding a Streaming Endpoint to the Project
- Choosing the Right Tool: Async Endpoint, Background Task, and Streaming
- Verifying the New Behavioral Contract
- Freezing the Concurrent Version as the New Baseline

Starting Point: The Structured Products API

Before introducing concurrency, background work, or streaming behavior, it is essential to make the starting state of the application explicit. In *Chapter 5, Structuring an API Project with AI Guidance*, the Products API was refactored into a structured project layout. That refactor did not add new features. It added something more valuable, that is, clear responsibility boundaries. At this point, the application already works, and that is precisely why this is the right moment to ask a new kind of question. Not "how do I make it run?" or "how should I organize my files?", but rather "given the structure I now have, where should new behavior live, and how should I reason about it before I ask Artificial Intelligence (AI) to write code?"

That question matters because concurrency is one of the easiest places to lose control if the structure of the project is not already visible in your mind. If you ask for asynchronous code, background tasks, or streaming responses without first anchoring yourself in the current architecture, the assistant may generate code that works in isolation but violates the separation of concerns you just established. In this chapter, prompts must not only request functionality. They must also preserve architectural intent. This is a shift from "generate code" to "constrain generation." The assistant is no longer asked what to build, but rather how to extend without breaking what already exists.

The first step, then, is not to write new code. It is to restate the project as it currently exists. A useful prompt at this stage is not broad. It asks the assistant to describe the application in terms of modules and responsibilities, because that is the map you will need before extending behavior.

Prompt

Describe the current structure of this FastAPI Products API after refactoring.

Explain what each module is responsible for, and keep the answer focused on how routing, models, and service logic are currently separated.

A good answer should not drift into abstract architectural language. It should describe the project concretely. The application entry point is **`app/main.py`**, where the FastAPI instance is created, and the products router is included. The request and response schemas live in **`app/models.py`**. The HTTP boundary—paths, methods, response models, and HTTP exceptions—lives in **`app/routers/products.py`**. The internal product operations and in-memory state live in **`app/services/product_service.py`**. If the assistant begins proposing repositories, controllers, or additional layers, the prompt has already failed, because the goal here is not expansion, but rather orientation.

At the beginning of this chapter, the project should therefore appears as follows:

```
app/
├── main.py
├── models.py
├── routers/
│        └── products.py
└── services/
          └── product_service.py
```

Baseline Architecture (before Adding Concurrency)

main.py

- *Application assembly only*
- *Creates the FastAPI application*
- *Includes routers*

models.py

- *Defines request and response schemas*
- *Owns validation rules and API data shapes*

routers/products.py

- *Defines HTTP endpoints*
- *Handles status codes and HTTP exceptions*

- *Translates requests into service calls*

services/product_service.py

- *Owns product-related logic and in-memory state*
- *Performs operations used by the API*
- *Same architecture. New timing behaviors.*

The purpose of this chapter is not to change these responsibility boundaries. Instead, asynchronous endpoints, background tasks, and streaming responses will be introduced within the existing structure. The architecture remains stable while the application gains new ways of handling work over time.

Seeing the structure is not enough. The next step is to connect that structure to actual code, because prompts become more effective when they are grounded in the files the reader will really touch. The following code represents the complete baseline carried over from this chapter. It is important to show it in full because everything introduced later in the chapter will be added to this exact project, and not to an isolated demo.

The application entry point is minimal, demonstrated as follows:

```
# app/main.py
from fastapi import FastAPI
from app.routers.products import router as products_router

app = FastAPI()

app.include_router(products_router)

@app.get("/health")
def health() -> dict:
    return {
        "status": "ok"
    }
```

This file does almost nothing, which is a sign of success, not weakness. Its responsibility is composition. It creates the application and attaches the router. Nothing more should be added here unless the whole application needs to be assembled differently.

The schema module defines the shapes of the data exchanged at the API boundary in the following way:

```
# app/models.py
from pydantic import BaseModel, Field

class ProductCreate(BaseModel):
    name: str
    price: float = Field(..., gt=0)
    description: str
```

```
class Product(ProductCreate):
    id: int
```

These models are already familiar. "**`ProductCreate`**" defines what the client sends when creating or updating a product. Product extends that contract with an ID, which is generated by the system and returned in responses. This distinction will remain useful in this chapter, because new workflows should still speak the same schema language wherever appropriate.

The service module owns the internal state and the product-related operations in the following way:

```
# app/services/product_service.py
from typing import List, Optional
from app.models import Product, ProductCreate

# In-memory storage
# Not safe for concurrent production access
products: List[Product] = []
next_id = 1

def create_product(data: ProductCreate) -> Product:
    global next_id
    product = Product(id=next_id, **data.model_dump())
    products.append(product)
    next_id += 1
    return product

def list_products() -> List[Product]:
    return products

def get_product(product_id: int) -> Optional[Product]:
    for product in products:
        if product.id == product_id:
            return product
    return None

def update_product(product_id: int, data: ProductCreate) ->
Optional[Product]:
    for index, product in enumerate(products):
        if product.id == product_id:
            updated = Product(id=product_id, **data.model_dump())
            products[index] = updated
            return updated
    return None
```

```
def delete_product(product_id: int) -> bool:
    for index, product in enumerate(products):
        if product.id == product_id:
            products.pop(index)
            return True
    return False
```

This file matters because it provides the chapter a stable place where internal work can happen. When concurrency is introduced later, this is where slow product-related operations can be simulated or delegated. The service is not the HTTP boundary. It is where the application does its work. Finally, the router defines the current API contract in the following manner:

```
# app/routers/products.py
from fastapi import APIRouter, HTTPException, status
from typing import List
from app.models import Product, ProductCreate
from app.services import product_service

router = APIRouter()

@router.post("/products", response_model=Product, status_code=status.
HTTP_201_CREATED)
def create_product(product: ProductCreate) -> Product:
    return product_service.create_product(product)

@router.get("/products", response_model=List[Product])
def list_products() -> List[Product]:
    return product_service.list_products()

@router.get("/products/{product_id}", response_model=Product)
def get_product(product_id: int) -> Product:
    product = product_service.get_product(product_id)
    if product is None:
        raise HTTPException(
            status_code=status.HTTP_404_NOT_FOUND,
            detail=f"Product {product_id} not found",
        )
    return product

@router.put("/products/{product_id}", response_model=Product, status_
code=status.HTTP_200_OK)
def update_product(product_id: int, updated: ProductCreate) -> Product:
    product = product_service.update_product(product_id, updated)
    if product is None:
        raise HTTPException(
```

```
            status_code=status.HTTP_404_NOT_FOUND,
            detail=f"Product {product_id} not found",
        )
    return product

@router.delete("/products/{product_id}")
def delete_product(product_id: int) -> dict:
    deleted = product_service.delete_product(product_id)
    if not deleted:
        raise HTTPException(
            status_code=status.HTTP_404_NOT_FOUND,
            detail=f"Product {product_id} not found",
        )
    return {"message": f"Product {product_id} deleted"}
```

This is the baseline that this chapter must respect. If concurrency-related code is added directly into the wrong place, the application may still run, but the structure won in *Chapter 5: Structuring an API Project with AI Guidance* will start to dissolve. That is why the reader must learn to use prompts not just to ask for a feature, but rather to constrain where that feature should live.

A better prompt, therefore, forces the assistant to reason in terms of the existing structure rather than inventing a new one, which is as follows:

Prompt

Given this structured FastAPI Products API, where should new product-related behavior be added if I want to preserve the current separation of responsibilities?

Explain where HTTP concerns should go, where internal product logic should go, and what should remain unchanged in the application assembly.

A strong answer should say that new endpoints belong in **`app/routers/products.py`**, new internal product operations belong in **`app/services/product_service.py`**, and schema definitions belong in **`app/models.py`** only if new request or response shapes are needed. **`app/main.py`** should remain focused on assembling the application unless a change affects application-wide composition. This is the kind of answer that helps the reader to think before coding. It turns the prompt into a development tool rather than a code vending machine.

At this stage, it is also useful to ask a more analytical question: What does the API already do, and what does it still not do? This distinction is what will justify the rest of the chapter.

Prompt

Summarize what this Products API can already do, and what it cannot yet do.

Focus on observable behavior: current CRUD operations, validation, errors, and any missing support for slow, deferred, or progressive workflows.

A good answer should make the current capability visible. The API already supports product creation, listing, retrieval, update, and deletion. It validates request bodies through Pydantic models, returns consistent status codes, and raises structured 404 errors when a product is missing. From the client's point of view, it behaves like a solid Create, Read, Update, and Delete (CRUD) API. Yet, it still assumes that all meaningful work fits inside a simple request-response pattern. There is no endpoint that intentionally performs slow work, no operation that starts now and finishes later, and no response that arrives progressively while processing continues. In other words, the API is structured, but still temporally simple.

That last point is the real bridge into the rest of this chapter. The issue is not that the API is incomplete in a generic sense. The issue is that all of its workflows are still immediate and synchronous in their visible behavior. Once the reader sees that limitation clearly, concurrency stops being an advanced topic and starts being a practical extension of the current app.

Before moving forward, the reader should run the project once and observe the baseline behavior directly. From the project root, the application still starts with the same command used in previous chapters, which is as follows:

```
uvicorn app.main:app --reload
```

Once the server is running, the current endpoints can be exercised through Swagger UI. Product creation still returns "**`201 Created`**." Invalid bodies still trigger "**`422 Unprocessable Entity`**." Missing resources still return "**`404 Not Found`**." All these cases are shown in *Figure 6.1*:

Figure 6.1: *Baseline Behavior before Introducing Concurrency*

The value of doing this again is not repetition for its own sake. It is to confirm that this chapter begins from a known and stable contract.

At this point, the reader should be able to explain not only what the API does, but also how to ask for its evolution in a disciplined way. That is the real purpose of this opening section. The application is not just a codebase; rather, it is now a structured environment in which prompts must preserve architectural intent while extending behavior. The next step is, therefore, not to make it async in abstract. It is to identify a concrete situation where the current request-response model becomes limiting, and then extend the system without breaking the structure you just built.

Concurrency Matters Only When Behavior Requires It

At this point in the book, the Products API is stable and predictable. Requests arrive, router translates them into service calls, service manipulates the in-memory product collection, and then a response is returned. Every endpoint follows the same behavioral pattern: a request enters, work is performed immediately, and a final result is returned before the connection closes.

For many APIs, that model is sufficient. CRUD operations often complete quickly and synchronously. Yet, the moment an application begins to interact with slower processes—file generation, external services, data processing, or progressive computation—the simple request-response pattern becomes less comfortable. The question that emerges is not "how do I write async code?" but rather something more practical: "What should happen when the work takes longer than the client should reasonably wait?"

This is where concurrency enters the discussion—not as a theoretical concept or a fashionable architectural trend, but rather as a response to timing constraints that appear naturally in real systems.

A common mistake is to treat asynchronous programming as an automatic improvement. Not every endpoint should become async. If an operation is already fast, immediate, and purely in-memory, converting it to async may add complexity without improving the client-visible API behavior. Concurrency should solve a behavioral problem, not become a default coding style.

If the API must perform slow work, three timing behaviors become possible: the client may wait for a final result, receive an immediate acknowledgment, or observe progress as work unfolds. Before writing the code, it is useful to transform this question into a prompt that frames the problem clearly in the following manner:

Prompt

In a small FastAPI Products API, what kinds of workflows suggest the need for

1) an async endpoint,

2) a background task,

3) a streaming response?

Keep the answer practical and tied to observable API behavior.

A useful response does not mention event loops, schedulers, or low-level concurrency primitives. Instead, it describes situations that a client interacting with the API might actually experience.

An async endpoint becomes relevant when the API performs a task that may take noticeable time but still produces a single final result. Imagine a product analysis endpoint that performs an expensive computation, checks availability across multiple services, or generates pricing recommendations. The client is willing to wait for the answer, but the server should not block the entire application while that work is happening.

A background task becomes appropriate when the client does not need to wait for the result at all. Consider an operation that exports the current product catalog to a report, sends a notification, or updates a search index. In those cases, the client only needs confirmation that the process started successfully. The real work can continue after the HTTP response has already been sent.

A streaming response appears when the client benefits from seeing partial progress rather than waiting for a single final payload. Instead of computing everything and returning one large response, the API can emit incremental updates as the work unfolds. For example, a product export process could progressively stream product records as they are processed, allowing the client to consume data immediately rather than waiting for the entire operation to complete.

Figure 6.2 illustrates these three timing patterns at the API boundary. An async endpoint returns a final result after some delay, but the server remains responsive to other requests during that time. A background task returns an immediate acknowledgment while the real work continues independently. A streaming response keeps the connection open and progressively emits data as it becomes available.

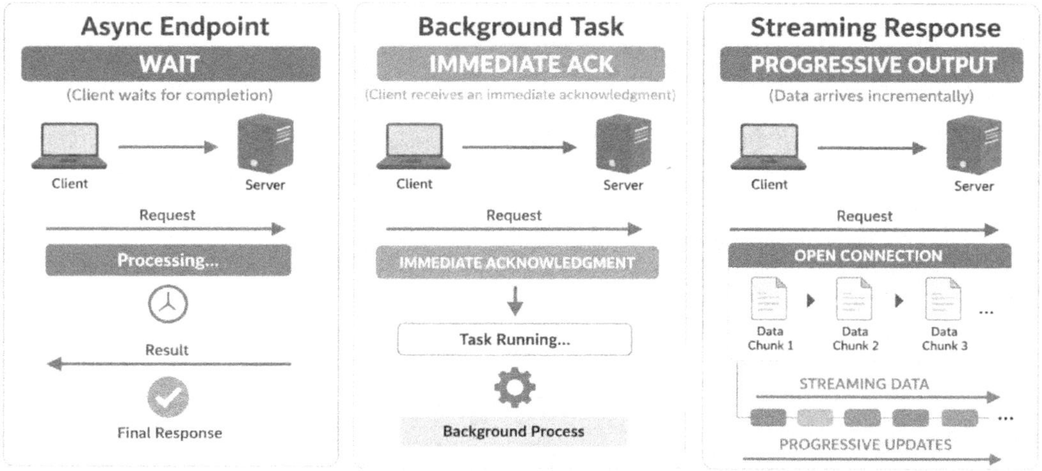

Figure 6.2*: Three Timing Patterns at the API Boundary*

The important point is that none of these mechanisms is introduced for its own sake. If every endpoint in the Products API remained fast and predictable, there would be no reason to change the execution model. Concurrency appears only when the workflow's timing behavior demands it.

To make this reasoning concrete, it helps to look again at the current code. The router translates HTTP requests into service calls, and the service performs operations on the in-memory product collection. Every operation returns immediately.

For example, the listing endpoint in the router still appears as follows:

```
@router.get("/products", response_model=List[Product])
def list_products() -> List[Product]:
    return product_service.list_products()
```

The service operation behind it is equally straightforward, demonstrated as follows:

```
def list_products() -> List[Product]:
    return products
```

Nothing about this operation requires concurrency. It reads from memory and returns immediately. Introducing asynchronous code here would not improve clarity, behavior, or performance. It would simply add complexity without solving a real problem.

This distinction is important because many developers encounter asynchronous programming as an abstract requirement: "Modern APIs should be async." In practice, the decision is behavioral, not ideological. If an operation is fast and immediate, synchronous code is perfectly appropriate. If an operation introduces delay, background processing, or progressive output, then the execution model must change accordingly.

A second prompt can sharpen that reasoning before any new code is introduced is as follows:

Prompt

Looking at the current Products API, which operations could realistically become slow or long-running in a real system? Suggest examples that would require either async execution, background work, or streaming results.

A thoughtful answer should identify realistic extensions of the existing domain. A product availability check might involve contacting multiple inventory systems. A catalog export could require generating a large report file. A price analysis endpoint could perform expensive calculations or call external services. In each of these situations, the API is still conceptually about products, but the workflow's timing behavior changes.

This is the moment where the reader should pause and think like a developer rather than a student of concurrency theory. The question is not "how does asynchronous programming work internally?" rather the question is "what behavior do I want the client to observe when the work takes longer than expected?"

If the client should wait for the final result, the endpoint can become asynchronous while still returning a single response. If the client only needs confirmation that work has started, a background task is more appropriate. If the client benefits from receiving partial data progressively, streaming becomes the natural solution.

Figure 6.3 summarizes this decision process from the client's perspective. The choice between async endpoints, background tasks, and streaming responses is not determined by implementation details inside the server. It is determined by how the client should experience time and progress when interacting with the API.

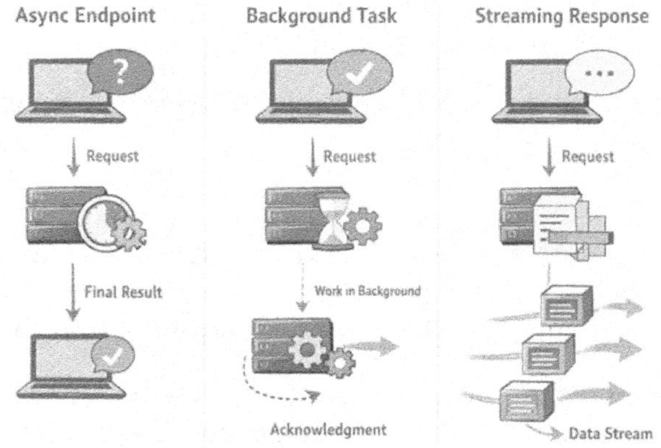

Figure 6.3: *Concurrency Behavior from the Client's Perspective*

With this perspective in place, the rest of the chapter becomes easier to navigate. Instead of learning concurrency as an isolated technical subject, the reader will be introduced to it only where the behavior of the Products API makes it necessary. The next step is to design the first workflow: A deliberately slow product-related operation that exposes the limitations of the current synchronous execution model and motivates the introduction of an asynchronous endpoint.

Identifying the First Real Need: A Slow but Observable Operation

The previous section made an important distinction: concurrency should not be introduced because it sounds modern, but rather because the behavior of a real workflow demands it. The next step is therefore not to write async def immediately; rather, it is to identify a concrete operation inside the current Products API that feels uncomfortable under the existing request-response model.

A good first candidate is an operation that is still simple enough to understand, still belongs clearly to the existing domain, and still returns a normal JSON response—but takes long enough to make the reader feel that the timing behavior matters. A simulated product analysis is a good fit. It stays close to the current application, does not require new infrastructure, and produces a final result that the client still wants in the response. The only difference is that the work is intentionally slow. A focused prompt makes that intention explicit, which is as follows:

Prompt

Add a new endpoint to this FastAPI Products API that simulates a slow operation for a single product and returns a JSON result. Use the existing project structure and keep the logic simple and runnable.

A useful answer should not invent a new architectural layer and should not yet drift into advanced asynchronous code. It should stay within the structure inherited from *Chapter 5: Structuring an API Project with AI Guidance*. The new endpoint belongs in **`app/routers/products.py`**, because it is part of the HTTP boundary. The product-related logic belongs in **`app/services/product_service.py`**, because it is internal work performed on behalf of the endpoint. The result should be a standard JSON object, as at this stage the client is still waiting for a final answer.

A reasonable response from the assistant would propose something such as a "GET **`/products/{product_id}/analyze`**" endpoint that checks whether the product exists, simulates a slow analysis, and returns a small JSON result describing the product. The key point is not the sophistication of the analysis, rather it is that it introduces a delay without changing the basic shape of the interaction.

The first code change belongs in the service layer. We add a slow analysis function to **`app/services/product_service.py`**. The rest of the file remains unchanged.

```
# app/services/product_service.py
import time

def analyze_product(product_id: int) -> Optional[dict]:
    product = get_product(product_id)
    if product is None:
        return None

    time.sleep(5)

    return {
        "product_id": product.id,
        "name": product.name,
        "analysis": "completed",
        "price_category": "premium" if product.price >= 100 else
"standard",
    }
```

The use of "**time.sleep(5)**" is intentional. This call blocks execution for five seconds, preventing the function from doing any other work during that time. The delay is not meant to simulate a realistic implementation; it is a simple way to make the waiting period visible during testing.

This intentionally blocks execution to demonstrate the limitation of a synchronous request-response workflow. In the next step, we will use this artificial delay to explore why asynchronous endpoints can be useful when an operation takes longer than the client should reasonably wait. The function itself is deliberately simple. It first checks whether the requested product exists and returns "None" if it does not. Otherwise, it waits for five seconds and returns a small analysis result. The goal is not to perform useful work, but rather to create a visible delay that we can use to explore different concurrency patterns. At this point, the service is doing exactly what we need pedagogically. It simulates slow internal work while still producing one final result. The implementation is deliberately imperfect from a concurrency point of view, and that is part of the chapter's design. The reader needs to feel the limitation before asking for a better execution model.

The second code change belongs in the router. We add a new endpoint to **app/routers/products.py**. The rest of the file remains unchanged.

```
# app/routers/products.py

@router.get("/products/{product_id}/analyze")
def analyze_product(product_id: int) -> dict:
    result = product_service.analyze_product(product_id)
    if result is None:
        raise HTTPException(
            status_code=status.HTTP_404_NOT_FOUND,
```

```
            detail=f"Product {product_id} not found",
        )
    return result
```

This endpoint fits neatly into the structure established in the previous chapter. The router still owns HTTP behavior. It declares the path, receives the "**`product_id`**," calls the service, and translates a missing product into an HTTP "**`404 response`**." The service still owns the internal product-related work. The new behavior, therefore, extends the application without violating the responsibility boundaries that are already established.

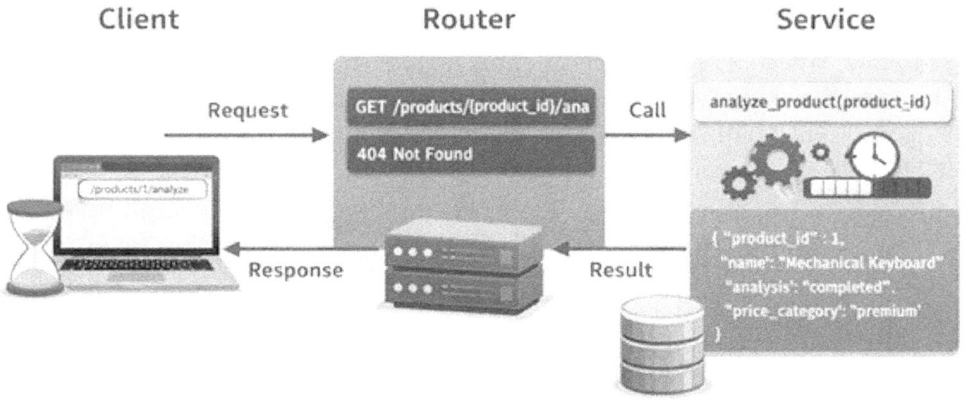

***Figure 6.4**: Introducing a Slow but Observable Workflow into the Products API*

A new endpoint is added to the router, but the slow operation itself remains in the service layer. The response is still a normal JSON result, making the workflow easy to observe while exposing the limitations of immediate synchronous execution.

The next step is to run the application and see what this new endpoint actually feels like. Start the server from the project root as usual in the following way:

```
uvicorn app.main:app --reload
```

If the server is already running, it will reload automatically after the file changes. Before testing the new endpoint, it is helpful to create at least one product through Swagger UI so that the analysis has something to operate on. For example, creating a product in the following way is enough (with **`POST /products`**):

```
{
  "name": "Mechanical Keyboard",
  "price": 129.99,
  "description": "Compact mechanical keyboard"
}
```

Once a product exists, call the new endpoint:

```
GET /products/1/analyze
```

The response will arrive, but not immediately. The browser or Swagger UI will wait for several seconds and then return something in the following manner:

```
{
"product_id": 1,
"name": "Mechanical Keyboard",
"analysis": "completed",
"price_category": "premium"
}
```

This result is intentionally ordinary. It is still a single JSON response returned at the end of the request. No background work has been introduced, and no data is streamed progressively. The goal of this experiment is not yet to introduce concurrency; rather, it is to make the timing of the operation visible while keeping the execution model unchanged. What changes is not the shape of the response, but the experience of waiting for it.

If you request a product that does not exist, the endpoint should still preserve the same error behavior used throughout the rest of the API in the following manner:

```
GET /products/999/analyze
```

The result should remain as follows:

```
{
"detail": "Product 999 not found"
}
```

with status code "404 Not Found."

Notice the difference between the two cases. When the product exists, the endpoint performs the slow analysis, and the client must wait. When the product does not exist, the request fails immediately, and no delay is observed. This tells us something important: The slowness is not a property of the endpoint itself, but rather of the work it performs. The delay appears only when real processing is required.

At this stage, it is important to help the reader analyze what has actually been achieved. The new endpoint works. It belongs to the "product" domain. It uses the current project structure correctly. It returns a normal JSON response. Yet, it feels different from the rest of the API. The structure is the same. The response format is the same. The error handling is the same. However, one element has changed: Time is now part of the observable behavior. The client is no longer interacting with an immediate system, but rather with one that requires waiting.

A good analytical prompt makes that difference explicit in the following way:

Prompt

What makes this new product analysis endpoint behave differently from the other CRUD endpoints in the current Products API? Focus on observable behavior, especially timing, and explain why this creates pressure for a different execution model.

A strong answer should highlight that all existing CRUD endpoints return almost immediately, while the analysis endpoint introduces a visible delay before producing its result. From the client's perspective, the contract has not changed: a request is sent, and a JSON response is eventually returned. What has changed is the time it takes to fulfill that contract. This is the key tension. The behavior is still correct, but the execution model no longer fits comfortably with the user experience. This is exactly the transition the chapter needs. The system still works. The structure is still correct. The endpoint is valid. Yet, the moment an operation becomes slow, the limitations of the current synchronous model become visible. This is not yet a concurrency problem in terms of implementation. It is a behavior problem. The question is no longer "how do we write this endpoint?", but rather "how should this endpoint behave when the work takes time, and the application should remain responsive?"

First Async Endpoint: Making a Slow Operation Non-Blocking

The previous section introduced a deliberately slow endpoint for a clear reason: to create pressure for a better execution model without changing the application domain. The endpoint worked, the project structure remained clean, and the client still received a normal JSON response. Yet, one detail changed the character of the workflow completely: Time became visible. The response no longer felt immediate.

That is the right moment to ask for a more appropriate implementation. Not because the endpoint has become more "advanced," but rather because the behavior now suggests that a slow operation should be handled differently from the rest of the CRUD API. The reader should resist the temptation to jump straight into abstract async theory. The important question is much narrower: What needs to change in the code so that this slow endpoint is implemented in a way that fits the new behavior, while preserving the structure established in *Chapter 5: Structuring an API Project with AI Guidance*?

A good prompt makes that intention precise and constrained, which is as follows:

Prompt

Refactor this new slow product-analysis endpoint so it uses async correctly.

Keep the existing router/service separation. Do not introduce new abstractions or low-level async internals. Explain only what changes in the endpoint and service code.

A useful answer should not redesign the application. It should not move logic into new layers. It should not explain the event loop or introduce benchmarking claims. It should focus on the two places that must change: the route in **`app/routers/products.py`** and the slow analysis logic in **`app/services/product_service.py`**.

The previous implementation used **`time.sleep(5)`** inside a normal service function. That made the delay visible, but it also kept the endpoint tied to a blocking model. To refactor it into an asynchronous version, the route must become async def, and the service function must become asynchronous as well, using a non-blocking delay.

The service file, therefore, changes first. The old synchronous "**analyze_product**" function is replaced with an asynchronous version.

```
# app/services/product_service.py

import asyncio

async def analyze_product(product_id: int) -> Optional[dict]:
    product = get_product(product_id)
    if product is None:
        return None

    await asyncio.sleep(5)

    return {
        "product_id": product.id,
        "name": product.name,
        "analysis": "completed",
        "price_category": ("premium" if product.price >= 100 else
"standard"),
    }
```

Notice that the API contract has not changed. The function still accepts the same input and returns the same result structure. What changes is the execution model: The delay is now handled asynchronously rather than blocking the thread. The endpoint contract stays identical while execution changes internally.

The important thing to notice here is not that the code has become longer or more sophisticated. In fact, the logical function behavior is almost identical to the previous version. It still checks whether the product exists. It still waits for five seconds. It still returns the same JSON-compatible dictionary. What changed is the way the delay is expressed. **`time.sleep(5)`** has been replaced with **`await asyncio.sleep(5)`**, and the function itself is now declared with async def.

This is exactly the kind of change the chapter wants to highlight. The domain logic did not become more complicated. The product analysis did not become more realistic. The response shape did not change. Only the execution model of the slow part changed.

The router must now be updated, so that it can call this new service function correctly. The endpoint becomes asynchronous too.

```
# app/routers/products.py

@router.get("/products/{product_id}/analyze")
async def analyze_product(product_id: int):
    result = await product_service.analyze_product(product_id)
```

```
    if result is None:
        raise HTTPException(
            status_code=status.HTTP_404_NOT_FOUND,
            detail=f"Product {product_id} not found",
        )
    return result
```

Again, the structural point is more important than the syntax itself. The route remains in **app/routers/products.py**, exactly where HTTP behavior belongs. The slow internal work remains in **app/services/product_service.py**, exactly where product-related operations belong. The response is still a normal JSON body, and the router still translates a missing product into a "**404 Not Found**." Nothing about the responsibility boundary, introduced in *Chapter 5: Structuring an API Project with AI Guidance*, has been broken. In *Figure* 6.5, the router remains the HTTP boundary, the service remains the home of product-related work, and only the slow execution path changes from blocking sleep to awaited delay.

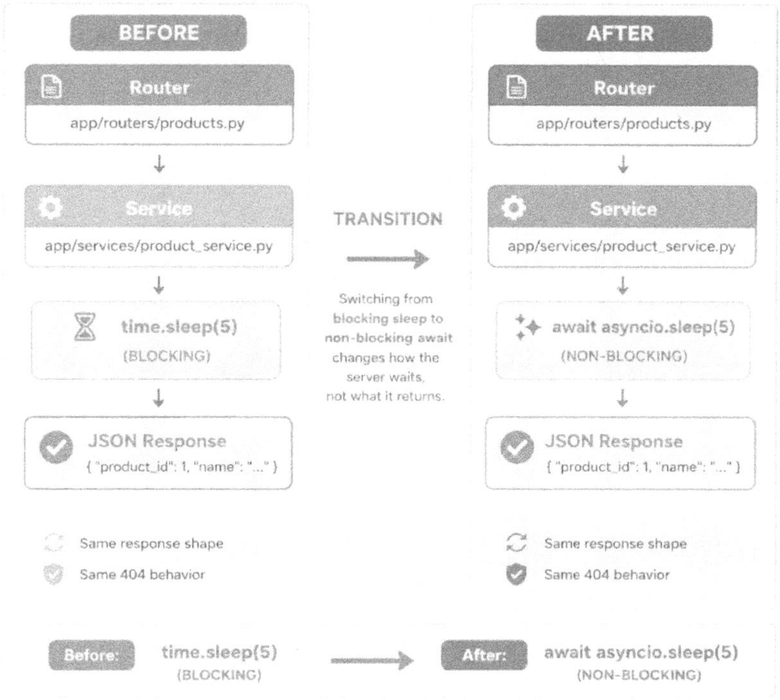

***Figure 6.5**: Refactoring the Slow Analysis Workflow into an Async Endpoint*

At this point, the reader should run the application and verify that the new endpoint is still observable in the same way as before. From the project root, the application starts exactly as usual in the following way:

```
uvicorn app.main:app --reload
```

Once the server is running, the existing CRUD endpoints still behave exactly as they did before. That continuity is important. The chapter does not introduce a new application. It is extending the current one. After creating at least one product, the new endpoint can be tested again through Swagger UI or directly in the browser.

Calling **`GET /products/1/analyze`** will still produce a delayed response, and the final body should still appears as follows:

```
{
"product_id": 1,
"name": "Mechanical Keyboard",
"analysis": "completed",
"price_category": "premium"
}
```

The delay is still there. The response shape is still there. The 404 behavior for a missing product is still there. From the client's perspective, the endpoint continues to behave as a normal API call that eventually returns JSON.

If the product does not exist, the endpoint still returns the same error contract in the following way:

```
{
"detail": "Product 999 not found"
}
```

with status code "**`404 Not Found`**." In *Figure* 6.6, the client still waits for a final JSON result after a simulated delay, but the internal implementation now expresses the slow operation through async code rather than a blocking sleep.

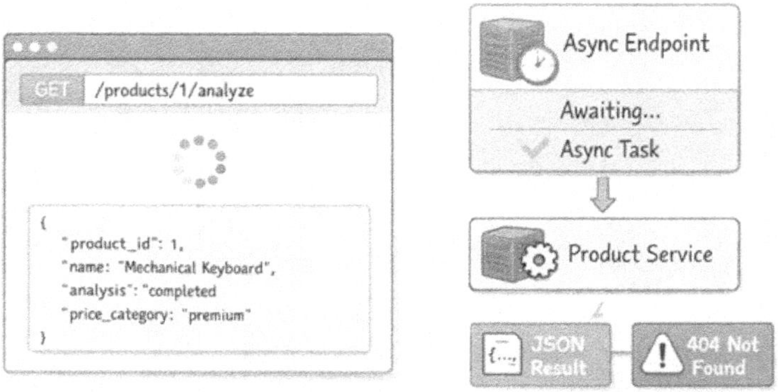

Figure 6.6: *Observable Behavior Remains Stable after the Async Refactor*

This is where the conceptual focus of the section becomes clear. This chapter is not asking the reader to memorize asynchronous programming rules in the abstract. It is asking a more disciplined question: What changed in code, and what stayed the same at the boundary?

A useful prompt for that reflection is the following:

Prompt

In this Products API, what changed when the slow analysis endpoint became async, and what stayed the same for the client using the endpoint? Focus only on the code changes and the observable API behavior.

A strong answer should identify the changes precisely. The route now uses async def, and the router awaits the service call. The service function is now asynchronous, and uses await "**`asyncio.sleep(5)`**" instead of "**`time.sleep(5)`**." However, the endpoint path did not change. The response body did not change. The error behavior did not change. The client still sees a delayed JSON response. In other words, the internal execution model changed, while the API contract remained stable.

That distinction is exactly what the reader needs to internalize. In *Chapter 5: Structuring an API Project with AI Guidance*, the structure changed while behavior stayed the same. In this section, the execution style changed while the boundary stayed the same. In both cases, the book is reinforcing the same discipline: Use prompts to guide controlled change, and verify carefully what has and has not changed.

This first async endpoint, therefore, serves two purposes. It gives the Products API its first runnable example of asynchronous behavior, and shows the reader how to use prompts not just to generate code, but rather to reason about where that code belongs and what kind of change it should represent. The next step will build on this distinction by moving to a different timing pattern altogether: Work that should continue after the response has already been sent.

Observing What Changed When the Endpoint Became Async

At this point in the chapter, the Products API contains its first asynchronous endpoint. The new route still belongs to the same application, still follows the structure introduced in *Chapter 5: Structuring an API Project with AI Guidance*, and still returns a normal JSON response. The only visible difference is that the endpoint intentionally waits a few seconds before producing the result.

This is exactly the moment where the reader should pause and observe what actually changed. The goal of this section is not to introduce more code or to dive into asynchronous internals. Instead, it follows the same method used throughout the book: Prompt → Code → Execution → Observation → Understanding. The async refactor already happened. Now, the reader needs to analyze the consequences.

Aspect	Synchronous Version	Asynchronous Version
Endpoint path	`/products/{id}/analysis`	`/products/{id}/analysis`
Request format	Unchanged	Unchanged
Response structure	Unchanged	Unchanged
HTTP status codes	Unchanged	Unchanged
Observable API contract	Unchanged	Unchanged
Waiting mechanism	time.sleep(5)	await asyncio.sleep(5)
Server behavior during wait	Blocking	Non-blocking
Purpose of the change	Simulate slow work	Handle slow work more efficiently

Table 6.1: *Sync versus Async: What Actually Changed?*

The important observation is that the API contract remains identical. Clients send the same request and receive the same response. What changed is the execution model inside the service layer. The refactor affects how the server waits, not what the endpoint returns.

A well-focused prompt guides that analysis in the following way:

Prompt

In this Products API, what changed when the slow endpoint became async, and what remained identical at the API boundary? Focus on code structure and observable behavior, not internals.

A useful answer should begin by pointing out that the most visible change happened in the router. The route definition that previously used a normal function now uses an asynchronous one. In practical terms, the declaration now begins with async def instead of def, and the router awaits the service call instead of executing it immediately. At this stage, no new code needs to be written. The endpoint was already updated in the previous section. What matters here is recognizing what has already changed in that existing code.

In the router, the product analysis endpoint still defines the same path, receives the same product_id, and returns the same responses as before. It still raises a "**`404 Not Found`**" error when the product is missing, and it still returns the same JSON result when the product exists. The only difference is that the call to the service layer is now awaited. From the point of view of HTTP behavior, nothing has changed. From the point of view of execution, the route is now explicitly asynchronous. A similar shift happened in the service module. The function that performs the slow analysis no longer uses a blocking delay. Instead, the delay is expressed as an awaited operation. The structure of the function is otherwise identical: it still retrieves the product, still returns "None" when the product does not exist, and still produces the same result after a short pause. What changed is not the logic, but rather the way that pause is represented and handled. Together, these changes highlight a precise distinction. The router still plays the same role at the HTTP boundary, and the service still owns the product-related logic. The outcome of the endpoint is identical. Only the execution model of the slow part has changed, moving from a blocking pause to an awaited one. *Figure* 6.7 summarizes this transformation from a structural perspective:

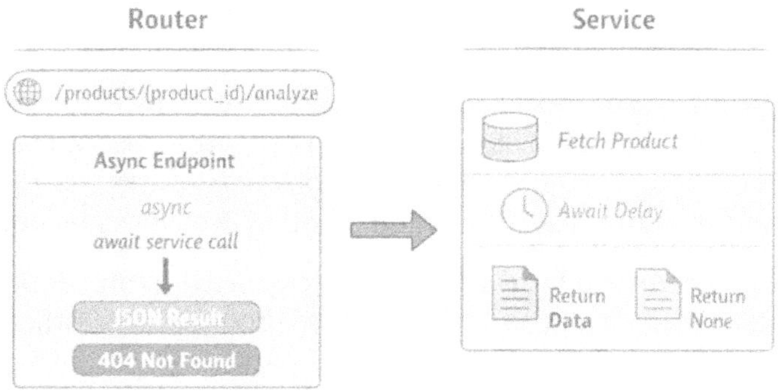

Figure 6.7: *Router and Service Changes after Introducing Async*

At this point, the reader should run the application again and observe how little has changed from the outside. The server still starts in the following same way:

```
uvicorn app.main:app --reload
```

Swagger UI still lists the same endpoints. The CRUD operations remain the same. The "GET **`/products/{product_id}/analyze`**" endpoint still appears in the documentation exactly where it did before.

Testing the endpoint produces the same observable experience. If a product exists, the request waits a few seconds and returns the analysis result in the following manner:

```
{
"product_id": 1,
"name": "Mechanical Keyboard",
"analysis": "completed",
"price_category": "premium"
}
```

If the product does not exist, the API still returns the same error contract in the following way:

```
{
"detail": "Product 999 not found"
}
```

`with status code` **`"404 Not Found."`**

This is the most important observation of the section: The API boundary did not change. The client still sees the same endpoint, delay, response body, and error behavior. The API contract is identical.

What changed is entirely inside the implementation. The endpoint is now capable of expressing slow work in a non-blocking way, and the service function expresses its delay through an awaited operation rather than a blocking sleep. From the point of view of the application's structure, this refactor preserved the same separation of responsibilities that was carefully introduced in *Chapter 5, Structuring an API Project with AI Guidance.*

The final question to ask at this stage is not about syntax but rather about behavior. What kind of situation is now represented more accurately by the code? The answer is that the application now models a slow operation explicitly. Instead of pretending that every endpoint is immediate, the code now acknowledges that some operations take time. That recognition is the real reason concurrency was introduced.

The reader should therefore take away a specific lesson from this section. Concurrency did not change the API contract. It changed how the system handles time internally while preserving the same external behavior. This pattern—internal improvement with stable observable behavior—should feel familiar by now. It is the same discipline used when the project was refactored structurally in the previous chapter.

Understanding that pattern prepares the reader for the next step. The async endpoint still waits for the result before responding. In other words, the client remains connected until the analysis completes. The next section will explore a different timing model altogether: Operations where the client should receive a response immediately while the real work continues afterward.

Background Tasks: Work That Continues after the Response

The asynchronous endpoint introduced in the previous section solved a very specific problem. The API now models a slow operation in a way that fits the structure of the application. The router declares an asynchronous endpoint, the service performs the delayed work, and the client eventually receives a JSON result once the operation completes. The endpoint still represents a request that begins, performs work, and returns a final answer.

However, not all slow operations belong in that category. In many real workflows, the client does not actually need to wait for the result. The client only needs confirmation that the process started successfully. Once that confirmation is delivered, the actual work can continue independently of the request-response cycle.

This distinction introduces a completely different timing pattern. Instead of waiting several seconds for a result, the client receives an immediate response while the server continues processing in the background.

This pattern appears naturally in many product-related scenarios. An API might generate a report describing product statistics. It might simulate sending a notification when a product price changes. It might export product data to an external system or log an inventory update. In all of these cases, the work may take time, but the client does not benefit from waiting for completion. The important signal for the client is simply that the process has started.

Before writing code, it is helpful to frame the need explicitly through a prompt that focuses on behavior rather than implementation, demonstrated as follows:

Prompt

In this FastAPI Products API, show a realistic example of a background task. The client should get an immediate response, while the real work continues after that. Use the current project structure and keep it runnable.

A good response to this prompt should not redesign the application. It should preserve the router-service separation already established in the project. The router should continue to own its HTTP behavior, while the service module should contain the logic that performs product-related work. The only new element is the introduction of a background task that runs after the HTTP response is sent.

In this example, the API will simulate exporting a product report. The client triggers the export, receives confirmation immediately, and the export process continues in the background. The first change belongs in the service module, where the simulated export operation will live. Insert this new function into your "**`app/services/product_service.py`**" file in the following way:

```
# app/services/product_service.py
import time
def export_product_report(product_id: int) -> None:
    product = get_product(product_id)
    if product is None:
        return

    time.sleep(5)
    print(f"[REPORT] Export completed for product {product.id}
({product.name})")
```

The use of **`time.sleep(5)`** is intentionally simplified for demonstration purposes. The goal is to make the background execution visible while testing. In a production system, report generation would typically involve real work such as file creation, database queries, or external service calls rather than an artificial blocking delay. The example focuses on the behavior of background tasks, not on how long-running jobs should be implemented in practice.

The new function "**`export_product_report`**" simulates a slow report generation process. It checks whether the product exists and then waits several seconds before printing a confirmation message. The function is intentionally simple because the purpose is to demonstrate timing behavior rather than export complexity. The second change happens in the router, where the endpoint that triggers the background task is defined. FastAPI provides a mechanism called "**BackgroundTasks**" that allows a task to be scheduled after the response is returned. Insert this new endpoint into your "**app/routers/products.py**" file and remember to also import **BackgroundTasks** in the following way:

```
# app/routers/products.py
from fastapi import APIRouter, HTTPException, status, BackgroundTasks

@router.post("/products/{product_id}/export")
def export_product(product_id: int, background_tasks: BackgroundTasks)
-> dict:
    product = product_service.get_product(product_id)

    if product is None:
        raise HTTPException(
            status_code=status.HTTP_404_NOT_FOUND,
            detail=f"Product {product_id} not found",
        )

    background_tasks.add_task(product_service.export_product_report,
product_id)

    return {
        "message": "Product export started",
        "product_id": product_id
    }
```

background_tasks.add_task() schedules execution after the HTTP response has been sent. The client receives an immediate acknowledgment while the export operation continues in the background. This endpoint makes the behavior easy to observe. The router verifies that the product exists and registers the export operation as a background task. The response is returned immediately, while the service continues processing the export independently. *Figure* 6.8 illustrates this timing pattern: The API acknowledges the request first, and completes the work afterward.

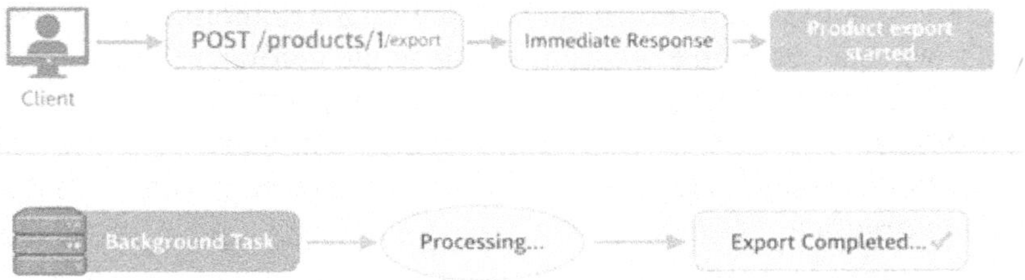

Figure 6.8: *Immediate Response with Background Processing*

The client receives an immediate confirmation while the server continues processing the export task after the response has been sent. The work is no longer tied to the request-response cycle. When the server is running, calling the new endpoint produces a response immediately in the following manner:

```
POST /products/1/export
```

The response appears almost instantly:

```
{
"message": "Product export started",
"product_id": 1
}
```

The export is not finished when this response is returned. The response only confirms that the work has been successfully scheduled. A few seconds later, the server console prints the simulated export result in the following way:

```
[REPORT] Export completed for product 1 (Mechanical Keyboard)
```

This message is not part of the HTTP response which is not visible in Swagger UI. It represents the work happening inside the server after the client has already received a response.

The delay still exists, but it is no longer experienced by the client. Instead of waiting for the export to finish, the client receives confirmation that the process has started. At this point, the reader should recognize a key difference between the two concurrency patterns introduced so far. The asynchronous analysis endpoint still waits for the result before returning the response. The background task endpoint does not. It acknowledges the request immediately and continues processing afterward.

A useful prompt helps to clarify this distinction in the following way:

Prompt

In the Products API, why would the export endpoint use a background task instead of simply making the endpoint async like the analysis endpoint?

Explain the difference in terms of client-visible behavior.

A strong answer should highlight the difference in timing expectations. The analysis endpoint returns a result that the client actually needs, so waiting for completion is reasonable. The export endpoint performs work that the client does not need to observe directly, so returning immediately is more practical. Background tasks, therefore, represent a different design decision about how the client experiences time and progress when interacting with the API.

This distinction is the real lesson of the section. Concurrency mechanisms are not interchangeable technical tricks. They represent different behavioral contracts between the API and its clients. Understanding that difference allows the developer to choose the right mechanism based on what the client actually needs to observe.

Adding a Background Task to the Products API

The previous section introduced the need for background work and showed why it differs from an async endpoint. Now, the goal becomes more precise: Add a concrete background-task workflow to the existing Products API without breaking the structure established in *Chapter 5: Structuring an API Project with AI Guidance*. The router must continue to own its HTTP concerns. The service must continue to own product-related work. The background task should fit into the project cleanly, not as an exception to the architecture.

At this point, the reader should not ask for "some background-task code." The better move is to ask for a change that is explicitly constrained by the current project structure. That makes the prompt more useful and the generated code easier to evaluate.

Prompt

Add a background task endpoint to the current Products API. Keep the router responsible for HTTP semantics and move product-related work into the service layer. Return an immediate JSON response confirming that processing has started.

A strong answer should not introduce a new architectural layer or move HTTP logic into the service. It should keep the endpoint in **app/routers/products.py**, add the product-related deferred operation in **app/services/product_service.py**, and preserve the existing style of the application: explicit 404 handling in the router, domain work in the service, and a simple JSON response at the boundary.

A concrete and easy-to-observe example is a product export process. The client triggers the export, receives confirmation immediately, and the real work continues afterward. The task itself can remain intentionally simple. The important thing is that it is visible and runnable.

The service module, therefore, needs a function that performs the simulated export work. At this stage, the function should be small and demonstrable rather than realistic. The following implementation is the same as that introduced in the previous section. No new code is added here. The goal is to examine the existing implementation and understand how it changes the behavior of the API.

```
# app/services/product_service.py

def export_product_report(product_id: int) -> None:
    product = get_product(product_id)
    if product is None:
        return
    import time
```

```
    time.sleep(5)
    print(f"[REPORT] Export completed for product {product.id}
({product.name})")
```

This function is intentionally plain. It looks up the product, waits for five seconds, and prints a confirmation message. The delay is enough to make the deferred work visible in the server console. The printed message is enough to make the task observable without introducing new infrastructure such as files, queues, or notifications. The router can now expose an endpoint that triggers this work in the background.

```
# app/routers/products.py
@router.post("/products/{product_id}/export")
def export_product(product_id: int, background_tasks: BackgroundTasks)
-> dict:
    product = product_service.get_product(product_id)
    if product is None:
        raise HTTPException(
            status_code=status.HTTP_404_NOT_FOUND,
            detail=f"Product {product_id} not found",
        )
    background_tasks.add_task(product_service.export_product_report,
product_id)
    return {
        "message": "Product export started",
        "product_id": product_id,
    }
```

At this stage, the focus is not on writing code, but rather on observing what this implementation actually does at runtime.

This endpoint is structurally important because it shows exactly where each responsibility lies. The router owns the path, the HTTP method, the error mapping, and the response body. The service owns the product-related operation itself. The background task is attached at the boundary through **`background_tasks.add_task(...)`**, but the real work remains outside the router. That is the architectural discipline the chapter wants to reinforce. The router accepts the request and schedules the task, while the service owns the product-related export work. The immediate response and the deferred processing remain clearly separated.

The result is now easy to observe. Start the server as usual in the following way:

```
uvicorn app.main:app --reload
```

Make sure at least one product exists. Then call the new endpoint:

```
POST /products/1/export
```

The response should return immediately in the following manner:

```
{
"message": "Product export started",
"product_id": 1
}
```

This immediate response is the key visible difference from the async analysis endpoint. The client does not wait for the export to finish. It only receives confirmation that processing has started.

A few seconds later, the server console should show the deferred work completing: This is not visible to the client.

```
[REPORT] Export completed for product 1 (Mechanical Keyboard)
```

This is what makes the task "background" in practical terms. The request–response cycle ends before the work does. If the client tries to export a product that does not exist, the endpoint should still preserve the same boundary behavior already used throughout the application in the following way:

```
POST /products/999/export
```

The response should remain:

```
{
"detail": "Product 999 not found"
}
```

with status code "**404 Not Found**."

Figure 6.9 shows how the client-visible contract ends with a confirmation response, while the actual export work continues afterward and becomes visible only through the server-side effect.

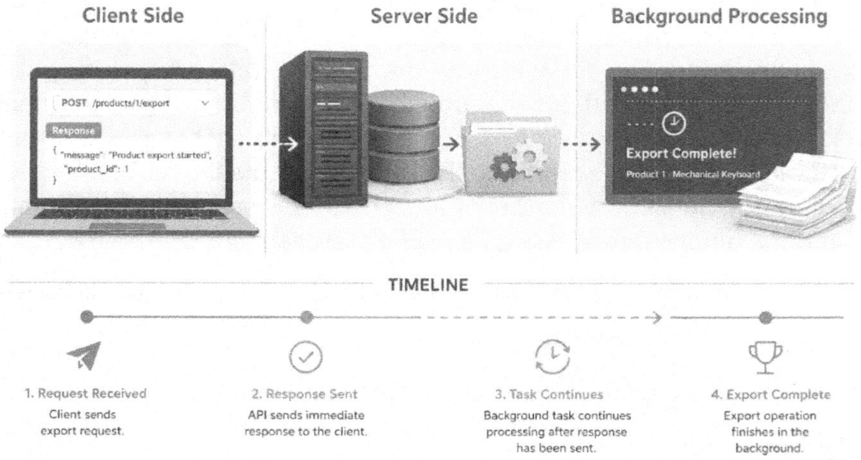

Figure 6.9: *Immediate Acknowledgment Followed by Deferred Product Processing*

At this stage, the reader should stop and analyze what was added. The new endpoint did not introduce new domain concepts. It introduced a new timing contract. The export request now means: "Start this process and tell me that it has started," not "Complete this process before answering me." That behavioral shift is more important than the specific code used to implement it.

A good follow-up prompt helps make that explicit, which is as follows:

Prompt

In this Products API, what makes the new export endpoint a background-task workflow rather than just another async endpoint? Explain the difference using only router behavior, service behavior, and what the client observes.

A strong answer should identify three things. First, the router returns immediately instead of waiting for the export to finish. Second, the service performs the actual product-related work after the response has already been sent. Third, the client observes only the acknowledgment, not the completion of the process. That is what makes the workflow fundamentally different from the async analysis endpoint.

This section, therefore, adds more than code. It adds a second concurrency pattern to the reader's mental model. The async endpoint still returns one final result after waiting. The background task endpoint returns immediately and lets the work continue. Both preserve the project structure from *Chapter 5, Structuring an API Project with AI Guidance*, but they express different client-visible behaviors. The next section will introduce a third pattern: workflows where the client should not wait silently and should not be disconnected immediately, but should instead receive output progressively while the work unfolds.

Streaming Responses: Returning Output Gradually

So far in this chapter, two timing patterns have been introduced in the Products API. The first was the async endpoint. In that case, the request begins, the server performs a slow operation, and the response is returned once the work completes. The client waits, but eventually receives a single final result. The second was the background task. There, the server returns immediately while the work continues elsewhere. The client receives confirmation that the process started, but does not observe the work itself. A third pattern now becomes useful in situations where the client should see progress while the work unfolds. Instead of waiting silently for a final response or disconnecting immediately after triggering a task, the API can return information gradually. Each piece of information is sent as soon as it becomes available. This is called a streaming response.

In practical product-related scenarios, this pattern appears in workflows such as:

- Previewing a product export while it is generated.
- Streaming updates from a product processing pipeline.
- returning a progressive feed of product-related events.
- Simulating a real-time inventory update stream.

The goal is not to build a real-time infrastructure system. The goal is to demonstrate observable progressive output inside a normal HTTP request.

Before writing any code, it is helpful to phrase the need through a prompt that explicitly describes the desired behavior in the following way:

Prompt

Show a simple streaming response example for this FastAPI Products API. The client should receive data progressively instead of waiting for one final JSON object. Keep the example runnable and easy to observe.

A useful response to this prompt should avoid adding architectural complexity. The router must still own HTTP semantics, and the service should still contain product-related logic. The only difference is that the endpoint will return a stream of messages instead of a single response object. A practical example is a progressive product export preview. Instead of generating a full report and returning it at the end, the API can stream status updates describing the export progress. To support this behavior, the service layer needs a generator function that produces pieces of output over time.

```
# app/services/product_service.py

import asyncio
from typing import AsyncGenerator

async def stream_product_export(product_id: int) -> AsyncGenerator[str, None]:
    product = get_product(product_id)
    if product is None:
        return
    yield f"Starting export for product {product.id} ({product.name})...\n"

    for step in range(1, 6):
        await asyncio.sleep(1)
        yield f"Processing step {step}/5...\n"

    yield "Export completed successfully.\n"
```

The defensive "**None**" check ensures that the generator exits safely if the requested product does not exist. Although the router validates the product before calling the generator, adding the check makes the service function more robust if it is reused elsewhere in the application.

This function behaves differently from anything used earlier in the chapter. Instead of returning a dictionary or a boolean result, it yields messages one at a time. Each message represents a small piece of the overall process.

The await "**asyncio.sleep(1)**" call simulates a delay between each stage of the export. As the function is asynchronous and uses yield, the caller can forward each message to the client immediately. The router can now expose an endpoint that returns these messages as a streaming HTTP response.

```
# app/routers/products.py

from fastapi.responses import StreamingResponse

@router.get("/products/{product_id}/export-stream")
async def stream_product_export(product_id: int) -> StreamingResponse:
    product = product_service.get_product(product_id)
    if product is None:
        raise HTTPException(
            status_code=status.HTTP_404_NOT_FOUND,
            detail=f"Product {product_id} not found",
        )

    generator = product_service.stream_product_export(product_id)
    return StreamingResponse(generator, media_type="text/plain")
```

The "**media_type="text/plain"**" parameter tells FastAPI to send each chunk as plain text rather than packaging the entire result as a JSON document. This makes it possible for the client to receive output incrementally as it is generated.

Keep in mind that some tools, including Swagger UI, may buffer streamed responses and display the output only after the stream completes. This behavior depends on the client, not on the FastAPI implementation. To observe streaming more accurately, command-line tools such as curl often provide a clearer view of the progressive output.

The structure of the router remains consistent with the architecture introduced in *Chapter 5: Structuring an API Project with AI Guidance*. The router defines the HTTP endpoint and delegates product-related logic to the service layer. The difference is that the response returned by the router is now a StreamingResponse.

Once the server is running, the behavior of this endpoint becomes immediately observable. The streaming behavior is easiest to observe with a browser, terminal, or a simple HTTP client, since interactive API tools may buffer the response.

Start the application in the following way:

```
uvicorn app.main:app --reload
```

Then, request the streaming endpoint in the following manner:

```
GET /products/1/export-stream
```

In this example, the stream is plain text rather than JSON. This keeps the behavior easy to observe while still demonstrating progressive output.

```
Starting export for product 1 (Mechanical Keyboard)...
Processing step 1/5...
Processing step 2/5...
Processing step 3/5...
Processing step 4/5...
Processing step 5/5...
Export completed successfully.
```

Each line arrives about one second apart, demonstrating that the response is being streamed while the process unfolds. *Figure 6.10* shows how the client receives multiple pieces of information over time instead of waiting for a final response:

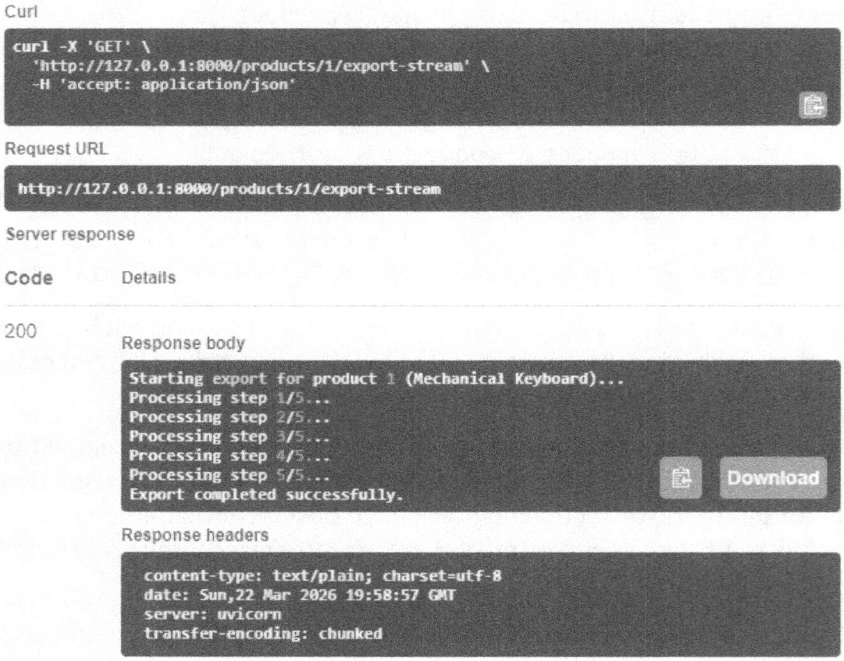

Figure 6.10: *Observable Progressive Output from a Streaming Endpoint*

This behavior clearly distinguishes streaming responses from the two earlier patterns in the chapter.

The **async analysis endpoint** waits several seconds, and then returns one JSON object.

The **background export endpoint** returns immediately and performs work after the response.

The **streaming export endpoint** begins responding immediately, but continues sending additional information, while the work progresses.

At this stage, the reader should again pause and analyze the behavior with the following prompt that focuses on observation rather than implementation:

Prompt

In this Products API, how does the streaming endpoint differ from the async analysis endpoint and the background export endpoint? Explain the difference in terms of what the client observes.

A good answer should highlight the difference in client-visible timing. The async endpoint produces one final response after waiting. The background task endpoint responds immediately and does not expose the progress of the work. The streaming endpoint keeps the connection open and progressively sends updates while the work continues.

This distinction is the real lesson of the section. Concurrency is not only about how code executes internally. It is about how time is represented at the API boundary. By introducing streaming responses, the Products API now supports three different ways of expressing time in a request–response interaction.

Adding a Streaming Endpoint to the Project

The previous section introduced streaming as a third timing pattern at the API boundary. The client does not wait silently for a final result, and the server does not simply acknowledge the request and continue elsewhere. Instead, the response begins immediately and continues progressively while the work unfolds. At this point, the goal is not to introduce a generic streaming example, but to extend the existing Products API without breaking its structure. The same rule still applies: the router owns HTTP behavior, and the service layer owns product-related logic. Streaming should fit into that structure, not bypass it. A well-formed prompt reflects both the desired behavior and the existing architecture, which is as follows:

Prompt

Add a streaming endpoint to the structured Products API. Use an async generator to return data progressively. Keep the implementation minimal and respect the current separation between router and service.

A strong answer should place the streaming logic in the service layer and use the router only to expose it through an HTTP response. No new layers are required, and no infrastructure needs to be introduced. The goal is to produce observable progressive output using the existing project. A natural extension of the current domain is a streaming version of the product export. Instead of waiting for the export to complete or running it entirely in the background, the API can expose the export as a sequence of incremental steps. The service layer is responsible for this behavior. It defines how the export progresses over time in the following way:

```
# app/services/product_service.py

from typing import AsyncGenerator
import asyncio

async def stream_product_export(product_id: int) -> AsyncGenerator[str,
None]:
    product = get_product(product_id)
    if product is None:
        return
    yield f"Starting export for product {product.id} ({product.
name})...\n"

    for step in range(1, 6):
        await asyncio.sleep(1)
        yield f"Processing step {step}/5...\n"

    yield "Export completed successfully.\n"
```

This function does not build a final result and return it. It produces the result incrementally. Each yield emits a new piece of information, and each await **asyncio.sleep(...)** introduces a visible delay between steps. Notice that this function does not handle the case where the product does not exist. That responsibility remains at the router boundary, where HTTP behavior is defined consistently across the application. The router exposes this generator through a streaming response in the following way:

```
# app/routers/products.py

from fastapi.responses import StreamingResponse

@router.get("/products/{product_id}/export-stream")
async def stream_product_export(product_id: int) -> StreamingResponse:
    product = product_service.get_product(product_id)
    if product is None:
        raise HTTPException(
            status_code=status.HTTP_404_NOT_FOUND,
            detail=f"Product {product_id} not found",
        )

    return StreamingResponse(
        product_service.stream_product_export(product_id),
        media_type="text/plain"
    )
```

The router remains responsible for the HTTP contract. It defines the path, checks whether the product exists, and returns a "**404 Not Found**" error if necessary. It also decides how the response is delivered by wrapping the service generator in a StreamingResponse. The service, on the other hand, remains focused on product-related behavior. It defines how the export progresses, but it does not know anything about HTTP semantics. This separation is the same one established in *Chapter 5: Structuring an API Project with AI Guidance*. The behavior becomes more sophisticated, but the boundaries remain stable. At this point, the code is ready to run. Start the application as usual in the following manner:

```
uvicorn app.main:app --reload
```

Ensure that at least one product exists. Then, call the new endpoint: "**GET /products/1/export-stream**." Instead of receiving a single JSON response, the client receives output progressively in the following manner:

```
Starting export for product 1 (Mechanical Keyboard)...
Processing step 1/5...
Processing step 2/5...
Processing step 3/5...
Processing step 4/5...
Processing step 5/5...
Export completed successfully.
```

Each line arrives with a short delay. The response is not assembled first and returned later. It is delivered while the work is happening.

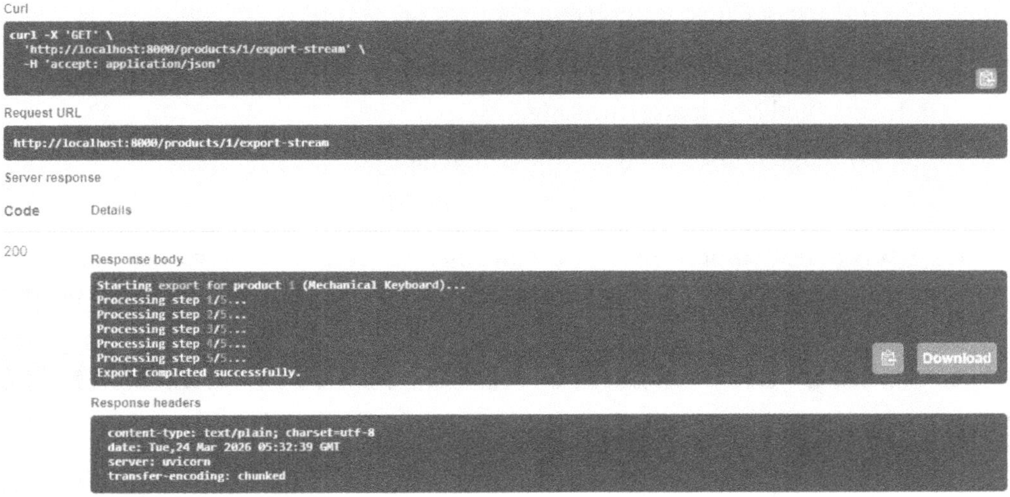

Figure 6.11: *Observable Progressive Output from the Streaming Export Endpoint*

The client receives multiple chunks over time instead of a single final payload, making the progress of the operation visible at the API boundary. Depending on the client used, the streaming behavior may appear progressively or may be buffered and displayed all at once. The progressive effect is easiest to observe in a browser or terminal. If the product does not exist, the endpoint preserves the same contract used throughout the API:

`GET /products/999/export-stream`

The response remains:

```
{ "detail": "Product 999 not found" }
```

with status code "**`404 Not Found`**."

At this stage, it is important to reflect on placement. The streaming logic did not move into main.py because the application assembly has not changed. It did not become an isolated utility because it still belongs to the product domain. It lives in the service layer because it represents product-related work over time. The router exposes that work through a different response pattern.

A good follow-up prompt makes this explicit, which is as follows:

Prompt

In this structured Products API, why does the streaming generator belong in the service layer while the StreamingResponse belongs in the router? Explain the answer in terms of responsibility boundaries.

A strong answer should point out that the generator defines how the product-related operation unfolds over time, which makes it service logic, while "**`StreamingResponse`**" is an HTTP concern because it determines how that output is delivered to the client.

This completes the introduction of the third timing pattern. The API can now:

- Return a final result after waiting,
- Acknowledge immediately and continue later, or
- Emit output progressively while work unfolds.

The next step is not to add more mechanisms, but rather to learn how to choose between these patterns intentionally based on the behavior the client should observe.

Choosing the Right Tool: Async Endpoint, Background Task, and Streaming

At this point in the chapter, the Products API supports three different timing behaviors. Each was introduced through a concrete implementation: A slow analysis endpoint, a background export process, and a streaming product export workflow. All three mechanisms are valid, which are now part of the application. The natural question for the reader is no longer how to implement them, but rather when each one should be used.

Question	Async Endpoint	Background Task	Streaming Response
Client waits for completion?	Yes	No	Partially
Immediate acknowledgment?	No	Yes	Yes
Receives progress updates?	No	No	Yes
Final result returned in response?	Yes	No	Incrementally
Typical use case	Slow computation	Long-running job	Progressive output

Table 6.2: *Comparing the Three Timing Patterns*

The comparison in *Table* 6.2 highlights that the choice is not primarily about implementation details. It is about selecting the interaction model that best matches the client's expectations.

This is one of the most important decision points in the chapter. The goal is not to memorize syntax or internal mechanics. The goal is to connect each mechanism to the situation it represents at the API boundary. In other words, the decision should be based on what the client should experience when interacting with the endpoint. Choosing between asynchronous endpoints, background tasks, and streaming responses is primarily a behavioral decision. As shown in *Figure* 6.12, each pattern corresponds to a different client experience and should be selected based on how the API is expected to communicate progress and results.

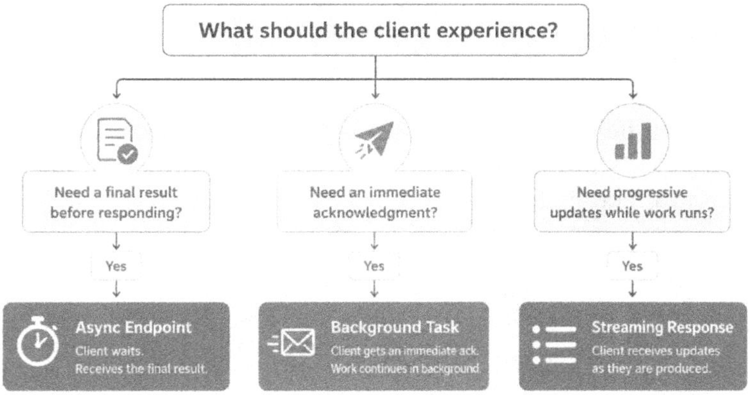

Figure 6.12: *Choosing the Appropriate Concurrency Pattern Based on Client Experience*

The best way to explore that decision is through a prompt that explicitly asks for behavioral guidance rather than a technical explanation.

Prompt

Given this Products API, how do I decide whether a workflow should be implemented as

1) an async endpoint,

2) a background task,

3) a streaming response?

Answer in terms of client-visible behavior and development intent.

A good answer does not begin with implementation details. It begins with the question that the client implicitly asks when calling an endpoint: "When will I see the result of this operation?"

The difference between these three patterns is not what the server does, but when the client observes the result. The first situation is when the client must wait for the final result. The client sends a request and expects the response to contain the completed outcome. In this case, the operation remains part of the request–response cycle. This is where an async endpoint is appropriate. The endpoint models a slow operation, but the result still belongs to the response. The second situation appears when the client does not need the final result immediately. The client only needs confirmation that a process has started. The export endpoint introduced earlier is a good example. A product export may take several seconds or minutes, but the client only needs to know that the export has begun. Waiting for the entire process to complete would not improve the user experience.

In that case, the request should end quickly while the work continues separately. The endpoint acknowledges the request and schedules the real work to happen afterward. This is precisely the role of a background task. The third situation occurs when the client benefits from observing the progress of an operation while it unfolds. Instead of waiting silently for the final result or disconnecting immediately, the client receives incremental updates. The streaming endpoint added earlier demonstrated this pattern by sending progressive product-related messages during the export simulation. In these cases, the endpoint begins responding immediately and continues sending pieces of information while the work progresses. The client does not wait in silence and does not disconnect. Instead, the connection becomes a channel for progressive output. This is where a streaming response becomes the right tool.

Side-by-side, the three mechanisms are less about concurrency techniques and more about timing expectations between the API and its clients.

An async endpoint answers the question: "Give me the final result, even if it takes a moment."

A background task answers: "Start the work and tell me that it has started."

A streaming response answers: "Let me see what is happening while the work progresses."

In *Figure* 6.13, async endpoints return a final result after waiting, background tasks acknowledge immediately while work continues elsewhere, and streaming responses deliver incremental output during execution.

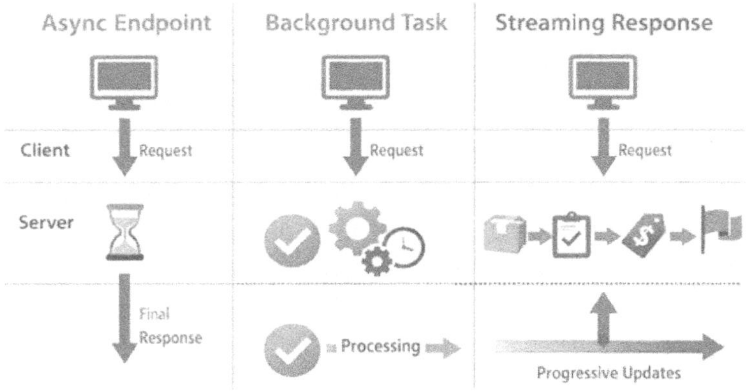

Figure 6.13: *Three Timing Models at the API Boundary*

From the perspective of the application's architecture, all three mechanisms still follow the same structural discipline introduced in the previous chapter. The router remains the HTTP boundary. The service layer remains responsible for product-related logic. Only the timing of the response changes. This is an important observation because it shows that concurrency mechanisms do not require restructuring the entire application. The structure remains stable while the execution model becomes more expressive.

A final prompt can consolidate that reasoning, which is as follows:

Prompt

Looking at the Products API now, explain how the three concurrency patterns introduced in this chapter expand the behavior of the system without changing the architecture introduced in "Chapter 5, Structuring an API Project with AI Guidance." Focus on responsibility boundaries and observable behavior.

A strong answer should emphasize that the router still defines HTTP semantics, the service layer still contains product-related logic, and the main application still assembles the components. The only difference introduced in this chapter is how time is represented in the interaction between client and server. This is the key lesson of the section. Concurrency is not just an internal optimization. It is a way of expressing different kinds of workflows at the API boundary. By learning to select the right mechanism based on client-visible behavior, the developer moves from simply implementing features to intentionally designing interactions.

Verifying the New Behavioral Contract

At this point, the Products API has changed importantly. It no longer exposes only immediate CRUD behavior. It now includes three new timing patterns: a slow async analysis endpoint, a background export endpoint, and a streaming events endpoint.

Each one was introduced for a specific reason, and each one changed what the client can observe when interacting with the API.

As in *Chapter 5, Structuring an API Project with AI Guidance*, this is the moment to stop adding features and freeze behavior.

That pause matters because concurrency is easy to misunderstand if it is only judged from the code. Two implementations may look different internally but behave the same at the API boundary. Conversely, two implementations may look similar in code while producing very different client-visible behavior. The purpose of this section is therefore not to inspect internals, but rather to define what must now be true from the client's point of view.

As shown in *Table* 6.3, the goal is not to verify how the implementation works internally. The goal is to verify that each endpoint exhibits the intended client-visible behavior. A concurrency feature is considered correct only if the observable behavior matches the contract.

Endpoint	Expected Behavior	Behavioral Failure
Async Analysis	Client waits and receives a final result after a delay	Endpoint returns immediately or never returns a result
Background Export	Client receives an immediate acknowledgment while work continues	Client waits for the export to finish before receiving a response
Streaming Export	Client receives output progressively over time	All output appears only after processing completes
Missing Product	Client receives a 404 response	Request hangs or returns an incorrect status code
Response Format	Response structure matches the documented contract	Response shape differs from the documented schema

Table 6.3: *Behavioral Contract Verification*

A useful prompt at this stage should explicitly ask for observable checks rather than implementation details, which is as follows:

Prompt

List the observable behaviors I should verify for the new async endpoint, background task endpoint, and streaming endpoint in this FastAPI Products API.

Focus only on what a client can observe.

A strong answer should produce a checklist centered on behavior at the boundary. The async endpoint should still return a structured final response after a delay. The background-task endpoint should return immediately with a confirmation message. The streaming endpoint should produce multiple pieces of output progressively, instead of returning one final JSON object. Swagger UI should still document the routes that can be described normally through the OpenAPI schema, and the behavior of each route should remain consistent with the intent that motivated its introduction.

That answer is useful because it turns the chapter's examples into something testable. The API is no longer just a collection of code snippets. It is a set of contracts about time and response behavior.

The first behavior to verify is the async endpoint. The route, "**`GET /products/{product_id}/analyze`**," should still behave like a normal request from the client's point of view, except that it takes time before returning a result. The response should remain a single structured JSON object. If the product exists, the client should wait a few seconds and then receive a result in the following manner:

```
{
  "product_id": 1,
  "name": "Mechanical Keyboard",
  "analysis": "completed",
  "price_category": "premium"
}
```

If the product does not exist, the endpoint should still return the same error structure already used elsewhere in the Products API, which is as follows:

```
{
  "detail": "Product 999 not found"
}
```

with status code "**`404 Not Found`**."

Nothing about this check depends on knowing how the code is implemented internally. The client only needs to observe that the endpoint waits, then returns the final result. That is the behavioral contract of the async endpoint.

The second behavior to verify is the background-task endpoint. The route, "**`POST /products/{product_id}/export`**," should not behave like the async analysis endpoint. The client should not wait several seconds for completion. Instead, the response should arrive almost immediately and confirm that processing has started.

A successful response should appear as follows:

```
{
  "message": "Product export started",
  "product_id": 1
}
```

The exact server-side completion of the task may appear later in the console, but from the client's point of view, the important fact is that the acknowledgment is immediate. That timing difference is the behavioral contract. If the endpoint starts behaving similarly to a slow final-result endpoint, the contract has drifted. If it stops confirming that the work has started, the contract has also drifted.

If the product does not exist, the boundary should remain consistent with the rest of the API:

```
{
  "detail": "Product 999 not found"
}
```

with status code "**404 Not Found**."

The third behavior to verify is the streaming endpoint. The route "GET **/products/{product_id}/export-stream**" should not return a single JSON document and should not merely acknowledge the request. Instead, it should start responding immediately and continue sending output progressively while the workflow unfolds.

A valid observable result might appear in the following way:

```
Starting export for product 1 (Mechanical Keyboard)...
Processing step 1/5...
Processing step 2/5...
Processing step 3/5...
Processing step 4/5...
Processing step 5/5...
Export completed successfully.
```

The critical point is not only the content of the messages, but also the fact that they arrive over time rather than as final payload. That progressive output is what defines the behavioral contract of the streaming endpoint.

If the product does not exist, the endpoint preserves the same HTTP contract and returns a "404 Not Found" response. Again, the reader does not need to inspect the generator implementation to verify this contract. The client only needs to observe that the endpoint opens a response and emits content progressively.

Swagger UI also plays an important role in this verification process. The streaming endpoint may not display progressive output clearly in Swagger UI and may appear as a single response. It should continue to document the routes that belong to the Products API and expose their paths exactly as expected. The reader should confirm that the new routes appear in the interface and that the documented request and response shapes remain meaningful where applicable. The async analysis endpoint should still appear as a normal "**GET**" route with a structured response. The background export endpoint should still appear as a normal **POST** route returning a confirmation body. The streaming endpoint may be more limited in how clearly it is represented in Swagger, but its path and availability should still be visible in the documented API. *Figure 6.14* shows how the new endpoints appear alongside the existing CRUD API, making the behavioral system expansion visible at the boundary even though the timing patterns now differ.

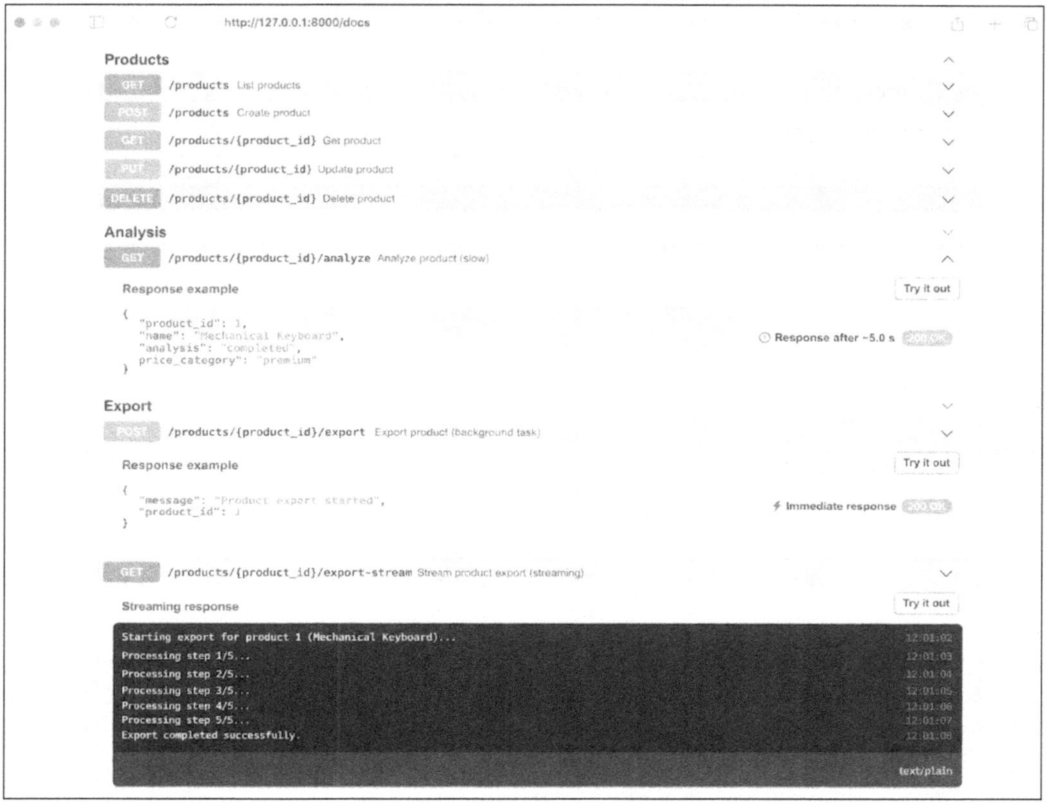

Figure 6.14: *Swagger UI after Adding Concurrency-Related Routes*

At this stage, the reader should think like a reviewer, not like an implementer. The question is no longer "Does the code run?" The question is now "Does each endpoint now express the timing behavior it was supposed to express?"

A useful follow-up prompt can reinforce that mindset, which is as follows:

Prompt

For each of the three new endpoints in this Products API, explain what specific timing behavior the client should observe and what would count as a behavioral failure for that endpoint.

A strong answer should say that the async endpoint fails behaviorally if it no longer returns a final structured response after waiting. The background-task endpoint fails if it does not return immediately or if it stops confirming that processing has started. The streaming endpoint fails if it collapses into a single final response instead of delivering progressive output. These are not low-level implementation failures. They are failures of the API contract as experienced by the client.

This is the deeper lesson of the section. In earlier chapters, verification focused on paths, status codes, validation, and error responses. In this chapter, verification expands to include time as part of the contract. The API is no longer defined only by what it returns, but also by when and how it returns it.

That understanding is what makes the chapter complete. The Products API has not merely gained new code. It has gained three new observable behaviors, and those behaviors must now be treated as part of the system's stable contract. Time is now part of the API contract. The final section of the chapter will therefore freeze this concurrent version of the application as the new baseline for everything that follows.

Freezing the Concurrent Version as the New Baseline

At this point in the chapter, the Products API has evolved again. Earlier chapters focused on building a working API and then reorganizing its structure so that responsibilities were clear and stable. The current chapter did not change that structure. Instead, it expanded what the system can express in terms of timing and workflow behavior.

Before moving forward in the book, it is important to freeze this version of the application in the same disciplined way used at the end of *Chapter 5: Structuring an API Project with AI Guidance*. The purpose is not to add new code or abstractions, but to confirm that the system now supports several kinds of observable workflows while maintaining the same structural clarity introduced earlier.

The first observation is that the project structure itself has not changed. No additional architectural layers were required to introduce asynchronous endpoints, background tasks, or streaming responses. The same modular structure created in *Chapter 5: Structuring an API Project with AI Guidance* remains the foundation of the system.

The project layout should still look as follows:

```
app/
    main.py
    models.py
    routers/
        products.py
    services/
        product_service.py
```

Same structure. Different timing behaviors. The architecture remains unchanged. What evolves in this chapter is not the organization of the project, but rather the way the API handles work over time through asynchronous execution, background processing, and streaming responses.

The main module continues to assemble the FastAPI application and register routers. The router module continues to define HTTP endpoints and translate domain outcomes into responses. The models module continues to define the request and response schemas used by the API contract. The service module continues to encapsulate product-related logic and in-memory state. This stability is intentional. Concurrency was added without reorganizing the project again. That decision reinforces an important principle: architectural structure should remain stable while behavior evolves inside the existing responsibility boundaries.

Within that structure, three new capabilities now exist:

The first capability is an **async endpoint** that models a slow operation returning a final result. The route "`/products/{product_id}/analyze`" simulates a time-consuming product analysis. The endpoint waits for the operation to complete and then returns a structured JSON response to the client. From the client's perspective, the behavior is a normal request-response interaction, but the API now explicitly represents the passage of time.

The second capability is a **background task workflow**. The route "`/products/{product_id}/export`" accepts a request and immediately acknowledges that processing has started. The export operation continues after the response has been sent. This behavior expresses a different contract with the client: confirmation now, work later.

The third capability is a **streaming response**. The route "`/products/{product_id}/export-stream`" produces progressive output as the operation unfolds. Instead of waiting silently or disconnecting immediately, the client receives multiple pieces of information over time.

These are not three different implementations, but rather three different ways of expressing time at the API boundary.

What is notable about these additions is that they did not require architectural sprawl. The router still owns HTTP semantics. The service still owns product-related workflows. No new layers, frameworks, or patterns were introduced. The project gained expressive behavior without losing structural clarity. This outcome reflects the discipline established in the previous chapter. The architecture was intentionally simple and modular so that new capabilities could be added without forcing another structural redesign. To consolidate this evolution, it is useful to ask the assistant for a summary that focuses on the reasoning process rather than the syntax.

Prompt

Summarize how this Products API evolved in this chapter. Focus on how concurrency expanded the behavior of the system without changing the project structure introduced in "Chapter 5, Structuring an API Project with AI Guidance."

A strong answer should emphasize several key points. The API began the chapter with a stable, modular structure and synchronous request-response behavior. The chapter then introduced three different concurrency patterns, each motivated by a specific workflow requirement. These patterns changed how time is represented in API interactions, but did not require restructuring the application.

The async endpoint demonstrated how to represent slow operations that still produce a final response. The background-task endpoint demonstrated how to acknowledge requests immediately while continuing work afterward. The streaming endpoint demonstrated how to deliver progressive output while a workflow unfolds.

The important insight is that these behaviors expanded the expressive power of the system without altering its responsibility boundaries. The router still defines the API boundary. The service layer still implements product-related logic. The models still define the schema contract. The architecture remained stable while the execution model became more flexible.

At this stage, the Products API has moved beyond simple CRUD behavior. It now supports workflows that unfold over time, acknowledging that real systems often need to represent delays, background processing, and progressive output. Yet it achieves this without sacrificing clarity or introducing unnecessary complexity.

This concurrent version of the application, therefore, becomes the new baseline for the chapters that follow. Future extensions—whether they involve persistence, security, testing, or deployment—will build on a system that is not only structurally organized but also capable of expressing realistic asynchronous workflows.

Conclusion

In this chapter, the Products API learned to represent different kinds of time-based behavior. Instead of every request following the same immediate request–response pattern, the application now supports three practical workflows. An async endpoint models slow operations that still return a final result. A background task allows the API to acknowledge a request immediately while the real work continues afterward. A streaming response lets the client observe progress as the operation unfolds.

These capabilities expand the behavior of the system without changing the architecture introduced in *Chapter 5, Structuring an API Project with AI Guidance*. The router still defines the HTTP boundary, the service layer still owns product logic, and the project structure remains stable.

The key lesson is simple: concurrency is not just about performance. It is about choosing the right interaction model for the workflow that the API needs to represent. So far, however, all product data still lives only in memory. The API can process requests more effectively, but it cannot preserve information once the application stops. In *Chapter 7: Building Data-Driven* APIs, we will introduce database persistence, connect the application to a real data store, and migrate the existing CRUD operations from temporary memory to durable storage. The API contract will remain unchanged, but the system will finally retain its data between executions.

Points to Remember

- Use concurrency when the workflow requires it.
- Async endpoints return a final result after waiting.
- Background tasks continue work after the response.
- Streaming responses expose progress while work runs.
- Choose the pattern based on client-visible behavior.
- Concurrency can expand capabilities without changing architecture.
- Keep HTTP concerns in the router and domain logic in the service layer.
- Verify timing behavior through observable results.
- Use prompts to select the right concurrency pattern for the problem.

Multiple Choice Questions

1. What is the main objective of *Chapter 6: Handling Concurrency and Real-Time Workflows*?
   a. To replace the service layer with asynchronous frameworks
   b. To introduce concurrency patterns while preserving the existing project structure
   c. To optimize API performance through benchmarking
   d. To migrate the API to a distributed architecture
2. When should an async endpoint typically be used in the Products API?
   a. When the client does not need any response
   b. When the client must wait for a final result produced by a slow operation
   c. When the server should ignore the request
   d. When the endpoint must run in the background indefinitely
3. What is the main purpose of a background task in FastAPI?
   a. To execute code before the request arrives
   b. To run a task after the HTTP response has already been returned
   c. To replace asynchronous endpoints
   d. To improve Swagger documentation
4. What observable behavior defines a streaming response?
   a. The server returns multiple JSON responses at once.
   b. The server returns data progressively while the operation unfolds.

   c. The server closes the connection immediately.
   d. The server executes tasks in parallel.

5. In the Products API example, what does the background export endpoint demonstrate?
   a. A workflow where the client waits until the export completes
   b. A workflow where the client receives an immediate confirmation while work continues afterward
   c. A workflow that replaces CRUD operations
   d. A workflow that blocks all other requests

6. Where should streaming logic be placed in the structured project introduced in *Chapter 5: Structuring an API Project with AI Guidance*?
   a. Inside the main application module
   b. Inside the router file only
   c. Inside the service layer, with the router exposing it through a streaming response
   d. Inside the models module

7. What remained unchanged when concurrency features were added in this chapter?
   a. The HTTP server implementation
   b. The modular architecture separating routers, models, and services
   c. The FastAPI framework itself
   d. The API endpoints themselves

8. What is the key factor when deciding whether to use an async endpoint, background task, or streaming response?
   a. The number of files in the project
   b. The complexity of the Python syntax
   c. The timing behavior the client should observe
   d. The number of developers working on the project

9. A client should immediately receive confirmation that a report export started, while the export continues afterward. Which concurrency pattern best fits this behavior?
   a. Async endpoint
   b. Background task

c. Streaming response
d. Standard synchronous route

Answers

1. b
2. b
3. b
4. b
5. b
6. c
7. b
8. c
9. b

Questions

1. Why is concurrency introduced in this chapter only after the API structure was stabilized in *Chapter 5, Structuring an API Project with AI Guidance*?
2. What kinds of real workflows in an API suggest the need for asynchronous behavior rather than immediate synchronous responses?
3. How does an async endpoint differ from a normal endpoint in terms of observable behavior from the client's perspective?
4. In what situations is a background task more appropriate than an async endpoint that waits for the final result?
5. What advantages does a streaming response provide compared to returning a single JSON response after a delay?
6. How do async endpoints, background tasks, and streaming responses represent three different timing contracts between client and server?
7. Why is it important that the introduction of concurrency mechanisms did not require changing the architecture established in *Chapter 5: Structuring an API Project with AI Guidance*?
8. How does verifying observable behavior—such as delayed responses, immediate acknowledgments, and progressive output—help confirm that the API behaves as intended?
9. In what ways does prompt-driven development help decide which concurrency mechanism to use when designing a new workflow?

10. How does thinking in terms of client-visible behavior lead to better decisions about asynchronous design than focusing only on implementation details?

Key Terms

- **Concurrency Workflow**: A pattern describing how an API handles operations that take time, determining whether the client waits for completion, receives an immediate acknowledgment, or observes progressive output.
- **Async Endpoint**: A FastAPI route defined with async def that performs non-blocking work and returns a final response once the operation completes.
- **Non-Blocking Operation**: A task that allows the server to continue handling other requests while waiting for an external or delayed operation to finish.
- **Background Task**: A FastAPI mechanism that schedules work to run after the HTTP response has already been returned to the client.
- **Deferred Processing**: A workflow where the API acknowledges a request immediately, while the actual work continues asynchronously in the background.
- **Streaming Response**: An HTTP response that sends data progressively over time instead of returning a single final payload.
- **Async Generator**: A Python function defined with async def and yield that produces multiple pieces of output asynchronously, often used to implement streaming responses.
- **Progressive Output**: A response pattern in which the client receives incremental updates while an operation unfolds instead of waiting for a final result.
- **Timing Contract**: The observable expectation between client and server describing when a response is delivered and whether work continues after or during the response.
- **Observable Behavior**: The aspects of an API interaction that a client can perceive, such as response timing, progressive output, or immediate acknowledgment.
- **Concurrency Pattern**: A practical strategy for structuring asynchronous work in an API, such as async endpoints, background tasks, or streaming responses.
- **Execution Model**: The way an API performs work internally while maintaining a stable external contract at the HTTP boundary.

CHAPTER 7
Building Data-Driven APIs

Introduction

In the previous chapters, the Products API learned how to organize its structure, and manage concurrent workflows. However, one important limitation still remains: product data exists only while the server is running. Once the application stops, everything disappears.

This chapter introduces the **first persistent storage layer** in the book, transforming the API from a temporary runtime system into a durable application. Until now, every feature has depended on in-memory state. Persistence changes that foundation by allowing data to survive application restarts, and become part of a long-lived system.

This chapter introduces persistence. Instead of storing products in memory, the API will begin storing them in a database. Using prompt-driven development, you will generate a database model, connect the application to a database, implement CRUD operations, and manage schema changes through migrations. By the end of the chapter, the Products API will become a **data-driven system** capable of storing and retrieving the persistent data, while keeping the same API contract introduced in earlier chapters.

Structure

In this chapter, we will discuss the following topics:

- The Next Limitation: Data Disappears When the Server Stops
- Choosing a Practical Persistence Approach
- Creating the First Database Model
- Creating the Database Session Layer
- Generating CRUD Operations with AI

- Refactoring the Router to Use Database Persistence
- Introducing a Migration Workflow
- Verifying the Database-Backed API
- Using AI to Review Data Access Logic
- Freezing the Data-Driven Version as the New Baseline

The Next Limitation: Data Disappears When the Server Stops

At the end of *Chapter 6 - Handling Concurrency and Real-Time Workflows*, the Products API had become more expressive. It could still perform normal CRUD operations, but it could also represent slower workflows through an async analysis endpoint, a background export process, and a streaming export endpoint. The structure of the project remained stable throughout those changes. The router still owned the HTTP boundary, the service layer still owned product-related behavior, and the application had begun to look like a real system, rather than a toy example. And yet, one important limitation remained.

Observable Limitation

Create Product

↓

Restart Server

↓

Product Gone

The limitation is visible from the outside. The API appears to work correctly while the server is running, but the data disappears when the process stops. Persistence is introduced to solve this observable behavior, not because a database is inherently more sophisticated than in-memory storage.

Create a few products. Stop the server. Start it again. Then open Swagger UI and call:

```
GET /products
```

The response will most likely be:

```
[]
```

Everything you created is gone. This is not a bug, and it is not an accident. It is the direct consequence of how the application still stores its data. Even after all the improvements introduced in the previous chapters, products still live only inside the running Python process. As long as the server is alive, the API can create, list, update, and delete them. The moment the process stops, that state disappears with it. This is the right moment to pause, because it reveals a new kind of limitation. Earlier chapters were concerned with behavior at the API boundary, such as: request validation, error handling, asynchronous waiting, background execution, and progressive output. Now the problem is different. The API can behave well during a session, and still fail to behave like a real catalog across sessions. That distinction matters. From the client's point of view, a product catalog is expected to remember products. If a client creates records today, and the server restarts tonight, those records should still exist tomorrow. An API that forgets everything each time the process restarts may still be useful for learning, but it is no longer sufficient for a realistic application. This is where persistence enters the story. Notice how the chapter arrives at that idea. It does not begin with database theory. It does not begin with schemas, tables, or SQL. It begins with an observable failure of memory at the system boundary. The API still responds correctly, but it does not retain anything beyond the lifetime of the running process. That is the real limitation we need to solve. *Figure* 7.1 shows the core limitation of the current API. Product data lives only in memory, while the FastAPI process is running. When the server stops, that data disappears. From the client's perspective, the system has no memory across restarts.

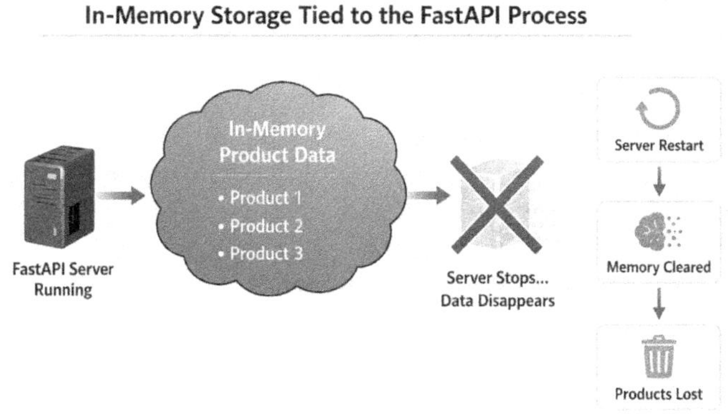

Figure 7.1: *In-memory Storage Tied to the Running Application Process*

Product data exists only while the FastAPI process is running. When the server stops, the in-memory state disappears with it. Before introducing any persistence technology, it is useful to frame the problem through a prompt that focuses on consequences, rather than tools.

Prompt

In this FastAPI Products API, what practical problems arise from storing products only in memory, and what would change if the data were stored persistently? Focus on observable behavior rather than database theory.

A useful answer should stay close to what a developer or client can actually observe. The first and most obvious problem is that all records disappear when the application restarts. A product created in one session is unavailable in the next. The second problem is that the API cannot behave consistently across multiple running instances, because each process would maintain its own isolated in-memory list. The third is that the data cannot be treated as a stable source of truth outside the lifetime of the application. The system can simulate a catalog, but it cannot actually preserve one. All of these observations lead to the same conclusion: the API needs a storage layer that exists independently of the server process. Once that requirement is stated clearly, persistence stops feeling like abstract infrastructure, and starts looking like the next practical step in the evolution of the application. The question is no longer whether the Products API should remember data. It is how to introduce that memory in the simplest possible way, while preserving the same structured architecture established in the previous chapters.

Choosing a Practical Persistence Approach

The previous section established the need for persistence through direct observation. The Products API behaves correctly while it is running, but it forgets everything as soon as the process stops. The problem is not theoretical. It is visible at the API boundary.

At this point, the question is no longer whether persistence is needed. The question becomes how to introduce it without breaking the clarity of the system built so far. There are many possible answers. Modern applications can use relational databases, NoSQL systems, distributed storage, or managed cloud services. Exploring all of these options would add complexity without improving understanding. The goal of this chapter is not to compare database technologies. It is to introduce persistence in a way that is immediately usable and easy to reason about within the existing project. For that reason, the guiding principle here is minimalism.

Table 7.1 shows as ach tool serves a specific purpose. SQLite provides persistence, SQLAlchemy acts as the bridge between Python code and database tables, and Alembic keeps the database schema synchronized as the application evolves.

Component	Responsibility
SQLite	Stores application data on disk
SQLAlchemy	Maps Python objects to database tables and queries
Alembic	Manages database schema changes over time
FastAPI	Exposes the HTTP API and coordinates requests
Pydantic	Validates request and response data

Table 7.1: *Persistence Components Used in This Chapter*

The persistence layer should:

- Require very little setup
- Integrate naturally with the current FastAPI structure
- Remain representative of real-world applications

Instead of starting from theory, the decision can again be framed through a prompt that focuses on practicality.

Prompt

Suggest a minimal database setup for this FastAPI Products API. Use SQLite for simplicity and generate SQLAlchemy models. Avoid advanced configuration and keep it runnable.

A useful answer to this prompt typically converges toward a simple and effective stack composed of three elements. The first element is SQLite, which acts as the database engine. SQLite stores all data in a single file, and does not require a separate server process. This makes it ideal for local development and learning environments. The application can begin storing data persistently without introducing infrastructure concerns. The second element is SQLAlchemy, which provides the Object-Relational Mapping (ORM) layer. SQLAlchemy allows Python classes to represent database tables, and offers a consistent way to perform create, read, update, and delete operations. Instead of writing raw SQL queries, the application can work with Python objects that map directly to persistent records. The third element is Alembic, which manages database migrations. As the application evolves, the structure of the database will change. Alembic records those changes, and applies them in a controlled, versioned way. This ensures that the database schema evolves alongside the application code, instead of drifting out of sync.

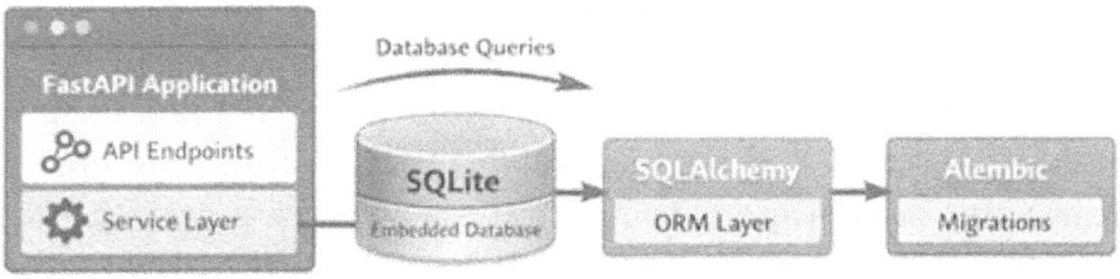

Figure 7.2: *Minimal Persistence Stack for the Products API*

The FastAPI application interacts with a SQLite database through SQLAlchemy models, while Alembic manages schema evolution through migrations. Together, these three components provide a complete but minimal persistence solution. SQLite removes the need for external services, SQLAlchemy integrates database access into the Python codebase, and Alembic introduces a disciplined way to manage schema changes over time. Before integrating these components into the project, the required dependencies must be installed. In addition to the packages already used in earlier chapters, the persistence layer introduces:

- `fastapi`

- `uvicorn`
- `sqlalchemy`
- `alembic`

They can be installed with:

```
pip install fastapi uvicorn sqlalchemy alembic
```

At this stage, it is important to notice what has not changed. The API still behaves exactly as before. The same endpoints exist, the router still delegates work to the service layer, and the service layer still uses in-memory storage. No request or response behavior has been modified yet. What has changed is the preparation. The project now includes the tools required to introduce persistence, but it has not yet started using them. This incremental approach is consistent with the method used throughout the book. New capabilities are introduced step by step, and each step is verified before moving on. The next section will take the first concrete step in that transition by defining a database model for the Product entity.

Creating the First Database Model

The previous section introduced a minimal persistence stack, but at this stage, the API still behaves exactly as before. Products are still stored in memory, and nothing survives a server restart. The application now has the tools required for persistence, but it has not yet started using them. Before introducing the database model, it is useful to briefly clarify what that actually means in practice. Up to this point, product data has lived inside Python objects stored in memory. With persistence, that data will instead be stored in a database. In this chapter, the chosen database is SQLite. SQLite is a lightweight relational database that stores all data in a single file on disk. Unlike other databases, it does not require a separate server process. This makes it particularly suitable for learning, local development, and small applications. The FastAPI application can read and write persistent data simply by connecting to that file. Another important advantage is that SQLite is already supported by SQLAlchemy and does not require additional system-level installation in most environments. In practice, installing the Python dependencies is enough to start using it. This is why SQLite is chosen here. It allows the chapter to focus on persistence as a behavior, without introducing operational complexity.

At this point, it is important to clarify something that may look confusing at first. The project already contains a file:

```
app/models.py
```

That file defines the API schemas used for request validation and responses. Those models are part of the API contract, and must remain unchanged. In this chapter, we are introducing a different kind of model: a database model.

This means that the project will now contain two types of models:

- **Pydantic models** (`app/models.py`) → define how data enters and leaves the API
- **SQLAlchemy models** (`app/db/models.py`) → define how data is stored in the database

These two layers serve different purposes, and must coexist. The existing models. py file should not be removed or replaced. With that clarification in place, the next step becomes straightforward. The application already knows what a product looks like. That definition has appeared multiple times in earlier chapters through request models, response schemas, and service logic. A product has an identifier, a name, a description, and a price. What changes now is not the meaning of a product, but where that data is stored. Until now, the Product model defined how data moves through the API boundary. The next step is to define how that same data is stored persistently in a database. Because the structure is already known, this is not a design problem. It is a translation. As in previous sections, this translation can be guided through a prompt.

Prompt

Generate a SQLAlchemy model for the Product entity used in this API.

Fields: id, name, description, price.

Keep it minimal and compatible with SQLite.

A strong response should avoid unnecessary complexity. The goal is not to introduce relationships, advanced configuration, or abstractions. The goal is simply to define a table that can store product records. To keep database-related code organized, the project introduces a new directory:

`app/db/models.py`

This file will contain the SQLAlchemy representation of the Product entity.

Before defining the model, notice the call to **`declarative_base().`** This function creates the base class from which all SQLAlchemy models inherit. It provides the metadata SQLAlchemy uses to map Python classes to database tables.

A minimal implementation looks like this:

```
# app/db/models.py

from sqlalchemy import Column, Integer, String, Float
from sqlalchemy.orm import declarative_base

Base = declarative_base()

class Product(Base):
    __tablename__ = "products"

    id = Column(Integer, primary_key=True, index=True)
```

```
    name = Column(String, nullable=False, index=True)
    description = Column(String, nullable=False)
    price = Column(Float, nullable=False)
```

The **Product** class now represents a database table, rather than an in-memory data structure. The fields mirror the API schema introduced in earlier chapters: id uniquely identifies a product, while name, description, and price store its data. The **index=True** option on name is not required for the current CRUD operations, but it prepares the schema for future search and filtering scenarios.

Nothing fundamentally changes at the API boundary. The same product structure is preserved, but it now has a new responsibility: representing data that can be stored persistently. *Figure 7.3* illustrates this transition from an API schema and in-memory object to a database-backed entity.

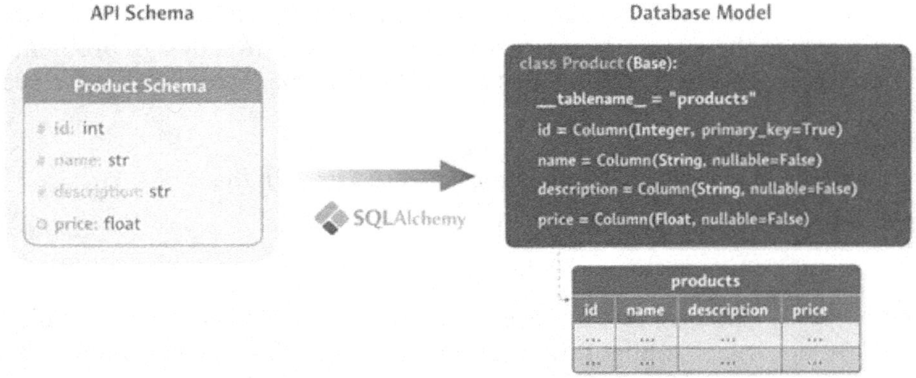

Figure 7.3: *Product Model Translated from API Schema to Database Model*

The Product entity moves from request/response schemas to a SQLAlchemy model mapped to a database table. It is important to notice what has not changed. The API endpoints are still the same. The router continues to define the same paths and responses. The service layer still uses the in-memory list introduced in earlier chapters. At this moment, the database model exists only as a definition. It has not yet been connected to the request lifecycle. This step is intentionally isolated. The chapter continues to follow the same incremental approach used throughout the book. Each capability is introduced, understood, and verified before being integrated into the system. The Product model now exists as a persistent entity definition. The next step is to create the database connection and session layer that allows the application to actually interact with this model.

Creating the Database Session Layer

In the previous section, the Products API gained its first persistent entity: a SQLAlchemy model representing the products table. That was an important step, but it was only a definition. At this point, the application still cannot actually read from or write to the database. A database model alone is not enough.

The API still needs a way to:

- Open a connection to the database
- Create sessions that perform operations through that connection
- Make those sessions available to the parts of the application that need them

This is the purpose of the database session layer. Before writing the code, it is useful to clarify one concept that often confuses readers the first time, they encounter SQLAlchemy: the difference between the engine and a session. The engine represents the application's connection to the database system. In this chapter, that means a connection to the SQLite database file. A session is different. A session is the object the application actually uses to perform work: querying records, adding new ones, updating them, and deleting them. If the engine is the connection mechanism, the session is the working context through which database operations happen in a FastAPI application, sessions should not be created manually inside every route. That would scatter connection logic throughout the code, and make resource management harder to reason about. Instead, the application should define one reusable dependency that provides a session when a route needs it and closes that session automatically when the request ends. That is the goal of this section.

The application needs only three elements:

- A database engine that knows how to connect to SQLite.
- A session factory that can create database sessions.
- a FastAPI dependency that provides one session per request.

As in earlier sections, the implementation can begin with a focused prompt.

Prompt

Generate a minimal SQLAlchemy database connection setup for this FastAPI project using SQLite. Create an engine, session factory, and dependency for FastAPI routes.

A useful response should produce a configuration that is small, explicit, and runnable. To keep database-related utilities organized, this logic belongs in a new file inside the **db** directory:

```
app/db/database.py
```

A minimal implementation looks like this:

```
# app/db/database.py

from sqlalchemy import create_engine
from sqlalchemy.orm import sessionmaker
```

```
DATABASE_URL = "sqlite:///./products.db"

engine = create_engine(
    DATABASE_URL,
    connect_args={"check_same_thread": False}
)

SessionLocal = sessionmaker(
    autocommit=False,
    autoflush=False,
    bind=engine
)

def get_db():
    db = SessionLocal()
    try:
        yield db
    finally:
        db.close()
```

This module introduces three pieces of infrastructure. The first is **`DATABASE_URL`**, which defines where the database lives. In this case, SQLite stores everything in a file named **`products.db`** in the project root. The triple slash (**`sqlite:///`**) indicates a relative file path. If the file does not yet exist, SQLite will create it automatically when the application first interacts with the database.

The second is the engine. This is the connection layer between the FastAPI application and the SQLite database. Notice the **`check_same_thread=False`** setting. SQLite restricts connections to the thread that created them by default. FastAPI may process requests across multiple threads, so this option relaxes that restriction for development use.

The third is **`SessionLocal`**, which is a factory that creates database sessions. Each session represents one active working context with the database.

Finally, the **`get_db()`** function turns that session into a FastAPI dependency. When a route depends on **`get_db`**, FastAPI creates a session, provides it to the route, and closes it automatically, once the request is finished. This lifecycle matters. The route does not need to know how to open or close a database connection. It simply receives a session when it needs one. That keeps the router focused on HTTP behavior, and keeps the database setup in a single, explicit place.

It is also important to notice what this file does not do.

- It does not yet create tables.
- It does not yet execute queries.
- It does not yet replace the in-memory product list.

At this stage, the application has only gained the ability to talk to the database. It has not yet started using that ability in the request lifecycle. *Figure* 7.4 illustrates how the FastAPI application interacts with the database through the session layer. The router does not connect to the database directly. Instead, it depends on the **`get_db()`** function, which provides a database session for each request. That session is created by the session factory, and is connected to the SQLite database through the engine. This flow makes the responsibility boundaries clear: the router handles HTTP behavior, while the database layer manages connections and data access.

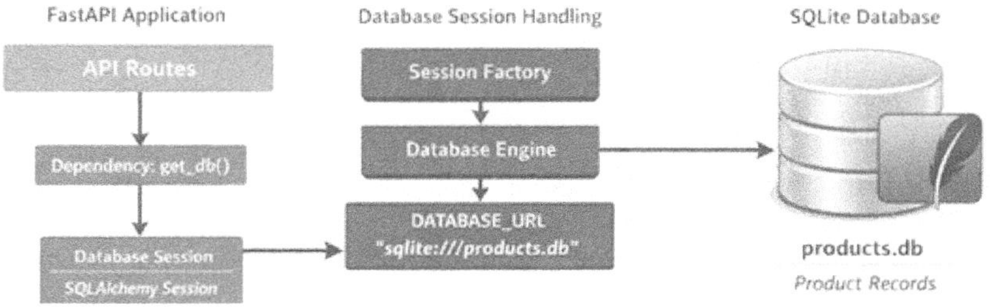

***Figure* 7.4:** *FastAPI Application Connected to a Database Session*

The application now has a database engine, a session factory, and a dependency that provides one database session per request. This separation is intentional. The chapter continues to follow the same incremental method used throughout the book. First, define the persistent model. Then define how the application connects to the database. Only after that do we replace the in-memory CRUD logic with database-backed operations. One final clarification is worth making before moving on. The **`get_db()`** dependency does not belong in the router, even though the router will use it. It belongs in the database layer because it is part of database access infrastructure, not part of HTTP behavior. The router should only consume that dependency, not define it. With this in place, the Products API now has a persistent model and a way to open database sessions. The next step is to connect those two pieces by generating CRUD operations that allow the service layer to create, read, update, and delete product records through the database.

Generating CRUD Operations with AI

At this point, the Products API has all the pieces required to move from temporary in-memory behavior to real persistence. The application already has a database model for products, and it already knows how to open a database session. What is still missing is the layer that actually performs operations against the database. So far, the service module has owned product-related logic using in-memory structures such as a Python list and a manual identifier counter. That approach was useful because it kept behavior simple and easy to observe. Now, however, persistence changes the nature of that responsibility. The service layer must stop treating products as temporary Python objects and start treating them as records stored in a database. This transition is important, but it does not change the role of the service layer. It still owns product-related operations. What changes is how those operations are implemented. As in earlier sections, this step can be guided through a focused prompt.

Keep them simple and compatible with the current FastAPI service layer. A useful response should avoid introducing new architectural layers. The goal is not to add repositories or abstractions. The goal is to replace the in-memory logic with database-backed operations, while preserving the existing structure. The file that changes is still:

```
app/services/product_service.py
```

A minimal implementation looks like this:

```
# app/services/product_service.py

from typing import List, Optional
from sqlalchemy.orm import Session
from app.db.models import Product as ProductDB
from app.models import ProductCreate

def create_product(db: Session, data: ProductCreate) -> ProductDB:
    product = ProductDB(
        name=data.name,
        description=data.description,
        price=data.price
    )
    db.add(product)
    db.commit()
    db.refresh(product)
    return product

def get_product(db: Session, product_id: int) -> Optional[ProductDB]:
    return db.query(ProductDB).filter(ProductDB.id == product_id).first()

def list_products(db: Session) -> List[ProductDB]:
    return db.query(ProductDB).all()

def update_product(db: Session, product_id: int, data: ProductCreate) ->
Optional[ProductDB]:
    product = get_product(db, product_id)
    if product is None:
        return None

    product.name = data.name
    product.description = data.description
    product.price = data.price

    db.commit()
    db.refresh(product)
```

```
    return product

def delete_product(db: Session, product_id: int) -> bool:
    product = get_product(db, product_id)
    if product is None:
        return False

    db.delete(product)
    db.commit()
    return True
```

For clarity, the examples use direct **`commit()`** calls. In production systems, database operations are typically wrapped in transaction-handling logic that performs a rollback, if an error occurs.

Refactoring the Router to Use Database

At this stage of the chapter, the Products API has already taken an important step toward persistence. The database model exists, the application can open database sessions, and the service layer now contains CRUD functions that operate through SQLAlchemy, instead of an in-memory list. But one important piece is still missing. The API routes themselves do not yet provide a database session to those functions. The persistence layer exists, but the request lifecycle is not connected to it yet. This is the moment where that connection is made. The key constraint remains the same one established in *Chapter 5, Structuring an API Project with AI Guidance*: the API boundary should stay stable. From the client's point of view, the same CRUD endpoints should still exist, the same request bodies should still be accepted, and the same responses should still be returned. What changes is not the contract of the API, but the internal mechanism used to fulfill each request. The router now needs access to a database session for every request. Earlier in the chapter, the **`get_db`** dependency was introduced for exactly this purpose. FastAPI can inject that dependency into route functions, allowing each route to receive a session, and pass it to the service layer.

Figure 7.5 shows how persistence becomes part of the request lifecycle. A database session is created through dependency injection, passed to the service layer, and used to access persistent storage.

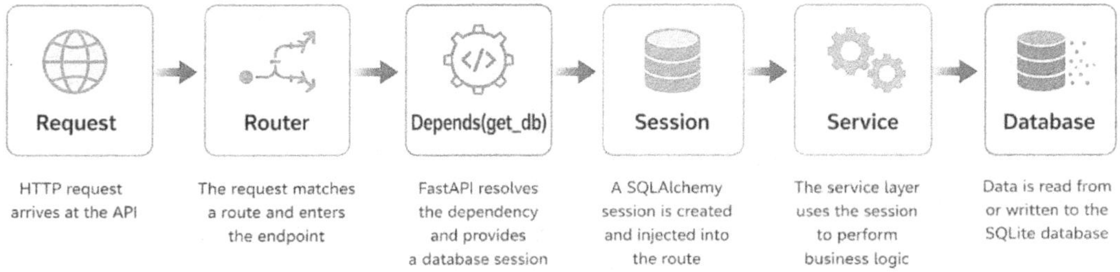

Figure 7.5: *Request Flow with Dependency-Injected Database Sessions*

At this point, it is important to keep the scope of the section clear. The project already contains additional endpoints introduced in *Chapter 6, Handling Concurrency and Real-Time Workflows*, but this section focuses specifically on reconnecting the CRUD routes to persistent storage. The goal here is not to rewrite the entire router, but to refactor the CRUD part of it so that requests now operate on database-backed records.

The relevant routes in **app/routers/products.py** are updated like this:

```
# app/routers/products.py

from fastapi import APIRouter, Depends, HTTPException, status
from sqlalchemy.orm import Session
from typing import List

from app.models import Product, ProductCreate
from app.services import product_service
from app.db.database import get_db

router = APIRouter()

@router.post("/products", response_model=Product, status_code=status.
HTTP_201_CREATED)
def create_product(product: ProductCreate, db: Session = Depends(get_
db)) -> Product:
    return product_service.create_product(db, product)

@router.get("/products", response_model=List[Product])
def list_products(db: Session = Depends(get_db)) -> List[Product]:
    return product_service.list_products(db)

@router.get("/products/{product_id}", response_model=Product)
def get_product(product_id: int, db: Session = Depends(get_db)) ->
Product:
    product = product_service.get_product(db, product_id)

    if product is None:
        raise HTTPException(
            status_code=status.HTTP_404_NOT_FOUND,
            detail=f"Product {product_id} not found",
        )
    return product

@router.put("/products/{product_id}", response_model=Product)
def update_product(product_id: int, updated: ProductCreate, db: Session
= Depends(get_db)) -> Product:
    product = product_service.update_product(db, product_id, updated)

    if product is None:
```

```
        raise HTTPException(
            status_code=status.HTTP_404_NOT_FOUND,
            detail=f"Product {product_id} not found",
        )
    return product

@router.delete("/products/{product_id}")
def delete_product(product_id: int, db: Session = Depends(get_db)) ->
dict:
    deleted = product_service.delete_product(db, product_id)

    if not deleted:
        raise HTTPException(
            status_code=status.HTTP_404_NOT_FOUND,
            detail=f"Product {product_id} not found",
        )

    return {"message": f"Product {product_id} deleted"}
```

The most visible change is the addition of the same parameter to each route:

```
db: Session = Depends(get_db)
```

This line tells FastAPI to create a database session for the request, pass it into the route function, and close it automatically when the request ends. That is the key integration point. The router does not open connections manually, and does not manage transactions. It simply receives the session, and forwards it to the service layer. This keeps the router focused on HTTP behavior, while allowing the service layer to operate on the persistent data.

In other words, the responsibilities remain stable:

- The router still defines paths, request handling, and HTTP errors.
- The service layer still performs product-related operations.
- The database now owns the actual storage of product records.

This is exactly the same architectural discipline established in the previous chapters. The behavior of the system evolves, but responsibility boundaries remain clear. One technical detail is worth keeping in mind here. The service layer now returns SQLAlchemy model instances, while the router still uses the existing Pydantic response models defined in app/models.py. For that to work correctly, the response models must be able to read attributes from ORM objects. That compatibility should already be present in the Pydantic model configuration; otherwise, the API will not serialize database objects correctly. At this point, a small practical check is useful. Start the application as usual:

```
uvicorn app.main:app -reload
```

Then open Swagger UI, and try the same CRUD workflow used in earlier chapters. Create a product with **POST /products** using a body such as:

```
{
  "name": "Mechanical Keyboard",
  "description": "Compact mechanical keyboard",
  "price": 129.99
}
```

Then call **GET /products**

The important thing to notice is that nothing looks different from the client's point of view. The same request still works. The same shape of response still comes back. The same routes still exist. That is exactly what should happen. The effect of this refactor is not that the API suddenly looks different. The effect is that the same requests are now fulfilled through the database, rather than through the in-memory list.

The deeper practical consequence will become visible in the next verification step, when the server is restarted, and the data remains available. A useful prompt at this stage helps make the architectural change explicit without drifting into implementation detail.

A strong answer should point out that the router still owns HTTP semantics, the service layer still owns product operations, and the database now owns storage and identity. The API boundary remains stable because the same requests still produce the same responses, even though the internal path taken to fulfill them has changed. This marks the point where the Products API becomes truly database-backed in its request lifecycle. The next step is to add a migration workflow so that the database schema itself can be created and evolved in a controlled way.

Introducing a Migration Workflow

At this point in the chapter, the Products API has crossed an important threshold. It no longer stores product data only in memory. It now has a database model, a database session layer, and routes that use persistent storage through the service layer. However, one practical problem remains. The application knows what the database schema should look like, but the database itself does not. Defining a SQLAlchemy model in Python does not automatically create a table in the database. There must be a controlled way to translate that model into an actual schema, and to evolve it over time. This is where migration becomes necessary. The goal of this section is not to explore migration theory in depth, but to make the current schema executable and manageable. By the end of this section, the application will be able to create its database tables, and track future schema changes in a controlled way.

Although Alembic can generate migration files automatically, they should not be treated as unquestionable output. A migration is executable database code. Before applying it, review the generated operations and verify that they match the intended schema change. This habit becomes increasingly important as applications grow, and schema changes become more complex.

The migration process follows a simple workflow. Each schema change begins in the SQLAlchemy model, and is translated into a migration file, reviewed, and only then applied to the database. *Figure 7.6* shows how the schema changes begin in the SQLAlchemy model, are converted into a migration file, reviewed for correctness, and then applied to the database:

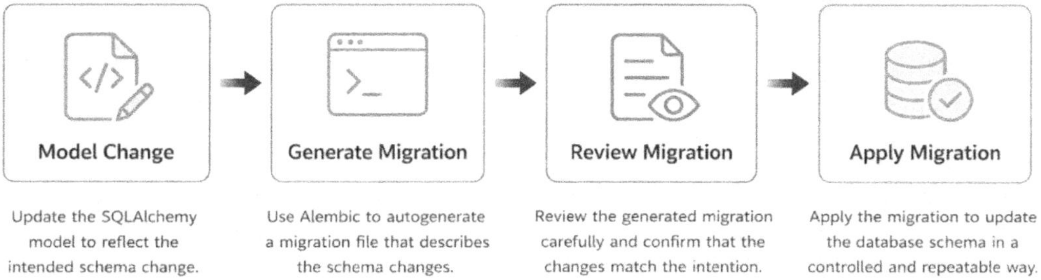

Figure 7.6: *Migration Workflow*

A focused prompt helps to guide this step toward a minimal and practical workflow.

Prompt

Explain how to set up Alembic migrations for this FastAPI project using the SQLAlchemy models that already exist. Keep the setup minimal.

A useful answer should converge on a small set of concrete steps that connect Alembic to the existing project without introducing unnecessary complexity. The first step is to initialize Alembic in the root of the project:

```
alembic init migrations
```

This command creates two things:

- a **`migrations/`** directory, which will contain migration files
- a configuration file named **`alembic.ini`**

At this point, Alembic is installed, but it does not yet know how to connect to the database or how to find the application's models.

The next step is to configure the database connection. Open **`alembic.ini`**, and update the database URL so that it matches the one used by the application:

```
sqlalchemy.url = sqlite:///./products.db
```

This ensures that Alembic and the FastAPI application are operating on the same database file. Next, Alembic needs access to the metadata that describes the

SQLAlchemy models. That metadata is defined in **Base.metadata** inside **app/db/models.py**. Open the file migrations/env.py, and import the Base object:

```
from app.db.models import Base
```

Then assign it to Alembic's **target_metadata**:

```
target_metadata = Base.metadata
```

This step is essential. It allows Alembic to compare the current database schema with the models defined in the code. Without it, Alembic would not know what changes to generate. At this point, Alembic is fully connected to the project. It knows where the database is, and how to read the model definitions. The first migration can now be generated:

```
alembic revision --autogenerate -m "create products table"
```

The **--autogenerate** flag tells Alembic to inspect the models and compare them with the current database state. Since the database is still empty, it will generate a migration that creates the products table. A new file will appear inside **migrations/versions/**. This file contains Python code describing the schema change, typically including a **CREATE TABLE** operation corresponding to the Product model.

Before applying the migration, inspect the generated file, and verify that the operations match the intended schema change. Autogeneration is a useful starting point, but generated migrations should always be reviewed before execution.

However, the migration has not been applied yet. To execute it, and create the table in the database, run:

```
alembic upgrade head
```

This command applies the latest migration, and updates the database schema. At this point, the database becomes concrete. If the **products.db** file did not exist before, it will be created. Inside it, a products table now exists, matching the structure defined in the SQLAlchemy model. This is a good moment to perform a simple practical check. After running the migration, start the API and create a product through Swagger UI. If everything is configured correctly, the request will succeed, and the data will be stored in the database, rather than in memory. Even without inspecting the database file directly, this confirms that the schema is now executable, and aligned with the application code. The key outcome of this step is that the database schema is now versioned. Until now, the Product model existed only in Python code. After applying the migration, the database itself reflects that model. More importantly, the change is recorded as a migration, which means it can be tracked, reapplied, and evolved over time.

A final prompt helps to clarify why this matters in practice.

Prompt

In this FastAPI Products API, what practical problem does Alembic solve once the Product database model already exists? Focus on execution and schema changes.

A strong answer should point out that defining a model in Python is not enough to create or update the database schema in a controlled way. Alembic fills that gap by turning schema changes into explicit, versioned steps that can be applied safely.

This becomes essential as soon as the API stores the real data. Tables can no longer be recreated freely, and changes must be applied without losing the existing records. Migrations provide that control. At this stage, the Products API now has everything required for persistence, such as: models, sessions, CRUD logic, router integration, and a migration workflow. The next step is to verify that this new setup produces a visible behavioral difference: product data should now survive server restarts, and behave like real persistent records, rather than temporary in-memory objects.

Verifying the Database-Backed API

At this stage of the chapter, the Products API has undergone a significant internal transformation. The service layer now performs database operations, the router provides a database session for each request, and the database schema is managed through migrations. However, as in previous chapters, new functionality should not be assumed to work. It must be verified through observable behavior. The guiding principle remains the same: verification happens at the API boundary. The goal is not to inspect internal database files or SQLAlchemy logs, but to understand what a client can actually observe when interacting with the API.

Figure 7.7 shows how a product is created through the API, stored in the database, and remains available after the server restarts. The observable behavior confirms that data is no longer tied to the lifetime of the application process.

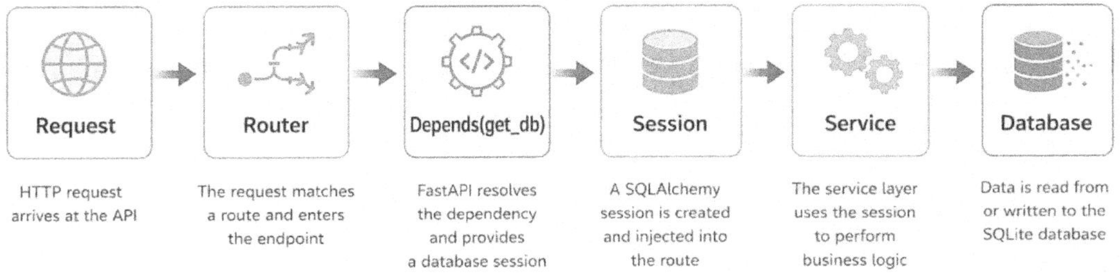

Figure 7.7: *Persistence Verification Workflow*

A focused prompt helps to make that perspective explicit.

Prompt

List the observable behaviors that confirm this FastAPI Products API is now backed by a persistent database instead of in-memory storage. Focus on what a client can observe.

A strong answer should immediately focus on one key idea: persistence becomes visible through time. In earlier chapters, product data existed only in memory. As soon as the server stopped, all data was lost. If persistence is now working correctly, that behavior must change.

Start the application, and create a product through Swagger UI:

POST /products

```
{
  "name": "Keyboard",
  "description": "Compact keyboard",
  "price": 49.99
}
```

The API should return a structured response with an assigned identifier:

```
{
  "id": 1,
  "name": "Keyboard",
  "description": "Compact keyboard",
  "price": 49.99
}
```

At this point, everything still looks exactly like before. The request works, and the response looks familiar. Nothing yet proves that persistence is in place. The difference appears when time is introduced into the workflow. Stop the server. Then start it again. Once the application is running again, call:

```
GET /products
```

If the API is truly backed by a database, the previously created product will still be present in the response. This is the most important verification in the entire chapter. It demonstrates that product data is no longer tied to the lifetime of the application process. Instead, it is stored in a persistent system that survives restarts. Once this behavior is confirmed, the rest of the verification becomes straightforward. The CRUD operations should behave exactly as before, even though their implementation has changed.

Retrieve the product:

```
GET /products/1
```

Update it:

```
PUT /products/1
{
  "name": "Mechanical Keyboard",
  "description": "Compact mechanical keyboard",
  "price": 79.99
}
```

Request it again, and confirm that the updated values are returned.

Delete it:

```
DELETE /products/1
```

Then try to retrieve it again:

```
{
  "detail": "Product 1 not found"
}
```

These checks confirm that all CRUD operations are now performed against persistent records, rather than temporary in-memory structures. At this point, it is also useful to verify that the database schema is under migration control. Run:

```
alembic history
```

and confirm that the migration responsible for creating the products table appears in the list. Then run:

```
alembic current
```

to verify that the database is at the latest revision.

This second verification does not affect client-visible behavior directly, but it confirms that the schema is managed in a controlled and versioned way.

Finally, inspect the API itself through Swagger UI. The same endpoints should still be present:

- **`POST /products`**
- **`GET /products`**
- **`GET /products/{product_id}`**
- **`PUT /products/{product_id}`**
- **`DELETE /products/{product_id}`**

The request bodies, response models, and status codes remain unchanged. This is an important observation. The internal storage mechanism of the API has changed completely, but the external contract exposed to clients has remained stable. Clients interact with the same API, in the same way, without needing to know whether the data is stored in memory or in a database. The only difference is that the system now behaves like a real data-driven application. It remembers what it stores, survives restarts, and manages its data consistently over time. At this point, the Products API is no longer a temporary simulation. It has become a persistent system with a stable and verifiable behavior.

Using AI to Review Data Access Logic

At this point in the chapter, the Products API has become a fully persistent system. The service layer operates on database records, the router provides database sessions, and the schema is managed through migrations. The application works, and its behavior has already been verified from the client's perspective. This is exactly the moment where AI should be used differently. So far, prompts were used primarily to generate code, such as: models, database configuration, CRUD functions, and migrations. But once the system is working, the most valuable use of AI is no longer generation. It is review. This shift is important. Using AI only to generate code risks turning it into a code producer. Using it for review turns it into a second pair of eyes. The goal is no longer to add features, but to improve clarity, while preserving behavior.

When reviewing the working code, AI should prioritize readability and correctness before optimization. Performance improvements are meaningful only after the code is understandable, and the behavior is known to be correct.

At this stage, the objective is very specific: check whether the current CRUD logic is readable, consistent, and appropriate for the scale of the project—without introducing new layers or abstractions.

A well-constrained prompt makes that intention explicit.

Prompt

Review the database CRUD logic for this FastAPI Products API. Suggest improvements only if they simplify the code without adding architectural complexity.

The wording matters. Without constraints, the assistant may suggest patterns that are unnecessary at this stage, such as repositories, generic abstractions, or additional layers. The goal here is not to redesign the data layer, but to make small, focused improvements.

A useful review might notice that:

- Query patterns are repeated across functions.
- Return types are not explicitly defined.
- Some functions could reuse the existing logic for clarity.

At this point, it is helpful to look again at the current service layer:

```
 # app/services/product_service.py

from sqlalchemy.orm import Session
from app.db.models import Product as ProductDB
from app.models import ProductCreate

def create_product(db: Session, data: ProductCreate) -> ProductDB:
    product = ProductDB(name=data.name, description=data.description,
price=data.price)
    db.add(product)
    db.commit()
```

```
    db.refresh(product)
    return product

def get_product(db: Session, product_id: int):
    return db.query(ProductDB).filter(ProductDB.id == product_id).first()

def list_products(db: Session):
    return db.query(ProductDB).all()

def update_product(db: Session, product_id: int, data: ProductCreate):
    product = db.query(ProductDB).filter(ProductDB.id == product_id).
first()
    if product is None:
        return None

    product.name = data.name
    product.description = data.description
    product.price = data.price

    db.commit()
    db.refresh(product)
    return product

def delete_product(db: Session, product_id: int) -> bool:
    product = db.query(ProductDB).filter(ProductDB.id == product_id).
first()
    if product is None:
        return False

    db.delete(product)
    db.commit()
    return True
```

A second, more focused prompt helps to refine the result:

Prompt

Keep the current service-layer structure.

Suggest only small improvements to readability or consistency in the CRUD functions.

Do not introduce new architectural layers.

A minimal revised version might look like this:

```
# app/services/product_service.py

from typing import List, Optional
from sqlalchemy.orm import Session
from app.db.models import Product as ProductDB
```

```
from app.models import ProductCreate

def create_product(db: Session, data: ProductCreate) -> ProductDB:
    product = ProductDB(name=data.name, description=data.description,
price=data.price)
    db.add(product)
    db.commit()
    db.refresh(product)
    return product

def get_product(db: Session, product_id: int) -> Optional[ProductDB]:
    return db.query(ProductDB).filter(ProductDB.id == product_id).first()

def list_products(db: Session) -> List[ProductDB]:
    return db.query(ProductDB).all()

def update_product(db: Session, product_id: int, data: ProductCreate) ->
Optional[ProductDB]:
    product = get_product(db, product_id)
    if product is None:
        return None

    product.name = data.name
    product.description = data.description
    product.price = data.price
    db.commit()
    db.refresh(product)
    return product

def delete_product(db: Session, product_id: int) -> bool:
    product = get_product(db, product_id)
    if product is None:
        return False

    db.delete(product)
    db.commit()
    return True
```

Notice that **`update_product()`** and **`delete_product()`** now reuse **`get_product()`**, instead of repeating the same query. This improves readability, and keeps lookup behavior in a single location. **Avoid duplicating query logic when helper functions already exist.** Centralizing common operations reduces repetition, and makes future changes easier to maintain.

The changes are intentionally small:

- explicit type hints improve readability
- **`get_product`** is reused to avoid duplication

- the overall structure remains unchanged

Most importantly, nothing about the observable behavior of the API changes. This is a good moment for a quick practical check.

Start the server, and repeat a simple workflow:

- create a product
- retrieve it
- update it
- delete it

All operations should behave exactly as before. The responses, status codes, and data structures remain identical. This confirms the key idea of the section: the code has been improved without changing the API contract. This is what responsible AI-assisted development looks like at this stage. The assistant is not used to introduce new abstractions, but to highlight small improvements. The developer remains in control, deciding which suggestions are appropriate and which would introduce unnecessary complexity. The result is a system that becomes slightly clearer and more consistent, while preserving the structure and behavior established earlier in the chapter. The next step is to freeze this version of the application as the new baseline for future work.

Freezing the Data-Driven Version as the New Baseline

At the end of this chapter, the Products API reaches a new stage in its evolution. In earlier chapters, the application behaved like a temporary system. Product data existed only while the server was running because it was stored in memory. Restarting the application meant losing everything. This limitation is now gone. The API has transitioned from simulated storage to real persistence. Product data is stored in a database, CRUD operations work on persistent records, and the schema is managed through migrations. Internally, the system has changed significantly. Externally, however, nothing has changed. The API contract remains exactly the same. This is the key result of the chapter. Clients still interact with the same endpoints, send the same requests, and receive the same responses. The difference is no longer visible in the interface, but in the behavior of the system over time. The API now remembers. As in *Chapter 5 - Structuring an API Project with AI Guidance* and *Chapter 6, Handling Concurrency and Real-Time Workflows*, this chapter concludes by freezing the current architecture as the new baseline. Freezing does not mean that development stops. It means that this version becomes the stable reference point for everything that follows. The project structure now includes a persistence layer alongside the components introduced earlier:

```
app/
    main.py
    models.py
    routers/
        products.py
    services/
        product_service.py
    db/
        database.py
        models.py
migrations/
```

The directory structure shows where responsibilities are located. *Figure* 7.8 summarizes how those responsibilities now interact at runtime. The architecture remains simple, that is requests enter through the router, business operations are handled by the service layer, database access is provided through a session, and data is stored persistently in SQLite.

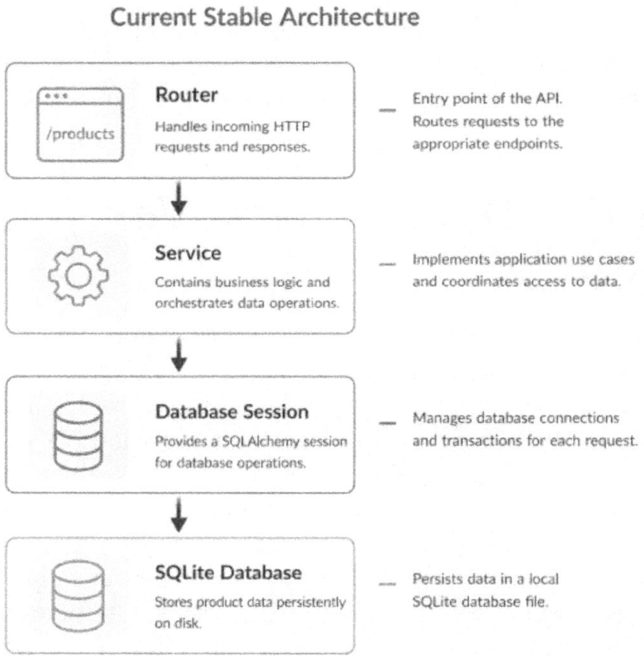

Figure 7.8: *Stable Architecture after Introducing Persistence*

Each part of the system now has a clear role. The router still defines the HTTP boundary, and handles request/response behavior. The service layer still owns product-related operations. The database layer now owns persistence, including how data is stored and retrieved. The migrations directory ensures that the database schema evolves in a controlled and repeatable way. What has changed is not the structure, but what each layer is responsible for. This structure introduces persistence without increasing architectural complexity. The system is still simple, but it is no longer temporary. Data survives restarts, operations interact with real records, and the application can evolve safely over time. Most importantly, the boundary of the system remains stable. This is a recurring principle throughout the book, such as: internal implementation can change, but the API contract should remain consistent. Clients should not need to know whether data is stored in memory, in a database, or elsewhere. They interact with the same interface. To consolidate this transition, the final step is to reflect on what changed.

Prompt

Summarize how this FastAPI Products API evolved from an in-memory service to a persistent database-backed system. Focus on behavior and architecture.

A useful summary highlights a clear progression. The application started with in-memory storage managed directly by the service layer. The introduction of SQLAlchemy models allowed data to be represented as persistent records. The router was then connected to a database session, enabling real database operations. Finally, migrations were added to manage schema changes over time. Throughout this evolution, the external API remained stable, while the internal behavior became more reliable and durable. At this point, the Products API is no longer a temporary example. It is a real data-driven system. This version now serves as the foundation for the next chapters, where new features will build on top of persistent storage, rather than transient state.

Conclusion

In this chapter, the Products API evolved from a temporary in-memory system into a persistent, data-driven application. Product data is now stored in a database, CRUD operations interact with real records, and migrations manage schema changes over time. Despite these internal changes, the API contract remained unchanged. The same endpoints, responses, and validation rules still define the boundary of the system. This chapter shows how new capabilities can be added without disrupting the external behavior of an API.

With persistence now in place, the Products API has become a stable foundation for future development. Data survives application restarts, the schema can evolve in a controlled way, and the system behaves like a real application, rather than a temporary runtime process. However, one important question remains unanswered: who is allowed to access that data? Up to this point, any client can call any endpoint as long as the request is valid.

In the next chapter, the focus shifts from persistence to control. The API will begin to recognize identity, enforce permissions, and respond differently depending on who is making the request. The system will not simply store data—it will start deciding who is allowed to use it.

Points to Remember

- Persistence solves an observable limitation: data survives server restarts.
- Adding a database should not change the API contract.
- The router handles HTTP behavior; the service layer handles data operations.
- SQLAlchemy models map API entities to database tables.
- CRUD logic should stay simple and readable.
- Database sessions separate persistence concerns from routing logic.
- Alembic manages schema creation and evolution through migrations.
- AI should review code for clarity and correctness, not just generate it.
- Persistence is verified through observable behavior, that is data remains available even after restart.

Multiple Choice Questions

1. What is the main objective of this chapter?
    a. To redesign the API routing system
    b. To introduce persistent storage using a database
    c. To replace FastAPI with another framework
    d. To implement advanced SQL queries
2. Why is persistence introduced in this chapter?
    a. Because every API must always use a database
    b. Because product data disappears when the server stops
    c. Because SQLAlchemy requires **`itd`**
    d. Because Swagger UI needs a database
3. What is the role of the SQLAlchemy Product model in this chapter?
    a. To replace the API schema used by FastAPI
    b. To translate the Product entity into a database table
    c. To generate Swagger documentation
    d. To manage HTTP routing
4. What is the purpose of the database session dependency in FastAPI routes?
    a. To automatically generate database tables
    b. To provide each request with access to the database connection

   c. To validate incoming request data
   d. To replace the service layer

5. Why are CRUD operations implemented in the service layer, rather than directly in the router?
   a. Because routers cannot access databases
   b. Because the service layer owns domain operations, while the router handles HTTP behavior
   c. Because SQLAlchemy requires a separate module
   d. Because Swagger UI depends on the service layer

6. What practical problem does Alembic solve in this chapter?
   a. It improves API performance.
   b. It replaces SQLAlchemy models.
   c. It manages database schema changes through versioned migrations.
   d. It generates API documentation.

7. After persistence is introduced, what observable behavior should change?
   a. Swagger documentation becomes different.
   b. Endpoints change their URLs.
   c. Product data remains available after the server restarts.
   d. The API returns different response structures.

8. What should remain unchanged after the API becomes database-backed?
   a. The internal implementation of the service layer.
   b. The database schema.
   c. The external API contract exposed to clients.
   d. The SQLAlchemy model definitions.

9. Which chapter feature made this possible?
   a. Swagger
   b. SQLAlchemy persistence
   c. Background tasks
   d. Streaming responses

Answers

1. b
2. b
3. b
4. b
5. b
6. c
7. c
8. c
9. b

Questions

1. Why does storing product data only in memory create limitations for a real API, and how does persistence change the behavior of the system?
2. How does introducing a database improve the reliability of the Products API without changing its external endpoints?
3. What role do SQLAlchemy models play in translating API entities into database tables?
4. Why is it important to keep database logic inside the service layer, rather than directly inside the router?
5. How does the database session dependency allow FastAPI routes to interact safely with the database?
6. Why are migrations necessary, once a database schema exists, and what problems could occur if schema changes were applied manually?
7. How does verifying API behavior after introducing persistence confirm that the external API contract has remained stable?
8. In what ways can AI assist with generating database models and CRUD logic, while still requiring human judgment to maintain architectural clarity?

Key Terms

- **Persistence:** The ability of an application to store data in a durable system (such as a database) so that it remains available even after the server restarts.
- **Database Model:** A representation of an application entity as a database table, typically defined using an ORM such as SQLAlchemy.

- **ORM (Object-Relational Mapping):** A programming technique that allows developers to interact with a relational database using objects and classes, instead of writing raw SQL queries.
- **SQLAlchemy:** A Python library used in this chapter to define database models, and perform database operations through an ORM interface.
- **Database Session:** A SQLAlchemy object that manages communication with the database during a request, handling queries, transactions, and persistence operations.
- **CRUD Operations:** The four basic database operations: Create, Read, Update, and Delete, which correspond to the core actions performed on persistent data.
- **Migration:** A versioned change to the database schema that allows tables and structures to evolve safely as the application grows.
- **Alembic:** A migration tool used with SQLAlchemy to generate, track, and apply database schema changes.
- **Schema Evolution:** The process of modifying a database structure over time, while preserving the existing data, and maintaining compatibility with the application.
- **Database-Backed API:** An API whose data is stored in a persistent database, rather than temporary in-memory structures, allowing information to survive server restarts.
- **Prompt-Driven Generation:** The use of AI prompts to generate implementation code, such as database models or CRUD logic, which is then reviewed and integrated into the application.
- **Persistent Architecture:** An application structure in which routing, service logic, and database layers collaborate to provide stable data storage, while maintaining a consistent API boundary.

CHAPTER 8
Securing an API System

Introduction

Up to this point, the API has grown in structure, behavior, and capability. It is modular, it handles different execution patterns, and it persists data reliably. From a functional perspective, it works. But there is a fundamental question that has not yet been addressed: *who is allowed to use it?*

So far, every request has been accepted as long as it was valid. The system processes input correctly, but it does not question the origin of that input. It does not distinguish between different clients, and it does not restrict access to any operation. This is not a limitation of implementation. It is a limitation of behavior. Real APIs do not operate in open environments. They must recognize who is making a request, and decide what that request is allowed to do.

Consider a simple e-commerce API. Any customer should be able to browse products, but only administrators should be allowed to delete them. The API must therefore answer two different questions: Who is making the request? And what is that user allowed to do? Authentication answers the first question. Authorization answers the second.

Without this capability, even a well-structured and persistent system remains exposed. This chapter introduces that missing dimension. Instead of starting with security theory, we begin with observable behavior. What should happen when a request arrives without identity? What should change when different users interact with the same endpoint? When should an operation be allowed, and when should it be rejected? These questions define the need for authentication and authorization.

As in previous chapters, the goal is not to build a complete security system, but to introduce minimal, runnable mechanisms that make these behaviors visible and testable. Identity will be added to requests, permissions will be enforced on specific operations, and the system will begin to respond differently depending on who is interacting with it. Throughout the process, AI will be used not only to generate authentication flows, but also to analyze and challenge their correctness. This dual role is essential, because security is not something that can be assumed—it must be verified. By the end of the chapter, the API will no longer be open. It will enforce identity, restrict access where necessary, and still preserve the same structure and external contract. The system will not become more complex. It will become more controlled.

Structure

In this chapter, we will discuss the following topics:

- The Next Limitation: Open Access without Identity
- Introducing Authentication as a Behavioral Requirement
- Generating a Minimal Auth Flow with AI
- Adding User Identity to the System
- Protecting Routes with Authentication
- Introducing Authorization: Not All Users are Equal
- Securing Product Operations
- Observing What Changed at the API Boundary
- Using AI to Detect Security Weaknesses
- Verifying the Secured API Behavior
- Freezing the Secured Version as the New Baseline

The Next Limitation: Open Access without Identity

At the end of *Chapter 7, Building Data-Driven* APIs, the Products API reached an important milestone. It is now persistent. Data is stored in a database, CRUD operations are stable, and the application behaves like a real system, rather than a temporary example. But a new limitation becomes immediately visible—one that is not technical, but behavioral. Anyone can do anything. There is no concept of identity in the system. No user. No login. No distinction between different clients. Every endpoint is publicly accessible, and every operation can be performed by anyone who knows the URL. This is not a theoretical issue. It is directly observable.

Run the API and open Swagger UI. Try the following:

- Create a product
- Update
- Delete

Every operation succeeds without any form of verification. There is no question asked about who is making the request. At this point, the system behaves correctly, but not safely. This is the exact moment where security is introduced in this book—not because APIs "should be secure," but because the current behavior is incomplete. The API has no way to distinguish between legitimate and illegitimate actions. To make this explicit, we turn the observation into a prompt.

Prompt

In this FastAPI Products API, what are the risks of having no authentication?

Focus on observable behavior and potential misuse.

A useful answer should not talk about abstract security principles. It should describe concrete consequences of the current system. It should highlight that any client can create unlimited products, modify or delete the existing ones, and manipulate the entire dataset without restriction. There is no way to associate actions with a specific user, no way to limit operations, and no way to prevent abuse. The API cannot answer a fundamental question: who is making this request?

This leads to a critical insight. The problem is not that the API lacks a specific technology like JWT or OAuth. The problem is that the system has no concept of identity. Without identity, there is no control. Without control, there is no security.

This is the same pattern used in previous chapters.

- In *Chapter 6, Handling Concurrency and Real-Time Workflows*, concurrency was introduced because some operations required different timing behavior.
- In *Chapter 7, Building Data-Driven* APIs, persistence was introduced because data disappeared after restart.
- In this chapter, authentication is introduced because actions cannot be attributed to a user.

Security, therefore, is not an addition. It is a response to a missing behavior. At this stage, the goal is not to fix the problem immediately, but to define it clearly. The API needs a way to recognize who is making a request, and to use that information to control access to its operations. The next step is to turn this requirement into something concrete: how can this API introduce identity in a minimal, runnable, and observable way?

Introducing Authentication as a Behavioral Requirement

Once the limitation is clear, the next step is not to choose a technology, but to define the missing behavior. Right now, the API processes every request in the same way, regardless of who is sending it. There is no distinction between a legitimate client and an unknown one, because the system does not ask for identity, and therefore, cannot enforce any rule based on it. This leads to a simple and concrete question:

What should happen before a request is allowed to access or modify data?

At this stage, the answer is not "implement JWT" or "add OAuth." Those are technical solutions. What we need first is a behavioral requirement. The API must be able to recognize who is making the request, and associate that identity with the request itself. This is, in practice, what authentication means. *Table* 8.1 shows that authentication establishes identity, and the authorization uses that identity to decide whether an operation should be allowed.

Concept	Question
Authentication	Who is making the request?
Authorization	What is this user allowed to do?

Table 8.1: *Identity vs Permission*

Figure 8.1 illustrates the first step in the security workflow. Before the API can enforce permissions, it must first establish identity.

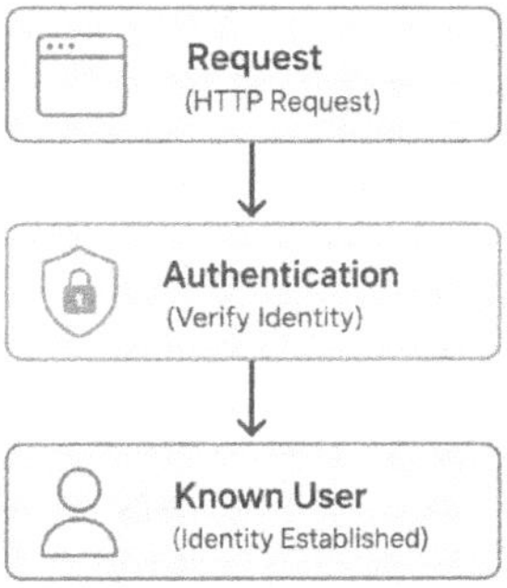

Figure 8.1: *Authentication Establishes Identity. Before the API Can Make Permission Decisions, It Must Associate the Incoming Request with a Known User*

To clarify this requirement, we turn it into a prompt.

Prompt

In this FastAPI Products API, how can the system recognize who is making a request?

Describe a simple and practical authentication approach suitable for this project.

Avoid advanced configurations and keep it runnable.

A useful answer will usually describe a simple flow: the client sends credentials such as a username and password, the API validates them, and if they are correct, it returns a token. That token is then included in future requests, allowing the API to identify the user without asking for credentials every time. What matters here is not the specific format of the token, but the flow itself. The API moves from "any request is accepted" to "requests must carry identity." This introduces a new observable behavior: some requests will now fail. If a client tries to access a protected endpoint without providing identity, the API should reject the request. This is a fundamental shift. The API is no longer purely functional; it becomes conditional.

At this point, it is important to notice what does not change. The endpoints remain the same, the request and response models remain the same, and the database layer is untouched. What changes is the condition under which those endpoints can be executed. This is consistent with the method used throughout the book. We are not redesigning the system but introducing a new constraint at the boundary.

Figure 8.2 illustrates this transition: on one side, an open API that accepts every request without distinction; on the other, an identity-aware API where each request must carry credentials, and is validated before the access is granted.

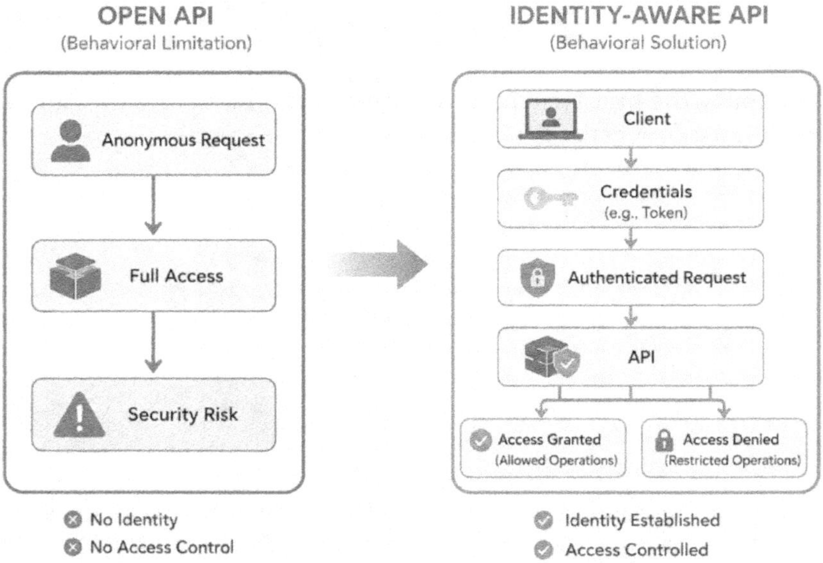

Figure 8.2: *From Open API to Identity-aware Requests*

Requests are no longer accepted blindly. Each request must now carry identity information that the API can validate before executing any operation. The system is now ready for its next step. The requirement is clear: requests must carry identity. The next question becomes practical:

How do we implement this behavior in the simplest possible way, using the current structure of the project?

That is where the first authentication flow will be generated.

Generating a Minimal Auth Flow with AI

Now that the requirement is clear, the next step is to turn it into something executable. We do not start by designing a full authentication system. We do not introduce external providers, password hashing strategies, or complex token validation. At this stage, the goal is much narrower: introduce identity into the request flow in the simplest possible way. This is consistent with the method used throughout the book. We are not building a production-ready security system, but a minimal, runnable authentication flow that allows us to observe how identity affects behavior. We start by asking the AI for a concrete implementation.

Prompt

Generate a minimal authentication flow for this FastAPI Products API.

Include:

- a login endpoint

- a simple token-based mechanism

- a dependency to retrieve the current user from the request

Keep everything simple, runnable, and compatible with the current project structure. Do not use external services. A useful answer should produce three essential elements: a login endpoint that returns a token, a simple way to represent users, and a mechanism to extract the user from incoming requests. At this stage, users are intentionally kept simple. No database integration is required. A minimal in-memory user store is enough to make the flow observable.

Create a new file **app/services/auth_service.py** and add the following implementation:

```
# app/services/auth_service.py

from typing import Optional

# simple in-memory users
fake_users_db = {
    "alice": {"username": "alice", "password": "password123"},
    "bob": {"username": "bob", "password": "secret"},
}

def authenticate_user(username: str, password: str) -> Optional[dict]:
    user = fake_users_db.get(username)
    if not user or user["password"] != password:
        return None
    return user

def create_token(user: dict) -> str:
```

```
    # Educational example only.
    # This token format is intentionally insecure and
    # should never be used in production.
    return f"token-{user[‹username›]}"

def get_user_from_token(token: str) -> Optional[dict]:
    if not token.startswith("token-"):
        return None
    username = token.replace("token-", "")
    return fake_users_db.get(username)
```

Now, we expose this behavior through the API by adding a login endpoint. The token implementation in this example is intentionally simplified. It does not provide encryption, signing, expiration, or tamper protection. Its purpose is only to make the authentication flow visible and easy to understand. This token format is intentionally insecure, and exists only to demonstrate authentication flow concepts. It should never be used in production systems.

Open **app/routers/products.py** and add:

```
from fastapi import APIRouter, HTTPException, status
from pydantic import BaseModel
from app.services import auth_service

router = APIRouter()

class LoginRequest(BaseModel):
    username: str
    password: str

class TokenResponse(BaseModel):
    access_token: str

@router.post("/login")
def login(data: LoginRequest) -> TokenResponse:
    user = auth_service.authenticate_user(data.username, data.password)
    if user is None:
        raise HTTPException(
            status_code=status.HTTP_401_UNAUTHORIZED,
            detail="Invalid credentials",
        )

    token = auth_service.create_token(user)
    return { "access_token": token}
```

LoginRequest represents credential input sent by the client during authentication. It is not a persistent user record and is not stored in the database. Its only purpose is to capture the username and password supplied to the login endpoint.

At this point, run the application, and interact with the new endpoint through Swagger UI or a client. You can send a request to **`/login`** with valid credentials:

```
{
  "username": "alice",
  "password": "password123"
}
```

If the credentials are correct, the API responds with:

```
{
  "access_token": "token-alice"
}
```

This is the first moment in which the API produces identity. Nothing else has changed yet. All product endpoints are still accessible without restriction. The token is generated, but it is not enforced. This is intentional. We are building the authentication flow incrementally. First, the system learns how to create identity. Only later will that identity be attached to the incoming requests, and used to control access.

Figure 8.3 visualizes this initial authentication step: a client submits credentials to the login endpoint, receives a token, and begins using that token as a representation of identity in subsequent interactions with the API.

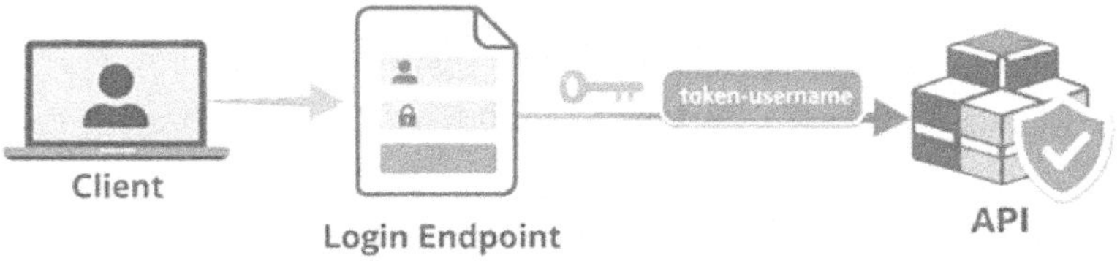

***Figure* 8.3**: *Minimal Authentication Flow Introduced in the API*

A client sends credentials to the login endpoint, receives a token, and uses that token to represent identity in subsequent requests. At this stage, the system can answer a new question:

Who are you?

But it still does not use that answer. The next step is to connect identity to incoming requests, and make it influence how endpoints behave.

Adding User Identity to the System

At this point, the API can generate identity, but it does not yet use it. A client can call /login, receive a token, and then nothing changes. All product endpoints still behave exactly as before. The system can answer the question "who are you?", but it does not use that information to influence any request. This is the next gap to close. The objective now is to attach the identity to incoming requests so that the API can recognize the current user during execution. We are not introducing authorization yet, and we are not restricting actions. We are only making identity available inside the request lifecycle. In FastAPI, this is achieved through a dependency. We express this need as a prompt.

Prompt

In this FastAPI Products API, implement a dependency that extracts the current user from a token passed in the request headers.

Keep it simple and compatible with the existing auth_service.

A useful answer should describe a minimal flow in which the client sends the token as part of the request, the API extracts it, resolves the corresponding user, and rejects the request if the token is invalid. We now implement this behavior inside the authentication service.

Open **`app/services/auth_service.py`** and add:

```
from fastapi import Header, HTTPException, status
from typing import Optional

def get_current_user(authorization: Optional[str] = Header(None)):
    if authorization is None:
        raise HTTPException(
            status_code=status.HTTP_401_UNAUTHORIZED,
            detail="Missing Authorization header",
        )

    # expected format: "Bearer token-username"
    if not authorization.startswith("Bearer "):
        raise HTTPException(
            status_code=status.HTTP_401_UNAUTHORIZED,
            detail="Invalid Authorization format",
        )

    token = authorization .split(" ", 1)[1]
    user = get_user_from_token(token)

    if user is None:
        raise HTTPException(
            status_code=status.HTTP_401_UNAUTHORIZED,
            detail="Invalid token",
        )

    return user
```

The authorization parameter is declared using **`Header(),`** which tells FastAPI to read the value from the incoming HTTP Authorization header. FastAPI automatically extracts the header, and injects it into the dependency function, just as it injects query parameters or request bodies into route functions.

This means the router does not need to read headers manually. Any route that depends on **`get_current_user()`** automatically receives authentication behavior through FastAPI's dependency system.

This function reads the Authorization header, extracts the token, and resolves the user. FastAPI automatically injects the Authorization header into the dependency through the **`Header()`** parameter. If any step fails, the request is rejected with a 401 Unauthorized response. At this stage, it is useful to observe how client behavior changes. A request is no longer just a path and method; it can now include identity information:

```
GET /products
Authorization: Bearer token-alice
```

After obtaining a token through the /login endpoint, you can verify the API behavior directly from the command line.

Linux / macOS

```
curl -X GET \
  "http://127.0.0.1:8000/products" \
  -H "Authorization: Bearer token-alice"
```

Windows (PowerShell)

```
curl.exe -X GET "http://127.0.0.1:8000/products" `
  -H "Authorization: Bearer token-alice"
```

A **`200 OK`** response confirms that the token is being transmitted correctly, and that authentication succeeded. A **`401 Unauthorized`** response indicates that the Authorization header is missing, malformed, or contains an invalid token.

The token is no longer just a value returned by **`/login`**. It becomes part of the request itself. *Figure* 8.4 illustrates this shift: identity is now carried within each request through the Authorization header, allowing the API to resolve the current user before executing any endpoint logic.

***Figure* 8.4:** *Identity Attached to Incoming Requests through Headers*

Each request now carries a token in the Authorization header, allowing the API to resolve the current user before executing endpoint logic. However, nothing is protected yet. The dependency exists, but it is not used. Endpoints still do not require authentication. If you call **/products** without a token, the request still succeeds because the dependency is not enforced. This is intentional. The system is being built incrementally. First, identity is created through login. Then, it is attached to requests through a dependency. Only in the next step will that identity be enforced to control access. At this point, the API can finally answer a new question during request execution: *who is making this request?*

The next section is where behavior will actually change: identity will begin to affect which requests are allowed to proceed.

Protecting Routes with Authentication

At this point, the API can generate identity, and extract it from incoming requests. However, there is still no consequence if identity is missing. This is the moment where behavior actually changes. Until now, every endpoint was accessible, and identity was optional. From this point on, some endpoints will require identity, and requests without it will fail. This is the first real enforcement of authentication. The objective is simple: require a valid user before executing certain endpoints.

Figure 8.5 illustrates the new request flow. Before any protected endpoint can execute its logic, the authentication dependency must resolve the current user.

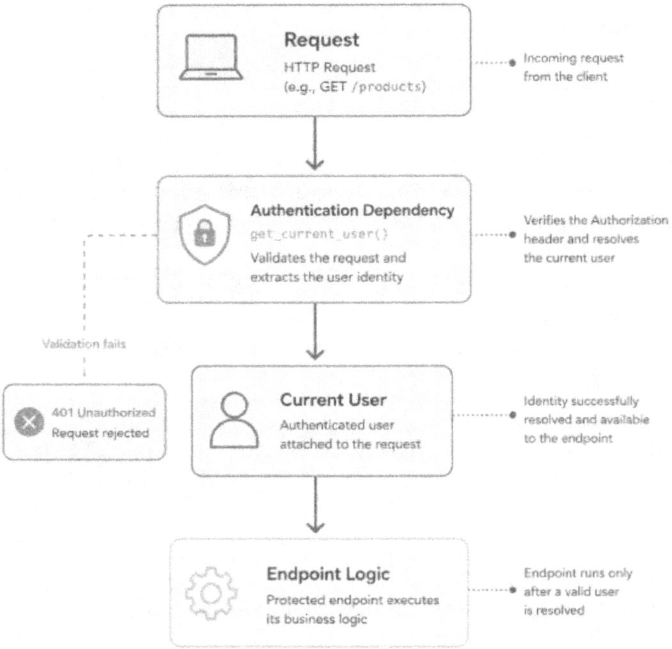

Figure 8.5: *Authentication Enforcement Flow*

We express this as a prompt.

Prompt

Protect the product endpoints in this FastAPI API so that only authenticated users can access them.

Use a dependency-based approach and keep the current structure.

A useful answer should not redesign the system. It should apply the dependency, we already created: **`get_current_user`**. This is how authentication becomes part of the request lifecycle.

Open **`app/routers/products.py`** and update the endpoints.

```
from fastapi import APIRouter, Depends, HTTPException, status
from typing import List
from sqlalchemy.orm import Session
from app.models import Product, ProductCreate
from app.services import product_service, auth_service
from app.db.database import get_db

router = APIRouter()

@router.post("/products", response_model=Product, status_code=status.
HTTP_201_CREATED)
def create_product(
    product: ProductCreate,
    db: Session = Depends(get_db),
    current_user: dict = Depends(auth_service.get_current_user),
) -> Product:
    return product_service.create_product(db, product)

@router.get("/products", response_model=List[Product])
def list_products(
    db: Session = Depends(get_db),
    current_user: dict = Depends(auth_service.get_current_user),
) -> List[Product]:
    return product_service.list_products()

@router.get("/products/{product_id}", response_model=Product)
def get_product(
    product_id: int,
    db: Session = Depends(get_db),
    current_user: dict = Depends(auth_service.get_current_user),
) -> Product:
    product = product_service.get_product(product_id)
    if product is None:
        raise HTTPException(
```

```
            status_code=status.HTTP_404_NOT_FOUND,
            detail=f"Product {product_id} not found",
        )
    return product

@router.put("/products/{product_id}",
             response_model=Product,
            status_code=status.HTTP_200_OK)
def update_product(
    product_id: int,
    updated: ProductCreate,
    db: Session = Depends(get_db),
    current_user: dict = Depends(auth_service.get_current_user),
) -> Product:
    product = product_service.update_product(db, product_id, updated)
    if product is None:
        raise HTTPException(
            status_code=status.HTTP_404_NOT_FOUND,
            detail=f"Product {product_id} not found",
        )
    return product

@router.delete("/products/{product_id}")
def delete_product(
    product_id: int,
    db: Session = Depends(get_db),
    current_user: dict = Depends(auth_service.get_current_user),
) -> dict:
    deleted = product_service.delete_product(db, product_id)
    if not deleted:
        raise HTTPException(
            status_code=status.HTTP_404_NOT_FOUND,
            detail=f"Product {product_id} not found",
        )
    return {"message": f"Product {product_id} deleted"}
```

At first glance, the change appears minimal. Each endpoint now includes a single additional parameter:

```
current_user: dict = Depends(auth_service.get_current_user)
```

This is dependency injection applied to security. Instead of validating identity inside every endpoint, the router declares a dependency on **`get_current_user()`.** FastAPI executes the authentication logic before the endpoint runs, and provides the resolved user automatically. If authentication fails, the endpoint is never executed.

This line does not modify the business logic. It does not affect the service layer, nor does it change the response models. What it changes is when the endpoint is allowed to execute. Before any endpoint logic runs, FastAPI resolves the dependency. The token is validated, the user is extracted, and if any of these steps fail, the request is rejected. The endpoint function is never executed. This introduces a new observable behavior.

Try calling **`/products`** without a token. The API responds with:

```
{
  "detail": "Missing Authorization header"
}
```

Or with an invalid token:

```
{
  "detail": "Invalid token"
}
```

Only when a valid token is provided, does the request succeed. *Figure* 8.6 illustrates this enforcement step: every request must pass through an authentication check, where valid tokens allow access to the API, while missing or invalid tokens are rejected before any endpoint logic is executed.

***Figure* 8.6:** *Authentication Enforced at the API Boundary*

Each request must now pass through an authentication check before reaching the endpoint logic, ensuring that only identified users can access the API. At this stage, the API is no longer open. It enforces a simple but strict rule:

```
no identity → no access
```

It is important to notice what did not change. The endpoints are the same, the request and response schemas are unchanged, the database logic is untouched, and Swagger still documents the same routes. Only the conditions of access have changed. This is consistent with the discipline established in previous chapters. The system is not being redesigned; a constraint is being introduced at the boundary. However, all authenticated users are still treated the same. A user can create, update, and delete products without restriction. The system now knows who is making the request, but it does not yet decide what they are allowed to do. That is the next step: introducing authorization.

Introducing Authorization: Not All Users are Equal

At this point, the API has crossed an important threshold. It is no longer open. Every request must include a valid identity, and the system can now answer the question: who is making this request? However, a new limitation immediately appears. All users are treated exactly the same. Any authenticated user can create products, update them, and even delete them without restriction. The system knows who you are, but it does not use that information to make decisions. This is where authorization enters the system.

- Authentication answers one question: *who are you?*
- Authorization answers a different one: *what are you allowed to do?*

This distinction becomes concrete as soon as we consider a simple scenario. Should every authenticated user be allowed to delete products? In most cases, the answer is "no". *Figure* 8.7 illustrates the basic idea behind Role-Based Access Control (RBAC). Identity alone is not enough. The system must associate users with roles and roles with permissions.

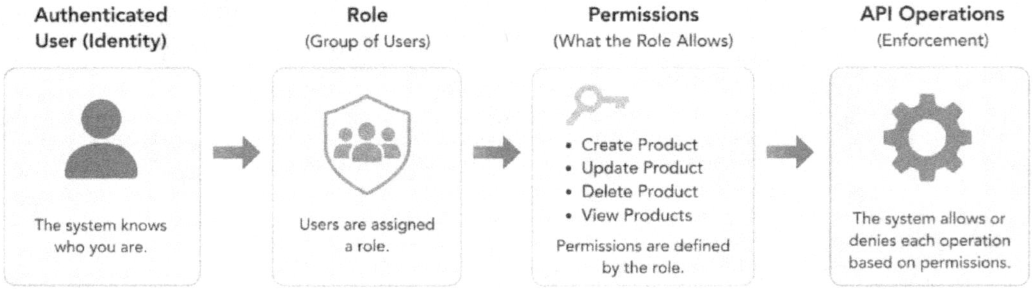

***Figure* 8.7:** *Role-Based Access Control (RBAC)*

Consider two authenticated users:

- **Alice** has the **`Admin`** role.
- **Bob** has the **`User`** role.

If both attempt to delete a product, the outcome is different. Alice is allowed to perform the operation because the Admin role includes the required permission. Bob is denied because the User role does not grant that permission.

The endpoint is the same. The request is the same. The difference is the role associated with the authenticated user.

This is the behavioral gap we now address. We turn it into a prompt.

Prompt

In this FastAPI Products API, how can I restrict some operations (like deleting products) to specific users while allowing others to access read operations?

Keep the solution simple and practical.

A useful answer should avoid introducing complex role systems or external identity providers. Instead, it should suggest a minimal approach in which each user is associated with a role, that role becomes part of the user representation, and endpoints use it to decide whether an operation is allowed. The key idea is simple: identity is not enough — identity must carry permissions.

We now extend the user model in the simplest possible way. Open **`app/services/auth_service.py`**, and update the in-memory user store:

```
fake_users_db = {
    "alice": {"username": "alice", "password": "password123", "role":
"user"},
    "bob": {"username": "bob", "password": "secret", "role": "admin"},
}
```

Nothing else changes. The login flow remains identical, the token format is unchanged, and the dependency still resolves the user in the same way. The only difference is that the user now carries an additional attribute: role. This small change enables a completely new behavior. The API can now make decisions based not only on identity, but on the attributes associated with that identity. *Figure* 8.8 illustrates this transition: requests are no longer treated equally, but are evaluated based on the user's role, allowing the system to differentiate between standard users and administrators when deciding which operations are allowed.

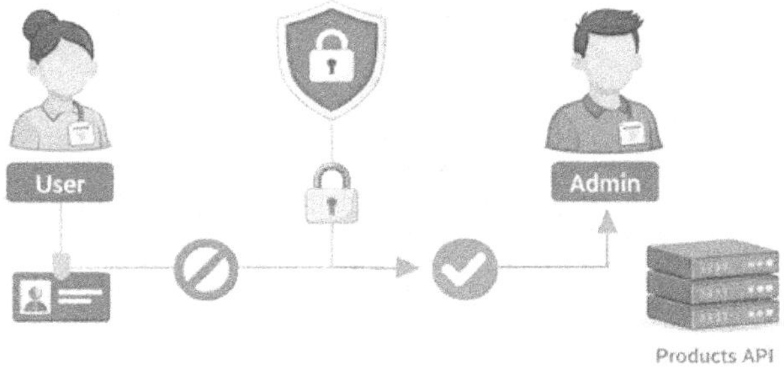

Figure 8.8: *From Identity to Permission-based Access*

Requests are no longer only authenticated; they now carry role information that allows the API to differentiate between users, and enforce different levels of access. At this stage, the system has all the information required to enforce authorization, but it is not yet doing so. The progression followed so far remains consistent. First, identity was introduced, then it was enforced, and now it has been enriched with additional meaning. The next step is where behavior changes again, that is using this information to restrict specific operations, such as allowing only admin users to delete products.

Securing Product Operations

At this point, the system has everything it needs to enforce authorization. Identity is present, it is required for every request, and it now includes a role. However, nothing is restricted yet.

All authenticated users can still perform all operations. The system knows the user's role, but it does not use it to influence behavior.

This is where authorization becomes observable.

The objective is simple: restrict specific operations based on user role.

We do not redesign the API, and we do not introduce a complex permission system. Instead, we apply a minimal and verifiable rule, such as: all authenticated users can read and create products, but only admin users can delete them.

We express this requirement as a prompt.

Prompt

Update the Products API so that only users with role "admin" can delete products.

Keep all other endpoints unchanged and preserve the current structure.

A correct response should modify only the relevant endpoint, without affecting the service layer or the overall architecture.

Open **app/routers/products.py** and update the delete endpoint:

```
@router.delete("/products/{product_id}")
def delete_product(
    product_id: int,
    db: Session = Depends(get_db),
    current_user: dict = Depends(auth_service.get_current_user),
) -> dict:
    if current_user["role"] != "admin":
        raise HTTPException(
            status_code=status.HTTP_403_FORBIDDEN,
            detail="Not enough permissions",
        )

    deleted = product_service.delete_product(db, product_id)
    if not deleted:
        raise HTTPException(
```

```
            status_code=status.HTTP_404_NOT_FOUND,
            detail=f"Product {product_id} not found",
        )
    return {"message": f"Product {product_id} deleted"}
```

The change in code is minimal, but its effect is significant. The authorization check happens before the service layer executes. The router first verifies that the authenticated user has the required role. Only after that check succeeds does the request proceed to the service layer, and interact with the persistent data.

The router no longer acts only as a translation layer between HTTP and the service. It now enforces an access rule. If the user does not have the required role, the request is rejected before any domain logic is executed. If the user is authorized, the request proceeds exactly as before. This introduces a new observable behavior. If you authenticate as a regular user (for example, alice) and attempt to delete a product, the API responds with:

```
{
  "detail": "Not enough permissions"
}
```

If you authenticate as an admin user (for example, bob) and perform the same operation, the request succeeds. *Figure* 8.9 illustrates this distinction: the same operation produces different outcomes depending on the user's role, making authorization visible at the API boundary.

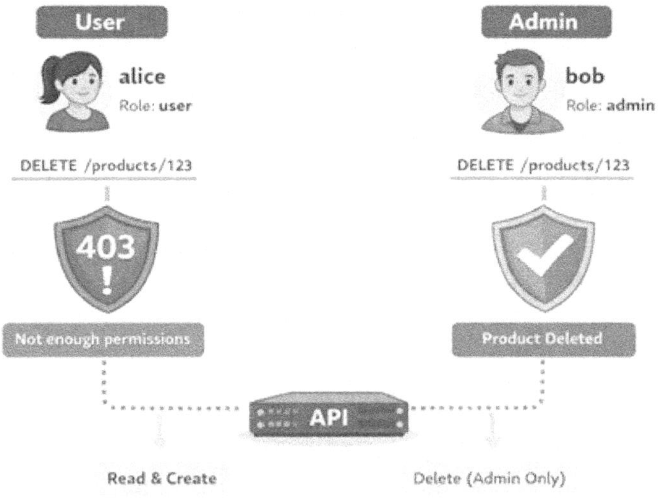

Figure 8.9: *Authorization Enforced on Specific Operations*

The API now differentiates between users based on their role, allowing only authorized users to perform sensitive actions such as deletion. At this stage, it is important to observe what has changed, and what has not. Some operations are now restricted, and unauthorized attempts result in a 403 Forbidden response. However, the external structure of the API remains identical. Endpoint paths, request and response schemas, service logic, and database structure are unchanged. The restriction is applied entirely at the HTTP boundary, inside the router. This is consistent with the architecture established earlier. The service layer remains focused on data operations, and is unaware of roles or permissions. Authorization is enforced where requests enter the system.

The API has now reached a new level of control. It can answer both:

- *who are you?*
- *what are you allowed to do?*

The next step is not to add more rules, but to step back, and observe the system as a whole: What changed in the API behavior after introducing authentication and authorization, and what remained exactly the same?

Observing What Changed at the API Boundary

At this stage, the API has changed in a fundamental way. It is no longer open, and it is no longer uniform. The system now reacts differently depending on who is making the request, and what they are allowed to do. To understand this change properly, we do not start from the internal code. Instead, we observe the system from the outside. This is consistent with the method used throughout the book:

```
prompt → code → execution → observation → understanding
```

We begin by turning the current state into a prompt.

Prompt

What changed in this API after adding authentication and authorization, and what remained identical at the API boundary?

Focus on observable behavior, not internal implementation.

A useful answer should describe what a client actually experiences when interacting with the API. Before security was introduced, every request succeeded as long as the input was valid. Identity was not required, and all users had the same capabilities. After introducing authentication and authorization, the behavior becomes conditional. Some requests now fail if no identity is provided. Others fail even when authenticated, depending on the user's permissions. The client must now include additional information in each request, such as the Authorization Header. These differences are directly observable. For example, a request without a token results in a response indicating a missing Authorization header. An invalid token produces a different error, and a valid token with insufficient permissions leads to a 403 Forbidden response. The API now rejects requests based on both identity and role. At the same time, it is equally important to observe what did not change. The endpoints remain the same, including paths such as **`/products and /products/{id}`**. Request bodies and response models are unchanged, and Swagger continues to document the same API structure.

If you open Swagger UI, everything appears familiar. The same routes are present, and the schemas are identical. What has changed is not the shape of the API, but the conditions under which it can be used. *Figure* 8.10 illustrates this contrast: while the API structure remains unchanged, access behavior now varies depending on authentication and authorization, making the boundary conditional, rather than open.

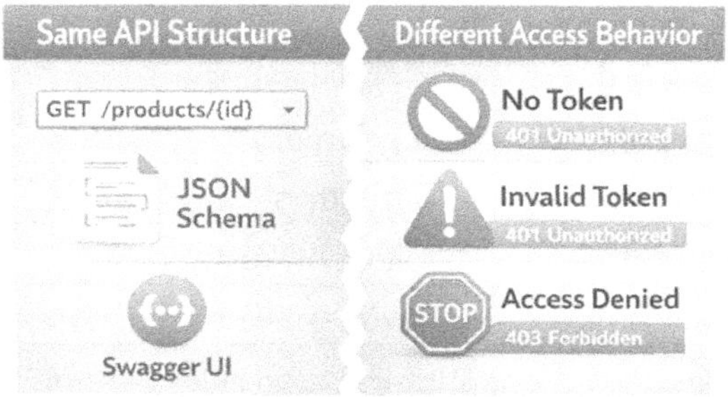

***Figure* 8.10:** *Same API Structure, Different Access Behavior*

The API endpoints and schemas remain identical, but access now depends on authentication and authorization, introducing conditional behavior at the boundary. This distinction is critical. The API contract has remained stable. A client that knows how to call /products still knows how to call it. However, the client must now satisfy an additional requirement: provide valid identity and sufficient permissions. This pattern follows the same discipline established in previous chapters. Earlier, structure was reorganized without changing behavior. Then execution changed without altering responses. Later, persistence was introduced without modifying the API contract. In this chapter, access rules have changed, while endpoints and schemas remain intact. Security, therefore, is not a redesign. It is a constraint applied at the boundary. At this point, the system behaves correctly, and is protected at a basic level.

However, one important question remains:

Is this implementation safe enough?

The next step is to use AI not to generate code, but to analyze what we built, and identify the potential weaknesses.

Using AI to Detect Security Weaknesses

Up to this point, AI has been used primarily to generate code. It helped create the authentication flow, structure the dependency, and apply authorization rules. Now, its role changes. The system works, the endpoints are protected, and the behavior is correct. This is precisely the moment when a different question becomes relevant:

Is this implementation actually safe?

Instead of asking AI to produce more codes, we now ask it to analyze what already exists. This marks an important shift. A developer who only uses AI to generate code risks introducing hidden problems. A developer who also asks for review begins to use AI as a security assistant, not just a code generator. A useful review does not simply identify flaws. It connects each weakness to the risk it creates. *Table* 8.2 summarizes the most important limitations of the current implementation, and why they matter.

Weakness	Risk
Plain-text passwords	Credential exposure
Predictable tokens	Token forgery
No token expiration	Unlimited token reuse
In-memory user storage	Data lost on restart
No password hashing	Password disclosure if data is leaked
No role persistence	Authorization rules cannot scale reliably
No token signature	Token tampering
No account lockout	Brute-force attacks

Table 8.2: *Security Review Summary*

None of these weaknesses prevent the example from demonstrating authentication and authorization behavior. However, they illustrate why security mechanisms should be reviewed critically before being considered production-ready.

We start with a focused prompt.

Prompt

Review this authentication and authorization implementation.

Identify potential security weaknesses or bad practices.

Keep suggestions minimal and practical for this project.

A useful answer should avoid introducing complex enterprise solutions. Instead, it should focus on concrete weaknesses that are directly visible in the current implementation. For example, the system stores passwords in plain text, making them immediately vulnerable, if exposed. Tokens are constructed using a predictable format such as token-username, which can be easily forged without authentication. There is no signature, no expiration mechanism, and no protection against reuse. Each of these issues weakens the reliability of the authentication system. These are not theoretical concerns. They can be observed directly in the code.

Consider the current token generation:

```
def create_token(user: dict) -> str:
    return f"token-{user[‹username›]}"
```

Anyone can construct a valid-looking token such as token-bob without logging in. The system is trusting something that can be guessed. This is a clear example of why code generation alone is not sufficient. The implementation behaves correctly, but it does not provide real security. At this point, the objective is not to fix everything, but to recognize limitations and improve them incrementally. We refine the prompt to keep the scope controlled.

Prompt

Given this simple auth implementation, suggest minimal improvements that increase security without adding complex external systems.

Do not redesign the architecture.

A useful answer should propose small, practical improvements. Passwords can be hashed, instead of stored in plain text. Tokens can be made less predictable, and a basic expiration mechanism can be introduced. Validation logic can be slightly strengthened without adding external dependencies. For example, a minimal improvement introduces password hashing, such as:

```
import hashlib

def hash_password(password: str) -> str:
    return hashlib.sha256(password.encode()).hexdigest()
```

and updating the user store:

```
fake_users_db = {
    "alice": {"username": "alice", "password": hash_
password("password123"), "role": "user"},
    "bob": {"username": "bob", "password": hash_password("secret"),
"role": "admin"},
}
```

And authentication logic updated accordingly:

```
def authenticate_user(username: str, password: str):
    user = fake_users_db.get(username)
    if not user:
        return None

    if user["password"] != hash_password(password):
        return None

    return user
```

This example uses SHA-256 only to demonstrate the idea of storing a transformed password, rather than plain text. In production systems, password storage should use dedicated password-hashing algorithms such as bcrypt, Argon2, or PBKDF2, which are specifically designed to resist brute-force attacks. The main aim here is to improve the example without introducing additional dependencies.

These changes do not make the system production-ready, but they improve it, while preserving simplicity and structure. *Figure* 8.11 illustrates this transition: after building a working authentication flow, AI is used to analyze the implementation, identify concrete weaknesses, and suggest targeted improvements, shifting its role from code generation to security-focused review.

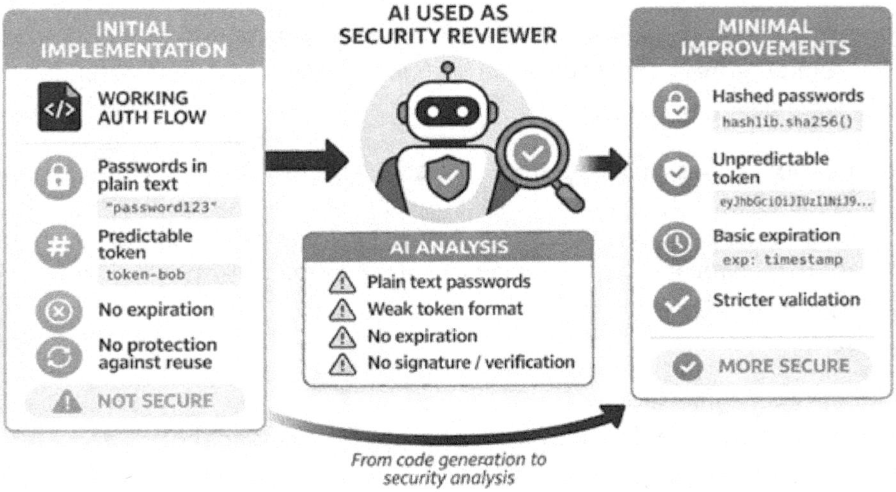

Figure 8.11: *AI Used as a Security Reviewer*

After implementing authentication, AI is used to identify weaknesses, and suggest minimal improvements, shifting from code generation to controlled analysis. This section introduces an important discipline. AI should not only be used to accelerate development or generate features. It should also be used to question assumptions, reveal hidden risks, and validate implementation choices. The responsibility remains with the developer. The assistant can highlight problems, but it cannot decide how far the system should evolve. At this stage, the API is protected, and its limitations are understood. The next step is to verify that the system behaves exactly as expected from the client's perspective, now that security constraints are in place.

Verifying the Secured API Behavior

At this point, the API has changed in a fundamental way. Before this chapter, every endpoint was publicly accessible, and requests succeeded as long as the input was valid. Now, the behavior is conditional. Some endpoints require authentication, others require specific roles, and requests may fail due to missing or invalid credentials. This is not just a code change. It is a new behavioral contract between the client and the API. As in previous chapters, we do not assume correctness. We verify it. The goal is to define what a client should observe and confirm that the system behaves exactly as expected. We start, as always, with a prompt.

Prompt

List the observable behaviors I should verify for this secured FastAPI Products API.

Focus on authentication, authorization, and what a client can observe.

A useful answer should describe visible outcomes, not internal logic. From this, we derive a concrete set of checks.

Security Verification Checklist

Missing token → 401 Unauthorized

✓ Invalid token → 401 Unauthorized

✓ Valid token → Request succeeds

✓ Insufficient role → 403 Forbidden

✓ Admin role → Protected operation succeeds

When accessing a protected endpoint without any authentication, the API should reject the request with a 401 Unauthorized response. Providing an invalid token should produce a similar result, confirming that authentication is enforced. When a valid token is used, the same request should succeed and return the expected data. At this point, authentication is working: identity is required and correctly validated. Authorization introduces a second layer of behavior. If a regular user attempts to perform an admin-only operation, such as deleting a product, the API should respond with a 403 Forbidden error. The same request, when executed by an admin user, should succeed without any change in the response structure. These differences are observable and intentional. The system now distinguishes between identity and permission. At the same time, it is important to observe what has not changed. The endpoints remain the same, request and response schemas are unchanged, and Swagger continues to document the same API structure. *Figure* 8.12 illustrates these outcomes: the same API requests produce different responses depending on authentication and authorization conditions, making success and failure paths clearly visible at the boundary.

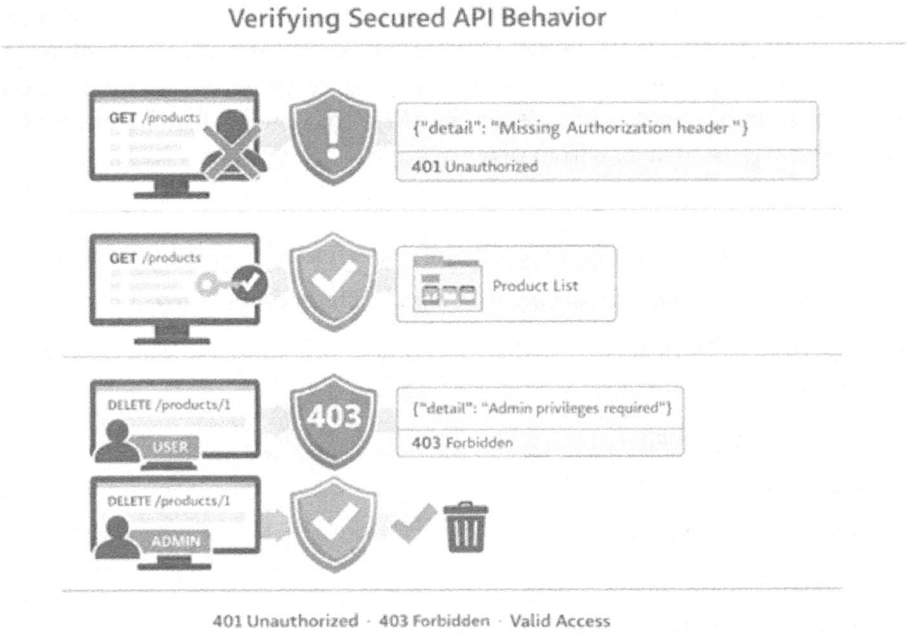

Figure 8.12: *Verifying Secured API Behavior through Client Interactions*

Requests without authentication fail with 401, role-restricted endpoints enforce 403, and valid credentials restore access without changing response structure. This confirms a key principle: security does not change the shape of the API, but the conditions under which it can be used. At this stage, the system is not only implemented but validated. Security is not something you "add and trust." It is something you observe and confirm, just like any other behavior. The development cycle remains consistent. An intention leads to a prompt, the prompt produces code, the code is executed, behavior is observed, and understanding is confirmed. With this verification complete, the secured version of the API becomes stable. The final step is to freeze this version as the new baseline for future chapters.

Freezing the Secured Version as the New Baseline

At the end of this chapter, something important has changed—and something equally important has stayed the same. The API is no longer open. It now enforces identity and permissions, and its behavior depends on who is making the request and what they are allowed to do. At the same time, the external structure remains stable. The endpoints are unchanged, request and response schemas are identical, and the system continues to behave in a predictable and observable way. This reflects the same discipline established in previous chapters: capabilities evolve, but the boundary remains controlled. Before moving forward, we freeze this new state of the system. The project structure now makes this evolution explicit:

```
app/
    main.py
    models.py
    routers/
        products.py
        auth.py
    services/
        product_service.py
        auth_service.py
    db/
        database.py
        models.py
migrations/
```

Identity Layer Added without Changing the API Contract

The API now includes authentication and authorization capabilities through dedicated routing and service components. Identity has become part of the request lifecycle, and permissions are enforced where required. However, the API contract remains unchanged: clients still interact with the same endpoints, request formats, and response structures introduced in earlier chapters.

No unnecessary layers have been introduced. The system has grown only where required: authentication logic, authorization checks, and secure route handling have been integrated into the existing structure without altering its clarity. We summarize this transformation through a prompt.

Prompt

Summarize how this FastAPI Products API evolved in this chapter.

Focus on how authentication and authorization changed the behavior of the API while preserving its structure.

A strong answer should highlight how identity was introduced, how permissions were layered on top of that identity, and how access rules began to influence behavior without changing the API contract itself. The system moved from anonymous access to authenticated interaction. It then evolved further by distinguishing between users based on roles, allowing some operations only under specific conditions. Throughout this evolution, the API boundary remained stable: endpoints, schemas, and response structures did not change. This is the key outcome of the chapter. Security has been introduced without redesigning the system. The router continues to manage HTTP semantics, the service layer remains responsible for domain logic, and the database continues to handle persistence. Security integrates into this structure, instead of replacing it.

The API now includes authentication and authorization layers, while preserving the same endpoints, schemas, and response behavior. At this point, the system has gained critical real-world capability. It can control access, protect sensitive operations, and adapt its behavior based on identity, while remaining understandable and predictable. This result is not accidental. It is the consequence of applying the same method throughout the book, that is starting from a concrete need, translating it into a prompt, generating minimal code, verifying observable behavior, and refining only where necessary. With this secured version frozen as the new baseline, the API is no longer just functional. It is structured, concurrent, persistent, and now secure. Everything that follows will build on this foundation—not by replacing it, but by extending it in controlled and observable steps.

Conclusion

In this chapter, the API evolved in a way that reflects real-world requirements. Until now, every request has been accepted. The system behaved correctly, but it trusted everything. This is no longer the case. Authentication was introduced to identify who is making a request, and authorization was added to control what that user is allowed to do. These capabilities were integrated without rewriting the application or breaking its external contract. The endpoints did not change, the schemas remained the same, and the request-response cycle is still identical. What changed are the conditions under which the access is granted.

This is the key shift: security is not a new layer that replaces behavior; it is a constraint that shapes it. Throughout the chapter, AI was used in two distinct ways. It helped generate the initial authentication flow, and it was later used to analyze and challenge its correctness. This second role is essential. Security is not something you generate and trust. It is something you question, verify, and refine.

By the end of this chapter, the API is no longer just functional or well-structured. It is aware of identity, capable of enforcing permissions, and resilient to common misuse patterns. At the same time, it remains understandable. That is the real goal. Not to build a secure system in the abstract, but to build a system whose security behavior can be explained, tested, and controlled. From this point on, every new feature will operate within these constraints. The system is no longer open. It is intentional.

However, one important question still remains: how do we know these behaviors will continue to work as the application evolves? So far, verification has been performed manually, and the application runs only in a specific local environment. In the next chapter, the focus shifts from securing behavior to validating and reproducing it. Automated tests will be introduced to verify correctness, and containerization will provide a consistent runtime environment. The goal is no longer just to build a working API, but to ensure that it behaves correctly, and runs consistently wherever it is deployed.

Points to Remember

- Security solves an observable limitation: unrestricted access.
- Authentication and authorization should not change the API contract.
- The router enforces access; the service layer handles business logic.
- Authentication establishes identity; authorization enforces permissions.
- Security rules should remain simple and explicit.
- Token-based authentication allows identity to travel with each request.
- Authorization checks should happen before protected operations execute.
- AI should review security for correctness, not just generate it.
- Security is verified through observable behavior: 401 for invalid identity, 403 for insufficient permissions, and success for authorized users.

Multiple Choice Questions

1. What is the main objective of this chapter?
    a. To redesign the database schema
    b. To introduce authentication and authorization into the API
    c. To optimize API performance
    d. To replace FastAPI with another framework
2. Why is security introduced in this chapter?
    a. Because every API must always use authentication
    b. Because the API currently allows unrestricted access to all operations
    c. Because SQLAlchemy requires authentication
    d. Because Swagger UI enforces security
3. What is the role of authentication in this chapter?
    a. To validate request payloads
    b. To identify the user making the request
    c. To generate database records
    d. To manage HTTP routing
4. What is the purpose of token-based authentication?
    a. To replace database queries
    b. To attach user identity to each request

   c. To validate API schemas
   d. To simplify Swagger documentation
5. Why are authorization checks implemented at the router level?
   a. Because routers cannot access services
   b. Because the router controls HTTP behavior and access to endpoints
   c. Because SQLAlchemy requires it
   d. Because tokens cannot be decoded elsewhere
6. What practical problem does authorization solve in this chapter?
   a. It improves database performance.
   b. It ensures that only allowed users can perform specific actions.
   c. It replaces authentication logic.
   d. It generates API documentation.
7. After security is introduced, what observable behavior should change?
   a. Endpoint URLs are modified.
   b. Swagger documentation disappears.
   c. Requests without valid credentials fail with 401 or 403.
   d. The API returns different data structures.
8. What should remain unchanged after securing the API?
   a. The internal authentication logic.
   b. The token format.
   c. The external API contract exposed to clients.
   d. The user roles.
9. A user successfully logs in but receives a 403 Forbidden response when attempting to delete a product. What is the most likely reason?
   a. Invalid password
   b. Missing token
   c. User lacks required role
   d. Product does not exist

Answers

1. b
2. b

3. b
4. b
5. b
6. b
7. c
8. c
9. c

Questions

1. Why does leaving an API unprotected create risks in a real system, and how does introducing authentication change the observable behavior of requests?
2. How does adding authentication and authorization improve the reliability and safety of the Products API without changing its external endpoints?
3. What is the difference between authentication and authorization, and why is it important to separate these two concerns?
4. Why is it important to keep authentication logic and user validation inside a dedicated service layer rather than directly inside the router?
5. How do token-based requests allow FastAPI routes to identify users without modifying endpoint definitions or request bodies?
6. Why is it necessary to explicitly verify behaviors such as 401 Unauthorized and 403 Forbidden responses after introducing security?
7. How does enforcing authorization at the router level preserve a clear boundary between HTTP behavior and business logic?
8. In what ways can AI assist with generating authentication flows and security logic, while still requiring human judgment to detect vulnerabilities, and avoid oversimplified or insecure implementations?

Key Terms

- **Authentication:** The process of verifying the identity of a user making a request, typically through credentials such as username and password, and confirmed via a token.
- **Authorization:** The process of determining what an authenticated user is allowed to do, such as accessing specific endpoints or performing restricted operations.

- **Access Token:** A piece of data (often a string) sent with a request that represents the authenticated user and allows the API to identify and validate them.
- **Token-Based Authentication:** A mechanism where each request includes a token (for example, in the Authorization header) instead of sending credentials repeatedly.
- **Security Dependency:** A FastAPI dependency (such as `get_current_user`) that enforces authentication and can be reused across multiple routes to protect endpoints.
- **Protected Route:** An endpoint that requires authentication and possibly authorization before it can be accessed successfully.
- **401 Unauthorized:** An HTTP status code indicating that a request lacks valid authentication credentials or includes an invalid token.
- **403 Forbidden:** An HTTP status code indicating that the user is authenticated but does not have permission to perform the requested operation.
- **Role-Based Access Control (RBAC):** A method of restricting access based on user roles (for example, user vs admin), used to enforce different permissions within the API.
- **Security Boundary:** The layer at which authentication and authorization are enforced, typically at the router level where HTTP requests are processed.
- **Credential Validation:** The process of verifying user-provided login data (such as username and password) before issuing an access token.
- **Prompt-Driven Security Design:** The use of AI prompts to generate and refine authentication and authorization logic, combined with human validation to ensure correctness and safety.

CHAPTER 9
Testing and Deploying an API

Introduction

Up to this point, the API has become structured, persistent, and secure. It behaves correctly, enforces identity, and stores data reliably. But one important question still remains: *how do we know it will keep working?*

So far, every verification has been manual, and the system runs only in a specific environment. This means that correctness depends on repetition and memory, and execution depends on local setup. This chapter addresses both limitations. Instead of introducing testing and deployment as separate topics, we approach them as new behavioral requirements. The API must be able to confirm its own correctness, and it must be runnable in a consistent way, regardless of where it is executed. To achieve this, automated tests are introduced to verify behavior, and containerization is used to define a reproducible runtime environment.

By the end of this chapter, you will be able to create automated tests for API behavior, interpret test failures, package an application with Docker, and run the same system consistently across different environments. Throughout the process, AI is used both to generate initial implementations, and to analyze failures when they occur. Thus, by the end of the chapter, the API will not only work—it will be able to prove that it works, and it will run the same way everywhere.

Structure

In this chapter, we will cover the following topics:

- The Next Limitation: A Working API is Not Yet a Verifiable System
- Defining What Must Be Tested First
- Generating the First Automated Tests with AI

- Testing Authentication and Authorization Behavior
- Testing Persistence and CRUD Behavior
- Using AI to Debug Failing Tests
- Making the API Runnable Anywhere: Why Containerization Matters
- Generating a Minimal Docker Setup with AI
- Adding Deployment Scripts without Overengineering
- Verifying the Dockerized API
- Freezing the Testable and Deployable Version as the New Baseline

The Next Limitation: A Working API is Not Yet a Verifiable System

At the end of *Chapter* 8, *Securing an* API *System*, the Products API reached an important level of maturity. It is no longer a temporary prototype. It has a stable project structure, persists data in a database, and protects access through authentication and authorization. From the outside, it behaves like a real system. And yet, one important limitation still remains. The API works, but its behavior is still being verified manually. The API works, but its behavior is still being verified manually. Working software and verifiable software are not the same thing. An application may appear to function correctly today, yet provide no reliable way to confirm that the same behavior will remain correct after future changes.

If you want to know whether the system is healthy, you open /health in the browser. If you want to know whether login works, you try /login by hand. If you want to verify that a normal user cannot delete a product, you log in as one user, call the delete endpoint, and inspect the response. If you want to confirm that an admin can do the same operation successfully, you repeat the request with a different token.

All of this is useful while the system is still being learned. But once the API has several behaviors that matter—persistence, protected routes, role-based access, and structured responses—manual verification becomes fragile. The problem is not that manual testing is wrong. The problem is that it does not scale with the system. A system that depends entirely on manual checks may still work, but it cannot yet be considered verifiable. Each time the code changes, the developer must remember what to test, which routes matter, which credentials to use, and which failure cases are important. That memory eventually becomes unreliable. And once it does, confidence in the system begins to weaken. This is the next limitation that the chapter addresses. The API must become testable in a repeatable way. As in the previous chapters, we do not begin from theory. We begin from behavior and from the practical risks that emerge when the system is used as it currently stands. A good prompt at this stage asks the AI to make that limitation explicit.

Prompt

In this FastAPI Products API, what problems remain if all verification is still manual?

Focus on observable development risks, not testing theory.

A useful answer should not turn into a lecture about testing frameworks. It should describe the problem in terms that the developer can already recognize from experience. If verification is manual, the same behavior may not be checked the same way every time. One day, the developer may verify only the success path and forget the failure path. Another day, they may test a protected route with an admin token, and forget to verify what happens without authentication. Over time, the system can regress without anyone noticing immediately. A change that accidentally opens access to a protected endpoint, alters an error response, or breaks a CRUD path may survive simply because nobody happened to repeat the right sequence of manual requests. The risk, in other words, is not theoretical. It is behavioral. The system may stop behaving as expected, and the developer may discover it too late.

This becomes particularly visible if we look at the current API as it stands at the end of *Chapter 8, Securing an API System*. The application exposes a health endpoint, a login flow, authenticated product routes, and role-restricted deletion. All of these behaviors matter, and all of them are currently being trusted because they were observed manually, rather than because they are verified automatically. The code makes this clear that the application entry point includes /health, and all product routes are attached through the products router. At this point, it is useful to make the current verification process concrete.

A developer might currently check the system like this:

1. Start the API
2. Call GET /health
3. Call **`POST /login`** with valid credentials
4. Copy the returned token
5. Call **`GET /products`** with the token
6. Try **`DELETE /products/{id}`** as a normal user
7. Repeat DELETE /products/{id} as an admin

Nothing is wrong with this sequence. In fact, it reflects the same prompt-driven and observation-driven method used throughout the book. But it depends entirely on the developer remembering the sequence and interpreting the results correctly every time. That dependence is precisely what the chapter now needs to reduce. *Figure 9.1* highlights the limitation of manual verification. As the system grows, correctness depends increasingly on human memory and repetition, increasing the risk of missed regressions.

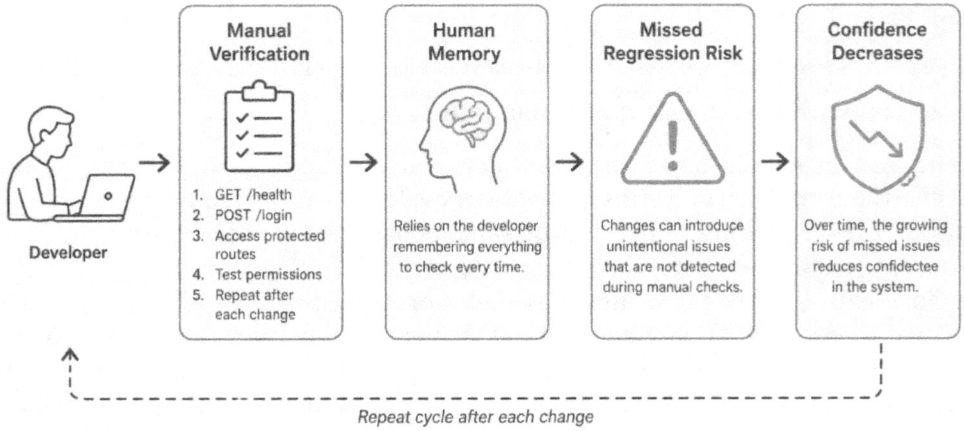

Figure 9.1: *The Growing Cost of the Human Verification*

Note: *A system with health checks, login, protected routes, and role-based behavior may still work correctly, but once verification depends entirely on repeated manual requests, confidence becomes difficult to maintain.*

At this point, an important distinction must be made. The system is already runnable. What it lacks is repeatable proof that it still behaves correctly after change. That distinction matters because this chapter is not about "adding tests because professional projects have tests." It is about responding to a new need in the same way the book has responded to every previous need. When the API could not remember data, persistence was introduced. When it could not distinguish users, authentication and authorization were introduced. Now the limitation is different: the API cannot yet confirm its own behavior in a reliable, repeatable way.

This is why testing becomes the next logical capability. The goal of the chapter is not to replace observation, but to preserve it. Automated tests turn observations that were previously manual and fragile into executable checks that can be repeated whenever the system changes. The developer does not stop thinking; the developer stops relying on memory alone. This also explains why the current chapter naturally belongs after security and persistence. The API is now complex enough that its behavior can no longer be trusted merely because it worked once. It must be made verifiable. The next step is therefore not to generate many tests at once. It is to decide what should be tested first, based on the behaviors that now define the system most clearly.

Defining What Must Be Tested First

Once the limitation is clear, the next step is not to immediately generate tests. The first step is to decide what actually matters. At this point, the API already exposes multiple behaviors: it responds to health checks, authenticates users, protects routes, persists data, and enforces role-based access. Not all of these need to be tested at once, and trying to do so would quickly introduce unnecessary complexity. Instead, we focus on observable behavior that defines the system. The goal of this section is simple: identify the minimum set of behaviors that must be verified to trust the API.

Minimum Verification Scope

Before expanding test coverage, verify the behaviors that define the system:

✓ *Health endpoint*

✓ *Login and token generation*

✓ *Protected route access*

✓ *Role enforcement on restricted operations*

✓ *Basic CRUD behavior*

Figure 9.2 shows the minimum behavioral path that should be verified before considering the API trustworthy.

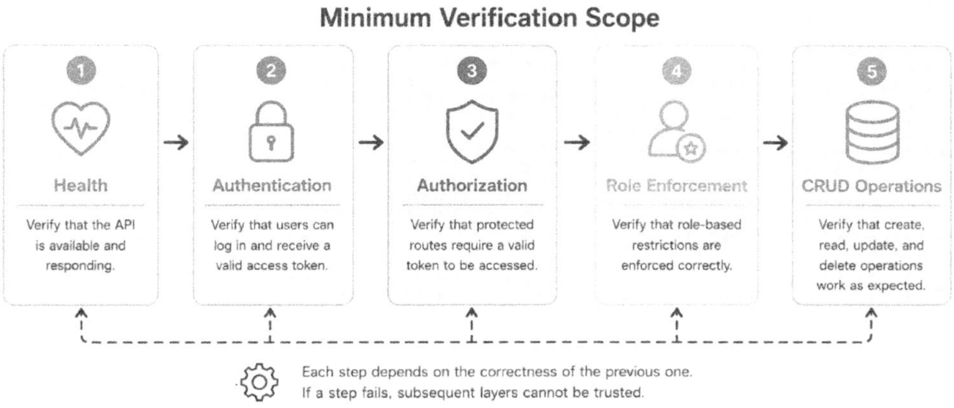

Figure 9.2: *Minimum Verification Scope*

Testing begins with the behaviors that define the system, such as: availability, authentication, authorization, and core CRUD functionality. Each layer builds on the correctness of the previous one.

We express this need through a prompt.

Prompt

List the most important behaviors that should be tested first in this FastAPI Products API.

Focus on health, login, protected product routes, and role-based delete behavior.

A useful answer should not produce test code yet. It should describe what a client expects to observe when interacting with the system. To make this concrete, consider the API as it currently exists. The application exposes a health endpoint:

```
@app.get("/health")
```

```
def health() -> dict:
    return {"status": "ok"}
```

This is the simplest observable behavior. If this endpoint fails, the system is not running correctly. The API also exposes a login endpoint:

```
@router.post("/login", response_model=TokenResponse)
def login(data: LoginRequest) -> TokenResponse:
    user = auth_service.authenticate_user(data.username, data.password)
    if user is None:
        raise HTTPException(status_code=401, detail="Invalid
credentials")
    token = auth_service.create_token(user)
    return {"access_token": token}
```

This is where identity is created. If login fails incorrectly, nothing else in the system can be trusted. Next, consider a protected endpoint:

```
@router.get("/products")
def list_products(
    db: Session = Depends(get_db),
    current_user: dict = Depends(auth_service.get_current_user),
):
    return product_service.list_products(db)
```

This endpoint introduces a new behavior: it requires authentication. A request without a valid token should not succeed.

Finally, consider a restricted operation:

```
@router.delete("/products/{product_id}")
def delete_product(
    product_id: int,
    db: Session = Depends(get_db),
    current_user: dict = Depends(auth_service.get_current_user),
):
    if current_user["role"] != "admin":
        raise HTTPException(status_code=403, detail="Not enough
permissions")

    deleted = product_service.delete_product(db, product_id)
    if not deleted:
        raise HTTPException(status_code=404, detail=f"Product {product_
id} not found",)

    return {"message": f"Product {product_id} deleted"}
```

This endpoint adds authorization. Not all authenticated users can perform this action. From these examples, four core behaviors clearly define the API:

- The system must respond correctly to /health.

- Login must succeed with valid credentials, and fail otherwise.
- Protected endpoints must reject unauthenticated requests.
- Restricted endpoints must enforce role-based permissions.

At this point, it is important to notice what we are not doing. We are not testing internal functions. We are not testing SQL queries directly. We are not validating individual helper functions. We are testing the system as a client experiences it. This is consistent with the approach used throughout the book: focus on the boundary. From this reasoning, we can define a minimal verification scope:

- The API responds correctly to **`/health`**.
- Login succeeds with valid credentials, and fails otherwise.
- Protected endpoints reject requests without authentication.
- Protected endpoints succeed with a valid token.
- Restricted operations enforce role-based access (403 vs success).

This list is intentionally small. It captures the behaviors that define the system after *Chapter* 8. Everything else can be added later, once this foundation is stable. At this stage, the system has moved from "*we know it works*" to "*we know what must be proven*". The next step is to turn this defined scope into executable tests that can be run automatically.

Manual Verification from the Command Line

Before converting behavior into automated tests,
you can verify API endpoints directly from the command line using curl.

(Linux / macOS):

```
curl -X GET \
"http://127.0.0.1:8000/products" \
-H "Authorization: Bearer token-alice"
```

(Windows - PowerShell)

```
curl.exe -X GET "http://127.0.0.1:8000/products" `
-H "Authorization: Bearer token-alice"
```

The -H option adds HTTP headers to the request. For protected endpoints,
include the token returned by /login in the Authorization header.

The same pattern can be used for any endpoint:

```
curl -X <METHOD> "<URL>" \
-H "Authorization: Bearer <TOKEN>"
```

For requests that send data (such as POST or PUT), add a JSON payload:

-H "Content-Type: application/json"

-d'{ ... }'

These commands provide a quick way to verify API behavior manually before expressing the same checks as automated tests.

Generating the First Automated Tests with AI

Once the behaviors to verify are clear, the next step is to turn them into something executable. Up to this point, every check has been performed manually. Now those same checks must become repeatable. The goal is not to introduce a testing framework as a topic of study, but to translate what we already know into automated verification. We start, as always, with a prompt.

Prompt

Generate initial automated tests for this FastAPI Products API using FastAPI TestClient.

Cover the health endpoint, login, and access to protected product routes.

Keep the tests minimal and runnable.

A useful answer should not attempt to cover every edge case. It should produce a small set of tests that can be executed immediately, and that reflect the behaviors defined in the previous section. Create a new file:

`tests/test_api.py` and add the following implementation:

```
from fastapi.testclient import TestClient
from app.main import app

client = TestClient(app)

def test_health():
    response = client.get("/health")
    assert response.status_code == 200
    assert response.json() == {"status": "ok"}

def test_login_success():
    response = client.post("/login", json={
        "username": "alice",
        "password": "password123"
    })
    assert response.status_code == 200
    assert "access_token" in response.json()

def test_login_failure():
```

```
    response = client.post("/login", json={
        "username": "alice",
        "password": "wrong-password"
    })
    assert response.status_code == 401

def test_protected_route_requires_auth():
    response = client.get("/products")
    assert response.status_code == 401
```

TestClient allows tests to interact with the API through HTTP requests without starting a real server. Each test can send requests, and inspect responses exactly as a client would, while the application runs entirely inside the test process.

This file introduces a new capability. The API is now testable. Each test corresponds directly to a behavior that was previously verified manually. The first test checks the **/health** endpoint. If this test fails, the application is not running correctly. The second and third tests verify the login flow. They confirm that valid credentials produce a token, and invalid credentials are rejected. The fourth test checks access control. It confirms that a protected endpoint cannot be accessed without authentication.

At this stage, it is important to notice what has not been introduced. There is no complex test structure. There are no fixtures, no configuration files, and no advanced assertions. The tests are simple functions that call the API, and verify observable outcomes. This is intentional. The goal is not to teach testing tools. The goal is to preserve the method used throughout the book. Each test is an executable version of a previously observed behavior. First install in your virtual environment:

```
pip install pytest httpx
```

Then in the tests and app folder, create **__init__.py** empty files. After the installation, you can run the tests:

```
pytest
```

and this is the output:

```
================================== test session starts =================
==================
platform win32 -- Python 3.11.6, pytest-9.0.3, pluggy-1.6.0
rootdir: C:\fastapi_app
plugins: anyio-4.12.1
collected 4 items

tests\test_api.py ....
[100%]

=================================== 4 passed in 1.62s ==================
=================
```

When executed, each test sends real HTTP requests to the application through the **`TestClient`**. The API is not mocked. It behaves exactly as it would in production, but inside a controlled environment. This is a critical shift. Instead of asking, "does the API work?" and answering manually, the system can now answer that question automatically.

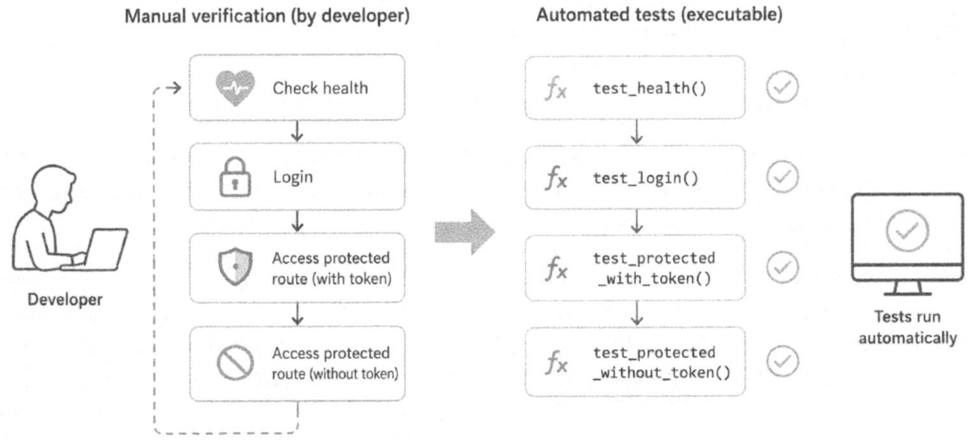

***Figure* 9.3:** *Manual Checks Become Executable Tests*

Note: *Each previously manual verification step is now expressed as a test function, allowing the system to confirm its behavior automatically.*

At this point, the test suite is still minimal. It does not yet verify authorization rules or database behavior. But it establishes something more important: a repeatable way to observe the system. The next step is to extend these tests to cover authentication and authorization more completely, ensuring that identity and permissions are enforced exactly as defined in *Chapter* 8.

Testing Authentication and Authorization Behavior

The first tests introduced a simple but important capability: the API can now confirm some of its behavior automatically. However, the most critical part of the system is still only partially verified. Authentication and authorization define how the API controls access. If these mechanisms fail, the entire system becomes unreliable, regardless of how well the rest of the logic works. This is the next behavior that must be made fully observable and repeatable. We begin, as usual, with a prompt.

A useful answer should extend the existing test file without introducing unnecessary complexity. The goal is to verify behavior at the API boundary, not to inspect internal functions.

Prompt

Add automated tests for authentication and authorization in this FastAPI Products API.

Verify 401 for missing or invalid tokens, 403 for non-admin delete, and success for admin delete. Keep the tests minimal and consistent with the current structure.

Open **tests/test_api.py** and extend it with the following tests:

```
def get_token(username: str, password: str) -> str:
    response = client.post("/login", json={
        "username": username,
        "password": password
    })
    return response.json()["access_token"]


def test_protected_route_with_invalid_token():
    response = client.get(
        "/products",
        headers={"Authorization": "Bearer invalid-token"}
    )
    assert response.status_code == 401


def test_protected_route_with_valid_token():
    token = get_token("alice", "password123")

    response = client.get(
        "/products",
        headers={"Authorization": f"Bearer {token}"}
    )
    assert response.status_code == 200


def test_delete_requires_admin():
    token = get_token("alice", "password123")

    response = client.delete(
        "/products/1",
        headers={"Authorization": f"Bearer {token}"}
    )
    assert response.status_code == 403


def test_delete_as_admin():
    token = get_token("bob", "secret")

    response = client.delete(
```

```
        "/products/1",
        headers={"Authorization": f"Bearer {token}"}
    )

    # product may or may not exist, but permission must be allowed
    assert response.status_code in (200, 404)
```

The **get_token()** helper keeps the tests focused on behavior, rather than repeated login code. Helper functions reduce duplication, and make tests easier to maintain.

These tests make security behavior explicit. The first test verifies that an invalid token is rejected. The API must not accept malformed or forged identity. The second test confirms that a valid token allows access to protected endpoints. This ensures that authentication works as expected. The third test verifies authorization. A normal user attempts to perform an admin-only operation, and is correctly rejected with a 403 Forbidden response. The fourth test confirms the opposite behavior. An admin user performs the same operation, and is allowed to proceed. The result may vary depending on whether the product exists, but the request must not be rejected due to permissions.

At this point, authentication and authorization are no longer assumptions. They are verified behaviors. It is important to notice how these tests reflect exactly what was introduced in *Chapter* 8, *Securing an* API *System*. The system does not just return data. It now enforces conditions. Some requests fail intentionally, and those failures are part of the correct behavior. This is a key idea. A secure system is not one that always succeeds. It is one that fails correctly when conditions are not met. At this stage, the API is not only protected—it is testably protected. The next step is to extend this verification to another critical aspect of the system: persistence and CRUD behavior backed by the database.

Testing Persistence and CRUD Behavior

So far, the tests have focused on access: who can call the API and under which conditions. Now, we turn to another critical aspect of the system: data. In *Chapter* 7 - *Building Data-Driven* APIs, the API moved from in-memory storage to a database-backed implementation. This introduced persistence. Products are no longer temporary; they are stored, retrieved, updated, and deleted through the database. Up to this point, this behavior has been trusted because it was observed manually. The next step is to verify it automatically.

Figure 9.4 shows the feedback loop created by automated testing. When a change introduces an inconsistency, a failing test exposes the problem immediately, allowing it to be corrected before it reaches the users.

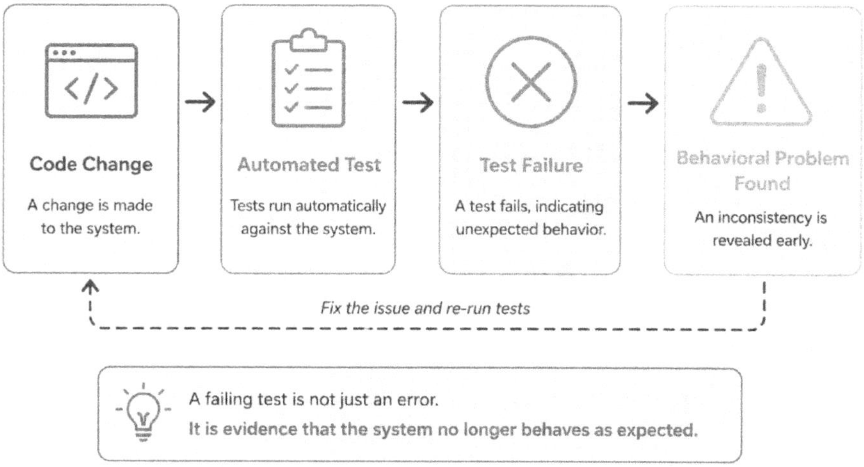

Figure 9.4: *Test Failures Expose Inconsistencies between Expected and Actual Behavior, Allowing Problems to be Detected Early*

As in previous sections, we begin with a prompt.

Prompt

Generate automated CRUD tests for the Product endpoints in this FastAPI API.

Keep them compatible with the current database-backed structure, and make them runnable. Focus on create, read, update, and delete behavior.

A useful answer should produce tests that interact with the API exactly as a client would, without directly calling database functions. The goal is not to test SQLAlchemy itself, but to confirm that the API correctly exposes CRUD behavior. Open **tests/test_api.py** and extend it with the following tests:

```
def test_create_product():
    token = get_token("alice", "password123")

    response = client.post(
        "/products",
        headers={"Authorization": f"Bearer {token}"},
        json={
            "name": "Test Product",
            "price": 10.5,
            "description": "Test description"
        }
    )

    assert response.status_code == 201
    data = response.json()
    assert data["name"] == "Test Product"
```

```
    assert data["price"] == 10.5
    assert "id" in data

def test_list_products():
    token = get_token("alice", "password123")

    response = client.get(
        "/products",
        headers={"Authorization": f"Bearer {token}"}
    )

    assert response.status_code == 200
    assert isinstance(response.json(), list)

def test_update_product():
    token = get_token("alice", "password123")

    create_response = client.post(
        "/products",
        headers={"Authorization": f"Bearer {token}"},
        json={
            "name": "Old Name",
            "price": 5.0,
            "description": "Old description"
        }
    )
    product_id = create_response.json()["id"]

    update_response = client.put(
        f"/products/{product_id}",
        headers={"Authorization": f"Bearer {token}"},
        json={
            "name": "New Name",
            "price": 7.5,
            "description": "Updated description"
        }
    )

    assert update_response.status_code == 200
    data = update_response.json()
    assert data["name"] == "New Name"
    assert data["price"] == 7.5

def test_delete_product_as_admin():
    token = get_token("bob", "secret")
```

```
    create_response = client.post(
        "/products",
        headers={"Authorization": f"Bearer {token}"},
        json={
            "name": "To Delete",
            "price": 3.0,
            "description": "Temporary"
        }
    )
    product_id = create_response.json()["id"]

    delete_response = client.delete(
        f"/products/{product_id}",
        headers={"Authorization": f"Bearer {token}"}
    )

    assert delete_response.status_code == 200
```

At this point, it is tempting to assume that these tests will simply pass. But this is exactly where testing becomes meaningful. When these tests are executed, they reveal a failure. In fact, running **pytest** again produces an output similar to the following:

```
============================================================ short test
summary info ==============================================================
FAILED tests/test_api.py::test_create_product - sqlalchemy.exc.
IntegrityError: (sqlite3.IntegrityError) NOT NULL constraint failed:
products.description
FAILED tests/test_api.py::test_update_product - sqlalchemy.exc.
IntegrityError: (sqlite3.IntegrityError) NOT NULL constraint failed:
products.description
FAILED tests/test_api.py::test_delete_product_as_admin - sqlalchemy.exc.
IntegrityError: (sqlite3.IntegrityError) NOT NULL constraint failed:
products.description
========================================================== 3 failed, 9
passed in 3.98s ==========================================================
==
```

The API raises a database error indicating that a required field is missing. Specifically, the description field is defined as required in both the API schema and the database model, but it is not being stored when a product is created. This is not a testing problem. It is a system inconsistency. The API accepts a field that the service layer silently ignores. As a result, the database receives a NULL value for a field that does not allow it, causing the operation to fail. This is a critical moment. Up to this point, the system appeared correct. Endpoints worked. Requests returned valid responses. But the tests have exposed a gap between different layers of the application. This is exactly the purpose of automated testing. Tests are not only used to confirm that behavior is correct. They are used to reveal when assumptions are wrong.

At this stage, we do not fix this issue yet. The goal of this chapter is to build a system that can be tested and executed reliably. The failure we have just observed is not caused by the tests—it reveals an inconsistency in the system itself. Rather than fixing it immediately, we keep it as a reference point. It will be analyzed and resolved in the next chapter, where AI will be used not just to debug, but to review the implementation and identify deeper issues. This reflects an important principle. Testing is not the final step of development. It is the bridge between implementation and understanding. At this point, the API is not only protected and testable—it is also revealing its own limitations. And that is exactly what we need in order to improve it.

Using AI to Debug Failing Tests

Up to this point, AI has been used mainly to generate code and test cases. It helped us define what to verify, produce the first automated tests, and expand them to cover authentication, authorization, and CRUD behavior. But once tests exist, AI takes on a different role. It is no longer used only to produce new code. It is used to interpret failures. This shift matters because automated tests do not just confirm correctness. They also expose inconsistencies that were previously hidden by manual verification. That is exactly what happened in the previous section. The CRUD tests did not simply fail; they revealed that different parts of the system no longer agreed on what a product actually is. At this stage, the developer is no longer asking: "*Does the API work?*". The question has changed: "*Why is this test failing, and what does that failure reveal about the system?*" That is where AI becomes useful in a new way. Instead of asking it to generate another feature, we ask it to analyze the mismatch between the test, the route, the schema, and the service logic. A good prompt should include the failing behavior, the error message, and the relevant code. For this specific case, the right prompt is not abstract. It is tightly grounded in what the tests just revealed.

Prompt

My FastAPI CRUD tests are failing with this error:

sqlite3.IntegrityError: NOT NULL *constraint failed: products.description*

The request body includes a description field, and both the API schema and the database model define description as required. Review the route and service code involved in product creation and update. Explain the most likely cause, and suggest the smallest fix that preserves the current structure. This prompt is effective because it does not ask for a redesign. It asks for diagnosis. To make the problem concrete, include the relevant code in the prompt. The route for product creation in the **`app/routers/products.py`** currently looks like this:

```
@router.post("/products",
```

```
response_model=Product, status_code=status.HTTP_201_CREATED)
def create_product(
    product: ProductCreate,
    db: Session = Depends(get_db),
    current_user: dict = Depends(auth_service.get_current_user),
) -> Product:
    return product_service.create_product(db, product)
```

The schema used by that route requires description in the **app/models.py** file:

```
class ProductCreate(BaseModel):
    name: str
    price: float = Field(..., gt=0)
    description: str

class Product(ProductCreate):
    id: int
```

And the database model also requires it in the **app/db/models.py** file:

```
class Product(Base):
    __tablename__ = "products"

    id = Column(Integer, primary_key=True, index=True)
    name = Column(String, nullable=False)
    description = Column(String, nullable=False)
    price = Column(Float, nullable=False)
```

At first glance, everything seems aligned. The request body includes description, the API schema requires it, and the database table expects it. But the service layer (**app/services/product_service.py**) reveals the actual problem:

```
def create_product(db: Session, data: ProductCreate) -> ProductDB:
    product = ProductDB(name=data.name, price=data.price)
    db.add(product)
    db.commit()
    db.refresh(product)
    return product
```

Here, description is silently ignored. The same inconsistency appears in the update logic:

```
def update_product(db: Session, product_id: int, data: ProductCreate) ->
Optional[ProductDB]:
    product = get_product(db, product_id)
    if product is None:
        return None
```

```
    product.name = data.name
    product.price = data.price
    db.commit()
    db.refresh(product)
    return product
```

Again, the incoming description exists in the API contract, but the service does not persist it. A useful AI response should identify this immediately. The failure is not caused by the tests. It is caused by a mismatch between layers of the application. The API accepts a field that the service layer does not forward to the database. As a result, SQLAlchemy tries to insert NULL into a column that explicitly forbids it. This is not a testing problem. It is a system inconsistency revealed by testing. The smallest fix preserves the current architecture, and updates only the service logic. Open **app/services/product_service.py** and update the relevant functions as follows:

```
from typing import List, Optional
from sqlalchemy.orm import Session
from app.db.models import Product as ProductDB
from app.models import ProductCreate

def create_product(db: Session, data: ProductCreate) -> ProductDB:
    product = ProductDB(
        name=data.name,
        price=data.price,
        description=data.description,
    )
    db.add(product)
    db.commit()
    db.refresh(product)
    return product

def get_product(db: Session, product_id: int) -> Optional[ProductDB]:
    return db.query(ProductDB).filter(ProductDB.id == product_id).first()

def list_products(db: Session) -> List[ProductDB]:
    return db.query(ProductDB).all()

def update_product(db: Session, product_id: int, data: ProductCreate) ->
Optional[ProductDB]:
    product = get_product(db, product_id)
    if product is None:
        return None

    product.name = data.name
```

```
    product.price = data.price
    product.description = data.description
    db.commit()
    db.refresh(product)
    return product

def delete_product(db: Session, product_id: int) -> bool:
    product = get_product(db, product_id)
    if product is None:
        return False

    db.delete(product)
    db.commit()
    return True
```

This is a small change, but it restores consistency across the system. Now the request schema, the service layer, and the database model all agree on the same definition of a product. At this point, run the tests again with **pytest**. The previously failing CRUD tests should now pass. In fact, you get this result:

```
============================================================ test
session starts ============================================================
=====
platform win32 -- Python 3.11.6, pytest-9.0.3, pluggy-1.6.0
rootdir: C:\fastapi_app
plugins: anyio-4.12.1
collected 12 items

tests\test_api.py ............
[100%]

============================================================ 12 passed
in 1.12s ============================================================
```

This sequence demonstrates why AI-assisted debugging is valuable. The assistant is not being asked to invent a new architecture. It is being asked to trace a failure back to its cause and suggest the smallest correction that preserves the structure already established in the project. That is a very different use of AI. Instead of saying: "*write this code*", the developer is saying: "*interpret this failure*" and then: "*show me the smallest fix that restores consistency.*"

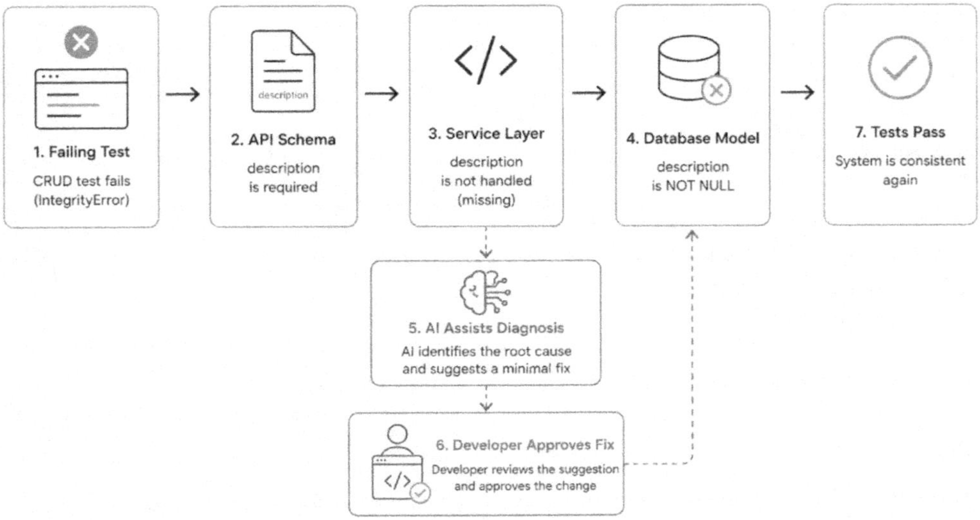

Figure 9.5: *A Failing Test Reveals a Behavioral Inconsistency*

Note: A *failing* CRUD *test reveals a mismatch between* API *schema, service logic, and database model.* AI *helps trace the failure to the missing description handling in the service layer, and guides a minimal correction.*

This section introduces an important discipline. Tests do not merely validate behavior. They expose the hidden disagreement between layers. And AI, when used well, does not replace debugging. It accelerates understanding. At this stage, the API is not only testable. It is becoming maintainable, because failures can now be interpreted systematically, rather than handled through guesswork. The next step is to move beyond local correctness. The API can now be tested reliably on the developer's machine, but it still depends on that machine's environment. The next question is no longer about failing behavior. It is about reproducible execution. How can the same API be run in the same way anywhere? That is where containerization becomes relevant.

Making the API Runnable Anywhere: Why Containerization Matters

At this point, the API has gained an important capability. It is verifiable. Tests can be executed automatically, failures can be analyzed, and behavior can be confirmed in a repeatable way. From a development perspective, the system is now under control. And yet, another limitation becomes visible. The API still runs only in a specific environment. It works on the developer's machine because the dependencies are installed, the database file is available, and the application is started in a particular way. If someone else tries to run the same project, they must recreate that environment manually. They need the correct Python version, the right dependencies, the same directory structure, and a compatible runtime configuration. Nothing in the project guarantees that this setup will be reproduced exactly. This is the next problem. The API is testable, but it is not yet reproducible.

A working application is not necessarily a portable application. An API may behave correctly in one environment, while failing in another due to differences in dependencies, runtime configuration, or operating system assumptions. *Figure 9.6* illustrates the limitation of environment-dependent execution. Even when an application works correctly on one machine, differences in runtime environments can introduce deployment problems elsewhere.

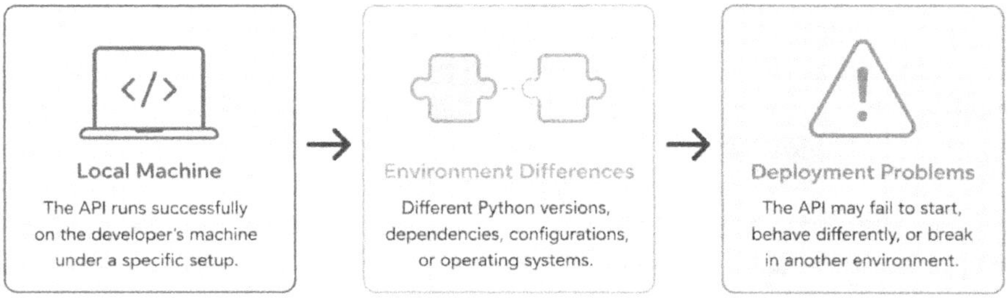

Figure 9.6: *Environment-dependent Execution Creates Reproducibility Risks*

An application that works correctly on a developer's machine may fail elsewhere if dependencies, configuration, or runtime assumptions differ. As in previous sections, we do not start with tools or theory. We start with behavior. A good prompt at this stage makes the limitation explicit.

Prompt

For this FastAPI Products API, what practical problem does Docker solve?

Focus on reproducibility and runnable deployment, not container theory.

A useful answer should not describe container internals. It should describe what changes from the developer's perspective. Without containerization, the API depends on the environment in which it is executed. With containerization, the environment becomes part of the application itself. Instead of saying, "install these dependencies and run this command," the project can define exactly how it should be built and executed. To understand this more concretely, consider how the API is currently started.

A developer runs:

```
uvicorn app.main:app -reload
```

This command assumes several things. It assumes that uvicorn is installed. It assumes that the current directory is correct. It assumes that the Python environment includes FastAPI, SQLAlchemy, and all required dependencies. It also assumes that the database file can be created and accessed without issues. If any of these assumptions fail, the

API will not start. This is not a problem for a single developer. It becomes a problem when the system needs to be shared, tested in a different environment, or prepared for deployment. Containerization addresses this limitation. Instead of relying on external conditions, the application defines its own execution environment. The same system that runs on one machine can be reproduced exactly on another. From the outside, the behavior changes in a simple but powerful way. Instead of asking: "*what do I need to install to run this* API?", the question becomes: "*how do I run this container*?". This is a shift in responsibility. The environment is no longer managed manually. It is defined as part of the project. At this stage, it is important to notice what is not changing. The API itself does not change.

The endpoints remain the same. The request and response schemas are unchanged. Authentication and authorization continue to behave exactly as before. The database layer remains the same. Containerization does not modify the system's behavior. It makes that behavior reproducible. This is consistent with the discipline used throughout the book. Each new capability extends the system without breaking its boundary. The next step is to turn this idea into something concrete. Instead of describing containerization, we will generate a minimal, runnable setup that allows the API to be built and executed inside a container.

Generating a Minimal Docker Setup with AI

Once the need for reproducibility is clear, the next step is to make it executable. As in the rest of the chapter, we do not begin by learning Docker as a tool. We begin by asking for a concrete outcome: a minimal way to run this API in a controlled environment. We turn this into a prompt.

Prompt

Generate a minimal Docker setup for this FastAPI Products API.

Include a Dockerfile and keep it simple, runnable, and compatible with the current project.

Do not add unnecessary complexity.

A useful answer should not introduce multiple services, orchestration tools, or production optimizations. It should produce a small, clear configuration that allows the API to be built and started in a container. Create a new file in the root of the project **`Dockerfile`,** and add the following content:

```
# Use a lightweight Python image
FROM python:3.11-slim

# Set working directory
WORKDIR /app
```

```
# Copy project files
COPY . .

# Install dependencies
RUN pip install --no-cache-dir fastapi uvicorn sqlalchemy alembic

# Expose the application port
EXPOSE 8000

# Run the FastAPI application
CMD ["uvicorn", "app.main:app", "--host", "0.0.0.0", "--port", "8000"]
```

This configuration introduces several important elements. The python:3.11-slim image provides a complete Python runtime, while keeping the container significantly smaller than the standard Python image. Smaller images download faster, consume less storage, and generally improve deployment efficiency.

The WORKDIR instruction defines **/app** as the working directory inside the container, while **COPY . .** copies the project files into that directory. The dependencies required by the application are then installed through **pip**.

For simplicity, dependencies are installed directly in the Dockerfile:

```
RUN pip install --no-cache-dir fastapi uvicorn sqlalchemy alembic
```

In production projects, dependencies are typically managed through a requirements.txt file (or a similar dependency specification) to ensure consistency between development, testing, and deployment environments. A more common production-oriented approach would be:

```
COPY requirements.txt .
RUN pip install --no-cache-dir -r requirements.txt
```

This approach makes dependency management easier as the project grows because all the required packages are maintained in a single version-controlled file.

Finally, `EXPOSE 8000` documents the port used by the application, and the CMD instruction starts the FastAPI server when the container is launched.

This file defines how the API is built and executed. The base image provides a clean Python environment. The working directory is set inside the container. The project files are copied, dependencies are installed, and the application is started using the same command that was previously executed manually. At this point, the system has a defined runtime. To make the setup cleaner, we also exclude unnecessary files from the build process. Create **.dockerignore** and add:

```
__pycache__/
*.pyc
*.pyo
```

```
*.pyd
.env
venv/
tests/
```

This ensures that temporary files and local environments are not included in the container image. Now the API can be built and run. Build the image:

```
docker build -t products-api.
```

Run the container:

```
docker run -p 8000:8000 products-api
```

Once the container is running, the API is accessible at:

```
http://localhost:8000
```

You can open **/health**, call **/login**, and interact with **/products** exactly as before. At this stage, it is important to observe what has changed. The API is no longer tied to a local Python environment. It runs inside a container that defines its own dependencies and execution context. The same container can be started on any machine with Docker installed. At the same time, what has not changed is equally important. The API behavior is identical. The endpoints are the same. Authentication and authorization behave the same way. The database is still used in the same way. From the client's perspective, nothing is different. This reflects the same pattern used throughout the book. Capabilities evolve, but the boundary remains stable.

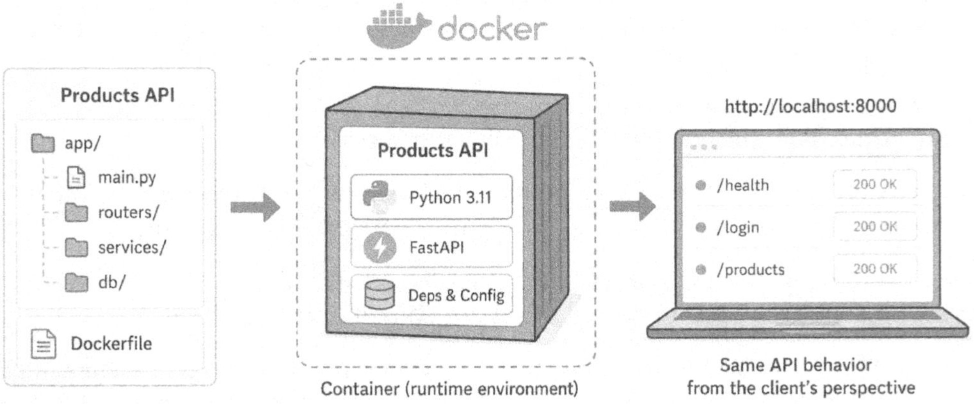

Figure 9.7: *Minimal Containerized API Setup*

Note: *The application is packaged into a container that defines its runtime environment, allowing the API to be built and executed consistently across different systems.*

At this point, the system is both testable and runnable. The next step is to simplify how these operations are performed, so that running tests, and starting the container does not require remembering multiple commands.

Adding Deployment Scripts without Overengineering

At this point, the API has gained two important capabilities. It can be verified through automated tests, and can be executed inside a container. From a technical perspective, the system is both testable and reproducible. However, there is still a practical limitation. Running the system requires remembering a sequence of commands. To execute tests, the developer must run **`pytest`**. To build the container, they must run docker build. To start the application, they must run docker run with the correct arguments. None of these steps are complex, but they are easy to forget or to execute inconsistently. This is the next problem to solve. The system is runnable, but it is not yet easy to operate. As in the rest of the chapter, we do not introduce complex infrastructure. We do not add CI/CD pipelines or deployment platforms. Instead, we focus on a simple goal: make common operations repeatable through small, explicit scripts. We express this as a prompt.

Prompt

Generate minimal scripts to run tests and start the Dockerized FastAPI API.

Keep them simple and executable. Do not introduce CI/CD pipelines or external tools.

A useful answer should produce a small number of scripts that encapsulate the commands already used. Create a new directory **`scripts/`** and inside it, create the first script **`scripts/run_tests.sh`** with the following content:

```
#!/bin/bash

echo "Running automated tests..."
pytest
```

This script does not introduce a new behavior. It simply makes the test execution explicit and easy to repeat. Next, create a script for building and running the container **`scripts/run_docker.sh`** with the following content:

```
#!/bin/bash

echo "Building Docker image..."
docker build -t products-api .

echo "Starting container..."
docker run -p 8000:8000 products-api
```

These scripts can now be executed directly:

```
chmod +x scripts/run_tests.sh
chmod +x scripts/run_docker.sh

./scripts/run_tests.sh
./scripts/run_docker.sh
```

At this point, it is important to observe what has changed. The commands themselves are the same. The system still uses **pytest** to run tests and Docker to build as well as run the application. Nothing new has been introduced at the level of behavior. Nothing new has been introduced at the level of behavior. Scripts reduce operational friction by turning multi-step processes into single commands. Instead of remembering and retyping a sequence of instructions, developers can execute a predefined script and obtain the same result in a consistent way.

What has changed is how that behavior is accessed. Instead of remembering commands, the developer runs a script. This reduces friction and makes the system easier to use consistently. At this stage, the system has reached a new level of usability. It can be tested automatically, executed in a controlled environment, and started with simple commands. The next step is to verify that the containerized version of the API behaves exactly like the local version, ensuring that reproducibility does not introduce inconsistencies.

Verifying the Dockerized API

At this point, the API can be executed inside a container. The build process is defined, the runtime environment is controlled, and the application can be started with a single command. From an operational perspective, the system is now reproducible. However, one important question remains. Does the containerized API behave exactly like the local version? As in every previous chapter, we do not assume correctness. We verify it. The goal of this section is simple: confirm that running the API inside a container does not change its observable behavior. We begin, as usual, with a prompt.

Prompt

List the observable behaviors I should verify after running this FastAPI Products API in a Docker container.

Focus on startup, health endpoint, authentication, and protected routes.

A useful answer should not describe container internals. It should describe what a client should observe when interacting with the API. Start the container using the script defined earlier:

```
./scripts/run_docker.sh
```

On Windows, shell scripts (**.sh**) are not executed directly, unless you are using a Unix-like environment such as Git Bash or WSL. To keep the workflow consistent, you can create equivalent PowerShell scripts.

Create the file **scripts/run_tests.ps1** with the following content:

```
Write-Output "Running automated tests..."
pytest
```

Then create **scripts/run_docker.ps1** with the following content:

```
Write-Output "Building Docker image..."
docker build -t products-api .

Write-Output "Starting container..."
docker run -p 8000:8000 products-api
```

You can execute these scripts from the VS Code terminal (PowerShell) using:

```
.\scripts\run_tests.ps1
.\scripts\run_docker.ps1
```

This approach provides the same repeatable workflow as the shell scripts, while remaining fully compatible with the Windows environment. Once the container is running, the API is available at:

```
http://localhost:8000
```

The first behavior to verify is startup. Open a browser or use a simple request to check the health endpoint:

```
curl http://localhost:8000/health
```

Expected response:

```
{
  "status": "ok"
}
```

This confirms that the application starts correctly inside the container. Next, verify authentication. Send a login request:

```
curl -X POST http://localhost:8000/login \
  -H "Content-Type: application/json" \
  -d '{"username": "alice", "password": "password123"}'
```

On Windows you have to use this:

```
echo '{"username": "alice", "password": "password123"}' > body.json

curl.exe -X POST http://localhost:8000/login `
-H "Content-Type: application/json" `
--data-binary "@body.json"
```

Expected response:

```
{
  "access_token": "token-alice"
}
```

This confirms that identity can be created in the containerized environment. Now verify protected routes. Try accessing a protected endpoint without a token:

```
curl http://localhost:8000/products
```

Expected response:

```
{
  "detail": "Missing Authorization header"
}
```

This confirms that authentication is enforced. Then repeat the request with a valid token:

```
curl http://localhost:8000/products \
  -H "Authorization: Bearer token-alice"
```

On Windows:

```
curl.exe http://localhost:8000/products `
-H "Authorization: Bearer token-alice"
```

The request should now succeed, and return a list of products. Finally, verify authorization.

Attempt to delete a product as a normal user:

```
curl -X DELETE http://localhost:8000/products/1 \
  -H "Authorization: Bearer token-alice"
```

On Windows

```
curl.exe -X DELETE http://localhost:8000/products/1 `
-H "Authorization: Bearer token-alice"
```

Expected response:

```
{
  "detail": "Not enough permissions"
}
```

Then repeat the same operation as an admin:

```
curl -X DELETE http://localhost:8000/products/1 \
  -H "Authorization: Bearer token-bob"
```

On Windows:

```
curl.exe -X DELETE http://localhost:8000/products/1 `
-H "Authorization: Bearer token-bob"
```

This request should succeed or return 404 if the product does not exist, but it must not fail due to permissions. At this point, several behaviors have been confirmed. The API starts correctly, responds to health checks, generates tokens, protects endpoints, and enforces role-based access—all inside the container.

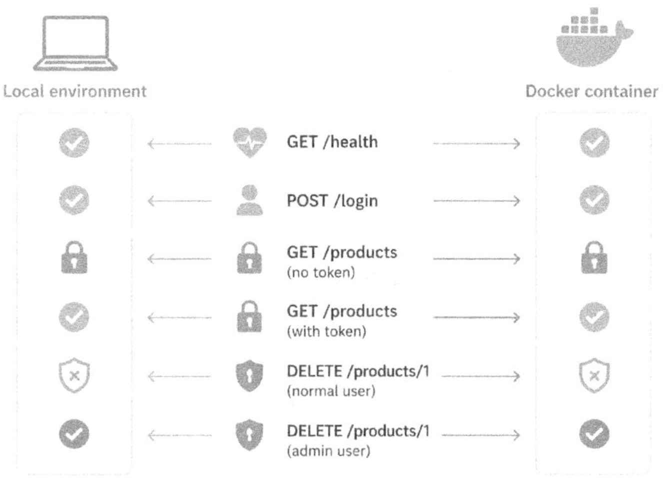

Figure 9.8: *Verifying Containerized API Behavior*

Note: *The same requests produce the same responses in both local and containerized environments, confirming that containerization preserves API behavior.*

This is the key outcome of the section. Containerization did not change what the API does. It only changed how the API is executed. The external contract remains identical. The same endpoints, the same responses, and the same error conditions are observed regardless of where the system runs. This is consistent with the method used throughout the book. Each new capability extends the system without breaking its boundary. At this stage, the API is not only functional, structured, persistent, secure, and testable. It is also reproducible. The final step is to freeze this version of the system as the new baseline, capturing both its behavior and its execution model for future development.

Freezing the Testable and Deployable Version as the New Baseline

At the end of this chapter, the API has gained two new capabilities. It is no longer only functional, structured, persistent, and secure. It is now also testable and reproducible. Automated tests verify its behavior. A container defines how it runs. And yet, something important has remained unchanged. The API boundary is still stable. The endpoints are the same. The request and response schemas are unchanged. Authentication and authorization behave exactly as before. From the client's perspective, nothing has been redesigned. This reflects the same discipline applied throughout the book. Capabilities evolve, but the boundary remains controlled. Thus, before moving forward, we freeze this new state of the system.

Current Baseline

✓ Tested

✓ Secure

✓ Persistent

✓ Dockerized

The Products API now combines the capabilities introduced throughout the previous chapters. Its behavior can be verified through automated tests, access is controlled through authentication and authorization, data is stored persistently, and the entire application can be executed consistently through containerization.

The project structure now makes this evolution explicit:

```
app/
    main.py
    models.py
    routers/
        products.py
    services/
        product_service.py
        auth_service.py
    db/
        database.py
        models.py
migrations/
tests/
    test_api.py
Dockerfile
.dockerignore
scripts/
    run_tests.sh
    run_docker.sh
```

No unnecessary layers have been introduced. The system has grown only where required: test files to verify behavior, container configuration to define runtime, and scripts to simplify execution. The existing architecture has not been modified. The router still handles HTTP semantics, the service layer still manages domain logic, and the database layer continues to handle persistence. We summarize this transformation through a prompt.

Prompt

Summarize how this FastAPI Products API evolved in this chapter.

Focus on how automated tests and deployment setup made the system verifiable and runnable.

A strong answer should highlight two key changes. First, the system became verifiable. Behavior that was previously confirmed manually is now expressed as automated tests. Health checks, authentication, authorization, and CRUD operations can be executed repeatedly, producing consistent results. The API no longer relies on memory to confirm correctness. Second, the system became reproducible. The runtime environment is now defined explicitly. The API can be built and executed inside a container, ensuring that the same behavior is observed regardless of where the system runs. Scripts simplify these operations, making them accessible and repeatable. At the same time, the API contract remained stable. Endpoints, schemas, and response formats did not change. Only the way the system is verified and executed has evolved. This is the key outcome of the chapter. The system did not become more complex. It became more controlled.

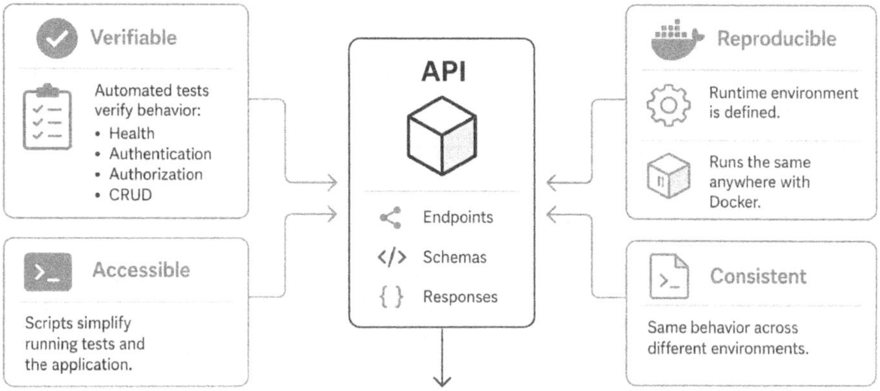

***Figure 9.9**: Testable and Deployable API as the New Baseline*

Note: *The API now includes automated tests and a defined runtime environment, while preserving the same endpoints, schemas, and observable behavior.*

At this point, the API has reached a new level of maturity. It can be tested automatically, executed consistently across environments, and verified with confidence after every change. These capabilities do not replace the previous ones—they reinforce them. The development method also remains consistent. A need is identified, translated into a prompt, implemented through minimal code, verified through observable behavior, and refined only where necessary. With this version frozen as the new baseline, the API is no longer just a working system. It is a system that can prove that it works. Everything that follows will build on this foundation—not by redesigning it, but by extending it in controlled, observable steps.

Conclusion

In this chapter, the API gained a new kind of capability. Until now, the system could be observed, structured, persisted, and secured. It behaved correctly, but that correctness still depended on manual verification and a specific runtime environment. That is no longer the case. Automated tests were introduced to make behavior verifiable. What was previously checked by hand—health, login, protected routes, and role-based access—is now expressed as executable code that can be run at any time. The system no longer relies on memory to confirm that it works.

At the same time, containerization was introduced to make execution reproducible. The API is no longer tied to a specific machine or local setup. Its runtime is defined explicitly, allowing the same behavior to be observed in any environment. These changes do not alter what the API does. They change how its correctness is established and how its execution is guaranteed.

This is the key shift of the chapter: verification and reproducibility become part of the system itself. Throughout the process, AI was used in two complementary ways. It helped generate initial test cases and configuration files, and it supported debugging by analyzing failing tests and suggesting minimal fixes. This dual role is essential. AI does not replace reasoning. It accelerates it. By the end of the chapter, the API is no longer just functional or secure. It is verifiable and runnable in a consistent way. Its behavior can be confirmed automatically, and its execution does not depend on hidden assumptions. And yet, the external contract remains unchanged. The endpoints are the same. The schemas are the same. The responses are the same. What has evolved is the level of control over the system. From this point on, every change can be validated, and every execution can be reproduced. The API is no longer something that "works on this machine." It is a system that can prove it works, wherever it runs.

In the next *Chapter 10, Debugging and Optimizing with AI*, the focus shifts from verification to evaluation. A system that passes its tests and runs consistently is not necessarily a well-designed system. Using AI as a reviewer rather than a code generator, we will examine the existing implementation, identify weaknesses, and explore how to improve readability, consistency, and maintainability without changing the observable behavior of the API. The goal is no longer to add capabilities, but to critically assess and refine the ones that already exist.

Points to Remember

- Automated tests become necessary when manual verification is no longer reliable.
- Testing should verify behavior without changing the API contract.
- Tests should interact with the API as a client would.
- Authentication and authorization require both success and failure tests.
- Focus on core behaviors: health, login, protected access, and CRUD operations.
- Containerization makes execution reproducible across environments.

- Docker changes how the API runs, not how it behaves.
- Scripts simplify repetitive operations and improve consistency.
- AI should review failures as well as generate tests and configurations.
- Consistent behavior across local and containerized environments confirms reproducibility.

Multiple Choice Questions

1. What is the main objective of *Chapter* 9?
   a. To redesign the API routing system
   b. To introduce automated testing and deployment setup
   c. To replace the database layer
   d. To remove authentication and authorization
2. Why are automated tests introduced in this chapter?
   a. Because FastAPI requires tests to run
   b. Because manual verification becomes unreliable as the system grows
   c. Because Docker cannot run without tests
   d. Because Swagger UI generates tests automatically
3. What is the primary focus of the tests generated in this chapter?
   a. Internal database queries
   b. Low-level Python functions
   c. Observable API behavior at the boundary
   d. Performance optimization
4. What is the role of FastAPI TestClient in this chapter?
   a. To deploy the API to production
   b. To simulate HTTP requests and verify responses
   c. To manage database migrations
   d. To generate API schemas
5. Why is it important to test authentication and authorization explicitly?
   a. Because they are optional features
   b. Because they define access control and failure behavior
   c. Because they improve performance
   d. Because they replace CRUD operations

6. What practical problem does containerization solve in this chapter?
    a. It improves database query speed.
    b. It ensures that the API runs consistently across environments.
    c. It replaces automated tests.
    d. It simplifies API routing.
7. After containerizing the API, what observable behavior should remain the same?
    a. The internal file structure.
    b. The Docker configuration.
    c. The API endpoints and responses.
    d. The operating system.
8. What is the purpose of adding simple scripts (for example, run_tests.sh, run_docker.sh)?
    a. To replace Docker
    b. To automate common commands, and reduce manual repetition
    c. To generate API documentation
    d. To modify API behavior
9. Which chapter capability is most likely to detect this regression automatically?
    a. Swagger UI
    b. Docker
    c. Automated Tests
    d. SQLAlchemy

Answers

1. b
2. b
3. c
4. b
5. b
6. b
7. c
8. b
9. c

Questions

1. Why does manual verification become unreliable as an API grows, and how do automated tests change the way system behavior is confirmed?
2. How does testing API behavior at the boundary improve confidence in the system without requiring knowledge of internal implementation details?
3. Why is it important to define a clear testing scope before generating automated tests, and what risks arise if tests are created without a clear focus?
4. How do automated tests for authentication and authorization (401 and 403 responses) ensure that security behavior remains consistent over time?
5. Why should CRUD operations be tested through API endpoints, rather than by directly interacting with the database layer?
6. How does containerization improve reproducibility, and what practical problems does it solve compared to running the API only in a local environment?
7. Why does containerizing the API not change its observable behavior, and how does this reinforce the concept of a stable API boundary?
8. In what ways can AI assist both in generating automated tests and in debugging failing ones, and why is human judgment still necessary to avoid incorrect assumptions or overengineering?

Key Terms

- **Automated Testing:** The process of verifying API behavior through executable test cases that can be run repeatedly without manual intervention.
- **TestClient (FastAPI):** A utility that allows tests to simulate HTTP requests to a FastAPI application, and verify responses as a client would.
- **Test Suite:** A collection of test cases that together verify the behavior of an API, including endpoints, authentication, and data operations.
- **Behavioral Verification:** The practice of confirming that an API behaves as expected by observing responses at the HTTP boundary rather than inspecting internal code.
- **Test Scope:** The defined set of behaviors and endpoints that automated tests are designed to verify, ensuring focus and avoiding unnecessary complexity.
- **Reproducible Environment:** A runtime setup that can be recreated consistently across different machines, ensuring that the API behaves the same way everywhere.

- **Containerization:** The process of packaging an application and its dependencies into a container, allowing it to run consistently across environments.
- **Dockerfile:** A configuration file that defines how a container image is built, including the base environment, dependencies, and startup command.
- **Docker Image:** A packaged snapshot of an application and its runtime environment, used to create containers.
- **Container Runtime:** The environment in which a containerized application executes, ensuring consistency regardless of the host system.
- **Deployment Scripts:** Simple executable scripts that automate common tasks such as running tests or starting the containerized API.
- **AI-Assisted Debugging:** The use of AI to analyze failing tests, identify the root cause of issues, and suggest minimal fixes without introducing unnecessary changes.

CHAPTER 10
Debugging and Optimizing with AI

Introduction

In the previous chapters, the API was built step by step. It started as a simple structure, then evolved to handle concurrency, persistence, authentication, testing, and deployment. At each stage, a new capability was added, and the system became more complete. By the end of *Chapter 9, Testing and Deploying an* API, the API reached an important milestone. It works. Its behavior is verified through automated tests. It can run consistently in a controlled environment. From the outside, it behaves correctly and predictably. But a new question now becomes unavoidable. Is the implementation actually good? A system can pass all tests and still contain weaknesses. It can behave correctly while hiding inconsistencies between layers. It can be functional, but difficult to maintain or extend. This is the limitation addressed in this chapter.

The goal is not to add new features. The goal is to examine the existing system and improve it. This requires a different approach. Up to now, AI has been used mainly to generate code. Prompts described what the system should do, and the assistant produced implementations that satisfied those requirements. In this chapter, AI is used differently. It is used as a reviewer. Instead of asking "*how do we build this*?", we ask: "*What is wrong with what we already built*?"

This shift is essential for professional development. Writing code is only part of the process. Reviewing, questioning, and refining that code is what makes a system reliable over time. Throughout the chapter, the same method will be applied repeatedly: the existing code will be analyzed, weaknesses will be identified, minimal improvements will be introduced, and behavior will be verified to ensure that functionality remains unchanged.

The objective is not to redesign the system. It is to improve it without breaking it. By the end of this chapter, the API will not look very different from the outside. The same endpoints will exist. The same requests will work. The same responses will be returned. But internally, the system will be clearer, more consistent, and more robust. This is the transition from a working system to a well-engineered one.

Structure

In this chapter, we will discuss the following topics:

- The Next Limitation: Working Code is Not Necessarily a Good Code
- Using AI as a Senior Reviewer
- Detecting Real Issues in the Current Code
- Reviewing Consistency between Layers
- Reviewing Authentication Logic
- Reviewing Error Handling and API Clarity
- Avoiding Overengineering with AI
- Reviewing Small Performance Improvements
- Verifying Improvements without Breaking Behavior
- Freezing the Reviewed Version as the New Baseline

The Next Limitation: Working Code is Not Necessarily a Good Code

At the end of *Chapter 9, Testing and Deploying an* API, the API reached a new level of maturity. It is no longer just functional. It is structured, persistent, secure, testable, and reproducible. Automated tests confirm its behavior. The application can be executed consistently across environments. From a development perspective, the system works. And yet, another limitation becomes visible. The code works, but that does not mean it is good. The code works, but that does not mean it is good. Correctness is the foundation of quality, but it is not the entirety of quality. A system can satisfy its functional requirements while still being difficult to understand, maintain, or evolve. Up to this point, correctness was the main objective. The API had to respond correctly, enforce authentication, persist data, and pass all tests. Now that these goals have been achieved, a different question becomes relevant: Is the implementation reliable, clear, and maintainable?

This is not a theoretical concern. It becomes concrete when we look at how the system evolved. In the previous chapter, automated tests exposed a real inconsistency in the system. The API accepted a description field, the database required it, but the service layer ignored it. The application appeared to work, but different parts of the system did not agree on the same definition of a product. The issue was not visible through manual testing. It only became clear when the system was observed systematically. This is the key insight. A system can be correct at the surface, and still contain structural problems underneath. At this stage, the API is no longer failing. The tests pass. The endpoints behave as expected. But this does not guarantee that the implementation is robust.

Figure 10.1 illustrates the progression from functional correctness to maintainability. A system that works and passes its tests is not necessarily ready for long-term evolution.

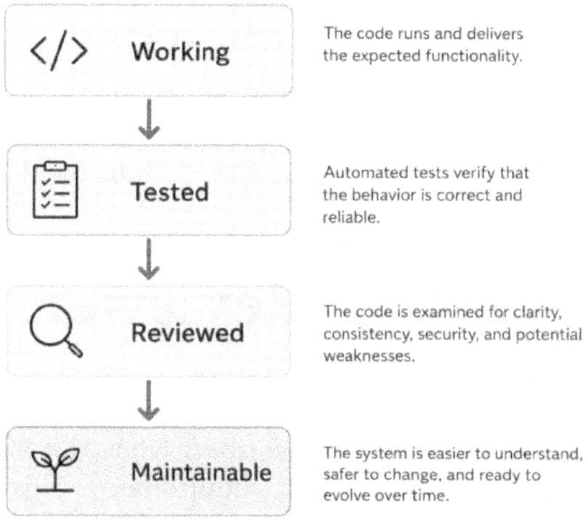

Figure 10.1: *Quality Evolves in Stages. Working Code Becomes More Trustworthy When it is Tested, and More Sustainable When it is Reviewed and Refined for Maintainability*

There may still be:

- Inconsistencies between layers
- Duplicated logic
- Unclear responsibilities
- Weak assumptions that could lead to future bugs

The goal of this chapter is not to add new features. It is to examine what already exists and improve it. This requires a different use of AI. So far, AI has been used to generate code, and help implement features. Now, it will be used to analyze the system as a whole, identify weaknesses, and suggest improvements—just as a senior engineer would during a code review. To make this shift explicit, we start with a prompt.

Prompt

Review this FastAPI Products API as a senior engineer.

Assume the system works and all tests pass.

What problems, risks, or weaknesses do you see in the current implementation? Focus on clarity, correctness, and maintainability. Avoid suggesting a complete redesign. A useful answer should not introduce new architectures or advanced frameworks. It should focus on what is already present in the code, and identify the concrete areas of improvement. This is a critical distinction. We are not asking the AI to build something new. We are asking it to understand what has already been built. At this point, the development process changes again. Previously, the cycle was:

prompt → code → execution → verification

Now, a new step is introduced:

prompt → review → reasoning → targeted improvement

The system is no longer evolving by adding capabilities. It is evolving by refining its existing structure. The next step is to apply this review process to the current codebase, and identify concrete issues that can be improved without changing the overall architecture.

Using AI as a Senior Reviewer

Once the limitation is clear, the next step is not to start modifying the code. The first step is to learn how to look at it differently. Up to this point, AI has been used to generate implementations. Prompts described what the system should do, and the assistant produced code to satisfy that requirement. This approach works well when building features, but it is not sufficient when the goal is to improve an existing system. A reviewer does not start from requirements. A reviewer starts from the code. The goal of this section is to define how AI should be used in that role.

Figure 10.2 illustrates the review workflow introduced in this chapter. Instead of generating new functionality, AI analyzes the existing code, produces observations, and supports human decision-making.

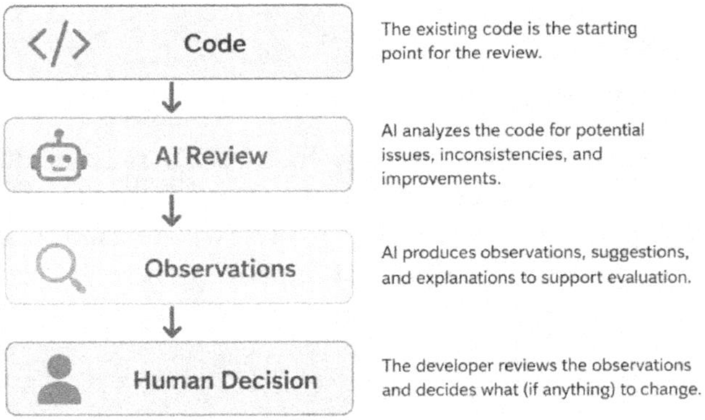

Figure 10.2: *AI-assisted Review Begins with the Existing Code Rather Than Requirements*

We begin with a prompt.

Prompt

Review this code as a senior engineer.

Identify problems, risks, or unclear parts in the implementation.

Focus on correctness, clarity, and maintainability.

Do not redesign the system.

Suggest only minimal and practical improvements.

This prompt introduces a different constraint. The quality of the review depends heavily on the constraints included in the prompt. The assistant is no longer free to propose new architectures or advanced patterns. It must work within the existing structure and focus on what can be improved without changing the system's design. This constraint is essential. Without it, the response would quickly move toward overengineering. The assistant might suggest introducing new layers, replacing authentication logic, or restructuring the entire project. These suggestions may be valid in a different context, but they are not useful here. The goal is not to rebuild the system. The aim is to understand and refine it. To see how this works in practice, consider a concrete part of the codebase. For example, the product creation route is:

```
@router.post("/products", response_model=Product, status_code=status.
HTTP_201_CREATED)
def create_product(
    product: ProductCreate,
    db: Session = Depends(get_db),
    current_user: dict = Depends(auth_service.get_current_user),
) -> Product:
    return product_service.create_product(db, product)
```

At first glance, this endpoint is correct. It defines the route, validates input, enforces authentication, and delegates logic to the service layer. It also returns the correct status code. A generation-focused prompt would stop here. A review-focused prompt goes further. It asks questions such as:

- Is the responsibility of this function clear?
- Are there hidden assumptions?
- Is error handling consistent with the rest of the system?
- Is the interaction with the service layer explicit and safe?

The purpose of the review is not to find obvious bugs. It is to identify areas where the code could become fragile over time. This is why the output of the prompt is different. A useful answer should not produce large code blocks. It should produce observations. For example, it might highlight that:

- The route depends on a generic dict for the current user, which weakens type clarity.
- Error handling is delegated entirely to the service layer without explicit guarantees.
- The boundary between HTTP logic and domain logic is correct, but not explicitly documented.

These are not failures. They are potential weaknesses. At this stage, it is important to understand what makes this approach effective. The quality of the review depends entirely on the constraints of the prompt. If the prompt is too open, the assistant will suggest redesigning the system. If the prompt is too narrow, it will miss important issues. The balance is to allow analysis while preventing unnecessary change. This leads to a simple rule. When using AI as a reviewer:

- Always define the scope.
- Always restrict the level of change.
- Always focus on observable improvements.

This keeps the system stable while allowing it to improve. At this point, the method is clear. The next step is to apply it to the current codebase, and identify real issues that can be improved through targeted changes.

Detecting Real Issues in the Current Code

Now that the review method is defined, the next step is to apply it to the actual system. The goal is not to search for theoretical problems. The goal is to identify real issues that already exist in the codebase. At this point, the API works. All tests pass. From the outside, the system behaves correctly. But as we have already seen in *Chapter 9, Testing and Deploying an* API, correctness at the surface does not guarantee consistency underneath. The most effective way to start is to revisit a concrete case. In the previous chapter, automated tests revealed a failure in the CRUD operations. The API accepted a description field, the database required it, but the service layer did not persist it. This resulted in a database error:

```
sqlite3.IntegrityError: NOT NULL constraint failed: products.description
```

That issue has already been fixed. But fixing it does not mean understanding it. This is where the review process becomes important. We turn the situation into a prompt.

Prompt

Review the product creation and update flow in this FastAPI API.

The system previously failed due to a missing "description" field in the service layer.

Explain why this inconsistency was possible and what this reveals about the current structure of the application.

Do not redesign the system. Focus on structural weaknesses.

This prompt does not ask for a fix. It asks for reasoning. To make the analysis concrete, we look at the relevant parts of the code. The API schema defines a product with a required description:

```
class ProductCreate(BaseModel):
    name: str
    price: float = Field(..., gt=0)
    description: str
```

The database model also requires it:

```
class Product(Base):
    __tablename__ = "products"

    id = Column(Integer, primary_key=True, index=True)
    name = Column(String, nullable=False, index=True)
    description = Column(String, nullable=False)
    price = Column(Float, nullable=False)
```

At the boundary of the system, the definition is consistent. The inconsistency appeared inside the service layer, where the field was simply not used. A useful AI review should identify the deeper issue. The problem is not just that a field was forgotten. The problem is that nothing in the system prevented that mistake. There is no mechanism that enforces alignment between:

- The API schema
- The service layer logic
- The database model

Each layer defines its own version of the same concept. As long as they remain aligned, the system works. But if they diverge, the error appears only at runtime—and in this case, only when the database rejects the operation. This is the key insight. The architecture separates concern correctly, but it does not guarantee consistency between them. The relationship between the API schema, service layer, and database model can be visualized as shown in *Figure* 10.3.

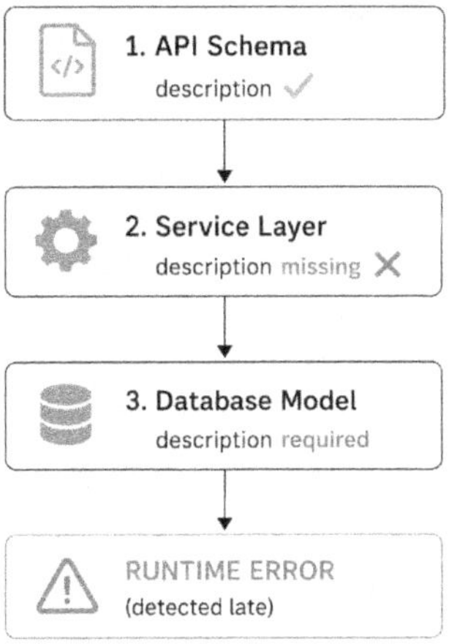

Figure 10.3: *Inconsistency between Layers*

At this stage, the goal is not to eliminate this separation. The separation is correct and necessary. The goal is to recognize the risk it introduces. A useful review should therefore highlight patterns such as:

- Data passed between layers is not explicitly validated or transformed.
- The service layer relies on manual field mapping.
- Inconsistencies are detected late (at the database level) rather than early.

These are not implementation errors. They are structural weaknesses. Understanding them changes how we approach improvements. Instead of reacting to bugs after they appear, we begin to ask: "*How can the system make these inconsistencies harder to introduce?*" This question does not require a redesign. It requires small, targeted improvements that increase clarity and reduce the chance of silent errors. The next section focuses on exactly that: improving consistency between layers, while preserving the existing structure.

Reviewing Consistency between Layers

The previous section revealed an important limitation. The system is correctly structured, but the alignment between layers depends entirely on manual discipline. The API schema defines one version of the data, the database model defines another, and the service layer is responsible for keeping them consistent. When that alignment breaks, the error appears late, often at runtime. The goal of this section is not to redesign the architecture. The aim is to reduce the risk of inconsistency, while preserving the existing structure. We start with a prompt.

Prompt

Given this FastAPI Products API, suggest minimal improvements to reduce inconsistencies between API schema, service layer, and database model.

Do not introduce new layers or redesign the architecture.

Focus on clarity and correctness.

A useful answer should not suggest replacing the service layer or introducing complex validation frameworks. It should focus on making the existing flow more explicit and less error-prone. To understand where improvements can be applied, consider the product creation logic in **`app/services/product_service.py`**:

```
def create_product(db: Session, data: ProductCreate) -> ProductDB:
    product = ProductDB(
        name=data.name,
        price=data.price,
        description=data.description,
    )
    db.add(product)
```

```
    db.commit()
    db.refresh(product)
    return product
```

This implementation is now correct, but it still relies on manual field mapping. Every field must be explicitly transferred from the API schema to the database model. If a new field is added to the schema, the service layer must be updated accordingly. If it is not, the inconsistency may go unnoticed until runtime. The improvement is not to automate everything. The improvement is to make the mapping more explicit and less fragile. One simple approach is to centralize the conversion between layers.

```
def create_product(db: Session, data: ProductCreate) -> ProductDB:
    product_data = data.model_dump()
    product = ProductDB(**product_data)

    db.add(product)
    db.commit()
    db.refresh(product)
    return product
```

In larger systems, developers may choose to explicitly filter fields before constructing database objects. For this project, the schema and model are intentionally kept aligned, so the direct **model_dump()** approach remains sufficient, and easier to maintain.

Instead of assigning each field manually, **model_dump()** converts the Pydantic model into a dictionary and passes all fields directly to the SQLAlchemy model. This reduces duplication, and lowers the risk of schema drift between layers. When new fields are added to the API schema, fewer manual changes are required in the service layer.

This change does not introduce a new abstraction. It simply uses the schema as the source of truth for the data being passed to the database model. Now, if a new field is added to `**ProductCreate**`, it will automatically be included in the mapping. The risk of forgetting a field is reduced. The same improvement can be applied to the update logic:

```
def update_product(db: Session, product_id: int, data: ProductCreate) ->
Optional[ProductDB]:
    product = get_product(db, product_id)
    if product is None:
        return None

    for key, value in data.model_dump().items():
        setattr(product, key, value)

    db.commit()
    db.refresh(product)
    return product
```

At this point, these changes can be applied directly. They do not alter the behavior of the API. All existing endpoints, responses, and tests should continue to work exactly as before. Run the test suite again:

```
pytest
```

All tests should still pass. This confirms that the improvement reduces duplication without changing the external behavior of the system. Again, the goal is not to introduce a new pattern. The goal is to reduce duplication and make the relationship between layers clearer. A useful AI review should also highlight another aspect. Even with improved mapping, the system still assumes that the API schema and database model are compatible. There is no explicit validation step between them. This is acceptable for a simple system, but it reinforces the idea that consistency is a responsibility shared across layers.

Instead of copying fields one by one, the service layer uses the schema as a structured input, reducing the risk of missing or inconsistent data. At this stage, it is important to observe what has changed. The architecture is the same. The router still handles HTTP logic. The service layer still manages data operations. The database model remains unchanged. What changed is the clarity of the data flow. The system is now less dependent on manual synchronization between layers, and therefore less likely to introduce silent inconsistencies. This is the pattern introduced in this chapter. We do not replace the system. We are making small, targeted improvements that reduce risk and increase clarity. The next step is to apply the same review approach to another part of the system where simplifications were intentionally introduced: authentication.

Reviewing Authentication Logic

Up to this point, the review process has focused on data consistency between layers. The next step is to apply the same method to another part of the system that was intentionally kept simple: authentication. The authentication flow introduced in *Chapter 8, Securing an API System* was designed to be minimal and runnable. It had to make identity visible in the request lifecycle without introducing unnecessary complexity. That choice was correct for the stage of the project. But now the system is no longer being judged only by whether it works. It is being reviewed. And under review, the current authentication logic immediately reveals several weaknesses. The review can be summarized by examining the most visible weaknesses, and the risks they introduce. *Table* 10.1 provides the following overview.

Current Implementation	Review Concern
Predictable tokens (token-username)	Tokens can be forged easily
In-memory user store	Data is lost when the application restarts
No token expiration	Tokens remain valid indefinitely

Current Implementation	Review Concern
Simplified authentication flow	Suitable for learning, not for production use
Minimal validation	Limited protection against misuse

Table 10.1: *Authentication Review Summary*

It is functional, but it is also clearly fragile. We begin with the same kind of prompt used throughout this chapter.

Prompt

Review the authentication logic in this FastAPI Products API as a senior engineer.

Focus on correctness, safety, and maintainability.

Do not redesign the system or introduce external services.

Suggest only minimal improvements.

A useful answer should not propose a complete replacement of the auth system. It should work within the current structure and identify the most obvious weaknesses in the existing implementation. To make that review concrete, consider the current code in **`app/services/auth_service.py`**:

```
# simple in-memory users
fake_users_db = {
    "alice": {"username": "alice", "password": "password123", "role":
"user"},
    "bob": {"username": "bob", "password": "secret", "role": "admin"},
}

def authenticate_user(username: str, password: str) -> Optional[dict]:
    user = fake_users_db.get(username)
    if not user or user["password"] != password:
        return None
    return user

def create_token(user: dict) -> str:
    # extremely simplified token (for learning purposes only)
    return f"token-{user['username']}"
```

This code is easy to understand, but a review should highlight two immediate issues. The first is that passwords are stored and compared in plain text. This makes the implementation simple, but it also means that credentials are handled in the weakest possible form. The second is that tokens are entirely predictable. A token such as token-bob is not really being issued securely; it can be constructed without authentication. These are not abstract concerns. They are direct consequences of the implementation. At this point, it is important to make a distinction. A good review does not mean applying every possible improvement immediately. It means identifying weaknesses and deciding which ones can be addressed safely at the current stage of the system. We start with the improvement that can be applied immediately without affecting the rest of the system: password handling. Instead of storing plain-text passwords, we hash them before storing and comparing them.

Open **app/services/auth_service.py** and update the relevant parts as follows:

```
import hashlib
from typing import Optional
from fastapi import Header, HTTPException, status

def hash_password(password: str) -> str:
    return hashlib.sha256(password.encode()).hexdigest()

fake_users_db = {
    "alice": {
        "username": "alice",
        "password": hash_password("password123"),
        "role": "user",
    },
    "bob": {
        "username": "bob",
        "password": hash_password("secret"),
        "role": "admin",
    },
}

def authenticate_user(username: str, password: str) -> Optional[dict]:
    user = fake_users_db.get(username)
    if not user:
        return None

    if user["password"] != hash_password(password):
        return None

    return user
```

This hashing approach is suitable only for demonstration purposes. While it improves on plain-text password storage, production systems should use dedicated password-hashing algorithms such as bcrypt, Argon2, or PBKDF2, which are specifically designed to resist brute-force and password-cracking attacks.

This change is small, but meaningful. The structure of the system remains identical. The login route still sends credentials to the service, and the service still returns a user if authentication succeeds. But the way passwords are handled is now more defensible. At this point, these changes can be applied directly. They do not alter the external behavior of the API. Login requests, tokens, and all existing tests continue to work exactly as before. Run the test suite:

```
pytest
```

All tests should still pass. You can also verify manually:

Before starting the server:

```
uvicorn app.main:app -reload
```

and then insert this command:

```
curl http://localhost:8000/login \
  -H "Content-Type: application/json" \
  -d '{"username": "alice", "password": "password123"}'
```

On Windows:

```
echo '{"username": "alice", "password": "password123"}' > body.json

curl.exe -X POST http://localhost:8000/login `
-H "Content-Type: application/json" `
--data-binary "@body.json"
```

The response should still include a valid token:

```
{
  "access_token": "token-alice"
}
```

This confirms that the improvement strengthens the implementation without changing the behavior.

The second issue identified by the review concerns the token format. The current token is predictable because it is derived directly from the username. A more robust approach would generate random tokens, and store them server-side, for example:

```
import secrets

issued_tokens = {}

def create_token(user: dict) -> str:
    token = secrets.token_hex(16)
    issued_tokens[token] = user["username"]
    return token
```

However, applying this change now would alter the behavior of the system. Tokens would no longer follow the **`token-username`** format, and all the existing tests, examples, and request flows would need to be updated. For this reason, we do not apply this change at this stage. Instead, we keep it as a **review finding**. This is an important distinction. A correct improvement is not always the right improvement to apply immediately. The role of the developer is to decide:

- Which changes are safe and local
- Which changes affect the system's behavioral baseline

In this case, password hashing is a safe, local improvement. Changing the token mechanism is a broader change that belongs to a future evolution of the system.

At this stage, it is important to observe what kind of improvement has been made. The system has not been re-architected. The router has not changed. The dependency-based access control remains the same. The improvement is local and deliberate. Weaknesses identified through review have been reduced without introducing complexity that the rest of the project is not ready to support. This is exactly the role of AI in this chapter. Not to replace the design, but to inspect it critically and suggest improvements proportional to the system's current level of maturity. The next step is to apply the same approach to another area where working code may still be unnecessarily fragile: error handling and the clarity of API responses.

Reviewing Error Handling and API Clarity

The previous sections focused on data consistency and authentication. Both revealed the same pattern: the system works, but some decisions make it more fragile than necessary. The same is true for error handling. At first glance, the API already handles errors correctly. It returns 401 for authentication failures, 403 for permission issues, and 404 when a resource is not found. From a functional perspective, everything is in place. But under review, another limitation becomes visible. Error handling is correct, but not consistent. Different parts of the system express errors in slightly different ways. Some messages are generic, others are specific. Some are defined directly in the router, others emerge indirectly from deeper layers. This does not break the API, but it makes the system harder to reason about and less predictable for clients. As in previous sections, we start with a prompt.

Prompt

Review the error handling in this FastAPI Products API.

Identify inconsistencies in how errors are raised and returned.

Suggest minimal improvements to make error responses clearer and more consistent.

Do not redesign the system.

A useful answer should not offer a full error-handling framework. It should focus on clarity and consistency within the current structure. To see the issue, consider how errors are currently handled in the router. For example, retrieving a product:

```
@router.get("/products/{product_id}", response_model=Product)
def get_product(
```

```
    product_id: int,
    db: Session = Depends(get_db),
    current_user: dict = Depends(auth_service.get_current_user),
) -> Product:
    product = product_service.get_product(db, product_id)
    if product is None:
        raise HTTPException(
            status_code=status.HTTP_404_NOT_FOUND,
            detail=f"Product {product_id} not found",
        )
    return product
```

And deleting a product:

```
@router.delete("/products/{product_id}")
def delete_product(
    product_id: int,
    db: Session = Depends(get_db),
    current_user: dict = Depends(auth_service.get_current_user),
) -> dict:
    if current_user["role"] != "admin":
        raise HTTPException(
            status_code=status.HTTP_403_FORBIDDEN,
            detail="Not enough permissions",
        )

    deleted = product_service.delete_product(db, product_id)
    if not deleted:
        raise HTTPException(
            status_code=status.HTTP_404_NOT_FOUND,
            detail=f"Product {product_id} not found",
        )
    return {"message": f"Product {product_id} deleted"}
```

These implementations are correct, but they reveal small inconsistencies:

- Error messages are written manually in each route.
- Similar errors are repeated across endpoints.
- Wording is not standardized ("**`Not enough permissions`**" versus "**`Product X not found`**").

This creates duplication and increases the chance of divergence over time. The improvement is not to centralize everything in a complex system. The improvement is to make error handling more explicit and reusable. A minimal step is to define small helper functions for common error cases.

Open **app/routers/products.py** and introduce simple helpers:

```
from fastapi import HTTPException, status

def not_found(resource: str, resource_id: int) -> None:
    raise HTTPException(
        status_code=status.HTTP_404_NOT_FOUND,
        detail=f"{resource} {resource_id} not found",
    )

def forbidden(message: str = "Not enough permissions") -> None:
    raise HTTPException(
        status_code=status.HTTP_403_FORBIDDEN,
        detail=message,
    )
```

For now, these helpers can remain inside **app/routers/products.py** because they are small and used only by this router. If the project grows, and the same error helpers are needed across multiple routers, they can be moved later to a shared module such as **app/utils/errors.py**. At this stage, keeping them close to the routes preserves clarity without introducing another layer.

Now the routes become slightly clearer:

```
@router.get("/products/{product_id}", response_model=Product)
def get_product(
    product_id: int,
    db: Session = Depends(get_db),
    current_user: dict = Depends(auth_service.get_current_user),
) -> Product:
    product = product_service.get_product(db, product_id)
    if product is None:
        not_found("Product", product_id)
    return product
```

And:

```
@router.delete("/products/{product_id}")
def delete_product(
    product_id: int,
    db: Session = Depends(get_db),
    current_user: dict = Depends(auth_service.get_current_user),
):
    if current_user["role"] != "admin":
        forbidden()

    deleted = product_service.delete_product(db, product_id)
```

```
    if not deleted:
        not_found("Product", product_id)

    return {"message": f"Product {product_id} deleted"}
```

At this point, these changes can be applied directly. They do not modify the behavior of the API. All endpoints return the same status codes and responses as before. Run the test suite again:

```
pytest
```

All tests should still pass. This confirms that the improvement standardizes error handling without affecting the external behavior of the system. This change is small, but it has two effects. First, it removes duplication. The same logic is no longer repeated across endpoints. Secondly, it standardizes error messages. All 404 responses follow the same format, and permission errors are expressed consistently.

At this stage, it is important to observe what has not changed. The API still returns the same status codes. The endpoints are identical. The service layer remains unchanged. The improvement is entirely at the boundary, where HTTP behavior is defined. This is consistent with the architecture established earlier. The router owns HTTP semantics. Error handling is part of that responsibility. This section reinforces a key principle. Clarity is not only about what the system does. It is also about how consistently it communicates when something goes wrong. The next step is to apply the same review discipline to another dimension of the system: avoiding unnecessary complexity when using AI for improvements.

Avoiding Overengineering with AI

At this point, the value of AI as a reviewer is clear. It can identify inconsistencies, suggest small fixes, and help make the system safer and easier to understand. But this usefulness comes with a risk. If the prompt is too open, the assistant will often suggest much more than the system actually needs. This is not a failure of the tool. It is a natural consequence of the request. A system like the current Products API could easily trigger suggestions such as:

- Replacing the simple token flow with a full JWT implementation
- Introducing repository classes between services and the database
- Adding a dedicated permissions module
- Splitting routers, schemas, and security concerns into even more layers
- Introducing caching, async database access, or advanced dependency injection

Some of these ideas may be reasonable in larger systems. But in this project, at this stage, they would introduce complexity faster than they would increase clarity. That is the problem this section addresses. The challenge is no longer how to get suggestions from AI. The challenge is how to get the right size of suggestion. A good way to make this visible is to compare two different prompts. A weak prompt looks like this:

Prompt

Improve this FastAPI API as much as possible.

This prompt gives the assistant no boundaries. It does not define the scope of change, the purpose of the review, or the level of complexity that is acceptable. As a result, the answer will usually drift toward redesign. A stronger prompt looks like this:

Prompt

Review the FastAPI Products API as a senior engineer.

Suggest only minimal improvements that increase clarity, correctness, or maintainability.

Do not redesign the system.

Do not introduce new architectural layers.

Do not replace the current authentication approach.

This second prompt does something essential. It constrains the assistant. It tells the AI not only what to do, but also what not to do. This is particularly important in a chapter like this one, where the goal is not to rebuild the API, but to improve it while preserving the structure established in earlier chapters. To see why this matters, consider the current codebase as a whole. The router already has a clear responsibility: it manages HTTP semantics, authentication dependencies, and access rules. The service layer owns product operations. The database layer owns persistence. The system is not incomplete. It is intentionally small. A useful AI review should respect that. For example, if we ask for a review of the current authentication logic without constraints, the assistant may suggest replacing the in-memory users with a user table, using JWT with signing and expiration, adding refresh tokens, or introducing password hashing libraries. These may all be legitimate improvements in the abstract. But not all legitimate improvements are appropriate in the current context. The book's method has never been to maximize sophistication. It has always been to add only what behavior requires.

The effect of prompt constraints on AI-generated recommendations is illustrated in *Figure* 10.4. Broad prompts tend to produce a wider range of suggestions, including unnecessary complexity, while constrained prompts encourage smaller, more targeted improvements that preserve the structure of the system.

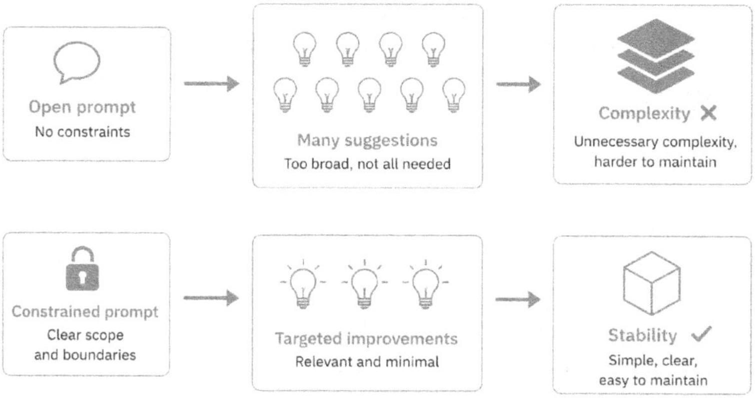

Figure 10.4: *Constraining AI to Avoid Overengineering*

This introduces an important discipline. When using AI for review, the developer must act as the keeper of scope. The assistant can produce many suggestions. The developer decides which suggestions belong to the current stage of the system and which ones belong to a future stage that has not yet been reached. This is not just a practical concern. It is part of professional engineering judgment. A mature workflow does not accept every possible improvement. It selects improvements that solve real problems without destabilizing the codebase. At this stage, it is useful to formulate a simple rule: ***if the system works and the architecture is already clear, improvements should reduce risk, not increase abstraction.***

This rule helps filter AI output. A suggestion is probably useful if it:

- Removes duplication
- Improves consistency
- Makes behavior easier to verify
- Reduces the chance of hidden bugs

A suggestion is probably premature if it:

- Adds layers that the system does not yet need
- Replaces simple, understandable code with generic patterns
- Solves a problem that has not actually appeared in the project

This distinction is what keeps AI-assisted review productive. The goal is not to reject ambitious ideas categorically. The goal is to make sure that improvements remain proportional to the system in front of us. At this point, the review process has already helped improve consistency, strengthen authentication, and clarify error handling. The next step is to apply the same disciplined review to another dimension of the system: performance and efficiency, but again, only at the level that the current project actually requires.

Reviewing Small Performance Improvements

At this stage, the system is correct, consistent, and easier to understand. The next question is natural: "*Can it be made more efficient?*" Performance is often introduced as a separate discipline, with its own tools and theories. But in this project, the goal is different. We are not building a high-load system. We are refining a small, controlled API. This means that performance improvements should follow the same rule established in the previous section: ***improve what is visible and relevant, without introducing unnecessary complexity***. We begin with a prompt.

Prompt

Review this FastAPI Products API for small performance improvements.

Focus on database usage and request handling.

Suggest only simple changes that improve efficiency.

Do not introduce caching layers or new infrastructure.

A useful answer should not propose large-scale optimizations. It should focus on small inefficiencies that can be improved without changing the structure of the system. To see where this applies, consider the current implementation of product listing in **app/services/product_service.py**:

```
def list_products(db: Session) -> List[ProductDB]:
    return db.query(ProductDB).all()
```

This is correct and simple. But it has one implicit assumption. It returns all products. In a small dataset, this is fine. But as the number of records grows, returning everything becomes inefficient. Even in a simple system, it is useful to make this behavior explicit. A minimal improvement is to introduce a limit.

```
def list_products(db: Session, limit: int = 100) -> List[ProductDB]:
    return db.query(ProductDB).limit(limit).all()
```

This does not change the structure of the system. It simply prevents unbounded queries and makes the behavior more predictable. To expose this at the API level, update the route. A small amount of validation can also be applied to prevent unreasonable values, while keeping the implementation simple.

```
@router.get("/products", response_model=List[Product])
def list_products(
    limit: int = Query(default = 100, ge = 1, le = 1000),
    db: Session = Depends(get_db),
    current_user: dict = Depends(auth_service.get_current_user),
```

```
) -> List[Product]:
    return product_service.list_products(db, limit)
```

This change is small, but it makes the endpoint safer. The API now communicates that listing products is a bounded operation. Another area where small improvements matter is unnecessary database work. Consider the update operation in the **app/services/product_service.py**:

```
def update_product(db: Session, product_id: int, data: ProductCreate) ->
Optional[ProductDB]:
    product = get_product(db, product_id)
    if product is None:
        return None

    for key, value in data.model_dump().items():
        setattr(product, key, value)

    db.commit()
    db.refresh(product)
    return product
```

This implementation updates every field, even if the values are unchanged. In a simple system, this is acceptable. But a review may suggest a small refinement: update only when necessary.

```
def update_product(db: Session, product_id: int, data: ProductCreate) ->
Optional[ProductDB]:
    product = get_product(db, product_id)
    if product is None:
        return None

    for key, value in data.model_dump().items():
        if getattr(product, key) != value:
            setattr(product, key, value)

    db.commit()
    db.refresh(product)
    return product
```

At this point, these changes can be applied directly. They do not alter the external behavior of the API. All endpoints, responses, and tests should continue to work as before. Run the test suite again:

```
pytest
```

All tests should still pass. This confirms that the improvements increase efficiency without changing the observable behavior of the system.

This change avoids unnecessary writes and makes the operation slightly more efficient, without adding complexity. A useful AI review might also point out that database sessions are created per request, which is already correct, and that queries are simple and predictable. In this context, no further optimization is required.

At this stage, it is important to observe what has not changed. The system does not introduce caching, asynchronous queries, or advanced optimization strategies. Those techniques are useful in larger systems, but they are not required here. This is consistent with the method of the book. Performance is not improved by adding complexity. It is improved by removing inefficiency where it is visible. The same principle applies as in previous sections. We do not redesign the system. We refine it. The next step is to verify that these improvements do not change observable behavior, and that the system continues to satisfy all the existing tests.

Verifying Improvements without Breaking Behavior

At this point, several improvements have been introduced. Data consistency between layers has been strengthened. Authentication has been made less fragile. Error handling is more consistent. Small performance refinements have been applied. Each change was minimal, local, and deliberate. But one question remains. Did these changes alter the behavior of the API? As in previous chapters, we do not assume correctness. We verify it. The goal of this section is simple: confirm that all improvements preserve the existing API contract.

Figure 10.5 illustrates the review cycle used throughout this chapter. Improvements are applied only after review, and tests are used to confirm that behavior remains unchanged.

Figure 10.5: *Review-driven Improvements Should Always be Verified through Testing. The Goal is to Improve Implementation Quality while Preserving the Existing API Contract*

We begin with a prompt.

Prompt

After applying small improvements to this FastAPI Products API, what behaviors should I verify to ensure nothing was broken?

Focus on observable API behavior, not internal implementation.

A useful answer should not describe code structure. It should describe what a client would observe when interacting with the API. From that, we derive a verification checklist. The API should still:

- Respond correctly to the **`/health`** endpoint
- Allow login with valid credentials
- Reject invalid credentials with 401
- Require authentication for protected routes
- Allow access with a valid token
- Enforce role-based authorization (403 for non-admin users)
- Support full CRUD operations on products
- Return consistent response formats

These behaviors were already tested in *Chapter 9, Testing and Deploying an* API. Now they serve a different purpose. They confirm that improvements did not introduce regressions. Run the test suite with **`pytest`**. All tests should pass. This result is significant. It shows that the system has improved internally while remaining stable externally. To make this more concrete, consider one of the changes introduced earlier: limiting the number of products returned by the listing endpoint. From the client's perspective, the endpoint still returns a list of products. The structure of the response is unchanged. The only difference is that the result is now bounded. This does not break existing tests, because they verify structure and behavior, not dataset size. The same applies to improvements in authentication and error handling. Passwords are now hashed, tokens are less predictable, and error messages are more consistent. But the external behavior—status codes, routes, and response formats—remains the same.

This is the key principle of this chapter. Improvements must be safe. A system that becomes more complex or more fragile after refactoring is not improving. It is regressing. Verification ensures that:

- Changes are controlled.
- Behavior remains predictable.
- The API contract is preserved.

At this stage, the development process is fully established. The system is not only built and tested. It is reviewed, improved, and verified again. The cycle is now:

prompt → review → improvement → verification

This is the foundation of professional-level problem solving. The final step is to capture this improved state of the system, and establish it as the new baseline for future development.

Freezing the Reviewed Version as the New Baseline

At the end of this chapter, the API has not gained new features. It has gained something more subtle and more important. It has been reviewed. Up to this point in the book, each chapter introduced a new capability: structure, concurrency, persistence, security, testing, and reproducibility. Each step expanded what the system could do. This chapter followed a different path. Instead of adding capabilities, it examined the existing ones. The API was analyzed, questioned, and improved without changing its external behavior. Weaknesses were identified. Small inconsistencies were corrected. Fragile assumptions were made more explicit. None of these changes altered what the API does. They changed how reliably it does it. This is the key distinction. A system can evolve not only by growing, but by becoming more precise. Thus, before moving forward, we freeze this new state of the system. The project structure remains the same:

```
app/
    main.py
    models.py
    routers/
        products.py
    services/
        product_service.py
        auth_service.py
    db/
        database.py
        models.py
migrations/
tests/
    test_api.py
Dockerfile
.dockerignore
scripts/
    run_tests.sh
    run_docker.sh
```

No new layers were introduced. No architectural redesign took place. All improvements were applied within the existing structure. The router still owns HTTP behavior. The service layer still manages business logic. The database layer still handles persistence.

The test suite still verifies observable behavior. The container setup still defines execution. Hence, we summarize this transformation with a prompt.

Prompt

Summarize how this FastAPI Products API improved in this chapter.

Focus on how AI was used to review and refine the system, and how the improvements increased clarity, consistency, and reliability

without changing the API contract.

A strong answer should highlight three key outcomes. First, the system became more consistent. Data flow between layers is clearer, and the risk of silent mismatches has been reduced. Improvements in the service layer ensure that API schemas and database models remain aligned. Secondly, the system became safer. Authentication handling was strengthened, predictable tokens were replaced with less trivial ones, and error handling became more uniform. These changes do not make the system production-grade, but they reduce obvious weaknesses. Thirdly, the system became easier to understand and maintain. Duplication was reduced, responsibilities are clearer, and behavior is more explicit. Therefore, the code is not only correct; it is more readable and predictable.

The resulting state of the reviewed system is summarized in *Figure* 10.6. Although the internal implementation has been refined, the overall architecture and external behavior remain unchanged. The review process improves consistency, security, and maintainability without altering the API contract.

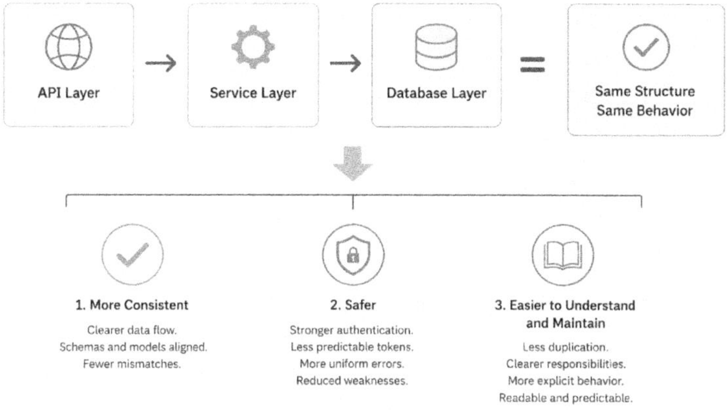

Figure 10.6: *Reviewed API as the New Baseline*

At this point, the API has reached a new level of maturity.

It is not only functional, structured, persistent, secure, testable, and reproducible. It is also:

- Reviewed

- Refined
- More resilient to future change

This is not the result of adding complexity. It is the result of removing uncertainty. The development method has now fully evolved. It began with building behavior. It continued with verifying that behavior. It now includes reviewing and improving that behavior under controlled constraints. With this version frozen as the new baseline, the system is ready for further evolution—not by replacing what exists, but by extending it with the same discipline that has been established throughout the book.

Conclusion

In this chapter, the API did not gain new features. It gained quality. Instead of expanding the system, the focus shifted to reviewing and refining what already existed. AI was used not only to generate code, but also to analyze it, identify weaknesses, and suggest targeted improvements under clear constraints.

Several refinements were introduced throughout the chapter. Data consistency between layers was improved, authentication logic was strengthened, error handling became more uniform, and small performance optimizations were applied. In every case, the goal was the same: improve the implementation without changing the API contract.

This chapter highlights an important principle. Correctness is only the beginning of quality. A system can work and still be difficult to maintain, evolve, or trust. Review and refinement help transform working code into code that is more robust, predictable, and understandable.

Another key lesson concerns the use of AI itself. Open-ended prompts often lead to unnecessary complexity, while constrained prompts produce focused and practical improvements. AI does not replace engineering judgment. It supports it.

By the end of the chapter, the API remains functionally identical, but it is more consistent, easier to maintain, and better prepared for future evolution.

In the next *Chapter 11, Designing Production-Ready Systems*, the focus shifts from code quality to production realism. Several simplifications introduced throughout the book will be revisited, their limitations evaluated, and targeted improvements applied to make the API behave more like a real-world system, while preserving clarity and simplicity.

Points to Remember

- Working code is not automatically maintainable code.
- Code review improves quality without changing the API contract.

- AI can review code as well as generate it.
- Constrained prompts reduce the risk of overengineering.
- API schemas, services, and database models must remain aligned.
- Improvements should be small, targeted, and low risk.
- Authentication can work correctly, while still requiring refinement.
- Consistent error handling improves clarity and maintainability.
- Simple performance improvements are often sufficient.
- Tests confirm that improvements preserve the existing behavior.

Multiple Choice Questions

1. What is the main objective of this chapter?
   a. To introduce automated testing
   b. To review and improve the existing API using AI
   c. To replace the database layer
   d. To redesign the entire system
2. Why is code review introduced after testing and deployment?
   a. Because tests are optional
   b. Because working code may still contain weaknesses
   c. Because Docker requires review
   d. Because FastAPI enforces it
3. What is the role of AI in this chapter?
   a. To generate new features
   b. To deploy the application
   c. To act as a senior reviewer, and identify improvements
   d. To replace the developer
4. Why must review prompts be constrained?
   a. To reduce the execution time
   b. To prevent AI from suggesting unnecessary redesign
   c. To improve performance
   d. To simplify testing

5. What issue was revealed by the missing description field?
   a. A database failure
   b. A network error
   c. A mismatch between system layers
   d. A routing issue
6. What is the goal of improving authentication logic in this chapter?
   a. To implement full production security
   b. To replace FastAPI security
   c. To reduce obvious weaknesses with minimal changes
   d. To remove authentication
7. Why is consistent error handling important?
   a. It improves database performance.
   b. It reduces API complexity.
   c. It makes API behavior more predictable for clients.
   d. It replaces validation.
8. What is the correct approach to performance improvements in this chapter?
   a. Introduce caching and async processing
   b. Redesign the database
   c. Apply small, targeted optimizations
   d. Ignore performance
9. What type of issue has been discovered?
   a. Functional failure
   b. Structural weakness
   c. Authentication error
   d. Deployment issue

Answers

1. b
2. b
3. c
4. b
5. c

6. c
7. c
8. c
9. b

Questions

1. Why can a system pass all tests and still contain structural weaknesses?
2. How does reviewing code differ from generating code, and why is this distinction important?
3. What risks arise when API schema, service logic, and database models are not aligned?
4. Why should improvements be minimal rather than based on a complete redesign?
5. How does constraining AI prompts help avoid overengineering?
6. In what ways can authentication be improved without introducing unnecessary complexity?
7. Why is consistent error handling important for API usability and maintainability?
8. How can small performance improvements provide value without increasing system complexity?
9. Why is it essential to verify behavior after making internal improvements?
10. How does AI-assisted review complement, rather than replace, developer judgment?

Key Terms

- **Code Review:** The process of analyzing the existing code to identify weaknesses, inconsistencies, and opportunities for improvement.
- **AI-Assisted Review:** The use of AI to evaluate code quality, detect risks, and suggest targeted improvements under defined constraints.
- **Maintainability:** The ease with which a system can be understood, modified, and extended over time.
- **Consistency between Layers:** The alignment of data definitions and behavior across API schema, service logic, and database models.
- **Structural Weakness:** A hidden issue in the system design that may not break functionality immediately but can lead to future bugs.

- **Overengineering:** Introducing unnecessary complexity or abstraction that does not provide proportional value.
- **Constrained Prompting:** The practice of limiting AI responses through explicit instructions to ensure focused and relevant output.
- **Error Handling Consistency:** The practice of returning uniform and predictable error responses across all API endpoints.
- **Incremental Improvement:** A method of refining a system through small, controlled changes rather than large-scale redesign.
- **Behavioral Stability:** The property of a system whose external behavior remains unchanged despite internal improvements.
- **Refactoring:** The process of improving code structure and clarity without altering its external behavior.
- **Verification Cycle:** The process of confirming that changes do not break the existing functionality through testing and observation.

CHAPTER 11
Designing Production-Ready Systems

Introduction

In the previous chapters, the API evolved step- by- step from a simple structure into a system that is secure, testable, and internally consistent. Each improvement focused on making the application behave correctly, while preserving a clear and stable interface. At this stage, however, correctness is no longer enough. A system can work, pass all tests, and still rely on assumptions that do not hold outside a controlled environment. Some of these assumptions were introduced intentionally to simplify earlier steps, but they now represent the main gap between a working application and a realistic one. This chapter addresses that gap.

The goal is not to redesign the system or introduce complex infrastructure, but to examine how it would behave under real conditions and to remove the most critical simplifications that limit its credibility. Using targeted prompts, the system will be evaluated, refined, and gradually aligned with the constraints that define production environments. By the end of the chapter, the API will not be a complete production system, but it will no longer behave like a simplified example. It will become a system whose behavior can be understood, trusted, and extended with a clear awareness of its limits.

In practical terms, readers will learn how to identify assumptions that are acceptable during early development but become problematic in more realistic environments. They will practice using AI to evaluate architectural decisions, recognize production-related risks, and apply focused improvements that increase reliability without introducing unnecessary complexity.

Structure

In this chapter, we will discuss the following topics:

- The Next Limitation: A Working API is Not Yet a Real System

- Persisting Users in the Database
- Strengthening Password Handling for Real Systems
- Making Token Handling More Realistic
- Adding Logout and Token Revocation
- Adding Basic Pagination for Product Listing
- Evaluating What Would Still Break in Production
- Consolidating a Production-Aware System
- Freezing the Production-Aware System

The Next Limitation: A Working API is Not Yet a Real System

At the end of *Chapter 10, Debugging and Optimizing with AI*, the API has reached a high level of quality. It is structured, consistent, tested, and internally coherent. Its behavior is predictable, its endpoints are stable, and its logic has been reviewed and refined through multiple iterations. From a development perspective, the system works. And yet, a new limitation becomes impossible to ignore. The system is still not realistic. This is not a problem of correctness, but of representation. Several aspects of the API were intentionally simplified in earlier chapters to make the system easier to understand, and evolve step by step. Those simplifications were appropriate at the time, but they now begin to stand out. The clearest example is the authentication system. Users exist only in memory, credentials are tied to the running process, and identity disappears as soon as the application is restarted. Tokens are generated without persistence, and do not reflect any durable relationship between the client and the system. In practice, authentication works, but it does so in a way that cannot exist outside a controlled environment. A real system behaves differently.

User data is stored in a database, credentials persist across executions, and authentication is tied to durable information rather than temporary state. Identity is not reconstructed at runtime—it is part of the system itself. This places the current API in an intermediate position. It behaves correctly, but it does not yet reflect the constraints of a real-world application. This is the purpose of the chapter. The goal is not to redesign the system or introduce complex infrastructure. Instead, the focus is on removing the last major simplifications that prevent the API from behaving in a realistic way. As in previous chapters, we begin by making the problem explicit through a prompt.

Prompt

What parts of this FastAPI Products API are still too simplified to be considered realistic in a production-like environment?

Focus on authentication, data persistence, and system behavior.

A useful answer should highlight what is already implicit in the current design: the in-memory user store does not reflect real systems, authentication is not tied to persistent data, and token handling remains fragile and temporary. These are not minor issues. They define how the system behaves over time and determine whether it can be trusted outside a controlled environment. At this stage, the goal is no longer just to identify limitations, but to address them directly. This introduces a new kind of step in the book. Until now, improvements have been local and incremental, each one solving a specific problem without significantly changing the nature of the system. From this point on, changes will still remain controlled, but they will begin to increase the realism of the application, even if that introduces a small amount of additional complexity. The balance we want to achieve is precise. The system should not become perfect, nor should it attempt to cover every possible scenario. It should become simple, but credible—a system that behaves like a real one, while remaining fully understandable. The shift from temporary identity to persistent identity can be visualized as shown in *Figure 11.1*. The goal is not to introduce new functionality, but to replace temporary assumptions with behaviors that remain consistent across restarts, executions, and environments.

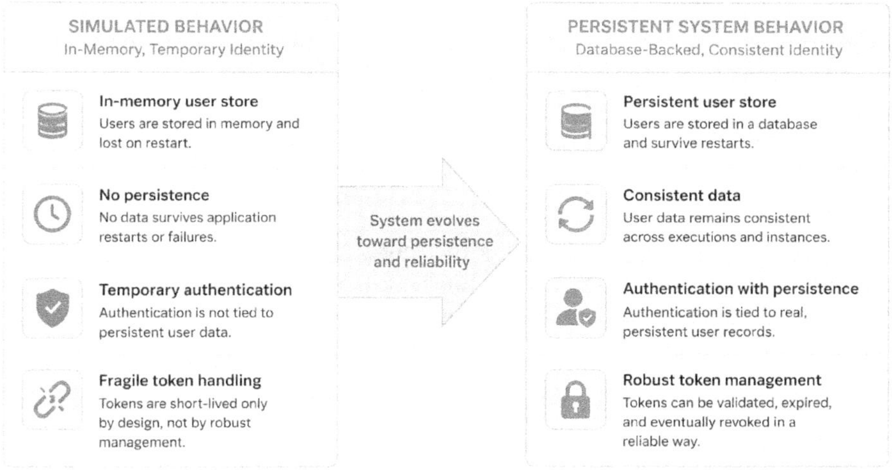

Figure 11.1: *From Simulated Behavior to Persistent System Behavior*

At this point, the direction is clear. The first step is to remove the most significant simplification in the current design: the in-memory user store. In the next section, we will introduce a persistent user model, and integrate it into the existing architecture without breaking the system.

Persisting Users in the Database

In the previous section, we identified a limitation that is no longer acceptable at this stage of the project. The API handles authentication, but it still does so through an in-memory structure. Users exist only while the application is running, credentials disappear on restart, and identity remains temporary. This is not a minor detail. It changes the nature of the system. A real API does not remember users only, while the process is alive. It stores them. It relies on persistent data. Authentication is not simulated; it is backed by the same database used for the rest of the application. The goal of this section is therefore precise: remove the in-memory user store and replace it with a database-backed model. We do not redesign the architecture. We do not introduce external services. We extend what already exists. As in previous chapters, we begin with a prompt that makes the intention explicit.

Prompt

Replace the in-memory user store in this FastAPI API with a database-backed model using SQLAlchemy.

Keep the current structure and avoid redesigning the system.

A useful answer should not introduce a new authentication system. It should integrate users into the existing database layer, just as products were integrated in *Chapter 7, Building Data-Driven APIs*.

We begin from the data model. Open **app/db/models.py**. This file already contains the database representation of products. We now extend it with a new entity: the user.

Add the following model:

```
class User(Base):
    __tablename__ = "users"

    id = Column(Integer, primary_key=True, index=True)
    username = Column(String, unique=True, nullable=False)
    password = Column(String(255), nullable=False)
    role = Column(String, nullable=False)
```

This model mirrors exactly what previously existed in memory. Nothing conceptually new is being introduced. Only the location of the data changes. At this point, the system knows what a user is, but the database does not yet contain the corresponding table. As in *Chapter 7, Building Data-Driven APIs*, this is handled through migrations. From the terminal, run:

```
alembic revision --autogenerate -m "add users table"
alembic upgrade head
```

After this step, the database structure includes users alongside products. Up to this moment, nothing in the API behavior has changed. The system has only gained the ability to persist user data. The next step is to connect authentication to this new model. Open **app/services/auth_service.py**. This file currently contains the in-memory dictionary **fake_users_db**. That structure must now be removed. In its place, authentication will query the database. First, import what is needed:

```
from sqlalchemy.orm import Session
from app.db.database import get_db
from app.db.models import User
```

Then update the authentication function so that it no longer reads from memory, but from the database:

```
def authenticate_user(db: Session, username: str, password: str) ->
Optional[User]:
    user = db.query(User).filter(User.username == username).first()
    if not user:
        return None

    if user.password != hash_password(password):
        return None

    return user
```

The logic remains the same. The system still retrieves a user, compares the password, and returns the result. The difference is that the source of truth is now persistent. However, authentication is not the only part of the system that depended on the old in-memory user store. Token resolution did as well. At this stage of the chapter, the token format remains intentionally unchanged, but the user associated with that token must now be retrieved from the database instead of from **`fake_users_db`**. For this reason, update the token creation and lookup logic as follows:

```
def create_token(user: User) -> str:
    # extremely simplified token (for learning purposes only)
    return f"token-{user.username}"


def get_user_from_token(db: Session, token: str) -> Optional[User]:
    if not token.startswith("token-"):
        return None

    username = token.replace("token-", "")
    return db.query(User).filter(User.username == username).first()
```

This lookup assumes that usernames are unique within the system. That assumption is enforced by the database model through the **`unique=True`** constraint on the username column, ensuring that a token can resolve to at most one user.

This is an important adjustment. The token is still simple, but the user is no longer a dictionary. It is now a database model instance, so access must happen through attributes rather than subscripting. This also means that **`get_current_user`** must now receive the database session. Update it as follows:

```
from typing import Optional
from fastapi import Depends, Header, HTTPException, status
from sqlalchemy.orm import Session
from app.db.database import get_db
```

```
def get_current_user(
    authorization: Optional[str] = Header(None),
    db: Session = Depends(get_db),
) -> User:
    if authorization is None:
        raise HTTPException(
            status_code=status.HTTP_401_UNAUTHORIZED,
            detail="Missing Authorization header",
        )
    if not authorization.startswith("Bearer "):
        raise HTTPException(
            status_code=status.HTTP_401_UNAUTHORIZED,
            detail="Invalid Authorization format",
        )
    token = authorization.split(" ", 1)[1]
    user = get_user_from_token(
        db,
        token,
    )
    if user is None:
        raise HTTPException(
            status_code=status.HTTP_401_UNAUTHORIZED,
            detail="Invalid token",
        )
    return user
```

At this point, the authentication flow still looks the same from the outside. A client logs in, receives a token, and uses that token in subsequent requests. Internally, however, both authentication and token resolution now depend on persistent data. The login endpoint must also be updated, because **authenticate_user** now requires a database session. Open **app/routers/products.py**, and modify the endpoint as follows:

```
@router.post(
    "/login",
    response_model=TokenResponse,
)
def login(
    data: LoginRequest,
    db: Session = Depends(get_db),
) -> TokenResponse:
    user = auth_service.authenticate_user(
        db,
        data.username,
```

```
        data.password,
    )

    if user is None:
        raise HTTPException(
            status_code=status.HTTP_401_UNAUTHORIZED,
            detail="Invalid credentials",
        )

    token = auth_service.create_token(user)

    return TokenResponse(
        access_token=token,
    )
```

At this stage, there is one more consequence of the change that must be made explicit. The current user is no longer represented as a dictionary. It is now a **`User`** model instance. Any route that previously accessed fields through dictionary syntax must therefore be updated to use attributes. This change reflects a broader transition in the system. User information is no longer retrieved from an in-memory dictionary but from a database-backed model, so that routes now interact with typed objects, rather than generic key-value structures.

For example, in the delete endpoint, check:

```
if current_user["role"] != "admin":
```

must become:

```
if current_user.role != "admin":
```

This is a natural consequence of moving from an in-memory representation to an ORM model. The behavior of the API is unchanged, but the internal representation has become more realistic. At this point, the structure is correct, but the system has no users yet. This is the first moment in the book where the API depends on data that must exist before it can function correctly. This is expected. A real system does not come with users unless they are created. Rather than asking the reader to open an interactive Python session and paste several lines manually, it is better to make this step explicit and repeatable. Create a new file named **`scripts/seed_users.py`** with the following content:

```
from app.db.database import SessionLocal
from app.db.models import User
from app.services.auth_service import hash_password

def main() -> None:
    db = SessionLocal()
    try:
        existing = {
```

```
            user.username
            for user in db.query(User).all()
        }
        if "alice" not in existing:
            db.add(
                User(
                    username="alice",
                    password=hash_password(
                        "password123"
                    ),
                    role="user",
                )
            )
        if "bob" not in existing:
            db.add(
                User(
                    username="bob",
                    password=hash_password(
                        "secret"
                    ),
                    role="admin",
                )
            )
        db.commit()
        print("Users created successfully.")
    finally:
        db.close()

if __name__ == "__main__":
    main()
```

This version is intentionally idempotent. If the reader runs it more than once, it does not try to recreate users that already exist. Now execute the script from the project root:

```
python -m scripts.seed_users
```

The -m flag is important here. It ensures that Python resolves the project modules correctly from the root of the application. This step replaces the old in-memory setup with actual persistent data. At this stage, the changes can be verified immediately. Run the test suite again:

```
pytest
```

All tests should still pass. This is a critical observation. The internal implementation of authentication has changed significantly, but the external behavior of the API remains identical. To confirm this from a client perspective, repeat a login request:

```
curl http://localhost:8000/login \
  -H "Content-Type: application/json" \
  -d '{"username": "alice", "password": "password123"}'
```

On Windows:

```
echo '{"username": "alice", "password": "password123"}' > body.json
```

```
curl.exe -X POST http://localhost:8000/login `
-H "Content-Type: application/json" `
--data-binary "@body.json"
```

The response should still be:

```
{
  "access_token": "token-alice"
}
```

This confirms the key property of the change. The system is now more realistic, but it has not broken its contract. At this point, it is useful to step back and observe the transformation carefully. Previously, identity existed only in memory. It disappeared when the process stopped. The system could authenticate users, but it could not remember them. Now, identity is part of the database. It is persistent, queryable, and consistent with the rest of the application. Nothing at the API boundary has changed. Everything in the internal behavior has. This is exactly the kind of evolution that defines production readiness. Not a new feature, but a more truthful representation of how the system works. The next step is to strengthen this model further. Persisting users make the system more realistic, but it does not yet make it safe.

Strengthening Password Handling for Real Systems

In the previous section, the system took a decisive step toward realism. Users are no longer simulated. They are stored in the database. Authentication now depends on persistent data, and identity survives across application restarts. At first glance, this may seem sufficient. The API now behaves like a real system. But if we look more closely, another limitation becomes evident. Passwords are still stored exactly as they are received. Even though we introduced a hashing function in the previous chapter, its role was mostly illustrative. It improved the situation, but it did not fully reflect how credentials should be handled in a real system. At this stage, the goal is not to introduce a complete security framework. The aim is to move from a "demonstration-level" solution to a minimally correct real-world approach. We start, as usual, with a prompt.

Prompt

Given this FastAPI API with database-backed users, how should password handling be improved to be acceptable for a simple production system?

Keep the solution minimal and practical. Do not introduce complex external systems. A useful answer should not propose enterprise-grade security. It should focus on one essential improvement: *password hashing must be handled by a dedicated, secure utility designed for credentials*. This is different from using a general-purpose hash function. In practice, this means replacing the current hashing approach with a library designed specifically for password security. We will use **passlib**, a widely adopted library that provides safe password hashing mechanisms.

At this point, install the dependency:

```
pip uninstall -y bcrypt passlib
pip install "passlib[bcrypt]==1.7.4" "bcrypt==4.0.1"
```

Unlike general-purpose hash functions such as SHA-256, **bcrypt** is specifically designed for password storage. It is intentionally slow, making password-guessing and brute-force attacks significantly more expensive. This does not make passwords impossible to crack, but it greatly increases the computational effort required to do so.

This step introduces no architectural change. It only replaces how passwords are processed. Now open **app/services/auth_service.py**. We replace the current hashing logic with a proper password context. Add the following at the top of the file:

```
from passlib.context import CryptContext

pwd_context = CryptContext(schemes=["bcrypt"], deprecated="auto")
```

This object defines how passwords are hashed and verified. Next, replace the existing **hash_password** function with:

```
def hash_password(password: str) -> str:
    return pwd_context.hash(password)
```

And update the comparison logic in **authenticate_user**:

```
def authenticate_user(db: Session, username: str, password: str) ->
Optional[User]:
    user = db.query(User).filter(User.username == username).first()
    if not user:
        return None

    if not pwd_context.verify(password, user.password):
        return None

    return user
```

This is the key change. Passwords are no longer compared directly. They are verified using a secure hashing algorithm designed for credentials. At this point, an important consequence appears. The passwords currently stored in the database were generated using the previous hashing method. They are no longer valid. This is not an error. It is a natural result of improving the system. To proceed, we must recreate the users with the new hashing mechanism. Instead of using an interactive Python shell, we make this step explicit and repeatable by creating a script. The transition from a simplified password hashing approach to a production-oriented mechanism has consequences beyond the authentication code itself. *Figure 11.2* illustrates how replacing SHA-256 with **bcrypt** changes the format of stored credentials, making the existing password hashes incompatible, and requiring users to be recreated.

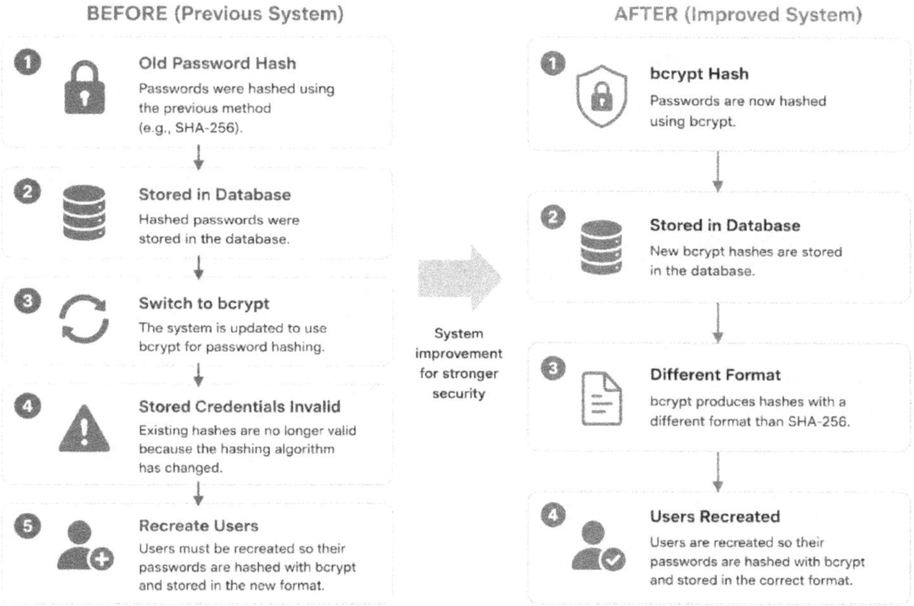

Figure 11.2: *Migrating from SHA-256 to Bcrypt*

Create a new file **scripts/reset_users.py** and add the following content:

```
from app.db.database import SessionLocal
from app.db.models import User
from app.services.auth_service import hash_password

def main() -> None:
    db = SessionLocal()
    try:
        # Remove existing users
        db.query(User).delete()
        # Recreate users with bcrypt hashes
        db.add(
            User(
                username="alice",
                password=hash_password(
```

```
                    "password123"
                ),
                role="user",
            )
        )
        db.add(
            User(
                username="bob",
                password=hash_password(
                    "secret"
                ),
                role="admin",
            )
        )
        db.commit()
        print("Users reset with secure password hashing.")
    finally:
        db.close()

if __name__ == "__main__":
    main()
```

Now execute the script from the project root:

```
python -m scripts.reset_users
```

If all is **OK**, as output, you get this message:

```
Users reset with secure password hashing.
```

This approach has two advantages: first, it is repeatable, and second, it keeps the operation explicit and versionable. This step ensures that stored passwords are compatible with the new verification method. Now the system can be verified again. Run:

```
pytest
```

All tests should still pass. This confirms that authentication behavior has not changed from the client's perspective. At this stage, it is important to observe the nature of this change. Nothing visible has changed: the login endpoint is identical, the response format is identical, and the test suite is unchanged. But internally, the system now handles credentials in a way that aligns with real-world expectations. This is a different kind of improvement compared to earlier chapters. It does not add functionality. It improves *correctness under real conditions*. Previously, passwords were simply data. Now, they are treated as sensitive information that must be protected. This is the transition from a working system to a system that respects real constraints. The next step is to address another remaining simplification in the authentication flow: the way tokens are generated and managed.

Making Token Handling More Realistic

At this point, the authentication system has undergone a significant transformation. Users are stored in the database. Credentials persist across application restarts. Passwords are no longer handled in plain form, but through a dedicated hashing mechanism designed for sensitive data. From the perspective of identity and credentials, the system now behaves in a way that closely resembles a real application. And yet, one part of the authentication flow still does not. The way tokens are generated. So far, tokens have been constructed directly from the username. A value such as token-alice is enough to authenticate as a specific user. This was an intentional simplification. It made the concept of authentication easy to understand, and easy to observe in earlier chapters. But at this stage, the limitation is no longer acceptable. A token should not be something that can be guessed. It should not be derived from user data in a predictable way. It should be issued by the system and recognized only if the system itself generated it.

Warning: The token registry introduced in this section is still process-local and disappears when the application restarts. It improves token unpredictability, but it does not yet provide production-grade token management.

To clarify what needs to change, we again translate the situation into a prompt.

Prompt

The current token format in this FastAPI API is predictable (token-username).

Suggest a minimal change to make tokens safer and less predictable, without introducing external authentication systems or redesigning the architecture.

A useful answer should not propose a complete authentication framework. It should focus on a single idea: tokens should be generated randomly and tracked by the system. This can be achieved with a small change. Instead of constructing tokens from the username, we generate them using a secure random generator and store the association between the token and the user inside the application. Open **`app/services/auth_service.py`**. At the top of the file, import the module that provides secure random values:

```
import secrets
```

Then introduce a simple structure that will keep track of issued tokens:

```
issued_tokens = {}
```

This dictionary will act as a temporary registry. Every time a token is created, it will be stored together with the user it represents. Now update the token creation function. Instead of returning a predictable string, it generates a random value:

```
def create_token(user: User) -> str:
    token = secrets.token_hex(16)
```

```
    issued_tokens[token] = user.username
    return token
```

At this point, tokens are no longer guessable. But the system must still be able to resolve them back to a user. The function responsible for this must also be updated. Previously, it extracted the username from the token itself. That is no longer possible. The username must now be retrieved from the registry and then used to query the database. Modify the token resolution logic accordingly:

```
def get_user_from_token(db: Session, token: str) -> Optional[User]:
    username = issued_tokens.get(token)
    if not username:
        return None

    return db.query(User).filter(User.username == username).first()
```

This change introduces a new dependency: resolving a token now requires access to the database. For this reason, the function that retrieves the current user must also receive the database session. Update **get_current_user** so that it follows the same pattern used throughout the API:

```
def get_current_user(
    authorization: Optional[str] = Header(None),
    db: Session = Depends(get_db),
) -> User:
    if authorization is None:
        raise HTTPException(
            status_code=status.HTTP_401_UNAUTHORIZED,
            detail="Missing Authorization header",
        )

    if not authorization.startswith("Bearer "):
        raise HTTPException(
            status_code=status.HTTP_401_UNAUTHORIZED,
            detail="Invalid Authorization format",
        )

    token = authorization.split(" ", 1)[1]

    user = get_user_from_token(
        db,
        token,
    )

    if user is None:
        raise HTTPException(
            status_code=status.HTTP_401_UNAUTHORIZED,
```

```
            detail="Invalid token",
        )

    return user
```

At this point, the structure of the authentication flow remains the same. A request still carries a token. The system still resolves that token into a user. Authorization rules are unchanged. But the behavior is fundamentally different. Tokens are no longer predictable. They are issued by the system and must be obtained through the login endpoint. This change becomes visible as soon as the system is tested again. Run the test suite:

```
pytest
```

If any test assumes that tokens follow the token-username format, it will fail. This is expected. The test suite must now rely on actual login responses instead of hardcoded values. Once this adjustment is made, all tests should pass again. To observe the new behavior directly, perform a login request:

```
curl http://localhost:8000/login \
  -H "Content-Type: application/json" \
  -d '{"username": "alice", "password": "password123"}'
```

On Windows:

```
echo '{"username": "alice", "password": "password123"}' > body.json

curl.exe -X POST http://localhost:8000/login `
-H "Content-Type: application/json" `
--data-binary "@body.json"
```

The response will now contain a token that has no visible relation to the username. It is simply a random string similar to this;

```
{"access_token":"adcea61a547167d31d82301df1e730ea"}
```

Use that token in a protected request:

```
curl http://localhost:8000/products \
  -H "Authorization: Bearer <token>"
```

For example, in Windows, you can send:

```
curl.exe http://localhost:8000/products `
-H "Authorization: Bearer adcea61a547167d31d82301df1e730ea"
```

The request succeeds, but only because the token was issued by the system itself. At this stage, the improvement may appear small, but its impact is significant. Previously, authentication could be bypassed by constructing a token. Now, it requires a valid interaction with the system. Identity is no longer something that can be inferred. It must be obtained. At the same time, it is important to recognize the limits of this approach. Tokens are still stored in memory. They disappear when the application stops. There is no expiration mechanism, and no way to revoke them explicitly. These are real limitations, and they would need to be addressed in a fully production-ready system. But they do not invalidate the improvement. The goal here is not to build a complete authentication system. The aim is to remove the most unrealistic behavior and replace it with something that reflects how real systems operate. The system is now closer to that point. Authentication is no longer only correct. It is now credible.

Adding Logout and Token Revocation

At this point, the authentication flow is much more realistic than it was at the beginning of the chapter. Users are stored in the database, passwords are handled through a proper password hashing mechanism, and tokens are no longer predictable values derived directly from usernames. A client must now authenticate through the system in order to obtain a valid token. And yet, one important part of the authentication lifecycle is still missing. A token can be created, but it cannot be invalidated deliberately. This is the next limitation that becomes visible as soon as the system is viewed as something more than a demonstration. In a real application, authentication is not only about logging in. It is also about ending a session, revoking access, and making sure that a token no longer remains usable once the user has chosen to disconnect. Without that capability, the system still behaves as if every token, once issued, remains valid until the application process disappears. That was already acceptable when tokens were a didactic simplification, but it is no longer sufficient now that the rest of the authentication model has become more credible. The goal of this section is therefore precise: *add a minimal logout mechanism that revokes the current token.*

Figure 11.3 illustrates the complete authentication lifecycle after logout support is introduced. Authentication is no longer limited to issuing tokens; it also includes a mechanism for explicitly revoking them.

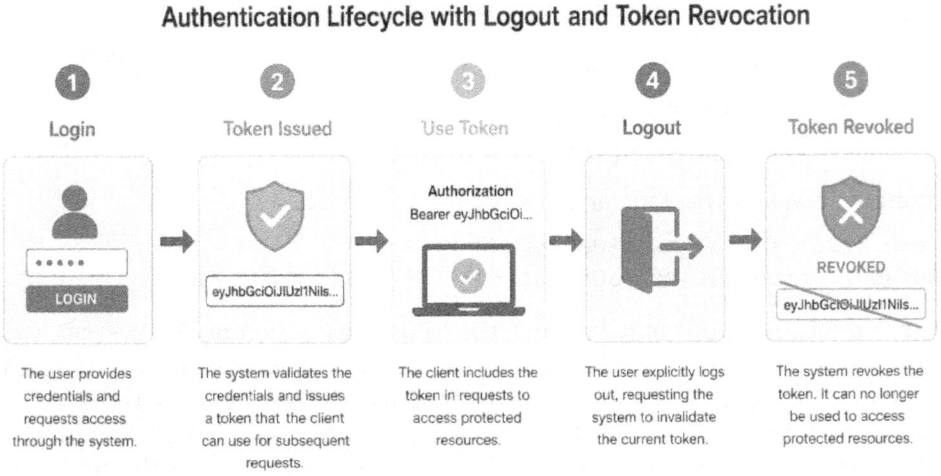

Figure 11.3: *Authentication Lifecycle with Token Revocation*

As in the rest of the chapter, we do not redesign the system. We do not introduce refresh tokens, token blacklists, or external session stores. We work within the current architecture and add the smallest missing piece that makes the authentication flow feel more complete. We begin, as usual, with a prompt.

Prompt

Add a minimal logout mechanism to this FastAPI API. The current authentication system issues random tokens stored in memory. Implement a logout endpoint that invalidates the current token without redesigning the system. Keep the solution simple and consistent with the current structure.

A useful answer should not propose a complete session management framework. It should introduce one new operation: remove the current token from the in-memory token registry so that it can no longer be used in subsequent requests. To do that, we first extend the authentication service. Open **`app/services/auth_service.py`**. This file already contains the token registry and the functions that create and resolve tokens. What is missing is a way to revoke one of them. Add the following function:

```
def revoke_token(token: str) -> bool:
    return issued_tokens.pop(token, None) is not None
```

This function is intentionally small. It checks whether the token exists in the in-memory registry, removes it if present, and returns a boolean indicating whether revocation actually took place. At this point, the service layer knows how to invalidate a token, but the API does not yet expose that behavior. We now need a route that allows a client to log out. Open **`app/routers/products.py`** and add a new endpoint:

```
from fastapi import Header
from app.db.models import User

@router.post("/logout")
def logout(
    authorization: str = Header(...),
    current_user: User = Depends(
        auth_service.get_current_user
    ),
) -> dict:
    if not authorization.startswith("Bearer "):
        raise HTTPException(
            status_code=status.HTTP_401_UNAUTHORIZED,
            detail="Invalid Authorization format",
        )
    token = authorization.split(" ", 1)[1]
    revoked = auth_service.revoke_token(token)
    if not revoked:
        raise HTTPException(
```

```
            status_code=status.HTTP_401_UNAUTHORIZED,
            detail="Invalid token",
        )
    return {"message": "Logged out successfully"}
```

This route follows exactly the same pattern used elsewhere in the API. It operates at the HTTP boundary, delegates token revocation to the service layer, and returns a simple structured response. It is also important to notice what this endpoint does **not** do. It does not remove the user from the database, it does not change any user data, and it does not alter the structure of the authentication system. It simply ends the validity of the current token. That is all a logout operation needs to do in the current design. At this point, the system has gained a missing behavior, but it must be verified immediately. The most direct way to understand the change is to try the flow from the client's perspective. First, authenticate as before:

```
curl http://localhost:8000/login \
  -H "Content-Type: application/json" \
  -d '{"username": "alice", "password": "password123"}'
```

On Windows:

```
echo '{"username": "alice", "password": "password123"}' > body.json
```

```
curl.exe -X POST http://localhost:8000/login `
-H "Content-Type: application/json" `
--data-binary "@body.json"
```

The response will contain an access token. Use that token to call a protected endpoint:

```
curl http://localhost:8000/products \
  -H "Authorization: Bearer <token>"
```

On Windows:

```
curl.exe http://localhost:8000/products `
-H "Authorization: Bearer 4ab19f8ea2e2948fcf7d8a14621fa162"
```

The request should succeed. Now use the same token to log out:

```
curl -X POST http://localhost:8000/logout \
  -H "Authorization: Bearer <token>"
```

On Windows:

```
curl.exe -X POST http://localhost:8000/logout `
  -H "Authorization: Bearer <token>"
```

The response should be:

```
{
  "message": "Logged out successfully"
}
```

Finally, repeat the same protected request using the token that was just revoked:

```
curl http://localhost:8000/products \
  -H "Authorization: Bearer <token>"
```

This time, the request should fail with:

```
{
  "detail": "Invalid token"
}
```

This is the key observation. The token has not merely "expired" because the application stopped. It has been actively invalidated by the system. Authentication now has a minimal but complete lifecycle: a token can be issued, used, and revoked. At this stage, the automated tests should also be extended so that this new behavior becomes part of the verified contract of the API.

Open **tests/test_api.py** and add the following test:

```
def test_logout_revokes_token():
    token = get_token(
        "alice",
        "password123",
    )

    response = client.post(
        "/logout",
        headers={
            "Authorization": f"Bearer {token}"
        },
    )
    assert response.status_code == 200
    assert response.json() == {
        "message": "Logged out successfully"
    }
    protected_response = client.get(
        "/products",
        headers={
            "Authorization": f"Bearer {token}"
        },
    )
    assert protected_response.status_code == 401
```

Now run the test suite again:

```
pytest
```

All tests should pass. That result matters. It confirms that the system has gained a more realistic authentication behavior without breaking the rest of the API. It is also important to understand the exact nature of this improvement. The logout mechanism is real, but it still belongs to the current level of simplicity. Tokens remain in memory, which means they still disappear when the application restarts, and revocation still works only inside a single running instance. In a more advanced deployment, the token lifecycle would need to be managed through persistent or shared state. But that does not make the improvement insignificant. On the contrary, it completes an essential part of the authentication story. The system no longer only proves that a user can authenticate. It also proves that authentication can end in a deliberate and observable way. This is what makes the application feel less like a demonstration and more like a real system. The next step is to apply the same production-aware reasoning to another area where the API still behaves more like a small teaching example than a realistic service: the way product collections are returned to the client.

Adding Basic Pagination to the Products List

At this stage, the API has become more credible in how it handles identity and authentication. Users are persistent, credentials are treated correctly, and tokens follow a realistic lifecycle. The system no longer behaves like a temporary simulation. However, another limitation becomes visible when we look at how data is returned to the client. So far, the product listing endpoint returns a collection of products using a simple query. A limit was introduced in the previous chapter to prevent unbounded results, but the behavior is still incomplete. The client can receive a subset of data, but it has no control over which subset is returned. There is no way to navigate through the dataset. This is a common gap between a working API and a usable one. A real API does not simply return "some data." It allows clients to request data in a controlled and predictable way, especially when the dataset grows over time. Without that capability, even a correct system becomes difficult to use in practice. The goal of this section is therefore clear: *introduce a minimal pagination mechanism that allows clients to navigate product data.* As in the rest of the chapter, the solution must remain simple. We do not introduce complex query languages, cursor-based pagination, or external libraries. We extend the existing endpoint with a small, explicit mechanism that makes the behavior more realistic. We begin with a prompt.

Prompt

Add basic pagination to the product listing endpoint in this FastAPI API. Use simple query parameters (skip and limit). Keep the implementation minimal and consistent with the current structure.

A useful answer should not redesign the endpoint. It should extend it by allowing the client to specify where to start and how many items to retrieve. To implement this, we begin from the service layer. Open **`app/services/product_service.py`**. The current implementation of **`list_products`** likely applies a limit, but does not support navigation. Replace it with the following:

```
def list_products(db: Session, skip: int = 0, limit: int = 100) ->
List[ProductDB]:
    return db.query(ProductDB).offset(skip).limit(limit).all()
```

This change introduces two parameters. The first, skip, defines how many records should be ignored from the beginning of the dataset. The second, limit, defines how many records should be returned. Together, they allow the client to request data in segments. At this point, the service layer supports pagination, but the API does not yet expose it.

Open **`app/routers/products.py`** and update the **`list_products`** endpoint:

```
@router.get("/products", response_model=List[Product])
def list_products(
    skip: int = Query(default=0, ge=0),
    limit: int = Query(default=100, ge=1, le=100),
    db: Session = Depends(get_db),
    current_user: dict = Depends(auth_service.get_current_user),
) -> List[Product]:
    return product_service.list_products(db, skip=skip, limit=limit)
```

This change is intentionally small. It introduces two query parameters that map directly to the service layer. The endpoint remains simple, and its structure is unchanged. At this stage, the API has gained a new capability, but it must be verified immediately. First, run the test suite:

```
pytest
```

All the existing tests should still pass. This confirms that the default behavior of the endpoint has not changed. A request without parameters still returns a list of products. To observe the new behavior, we interact with the API directly. Assume that the database contains several products. A basic request still works as before:

```
curl http://localhost:8000/products \
  -H "Authorization: Bearer <token>"
```

On Windows:

```
curl.exe http://localhost:8000/products `
-H "Authorization: Bearer <token>"
```

Now request only the first two items:

```
curl "http://localhost:8000/products?skip=0&limit=2" \
  -H "Authorization: Bearer <token>"
```

On Windows:

```
curl.exe "http://localhost:8000/products?skip=0&limit=2" `
  -H "Authorization: Bearer <token>"
```

The response will contain at most two products. Then request the next two:

```
curl "http://localhost:8000/products?skip=2&limit=2" \
  -H "Authorization: Bearer <token>"
```

On Windows:

```
curl.exe "http://localhost:8000/products?skip=2&limit=2" `
  -H "Authorization: Bearer <token>"
```

This returns the following segment of the dataset. At this point, the behavior is explicit. The client can move through the dataset by adjusting skip and limit. Even though the implementation is simple, the API now supports a fundamental pattern used in real systems. To make this behavior part of the verified contract, extend the test suite.

Open **tests/test_api.py** and add the following test:

```
def test_product_pagination():
    token = get_token("alice", "password123")

    # create multiple products
    for i in range(5):
        client.post(
            "/products",
            headers={"Authorization": f"Bearer {token}"},
            json={
                "name": f"Product {i}",
                "price": 10.0 + i,
                "description": "Test"
            }
        )

    response = client.get(
        "/products?skip=0&limit=2",
        headers={"Authorization": f"Bearer {token}"}
    )

    assert response.status_code == 200
    data = response.json()
    assert len(data) <= 2
```

Run the tests again:

```
pytest
```

All tests should pass. This confirms that pagination works correctly and that it does not interfere with existing behavior. At this stage, it is important to understand the nature of this improvement. The system has not become more complex in structure. No new layer has been introduced, and no existing component has been redesigned. The change is entirely local and directly visible at the API boundary. At the same time, the API is now more usable. Previously, the client could only retrieve a fixed subset of products. Now, it can navigate through the dataset in a controlled way. This is a small step, but it reflects a real requirement that appears in almost every production system. It is also important to recognize what has not been implemented. There is no total count of records, no next/previous links, and no advanced filtering. These features are useful, but they are not required to make the system credible at this stage. The goal is not to build a complete data access layer, but to remove the most obvious limitation. This is consistent with the approach of the chapter. We do not aim for completeness. We aim for realism. With this addition, the API is not only more secure and more consistent, but also more practical to use. It behaves less like a demonstration and more like a system that could support real interaction over time. The next step is to return to a broader perspective and evaluate how all these improvements fit together, and what limitations still remain when the system is observed as a whole.

Evaluating What Would Still Break in Production

At this point, the system has changed in a meaningful way. Users are stored in the database, passwords are handled through a secure mechanism, and tokens are no longer predictable values derived directly from user data. From a functional perspective, the API now behaves much more like a real application than it did in earlier chapters.

This is precisely the moment where a different question becomes necessary. Up to now, the main concern has been whether the system works. A limitation was identified, a change was introduced, and the result was verified. In this section, the goal is no longer to change the system immediately, but to evaluate it from a different point of view. The relevant question is no longer *whether it works*. It is: *would it survive in a real environment*?

Thus, before evaluating possible improvements, it is useful to summarize the most significant limitations that would still affect the system in a production environment. *Table 11.1* highlights the remaining gaps and their practical consequences.

Limitation	Consequence
In-memory token registry	Tokens are lost after application restart
No token expiration	Tokens remain valid indefinitely
No audit or security logging	Authentication issues are harder to investigate
Single-instance token state	Horizontal scaling becomes difficult
Simplified token management	Limited control over long-lived sessions

Table 11.1: *Production-readiness Gaps that Remain after Introducing Persistent Users, Secure Password Hashing, and Token Revocation*

As in previous chapters, we start by making that intention explicit through a prompt.

Prompt

Given this FastAPI API with database-backed users, hashed passwords, and random tokens, what would likely break or become problematic in a real production environment?

Focus on practical risks, not ideal architectures.

A useful answer should not suggest rewriting the system. It should look at what already exists and identify where it would begin to struggle under real conditions. To understand this properly, we need to shift perspective. Until now, the system has been used in a controlled setting. Requests arrive one at a time, data remains limited, failures are rare, and the application is assumed to keep running continuously. In production, none of these assumptions can be trusted. Requests arrive concurrently, users behave unpredictably, the process may restart, and failures happen under pressure rather than in isolation. When the current implementation is examined under these conditions, several limitations become visible. The first concerns token storage. Tokens are now random, which is a significant improvement over the predictable format used earlier, but they are still stored in memory. This means that every time the application restarts, all issued tokens disappear. From the client's perspective, a token that was valid a moment ago suddenly becomes invalid, not because of expiration or revocation, but simply because the process stopped and started again. This is not a programming error, but it is clearly a behavior that would become problematic in a real deployment. A second limitation concerns the token lifecycle. Tokens are created, but they never expire. There is no duration associated with them, no mechanism to invalidate them after a period of time, and no explicit way to revoke them.

Once a token has been issued, it remains valid for as long as the application continues to run. That behavior is acceptable for a didactic system, but incomplete for a real one. A third limitation emerges when we consider concurrency and deployment topology. The current system relies on a simple in-memory dictionary to store issued tokens. That approach works as long as the application runs in a single process and on a single instance. In a production environment, however, multiple replicas are often involved. Under those conditions, each instance would maintain its own token store, and a token issued by one instance would not necessarily be recognized by another. This problem does not appear in development, but it becomes critical as soon as the system grows beyond a single running process. Another area that deserves attention is error visibility. The API returns correct status codes and messages, but it does not record what happens internally. There is no logging, no tracing, and no structured way to reconstruct what led to a failure. In a controlled environment, this absence is easy to tolerate because the developer can often reproduce the problem directly. In a real system, that same absence makes debugging slow, uncertain, and expensive. Finally, there is the question of data growth. The product listing endpoint now includes a limit, which prevents completely unbounded queries, but the API still does not provide pagination, filtering, or a way to navigate large datasets in a controlled manner. As the amount of data increases, this becomes not only a performance concern but also a usability problem.

At this stage, it is important to interpret these observations correctly. They are not failures of the system. They are boundaries. They define the conditions under which the current implementation remains reliable, and they make visible the points at which further evolution would become necessary. This is the key shift introduced in this chapter. In earlier stages, the goal was to build and refine. Here, the goal is to understand limits before they become problems. This is how real systems are evaluated: not only by asking whether they work, but by asking under which conditions they would stop working reliably. No changes are applied in this section. The system remains exactly as it is. What has changed is the perspective. We now understand more clearly where the system stands, what assumptions it still makes, and what would need to evolve if it were deployed in a real environment. The next step is to take that understanding and make it more deliberate, moving from the identification of limitations to a more structured decision: which improvements matter now, and which ones can wait.

Consolidating a Production-Aware System

At this stage, the system has not been redesigned, and yet it is no longer the same. From the outside, nothing appears to have changed. The API still exposes the same endpoints, follows the same structure, and behaves in a predictable and testable way. A client interacting with the system would not notice any difference in how requests are made or how responses are returned. The transformation introduced in this chapter has taken place entirely within the system itself. Rather than adding new features, the focus has been on removing the most unrealistic assumptions that were still present in the earlier implementation. User data, which previously existed only in memory, is now stored in the database alongside the rest of the application state. Passwords are no longer treated as simple values, but as sensitive data handled through a dedicated mechanism. Tokens are no longer constructed from predictable patterns but generated by the system and validated through an internal process. These changes are small in terms of code, but they have a significant impact on behavior.

This distinction is important. Production-aware does not mean production-complete. The goal of this chapter has not been to eliminate every limitation, but to identify the most significant gaps between a learning-oriented implementation and a realistic one, and to address them without introducing unnecessary complexity.

The system no longer simply demonstrates how authentication works. It behaves in a way that can be trusted under normal conditions, because its assumptions are now aligned with how real applications operate. At the same time, the previous sections have made it equally clear that the system is not complete. There are still limitations, and they are not difficult to identify. Tokens are stored in memory and therefore do not persist across application restarts. There is no mechanism to control their lifecycle, which means they do not expire and cannot be explicitly revoked. The system assumes a single running instance and does not provide visibility into its internal operations, making it harder to observe and diagnose failures. These are not mistakes. They are known boundaries. To make this understanding explicit, we again turn it into a prompt.

Prompt

Summarize the current state of this FastAPI API.

Describe what makes it suitable for a simple production scenario, and what limitations remain for more advanced environments.

A useful answer should not reduce the system to a checklist of features. It should describe it as a whole, recognizing both what has been achieved and what remains intentionally incomplete. On one side, the API now satisfies a set of essential conditions. It is structured in a clear and maintainable way, persists data reliably, enforces authentication and authorization, protects credentials, and behaves consistently across requests. These properties are what make it suitable for a simple production scenario, not because it includes every possible feature, but because it avoids the most critical weaknesses.

On the other side, the system remains intentionally limited. It relies on a single application instance, keeps part of its state in memory, and does not implement full lifecycle management for authentication tokens. It also lacks the kind of visibility and monitoring that would be required in a more complex environment. These limitations are not the result of oversight. They are deliberate decisions that keep the system understandable and aligned with the scope of the project. This balance is the most important outcome of the chapter. A system does not need to be perfect to be usable. It needs to be clear about what it can do, and equally clear about where its limits are. At this point, it is important to verify that the system remains stable after all these changes. Each individual improvement has already been tested in the previous sections. The goal now is different. We want to confirm that, taken together, these changes have not altered the external behavior of the API. Run the test suite again:

```
pytest
```

Thus, all tests should pass, confirming that the external contract of the API has remained unchanged. The system has evolved internally, but from the perspective of the client, it behaves exactly as before. This is a pattern that has been applied throughout the book: capabilities evolve, but the boundary remains stable. To make this explicit, repeat a simple interaction that was used earlier. This is not a new test. It is a confirmation that existing behavior has been preserved. Authenticate as before:

```
curl http://localhost:8000/login \
  -H "Content-Type: application/json" \
  -d '{"username": "alice", "password": "password123"}'
```

Then use the returned token to access a protected endpoint:

```
curl http://localhost:8000/products \
  -H "Authorization: Bearer <token>"
```

The request succeeds, just as it did in previous chapters. This is the key observation. Nothing has changed at the API boundary. The same request produces the same response, even though the internal implementation has been significantly improved. This is what allows a system to evolve without breaking its clients. At this stage, the API has reached an important point in its evolution. It is not a fully production system, but it is no longer a simplified demonstration. It is a system that works, that is structured, and that reflects the most important constraints of real-world applications.

The next step is to freeze this state and use it as the reference point for everything that follows.

Freezing the Production-Aware System

At this stage, the idea of freezing the system takes on a different meaning compared to previous chapters. In earlier parts of the book, freezing the baseline meant establishing a stable starting point for further development. Each new chapter would extend the system from that reference. Here, the situation is different. This is the final stage of the API as a technical system. There is no next feature to implement, no additional layer to introduce, and no immediate extension that depends on this structure. Instead, freezing the system serves a different purpose: it marks the completion of its evolution from a simplified example to a production-aware application.

From the perspective of a client, nothing has changed. The same requests can be sent, and the same responses are returned. But internally, the system now reflects the essential constraints of real-world applications. Users are persistent. Passwords are handled securely. Tokens are generated and validated by the system. At the same time, its limitations are explicit and understood. This is what we freeze. Not a perfect system, but a complete one within its scope.

Current State

✓ *Persistent Users*

✓ *Secure Passwords*

✓ *Random Tokens*

✓ *Logout Support*

✓ *Pagination*

✓ *Verified Behavior*

Before concluding, we verify one last time that this evolution has not introduced inconsistencies. Run the test suite:

```
pytest
```

All tests should pass. This confirms the final property of the system: stability under change. Freezing the system at this point does not prepare it for the next implementation step. It makes it a reference. From this point forward, the API is no longer just a learning artifact. It is a complete, understandable, and credible system that can be used as a foundation for further exploration. The next chapter will not extend this system. It will extract the method used to build it.

Conclusion

In this chapter, the API became more realistic. Earlier versions of the system worked correctly, but some assumptions were intentionally simplified. Users existed only in memory, tokens were predictable, and parts of the authentication flow were designed primarily for learning. These limitations were addressed without redesigning the application. Users became persistent, password handling became more secure, and tokens were generated and managed by the system itself.

The most important outcome is not the individual improvements, but the perspective they introduce. A system should not be evaluated only by whether it works. It should also be evaluated by the assumptions it makes and the conditions under which those assumptions remain valid. Throughout the chapter, AI was used not only to generate changes, but also to identify gaps between a working implementation and a realistic one.

By the end of the chapter, the API is not production-complete, but it is production-aware. Its capabilities and limitations are both explicit, making the system easier to understand, trust, and evolve.

In the next *Chapter 12, Learning New Technologies with AI Prompts* the focus shifts from the API itself to the method used to build it. Throughout the book, AI has been used to explore requirements, generate implementations, review decisions, and refine behavior. The 12th is the final chapter that makes that process explicit, extracting the principles that can be applied to learn new technologies, and build systems beyond the scope of this project.

Points to Remember

- A system can work correctly and still be unrealistic.
- Internal improvements can increase reliability without changing the API contract.

- AI can evaluate assumptions as well as generate code.
- Production-focused prompts should be specific and constrained.
- Development shortcuts must be revisited as the system evolves.
- Persistent identity and data are essential for realistic behavior.
- Secure authentication requires proper password hashing and unpredictable tokens.
- Not every limitation needs to be solved immediately.
- Systems should be evaluated under real-world conditions, not only ideal ones.
- Production-aware means understanding both capabilities and limitations.

Multiple Choice Questions

1. What is the main objective of this chapter?
   a. To introduce automated testing
   b. To redesign the API from scratch
   c. To evaluate and improve the system with a production-aware mindset
   d. To remove authentication
2. Why is a working system not necessarily a realistic one?
   a. Because it may rely on assumptions that do not hold in real environments
   b. Because it lacks endpoints
   c. Because it cannot be tested
   d. Because it does not use a database
3. What was the main limitation of the authentication system before this chapter?
   a. It was too slow
   b. It used SQLAlchemy
   c. It relied on in-memory data and predictable tokens
   d. It did not use HTTP
4. What is the purpose of using AI prompts in this chapter?
   a. To generate new APIs
   b. To deploy the system
   c. To analyze system behavior under real conditions
   d. To replace the developer

5. Why are predictable tokens a problem?
    a. They increase performance
    b. They make authentication easier to bypass
    c. They reduce database load
    d. They simplify testing
6. What is a key improvement introduced in this chapter?
    a. Removing the database
    b. Introducing distributed systems
    c. Persisting users and improving credential handling
    d. Replacing FastAPI
7. Why are some limitations intentionally left unresolved?
    a. Because they are impossible to fix
    b. Because they are not relevant to any system
    c. Because they introduce unnecessary complexity at this stage
    d. Because FastAPI does not support them
8. What does it mean for a system to be production-aware?
    a. It supports every possible feature
    b. It has no limitations
    c. It behaves realistically and its constraints are understood
    d. It uses microservices
9. A user logs in successfully, receives a token, the server restarts, and the token stops working. What limitation does this reveal?
    a. Password hashing issue
    b. Database migration issue
    c. In-memory token storage
    d. Pagination problem

Answers

1. c
2. a
3. c
4. c

5. b
6. c
7. c
8. c
9. c

Questions

1. Why can a system behave correctly while still relying on unrealistic assumptions?
2. How does evaluating a system differ from simply testing its behavior?
3. What are the risks of relying on in-memory data for critical features such as authentication?
4. Why is it important for identity and credentials to be persistent?
5. How do small improvements, such as hashing passwords or generating random tokens, change the credibility of a system?
6. In what situations is it acceptable to defer improvements rather than implement them immediately?
7. How does thinking about concurrency and system restarts change the way an API is evaluated?
8. Why is it important to understand system boundaries rather than eliminate all limitations?
9. How does AI help identify weaknesses without requiring a full redesign?
10. What distinguishes a "working system" from a "production-aware system"?

Key Terms

- **Production-Aware System:** A system whose behavior reflects real-world constraints and whose limitations are explicitly understood.
- **System Evaluation:** The process of analyzing how an application behaves under realistic conditions, such as concurrency, failures, and restarts.
- **Persistent Identity:** The concept that users and credentials are stored durably and survive across executions of the application.
- **Credential Handling:** The methods used to store and verify sensitive data, such as passwords, in a secure manner.

- **Token-Based Authentication:** A mechanism in which access is granted based on tokens issued by the system after successful authentication.
- **Token Predictability:** A weakness in which tokens can be guessed or constructed without interacting with the system.
- **System Boundary:** The external interface of an API, including endpoints, requests, and responses, which should remain stable over time.
- **Realistic Constraints:** Conditions such as concurrency, failures, and scaling that affect how a system behaves in production.
- **Incremental Realism:** The process of improving a system step by step to better reflect real-world behavior without introducing unnecessary complexity.
- **Trade-off:** A design decision that balances benefits and costs, such as simplicity versus completeness.
- **System Credibility:** The degree to which a system behaves in a way that can be trusted in real usage scenarios.
- **Controlled Evolution:** The practice of improving a system gradually while maintaining stability and understanding of its behavior.

CHAPTER 12
Learning New Technologies with AI Prompts

Introduction

In the previous chapters, the API evolved step by step from a simple structure into a system that is persistent, secure, testable, and production-aware. Each improvement was introduced deliberately. New behavior was added, tested, reviewed, and refined. At every stage, the system remained understandable, and its external interface remained stable. At first glance, this may appear to be a book about FastAPI. But that is not what actually happened.

The framework was only the context. The real subject of the book has been the process used to explore, build, and refine a system with the support of AI. Every feature that was introduced—routing, persistence, authentication, testing, review—followed the same underlying pattern. A goal was defined, a prompt was written, an implementation was generated, and the result was verified and improved. This pattern was repeated consistently, even when it was not explicitly named.

By the end of *Chapter 11, Designing Production-Ready Systems*, the API was no longer the most important outcome. What matters is that the reader has already applied a method that can be used far beyond this specific project. The same approach can be used to explore a new framework, understand an unfamiliar tool, or build a system in a completely different context. This chapter makes that method explicit. The goal is not to introduce new features or extend the API further. The goal is to extract what has already been practiced, and turn it into something reusable. Instead of following instructions step by step, the reader will learn how to generate those steps independently.

Thus, by the end of this chapter, the focus shifts completely. The question is no longer, "*how do I build this API?*" It becomes: "*how do I learn something new, reliably, using AI as a tool?*"

Structure

In this chapter, we will discuss the following topics:

- Extracting the Learning Method
- The AI Learning Loop
- Prompt Patterns That Actually Work
- The Learning Checklist
- Applying the Method to a New Technology
- Avoiding Common Mistakes When Learning with AI
- Building Your Personal Prompt Library
- From Guided Learning to Independent Exploration

Extracting the Learning Method

Throughout the book, each chapter introduced a new capability. At first, the focus was on making the API work. Then it shifted to persistence, security, testing, and finally to production-aware reasoning. Each step appeared as a technical improvement, but underneath those changes, a consistent process was applied. That process was not always described explicitly, but it was present in every decision. To make it visible, we can reconstruct it by looking at how the system evolved. At no point was the entire application designed in advance. Instead, each stage began with a specific goal. The goal was translated into a prompt. The response produced an initial implementation, which was then executed, observed, and refined. When something failed, the failure itself became the next input. When something worked, it became the new baseline. This sequence is not specific to FastAPI. It is a general way of approaching any unfamiliar problem with AI. To make this transition explicit, we begin with a prompt that reflects what has already been done.

Prompt

Given the steps used to build this FastAPI API, extract a general learning method that can be applied to any new technology.

Focus on the sequence of actions, not on the framework itself.

A useful answer should not produce a generic list of advice. It should describe a pattern that can be recognized in the previous chapters. If we reconstruct that pattern carefully, the method becomes clear. Every new concept was approached by reducing it to a minimal, runnable example. The goal was never to understand everything at once. It was to reach a point where the system could be executed and observed. Once that point was reached, understanding followed through interaction.

Each step depended on verification. The code was not accepted because it looked correct. It was accepted because it could be executed, tested, and observed at the API boundary. This created a continuous feedback loop between expectation and behavior.

Failures were not interruptions. They were part of the process. When a test failed or a behavior was inconsistent, the failure was used as a precise input for the next prompt. Instead of guessing, the system was analyzed and corrected with targeted questions.

As the system grew, the same approach was applied at a different level. Instead of asking how to build a feature, the prompts began to ask how to review it, how to improve it, and how it would behave under real conditions. The interaction with AI shifted from generation to evaluation. This is the most important observation.

The reader has not only learned how to use a framework. They have learned a repeatable process for approaching unfamiliar systems. *Figure 12.1* summarizes that progression.

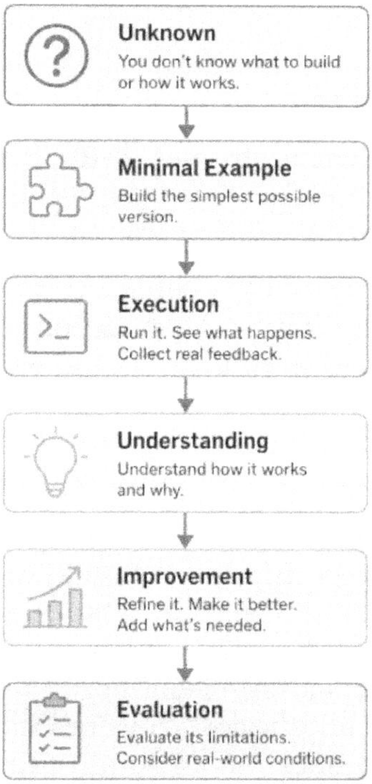

Figure 12.1: *The Learning Cycle Used throughout the Book*

This sequence is the real outcome of the book. At this stage, it becomes possible to detach the method from the specific implementation. The API is no longer required to apply it. The same process can be used to learn a new database, a messaging system, a frontend framework, or any other technology. The next step is to make this process even more explicit by turning it into a repeatable cycle—one that can be applied deliberately, rather than reconstructed after the fact.

The AI Learning Loop

In the previous section, the learning process that guided the entire book was made explicit. What initially appeared as a sequence of independent steps—building routes, adding persistence, introducing authentication, writing tests, and reviewing the system—can now be recognized as a consistent pattern. At this point, the goal is to make that pattern repeatable. A method becomes useful only when it can be applied intentionally. If the process remains implicit, it can only be followed by retracing the same path. Once it is made explicit, it can be reused in entirely different contexts. To do this, we reduce the process to its essential structure. As in previous chapters, we begin with a prompt.

Prompt

Given a new technology that I do not know, describe a repeatable learning loop using AI that allows me to go from zero knowledge to a working and understandable implementation.

Focus on practical steps, not theory.

A useful answer should not produce abstract advice. It should describe a sequence of actions that can be executed directly. When we compare this with the way the API was developed throughout the book, the same cycle emerges repeatedly.

Every new capability began with a clearly defined goal. That goal was never expressed in broad terms, such as "understand authentication" or "learn databases," but as a concrete and limited task, such as creating a login endpoint or storing products in a database. This constraint made the first step possible. From that goal, a minimal implementation was generated. The objective was not completeness, but execution. The system needed to run, even if it was incomplete or imperfect. A working example created a point of interaction.

Once the system could be executed, the next step was observation. Requests were sent, responses were examined, and behavior was verified. This transformed the code into something concrete. Instead of reasoning in the abstract, the system could be tested directly. At this point, understanding began to emerge. Questions were no longer generic, but grounded in behavior. Why does this endpoint return this result? Why does this test fail? Why does this value not persist? Each of these questions produced targeted prompts, and each prompt refined the system further.

Failures were not interruptions, but part of the process. When something did not work, the failure itself became a precise input for the next step. The interaction with AI shifted from generation to explanation, and from explanation to correction. This led to refinement. The system was adjusted, improved, and tested again. Each iteration brought the implementation closer to a stable and understandable state. At the same time, each successful step became the new baseline. The system did not restart from zero. It evolved in controlled increments, preserving what had already been verified.

If we make this process explicit, it can be understood as a continuous loop. A goal defines what needs to be built. A minimal implementation provides something that can be executed. Execution makes behavior observable. Observation leads to questions. Those questions drive refinement. The refined system becomes the new starting point, and the cycle repeats. This loop is simple, but it is also complete. It contains everything required to approach an unfamiliar technology without relying on predefined tutorials. Instead of following a fixed path, the process generates its own direction through interaction.

At this stage, it is important to notice what this loop does not require. It does not require full understanding at the beginning, nor perfect prompts, nor correct code on the first attempt. It only requires that each step produces something that can be executed and evaluated. This is what makes the method reliable. Instead of trying to understand everything before acting, the process creates understanding through interaction. Each iteration reduces uncertainty and increases clarity. The system itself becomes the source of feedback.

To apply this loop effectively, each step should be made explicit when working with a new tool. The first prompt should aim to produce a minimal, runnable example. Once that example is running, the next step should focus on explaining its behavior. From there, small modifications can be introduced, observed, and refined. The same pattern used to build the API can now be applied deliberately to any new context. The learning process described throughout the book can be summarized as the AI Learning Loop shown in *Figure* 12.2.

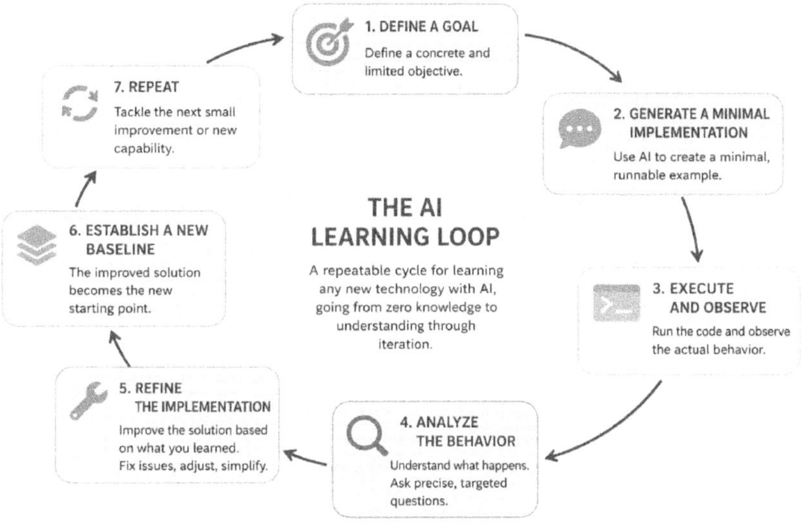

Figure 12.2: *The AI Learning Loop*

At this point, the method is defined, but it is not yet practical enough to use directly. In real scenarios, the quality of the process depends heavily on how prompts are written.

Some prompts lead to clear and usable results, while others produce responses that are too broad or too complex to apply. The next step is therefore to make the interaction with AI more precise by identifying prompt patterns that consistently produce useful outcomes.

Prompt Patterns That Actually Work

At this point, the learning loop is defined. It provides a clear sequence of actions that can be applied to any new technology: define a goal, generate a minimal implementation, run it, observe its behavior, refine it, and repeat. However, a practical limitation becomes immediately visible when this method is applied. The quality of the outcome depends heavily on how the prompt is written.

Two prompts that aim at the same goal can produce completely different results. One may generate a clear and minimal implementation that can be executed immediately. The other may produce a long and complex answer that is difficult to use or verify. The difference is not in the technology. It is in how the request is expressed. For this reason, the next step is not to introduce new concepts, but to make the interaction with AI more precise.

Instead of writing prompts from scratch every time, it is more effective to rely on a small set of patterns that consistently produce useful results. These patterns are not rigid templates. They are structured ways of asking questions that align with the learning loop described in the previous section. Each pattern corresponds to a specific moment in the process.

Before examining individual examples, it is useful to map common situations to the prompt patterns that support them. The following *Table* 12.1 summarizes the patterns used throughout this book.

Situation	Prompt Pattern
Start from zero	Minimal Example
Extend a working system	Incremental Change
Fix a problem	Smallest Fix
Evaluate an implementation	Senior Engineer Review
Assess realism and risks	What Would Break?

Table 12.1: *Prompt Patterns Aligned with Different Stages of the AI Learning Loop*

When starting from zero, the objective is not to understand everything, but to reach a point where the system can be executed. In this situation, a prompt such as the following is effective.

Prompt

Explain this technology in simple terms.

Show a minimal working example.

Avoid advanced features.

This prompt limits the scope deliberately. It prevents the response from expanding into unnecessary detail, and focuses on producing something that can be run and observed. It corresponds to the first step of the learning loop, such as: generating a minimal solution. Once the system is running, the next step is to extend it. At this stage, the goal is not to rewrite the implementation, but to evolve it incrementally. A prompt like this supports that transition.

Prompt

Extend this implementation step by step.

Do not rewrite everything.

Explain each change.

This pattern preserves continuity. It ensures that each new step builds on the previous one, making the evolution of the system easier to follow and verify. When something does not work as expected, a different kind of prompt is required. The goal is no longer to generate new code, but to understand a failure.

Prompt

This code fails.

Explain the most likely cause.

Suggest the smallest fix.

This pattern is critical. It transforms an error into a focused question. Instead of introducing large changes, it directs the response toward identifying the minimal correction required to restore correct behavior. As the system becomes more stable, the interaction with AI shifts again. The goal is no longer to fix errors, but to evaluate the quality of the implementation.

Prompt

Review this code as a senior engineer.

Focus on clarity, correctness, and risks.

Suggest minimal improvements.

This prompt reflects the transition from building to reviewing. It does not ask for new features. It asks for a critical analysis of what already exists, with an emphasis on targeted improvements rather than redesign. Finally, when the system is considered in a broader context, a different perspective is needed. The goal is to understand how the implementation behaves under real conditions.

Prompt

How would this behave in production?

What would break under real conditions?

This pattern introduces a production-aware view. It does not change the system directly, but it reveals its limitations and helps guide future decisions. Each of these patterns corresponds to a specific phase of the learning process. They are not interchangeable. Using the wrong pattern at the wrong moment often leads to confusion or unnecessary complexity. For example, asking for a full review before the system is stable produces results that are difficult to apply, while asking for a minimal example after the system has grown leads to oversimplification.

What makes these patterns effective is not their wording, but their constraint. Each prompt limits the scope of the response and directs it toward a specific outcome. This is what keeps the interaction with AI focused and aligned with the learning loop. At this stage, it is important to recognize that these patterns are sufficient for most situations encountered when learning a new technology. They cover the essential transitions, such as: from zero to a working example, from a working example to an extended system, from failure to correction, from implementation to review, and from correctness to production awareness. They also have another important property. They can be reused without modification.

A prompt that was used to build a FastAPI endpoint can be used in exactly the same form to explore a database, a messaging system, or a frontend framework. The technology changes, but the structure of the interaction remains the same. This is what transforms prompting from an ad-hoc activity into a reliable tool. At this point, the method is almost complete. The learning loop defines how to proceed, and the prompt patterns define how to interact with AI at each step. What is still missing is a way to verify progress systematically. The next section introduces a simple checklist that allows the reader to confirm whether a new technology has been understood at a practical level.

The Learning Checklist

At this stage, the learning loop defines how to proceed, and the prompt patterns define how to interact with AI at each step. The process is structured, repeatable, and adaptable to different technologies. However, one practical question remains. How do you know when you have actually learned something?

When working with a new tool, it is easy to confuse exposure with understanding. Reading explanations, generating code, or even running examples can create the impression of progress, but that impression is not always reliable. A system may appear familiar, while still hiding gaps that become visible only when something changes or fails. For this reason, a simple form of verification becomes necessary. Just as the API was tested throughout the book, the learning process itself must include a way to confirm that knowledge is not only theoretical, but operational. The goal is not to measure how much information has been covered, but whether the system can be used, modified, and understood in practice. To make this concrete, we begin with a prompt.

Prompt

Given a new technology that I am learning, define a minimal checklist that confirms I understand it at a practical level.

Focus on actions, not theory.

A useful answer should not produce abstract criteria. It should define a small number of concrete actions that can be executed directly. When we compare this with the way the API was developed and verified throughout the book, a consistent pattern emerges. Understanding is not demonstrated by explanation alone. It is demonstrated through interaction.

A practical checklist can therefore be expressed as a sequence of actions that the learner can perform directly on the system. The first step is execution. If a technology cannot be run in a minimal form, it cannot be observed or tested. Running the system creates the first point of contact between the learner and the tool. From there, the system must be modified. A working example is only a starting point. Understanding begins when the system can be changed deliberately, and the effect of that change can be observed. This confirms that the learner is not only following instructions, but actively interacting with the system.

At this point, it becomes important to explore the limits of the implementation. Breaking the system intentionally reveals how it behaves under incorrect conditions. This is not a failure of the process, but a way to expose hidden assumptions and verify how errors are handled. Once a failure has been introduced, the next step is to fix it. This reinforces understanding by connecting cause and effect. The learner no longer depends entirely on generated solutions, but begins to recognize patterns, and apply corrections.

Another essential step is explanation. If the system can be described clearly—what it does, how it works, and why it behaves in a certain way—then understanding has moved beyond execution and become conceptual. Finally, the system should be extendable. Adding a small feature or modifying existing behavior confirms that the learner can move beyond the original example and apply the same principles in a new context. Taken together, these actions form a minimal but complete checklist.

The following *Figure* 12.3 summarizes a practical definition of understanding that can be applied to any technology, framework, or system.

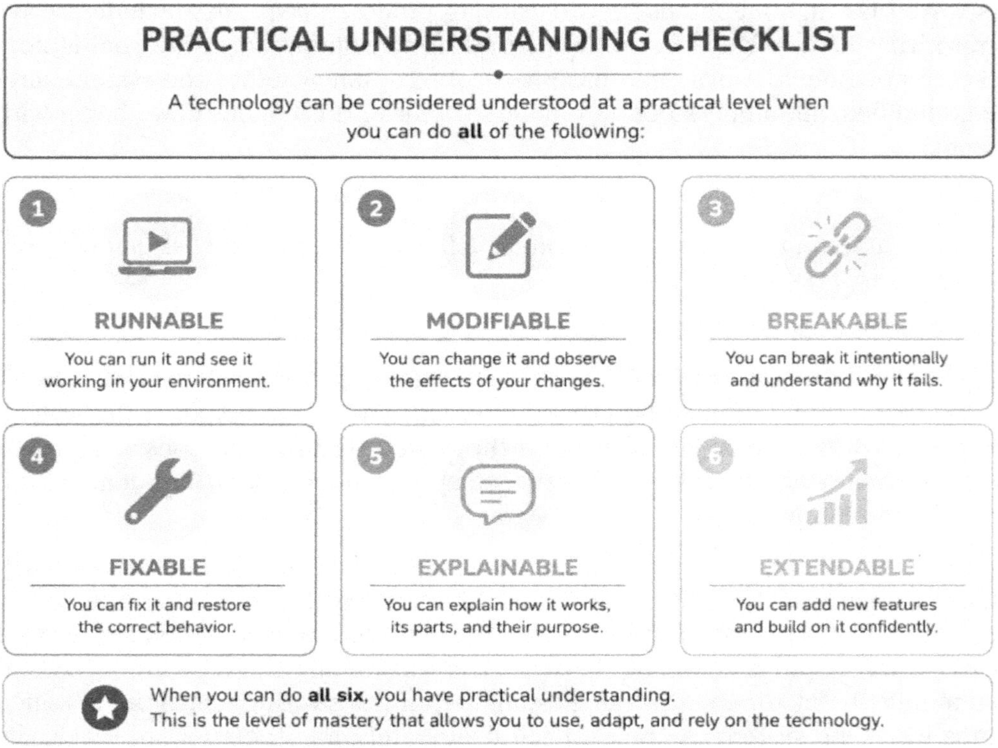

***Figure 12.3:** Practical Understanding Checklist*

If all of these steps can be performed, the technology is no longer unfamiliar. It has become something that can be used with confidence. At this stage, it is important to recognize what this checklist does not require. It does not require complete knowledge of the technology. It does not require familiarity with every feature or configuration option. It only requires that the learner can interact with the system in a controlled and deliberate way. This is what makes the checklist practical. It defines a stopping point that is both realistic and sufficient. Instead of aiming for complete mastery, the learner aims for operational understanding. From that point, further knowledge can be acquired incrementally, using the same loop and the same prompt patterns. In practice, this checklist can also guide the next step.

If the system can be run but not modified, the next prompt should introduce a small change. If it can be modified but not explained, the next prompt should focus on clarifying its behavior. In this way, the checklist becomes not only a tool for verification, but also a guide for what to do next. At this point, the method is fully defined. The learning loop provides the structure, the prompt patterns define the interaction, and the checklist ensures that progress is real. The next step is to apply this method to a completely new technology, showing how the same process can be used from the very beginning, without relying on any prior knowledge.

Applying the Method to a New Technology

Up to this point, the method has been defined in abstract terms. The learning loop describes how to proceed, the prompt patterns define how to interact with AI, and the checklist provides a way to verify understanding. What remains is to apply this method in a situation where no prior structure exists. This is the moment where the process becomes concrete. Instead of extending the existing API, we now approach a completely new tool. The objective is not to master it, but to reach a working and understandable state using only the method described so far. For this example, we introduce a simple but unfamiliar component: **Redis**.

Redis is often used as an in-memory data store, but at this stage, no prior knowledge is required. The only assumption is that it is something that can be integrated into a Python application. As in every other part of the book, we begin with a prompt that defines the goal clearly, and limits the scope.

Prompt

I want to learn Redis from scratch. Show a minimal example using Python that can connect to Redis, store a value, and retrieve it.

Keep the example simple and runnable. Avoid advanced features.

A useful answer should not attempt to explain everything about Redis. It should produce a minimal example that can be executed. The immediate objective is not deep understanding, but reaching a point where the system runs and produces observable behavior. Once that example has been generated, the next step is not to analyze it immediately, but to run it. Begin by installing the required dependency:

```
pip install redis
```

Then create a small file, for example, redis_example.py, and place the generated code inside it. A minimal version will typically look like this:

```
import redis

r = redis.Redis(host="localhost", port=6379, db=0, decode_
responses=True)

r.set("message", "Hello, Redis!")
value = r.get("message")

print(value)
```

Before running the script, Redis itself must be available. If it is not already installed locally, it can be started quickly using Docker:

```
docker run -p 6379:6379 redis
```

At that point, the script can be executed:

```
python redis_example.py
```

If everything is configured correctly, the output will be:

```
Hello, Redis!
```

This is the first important result. The system runs. That alone already confirms the first step of the checklist. Only now does analysis become useful. Instead of turning to documentation immediately, we use a second prompt that focuses on the current implementation.

Prompt

Explain what this Redis example is doing. Focus on how the connection works and how data is stored and retrieved.

A useful answer should clarify that the code establishes a connection to a running Redis instance, stores a key-value pair using set, and retrieves that value using get. At this point, the behavior is no longer opaque. It can be described, questioned, and understood.

The process then continues with modification. Instead of leaving the example unchanged, we introduce a small variation.

Prompt

Modify this example so that it stores multiple values and retrieves them in a loop.

Keep the changes minimal.

The resulting code may store several keys and iterate over them. Running the updated script confirms that the system can be modified and still behaves as expected. The next step is to explore its limits deliberately. To do that, we break it. For example, the port number can be changed to an incorrect value:

```
r = redis.Redis(host="localhost", port=9999, db=0, decode_
responses=True)
```

Running the script now produces an error. Instead of guessing, we again use a targeted prompt.

Prompt

This Redis connection fails.

Explain the most likely cause and how to fix it.

A useful answer should identify that the connection parameters are incorrect, and show how to restore them. This reinforces the relationship between configuration and behavior. At this point, the system has already passed through several essential stages. It has been executed, modified, broken, and fixed. The next step is to extend it slightly so that it moves beyond the original isolated script.

Prompt

Extend this example to integrate Redis into a FastAPI endpoint

that stores and retrieves a value.

Keep the implementation simple.

This produces a small integration that connects Redis with an API route. The result is not a complete system, but it demonstrates that the tool can already be used in a broader context. Only now do we return to the checklist. Redis was initially unfamiliar, but the method has allowed it to become something concrete. It can be run, modified, broken, fixed, explained, and extended. That is enough to conclude that it is no longer merely "something read about," but a tool that can already be used with confidence at a basic level. At this stage, it is important to observe what has happened. No tutorial was followed from beginning to end. No complete documentation was required before starting. No prior knowledge was assumed. The method generated its own path. This is the real outcome of the section. The same process that was used to build the API can now be applied independently. The framework has changed, but the method remains the same. In practice, this is what enables continuous learning. A new technology is no longer an obstacle that must be understood completely before it can be used. It becomes a system that can be approached step by step, through the same loop, the same prompt patterns, and the same verification process. The next step is to refine this approach further by identifying the mistakes that most often reduce its effectiveness, and by understanding how to avoid them.

Avoiding Common Mistakes When Learning with AI

At this point, the method has been applied end-to-end. A new technology was introduced, a minimal implementation was generated, the system was executed, observed, modified, and extended. The learning loop, the prompt patterns, and the checklist have all been used in a concrete scenario. And yet, there is an important aspect that has not been addressed directly. The method works, but it can also fail. Not because technology is complex, and not because AI is unreliable, but because the way the interaction is structured can introduce unnecessary friction. When the process is not followed carefully, the same tool that enables learning can produce confusion instead of clarity. For this reason, it is useful to make these failure points explicit.

Before examining individual examples, it is useful to summarize some common mistakes and their typical consequences. The following *Table* 12.2 highlights patterns that frequently slow down or distort the learning process.

Mistake	Consequence
Overly broad prompts	Large, unfocused responses
Not executing the generated code	False sense of understanding
Avoiding failure and experimentation	Missed learning opportunities
Rewriting entire solutions at once	Loss of context and harder verification
Skipping observation	Limited understanding of system behavior
Accepting AI output without review	Hidden errors and weak assumptions

Table 12.2: *Common Mistakes When Learning with AI*

A common mistake appears at the very beginning. When approaching a new technology, it is natural to want a complete explanation or a full implementation. Prompts such as "build a complete system" or "explain everything about this tool" often produce responses that are technically correct, but practically unusable. They are too broad, too detailed, and difficult to execute or verify. This breaks the learning loop before it even starts. The correct approach is to constrain the request. The goal is not completeness, but a minimal, runnable example. Understanding does not come from covering everything at once. It emerges from interaction.

Another source of confusion is accepting output without verification. Code generated by AI may look correct, but until it is executed, its behavior is unknown. Skipping execution removes the feedback loop that makes the method reliable. Without running the system, there is no way to observe what actually happens, and no way to detect inconsistencies. Throughout the book, every step was verified. This was not incidental. It was the mechanism that kept the process grounded in observable behavior. A different kind of mistake is avoiding failure. When something does not work, it is often perceived as an interruption. In practice, it is one of the most valuable moments in the learning process. A failure provides a precise and concrete input. It reduces ambiguity and makes it possible to ask focused questions.

If failures are ignored or bypassed, the opportunity to understand the system more deeply is lost. There is also a tendency to replace instead of refine. When code is unclear or incomplete, asking for a completely new implementation may seem faster. In reality, it removes context. The system changes too much at once, and it becomes difficult to track what has improved and why. Incremental changes are more effective. They preserve continuity, and make each step easier to understand and verify.

Another frequent issue appears once the system begins to work. It becomes tempting to move quickly toward more advanced features. While this is a natural progression, it can disrupt the learning process if it happens before the fundamentals are fully understood. The method described in this chapter depends on stability at each stage. Advancing too quickly introduces complexity before the underlying behavior is clear. Finally, there is the problem of vague prompts. A prompt that lacks constraints often produces responses that are not aligned with the current goal. Asking "how does this work?" without specifying context or depth can lead to explanations that are either too shallow or unnecessarily complex. To correct this, prompts must always reflect the current step of the learning loop. If the goal is execution, the prompt should request a minimal example. If the goal is debugging, the prompt should describe the failure precisely. If the goal is review, the criteria must be explicit. When a response is not aligned with expectations, it is often sufficient to adjust it with a small corrective prompt.

Prompt

Simplify this explanation.

Focus only on what is necessary to run the code.

This type of intervention reduces unnecessary detail and brings the output back to a usable form without restarting the process. At this stage, it is important to interpret these mistakes correctly. They are not errors in judgment. They are natural tendencies when working with a powerful tool. The purpose of identifying them is not to avoid them entirely, but to recognize when they occur and correct the course. The method itself does not change. A goal is defined. A minimal implementation is generated. The system is executed and observed. It is refined through iteration. When the process produces confusion, it is usually because one of these steps has been skipped, expanded too much, or applied at the wrong time. By maintaining the structure of the loop and using constrained prompts, the interaction with AI remains focused and productive. At this point, the method is not only defined and applied, but also stabilized. The next step is to make it personal, turning these patterns into a set of prompts that can be reused directly in future learning scenarios.

Building Your Personal Prompt Library

At this stage, the method is complete. The learning loop defines how to proceed. The prompt patterns define how to interact with AI. The checklist verifies that understanding is real. Common mistakes have been identified and can be avoided. What remains is to make this process practical in everyday use. Up to this point, prompts have always been written in context. Each one was adapted to a specific situation: building a feature, debugging a failure, reviewing code, or evaluating behavior. This approach works well in a guided environment, where each step is defined in advance. However, when approaching a new technology independently, this becomes inefficient. Reconstructing the same types of prompts every time slows down the process and introduces unnecessary variability. This is where a personal prompt library becomes useful. A prompt library is not a collection of random examples. It is a small, structured set of prompts that correspond to the key steps of the learning process. Each prompt has a clear purpose, and each one can be reused without modification across different technologies. The goal is not to have many prompts. The goal is to have the right ones.

To make this concrete, we can organize the patterns introduced earlier into a minimal and reusable set.

The core prompt library developed throughout this book can be summarized as a small reusable reference shown in the following *Figure* 12.4.

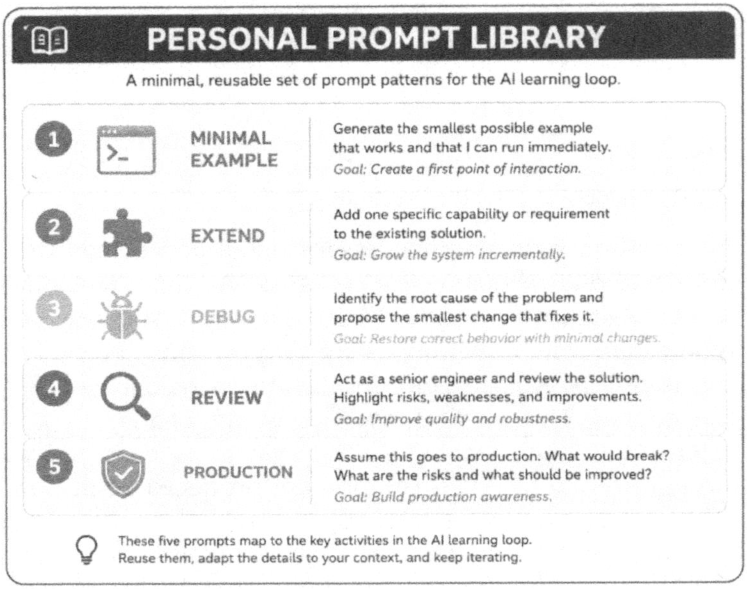

Figure 12.4: *Minimal Prompt Library*

When starting from zero, the objective is not to understand everything, but to create a point of interaction. This is captured by the first prompt.

Prompt

Explain this technology in simple terms. Show a minimal working example.

Avoid advanced features.

This prompt defines the entry point. It ensures that the response produces something that can be executed immediately, rather than an abstract explanation. Once the system is running, the next step is to evolve it without losing continuity.

Prompt

Extend this implementation step by step. Do not rewrite everything.

Explain each change.

This preserves the structure of the system, and makes each modification observable. The focus is not on adding complexity, but on understanding how the system evolves. When something does not work, the interaction changes again. The goal is no longer expansion, but correction.

Prompt

This code fails.

Explain the most likely cause.

Suggest the smallest fix.

This prompt is essential. It transforms an error into a precise question, and avoids unnecessary rewrites by focusing on minimal changes. As the system becomes stable, a different perspective is required. The goal shifts from making the system work to improving its quality.

Prompt

Review this code as a senior engineer.

Focus on clarity, correctness, and risks.

Suggest minimal improvements.

This introduces evaluation without breaking the structure. It refines the system, instead of replacing it. Finally, the system can be considered under real-world conditions.

Prompt

How would this behave in production?

What would break under real conditions?

This prompt does not produce immediate changes but reveals limitations. It helps guide decisions about what should be improved, and what can remain unchanged.

These five prompts are sufficient to cover the entire learning process. They correspond directly to the stages of the loop: starting, extending, debugging, reviewing, and evaluating. At this point, an important detail becomes visible. These prompts are intentionally simple. They do not reference any specific framework, language, or tool. This is what makes them reusable. The same prompt used to explore FastAPI can be applied without modification to a database, a messaging system, or a frontend framework.

In practice, this library can be stored as a small reference that is always available when starting something new. It reduces the effort required to formulate effective prompts, and ensures that interaction with AI remains consistent. The library itself is not fixed. As new situations are encountered, prompts can be refined or extended. What matters is not the number of prompts, but their clarity and usefulness. At this stage, the learning process is no longer dependent on external guidance. The prompts provide a structure that can be applied independently, without reconstructing the method each time. This is what transforms the approach from a guided experience into a reusable skill. The final step is to extend this independence further, moving from structured learning to open exploration, where the method can be applied without predefined boundaries.

From Guided Learning to Independent Exploration

Up to this point, every step of the process has been guided. Goals were defined in advance, prompts were suggested, and the sequence of actions was structured. Even when the system was explored incrementally, the direction was always clear. Each section provided a starting point, and each improvement followed a predictable path. This was intentional. A method is easier to understand when it is applied in a controlled context. The API provided that context. It allowed the process to be repeated, refined, and observed without unnecessary distractions. But the purpose of the method is not to remain inside that context. It is to be used independently. At this stage, the structure that supported the learning process is no longer required. The same steps can now be generated directly by the reader. Instead of following instructions, the reader can define them. This is the key transition. The transition from guided learning to independent exploration can be summarized as shown in the following *Figure* 12.5.

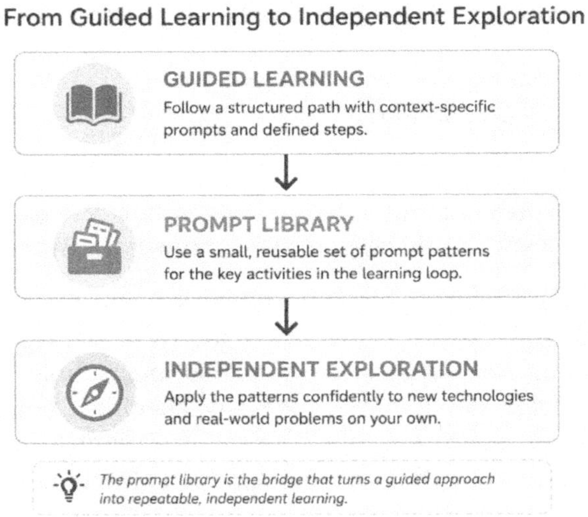

Figure 12.5: *Transition from Guided Learning to Independent Exploration*

When approaching a new technology, there is no predefined sequence. There is no chapter explaining what to do first, what to build next, or how to verify the result. The path is not given. It must be created.

The method described in this chapter provides the tools to do exactly that. A goal can be defined in concrete terms. A minimal implementation can be generated. The system can be executed and observed, its behavior analyzed, and then refined and extended. At every step, prompts guide the interaction, and the checklist confirms that progress is real. This changes the role of uncertainty. The absence of instructions is no longer a limitation. It becomes part of the process. When something is unknown, the first step is no longer to search for a complete explanation. It is to create a starting point. A prompt produces a minimal example, and that example becomes the basis for further exploration. Each iteration adds clarity, and each question becomes more precise.

In this way, learning is no longer dependent on external structure. It becomes self-directed. This does not eliminate uncertainty. New technologies will still introduce unfamiliar concepts, unexpected behaviors, and moments of confusion. The difference is that these moments no longer interrupt the process. They become inputs for the next step. The system itself provides feedback. At this stage, it is also important to recognize that independence does not mean isolation. Documentation, examples, and external resources remain useful. What changes is the role they play. They are no longer the only source of guidance. They are integrated into a process that is already defined. The reader is no longer following a path. They are constructing it. This is what makes the method transferable. The same approach can be applied to any tool, in any context, and at any level of complexity. The structure remains the same, even when the details change. The most important consequence of this shift is simple. You no longer need instructions. You can generate them.

At this point, the transition is complete. The method is no longer something that has been followed. It is something that can be applied deliberately, without relying on predefined steps. The final section closes the book by making explicit what this transformation represents, and what it enables beyond this specific project.

Conclusion: The Real Outcome of This Book

At the beginning of this book, the objective appeared straightforward, that is, build a FastAPI application, understand how its components work, and learn how to structure, test, and refine an API. Those objectives have been achieved. The system now includes a clear architecture, persistent data, authentication and authorization, automated tests, and a production-aware perspective. It behaves in a consistent and predictable way. It can be executed, verified, and extended. From a technical point of view, the result is complete. But this is not the most important outcome. At every stage, the system was not only built—it was constructed through a specific way of working. Each step began with a goal, continued with a prompt, and was verified through execution. When something failed, the failure was analyzed and corrected. When something worked, it became the new baseline. This process was applied repeatedly, across different problems and different levels of complexity. What has been developed is not only an application. It is a method. The value of that method is not limited to FastAPI. It does not depend on a specific framework or a specific language. It can be applied to any situation where something new must be understood, built, and refined.

A new technology is no longer an obstacle that requires complete preparation before action. It becomes something that can be explored step by step, starting from a minimal example and evolving through interaction. This changes the nature of learning. Instead of waiting to understand everything before building, the process creates understanding through building. Instead of relying on predefined paths, it generates its own structure. Instead of avoiding uncertainty, it uses it as part of the process. At this stage, it is important to recognize what this does—and what it does not imply. It does not remove the need for thinking. It does not replace judgment. It does not guarantee correct results on the first attempt. What it provides is a reliable way to move forward: a way to define a goal, create a starting point, verify behavior, and improve it iteratively. This is what allows progress to continue even when the path is not known in advance.

The API built in this book is an example of that process. It is not the final destination. It is the context in which the method was applied. The real outcome is the ability to repeat that process independently. The goal was never the API. The goal was to learn how to build one. From this point forward, the same approach can be used to explore new frameworks, integrate unfamiliar tools, or design systems that go beyond the scope of this project. The system can change, but the method remains.

Points to Remember

- Start with a minimal runnable example, not complete understanding.
- Use AI to support a learning loop of execution, feedback, and iteration.
- Clear prompts produce useful results; vague prompts create confusion.
- Interaction teaches more than exhaustive explanations.
- Failures accelerate learning by exposing what needs attention.
- Improve systems incrementally instead of rewriting them.
- Reuse the same prompt patterns across different technologies.
- Verify understanding through practice, not theory alone.
- Use AI to generate, debug, review, and evaluate solutions.
- Independent learning begins when you can define your own next steps.

Multiple Choice Questions

1. What is the main objective of this chapter?
    a. To introduce a new framework
    b. To optimize API performance
    c. To extract a reusable learning method using AI
    d. To redesign the application

2. Why is a minimal working example important when learning a new technology?
    a. Because it replaces documentation
    b. Because it allows execution and observation
    c. Because it improves performance
    d. Because it simplifies deployment
3. What is the role of AI in the learning process described in this chapter?
    a. To replace the developer
    b. To generate final solutions only
    c. To support iterative learning through prompts
    d. To deploy applications automatically
4. Why should prompts be constrained and focused?
    a. To reduce API complexity
    b. To improve execution speed
    c. To produce clearer and more usable results
    d. To avoid writing code
5. What is the purpose of the learning checklist?
    a. To test performance
    b. To verify practical understanding
    c. To generate documentation
    d. To replace testing
6. Why is it useful to break a system intentionally?
    a. To improve performance
    b. To simulate production
    c. To expose assumptions and understand behavior
    d. To simplify code
7. What is the benefit of building a personal prompt library?
    a. It replaces all documentation.
    b. It automates deployment.
    c. It provides reusable interaction patterns.
    d. It improves database performance.

8. What marks the transition to independent learning?
    a. Knowing all features of a technology
    b. Writing complex systems without AI
    c. Being able to generate your own learning steps
    d. Avoiding errors completely
9. You are learning a new technology, and immediately ask AI to build a complete production system. Which learning mistake does this represent?
    a. Incremental refinement
    b. Minimal example first
    c. Over-scoping the prompt
    d. Production review

Answers

1. c
2. b
3. c
4. c
5. b
6. c
7. c
8. c
9. c

Questions

1. Why is starting from a minimal example more effective than trying to understand a technology completely from the beginning?
2. How does the learning loop transform uncertainty into a structured process?
3. What are the risks of relying on AI without executing and verifying the generated code?
4. Why is failure considered a valuable part of the learning process in this method?
5. How do prompt patterns improve consistency when learning different technologies?

6. In what ways does incremental refinement support understanding better than full rewrites?
7. How does the learning checklist help distinguish between theoretical and practical knowledge?
8. Why is it important to separate the method from the specific technology used in the book?
9. How can a personal prompt library improve long-term learning efficiency?
10. What does it mean to move from guided learning to independent exploration?

Key Terms

- **AI Learning Loop:** A repeatable process of defining a goal, generating a minimal solution, executing it, analyzing behavior, and refining iteratively.
- **Minimal Working Example:** A simple, runnable implementation that demonstrates the core behavior of a technology.
- **Prompt Pattern:** A reusable structure for interacting with AI to achieve specific outcomes such as building, debugging, or reviewing.
- **Iterative Learning:** A process where understanding is built progressively through repeated cycles of execution and refinement.
- **Practical Understanding:** The ability to run, modify, explain, and extend a system, rather than only describing it theoretically.
- **Debugging with AI:** The use of targeted prompts to analyze failures, and identify minimal fixes.
- **Incremental Development:** The practice of improving a system step by step without rewriting it entirely.
- **Prompt Library:** A curated set of reusable prompts that support consistent interaction with AI across different contexts.
- **Learning Checklist:** A set of actions used to verify that a technology is understood at an operational level.
- **Independent Exploration:** The ability to learn new technologies without predefined instructions, using AI as a structured support tool.
- **Constraint in Prompting:** The practice of limiting scope and complexity in prompts to obtain clear and usable responses.
- **Feedback Loop:** The cycle of execution, observation, and refinement that drives continuous learning.

APPENDIX

From API Core to Real Applications

By the end of this book, you have built more than a FastAPI application. You have built an API core system. This means that you now have a structured backend that exposes a clear interface, persists data, enforces authentication and authorization, and behaves in a predictable and testable way. It is not tied to a specific interface or client. It does not assume how it will be used. It defines *what the system can do*, not *how it must be used*. This is what makes it a core. A core system can support different kinds of applications without being redesigned. It can serve different clients, evolve in multiple directions, and grow in complexity while preserving its structure. At this stage, the question is no longer how to build the API. It is how this core can be used. This appendix introduces a set of possible directions. Each one represents a different way of using the same system. The goal is not to provide complete implementations, but to show how the core can be extended, and to provide a starting point for exploration.

Each direction includes:

- The type of application it enables
- The technologies involved
- A prompt that can be used to begin

From that point, the same method applies: build something minimal, run it, observe it, and refine it.

Server-Side Web Application

The API can be extended to return HTML instead of JSON, turning it into a complete web application rendered on the server.

Technologies / Components:

- Jinja2Templates

- HTMLResponse
- FastAPI routing for pages

Prompt

Convert one API endpoint into a server-rendered HTML pageusing Jinja templates and HTMLResponse.

Keep the implementation minimal.

Frontend + API (Single Page Application)

The API can act as a backend for a separate frontend application, such as React or Vue.

Technologies / Components:

- JavaScript fetch / Axios
- React / Vue (optional)
- CORS middleware (CORSMiddleware)

Prompt

Create a minimal frontend page that calls this API, and displays product data using JavaScript fetch. Do not use frameworks.

Internal Tools and Admin Interfaces

The API can power internal dashboards or administrative tools for managing data.

Technologies / Components:

- FastAPI endpoints (existing)
- Simple HTML or frontend UI
- Role-based access (Depends, roles)

Prompt

Build a simple admin interface that allows creating, updating, and deleting products using the existing API endpoints.

Mobile Backend

The API can serve as a backend for mobile applications (iOS or Android).

Technologies / Components:

- JSON responses (already implemented)
- Token-based authentication

- HTTP clients (mobile side)

Prompt

Explain how this API could be used as a backend for a mobile application, including authentication flow.

Microservice Integration

The API can become one component in a larger system, interacting with other services.

Technologies / Components:

- REST communication
- Service-to-service authentication
- Modular architecture

Prompt

Describe how this API could be integrated as a microservice in a larger distributed system.

Background Tasks and Asynchronous Work

The system can handle operations that run outside the request-response cycle.

Technologies / Components:

- BackgroundTasks
- Task queues (Celery, RQ — optional extension)

Prompt

Add a background task to this API that runs after creating a product (for example, logging or notification).

Real-Time Communication

The API can be extended to support real-time interactions.

Technologies / Components:

- WebSockets (WebSocket)
- Event-driven communication

Prompt

Create a minimal FastAPI WebSocket example that allows sending and receiving messages.

Data API / Public API

The API can be exposed to external users or third-party developers.

Technologies / Components:

- OpenAPI / Swagger (already present)
- API versioning
- Rate limiting (external tools)

Prompt

Review this API as if it were public and suggest improvements for documentation and usability.

Caching and Performance Optimization

The API can be extended to handle higher load, and improve performance.

Technologies / Components:

- Redis
- Response caching
- Query optimization

Prompt

Integrate a simple Redis cache for the product listing endpoint.

Deployment and Production Environments

The API can be deployed, and made accessible in real environments.

Technologies / Components:

- Docker
- Cloud platforms (Render, AWS, and so on.)
- Environment variables

Prompt

Containerize this FastAPI application using Docker and explain how to run it in a production-like environment.

Final Note

Each of these directions represents a different way of using the same system. None of them requires starting from zero. All of them build on what already exists. Therefore, the purpose of this appendix is not to expand the system for you. It is to show that it can be expanded. You already have the structure and the method. So, from this point forward, the next step is yours.

Index

A

B

R

S

T

U

V

www.ingramcontent.com/pod-product-compliance
Lightning Source LLC
LaVergne TN
LVHW081737071126
851857LV00041B/1651
* 9 7 8 8 1 6 9 6 4 6 4 5 1 *